COPELAND'S
TREASURY FOR BOOKLOVERS

ELLEN TERRY AS "LADY MACBETH"

From the painting by John Singer Sargent

COPELAND'S TREASURY
FOR BOOKLOVERS

A PANORAMA OF ENGLISH
AND AMERICAN POETRY AND PROSE FROM THE
EARLIEST TIMES TO THE PRESENT

SELECTED AND EDITED

BY

CHARLES TOWNSEND COPELAND

BOYLSTON PROFESSOR OF
ORATORY AND RHETORIC AT HARVARD UNIVERSITY

VOLUME I

NEW YORK
CHARLES SCRIBNER'S SONS
1929

To Mrs. Swan

MY OLDEST AND MY YOUNGEST FRIEND

WITH GREAT REGARD

ACKNOWLEDGMENTS

For the use of the copyrighted material in The Copeland Reader, all rights in which are reserved by the holders of the copyrights, permission has been obtained from the following publishers and authors:

Boni & Liveright, Inc.: "And in the Hanging Gardens" from "Priapus and the Pool" by Conrad Aiken; "An Occurrence at Owl Creek Bridge" from "In the Midst of Life" and "The Damned Thing" from "Can Such Things Be?" by Ambrose Bierce. Copyright 1918, 1925, by Boni & Liveright, Inc.

Dodd, Mead & Company: "The Great Lover" and "The Soldier" from "Poems" by Rupert Brooke; "Ethandune: The Last Charge" from "The Ballad of the White Horse" by Gilbert Keith Chesterton; "The Roman Road" and "The Burglars" from "The Golden Age" by Kenneth Grahame; "Madeline of the Movies" from "Further Foolishness" and "My Financial Career" from "Literary Lapses" by Stephen Leacock; "Wordsworth's Grave" from "Poems" by William Watson. Copyright 1892, 1893, 1911, 1916, by Dodd, Mead & Company.

Doubleday Page & Company: "Youth" by Joseph Conrad; "A Municipal Record" from "Strictly Business," "Calloway's Code" from "Whirligigs," "The Gift of the Magi" and "Memoirs of a Yellow Dog" from "The Four Million," "Roads of Destiny," and "Thimble, Thimble" from "Options," by O. Henry; "The Bell Buoy," "Chant-Pagan," "The 'Eathen," "The Last Chantey," "Mandalay" and "The Truce of the Bear" from "Rudyard Kipling's Verse, Inclusive Edition, 1885-1918" by Rudyard Kipling. Copyright 1903, 1906, 1909, 1910, 1911, 1926, by Doubleday Page & Company.

Duffield & Company: Chapter I from "Fern Seed" by Henry Milner Rideout. Copyright 1921 by Duffield & Company.

Harcourt, Brace & Company: "The Fifty-First Dragon" from "Seeing Things at Night" by Heywood Broun; "Into Battle" by Julian Grenfell, from "Some Soldier Poets" collected by Sturge Moore. Copyright 1920, 1921 by Harcourt, Brace & Company.

Harper & Brothers: "Wanted: an Income Taximeter" from Harper's Magazine, by Frederick Lewis Allen; Chapter I from "The Mayor of Casterbridge," and "The Darkling Thrush" from "Poems," by Thomas Hardy; "The Philosophy of Ceilings" from Harper's Magazine, by David Watson McCord; "A Daring Deed" and "A Pilot's Needs" from "Life on the Mississippi," "The Yankee's Fight with the Knights" from "A Connecticut Yankee at the Court of King Arthur," and "The Notorious Jumping Frog of Calaveras County," by Mark Twain; "A Village Singer," "A Kitchen Colonel" and "The Revolt of 'Mother'," from "A New England Nun and Other Stories" by Mary E. Wilkins Freeman. Copyright 1883, 1886, 1889, 1920, 1926 by Harper & Brothers.

Henry Holt & Company: "Christmas Afternoon" from "Of All Things" by Robert Charles Benchley; "After Apple-Picking," "The Runaway" and "The Wood-Pile" from "North of Boston" by Robert Frost; "The Listeners," "The Sleeper" and "Winter Dusk" from "The Listeners" by Walter de la Mare. Copyright 1915, 1916, 1921 by Henry Holt & Company.

Houghton Mifflin Company: "Sargent's Portrait of Edwin Booth at 'The Players'" and "An Ode on the Unveiling of the Shaw Memorial on Boston Common" from "Poems" by Thomas Bailey Aldrich; "The Army of France" from "Zut and

Other Parisians" by Guy Wetmore Carryl; "Miggles," "Tennessee's Partner," and "The Outcasts of Poker Flat" from "The Luck of Roaring Camp and Other Tales" by Francis Bret Harte; "My Last Walk with the School-mistress" from "The Autocrat of the Breakfast Table," and "The Broom-stick Train," "The Chambered Nautilus," and "The Last Leaf," from "Poetical Works" by Oliver Wendell Holmes; "The Town Poor" and "A Winter Courtship" by Sarah Orne Jewett; "The High Woods" from "Admiral's Light" by Henry Milner Rideout. Copyright 1870, 1885, 1903, 1907, 1925 by Houghton Mifflin Company.

Alfred A. Knopf, Inc.: "The Burial in England" and "Gates of Damascus" from "Poems" by James Elroy Flecker.

Little, Brown & Company: "Harvard College in the War" from "Speeches" by Oliver Wendell Holmes II. Copyright 1913 by Little, Brown & Company.

The Macmillan Company: "An Old Woman of the Roads" from "Wild Earth" by Padraic Colum; "Devil's Edge," "Flannan Isle" and "The Hare" from "Poems" by Wilfrid Wilson Gibson; "Eve" and "Time, you Old Gipsy Man" from "Poems" by Ralph Hodgson; "The Western Islands" from "A Mainsail Haul," "Cargoes" and "O little self, within whose smallness lies" from "Collected Poems," by John Masefield; "Old King Cole" from "Poems" by Edwin Arlington Robinson; "The Snare" from "Poems" by James Stephens; "Immortality" from "The Seven Ages of Washington" and "Lee's Surrender" from "Ulysses S. Grant" by Owen Wister; "The Lake Isle of Innisfree" from "Poems" and a part of the play: "Cathleen ni Hoolihan" by William Butler Yeats. Copyright 1900, 1905, 1907, 1913, 1916, 1917, 1921, 1922, by The Macmillan Company.

The Modern Library, Inc.: Chapter I from "American Literature" by John Macy. Copyright 1918 by The Modern Library, Inc.

The Neale Publishing Company: "An Occurrence at Owl Creek Bridge" from "In the Midst of Life" and "The Damned Thing" from "Can Such Things Be?" by Ambrose Bierce. Copyright 1909 by the Neale Publishing Company.

G. P. Putnam's Sons: "Bernhardt" from "Enchanted Aisles" by Alexander Woollcott. Copyright 1924 by G. P. Putnam's Sons.

Small, Maynard & Company: "Mr. Booth off the Stage" from "Edwin Booth" by Charles Townsend Copeland; "On New Years' Resolutions," and "Rudyard Kipling" from "Mr. Dooley in the Hearts of His Countrymen" by Finley Peter Dunne. Copyright 1899, 1901 by Small, Maynard & Company.

The Viking Press: "I'm a Fool" from "Horses and Men" by Sherwood Anderson. Copyright 1923 by The Viking Press.

William Stanley Braithwaite: "Sandy Star" and "Twenty Stars to Match His Face."

Mark Antony De Wolfe Howe: "The Known Soldier," and "The Sailor-Man" from "The Known Soldier," and "Spring on the Land" from "Harmonies."

Rudyard Kipling: "The Bell Buoy," "Chant-Pagan," "The 'Eathen," "The Last Chantey," "Mandalay" and "The Truce of the Bear" from "Rudyard Kipling's Verse, Inclusive Edition, 1885-1918." Copyright 1891, 1892, 1893, 1894, 1895, 1896, 1897, 1899, 1900, 1901, 1902, 1903, 1904, 1905, 1906, 1907, 1909, 1910, 1911, 1912, 1913, 1914, 1915, 1916, 1917, 1918, 1919 by Rudyard Kipling.

Gretchen Warren: "The Garden."

INTRODUCTION

The title of this anthology to a great degree expresses its composition and purpose. Wide as is its range, the selection includes only what I have read aloud during thirty-four years of teaching, lecturing, and reading.

Many of the pieces I have used with classes and audiences in Harvard University and Radcliffe College, many in excursions to other colleges and to schools, many with a surprising variety of clubs and societies,— chief among them the Harvard Club of New York, which for twenty-one years has made me thrice welcome and thrice grateful. I remember with particular pleasure two visits, professional and social, to Bowdoin College, the best college in my own state, one of the few best in all the states. My own bright and beautiful town, flouting the proverb, has often encouraged native talent to do its best. As for Christmas Eve, it won't seem like itself if Mrs. Lowell stops allowing me to bring my book, to add a bit to genial, truly hospitable parties. Each year these parties, for a "two hours traffic," make crowds of young men forget that they are away from home and kin.

As to many good schools, as to groups, coteries, the patient family circle, and single victims, all these must wait for their places in a big book of recollections and opinions, promised and some day to be written.

I shall soon take a year off, and after a rest, and with more leisure, I know I shall have the wish and I think I shall have the energy to write reminiscences. Let me set down here one memory of a single victim,— exquisite poet, renowned wit, and best of all talkers. I had been reading to him certain of his own poems when suddenly he exclaimed: "Come, Copeland, give us some of that fool woman's poetry." My friend used the word poetry with full intention, for much as he detested the lady's rhymes and the lack of them, not all his conservatism kept him from recognizing her genius. Why, by the way, did this wise American woman speak in a letter published many years after her death, of *red* as the most frequent color in New England wild flowers? How about yellow? Or even pink?

I had intended, following the good example of the editors of "The Golden Treasury," "The Golden Treasury of Modern Lyrics," and indeed of most anthologists, to make my introduction or preface very brief and purely explanatory. According to this intention it remains only to be stated that, although I do not always read the best literature—audiences are great choosers—I almost never, for any audience, choose either verse or prose that is not literature. So that, however the collection may be lacking in method, it will seldom be found to lack quality.

With this explanation I had thought to be done. But my invaluable colleague, Dr. Hood, my publisher, Mr. Maxwell Perkins of Scribners, and other friends whose advice is not to be gainsaid, have suggested that certain unpublished addresses and essays of mine would be welcome to many former students who remember them, and especially welcome to teachers. Although I have been cherishing these papers to make a volume, with additions, I gladly offer here some of the briefer and more appropriate. Teachers may like to use such material as I constantly use it, to introduce, explain, and praise authors from whom I am about to read.

"Bacon as an Essayist" was read at the Boston Public Library in observance of the three-hundred-and-fiftieth anniversary of the birth of Lord Bacon. Professor R. B. Perry, I remember, on "Bacon as a Philosopher," and Professor R. B. Merriman on "Bacon as an His-torian," were among my fellow speakers and readers on a curiously interesting occasion. "Not 'Poor Charles Lamb' " is a fragment from an address in aid of the Radcliffe Fund three years ago. "Hawthorne's In-heritance and His Art" is a part of an anniversary discourse at Concord. "Dickens: His Best Book?" was written for the Harvard Club of New York. "Tennyson and Browning as Religious Poets" is taken from a college lecture, spoken, not written. "As to Margaret Ogilvy" is a bit from a lecture on Sir James Barrie to the Harvard Summer School. Here follow these addresses and other papers, in the order named.

BACON AS AN ESSAYIST

In Bacon's Essay, "Of Discourse," one of the brief original ten, printed in 1597, the author says: "To use too many circumstances ere one come to the matter, is wearisome; to use none at all is blunt." When a ten-minute speech is the matter in hand, one must be blunt. And so I abruptly inform the few unlettered persons in this great company that Bacon's Essays, like the lion in "A Midsummer Night's Dream," are not what they call themselves. They are not essays at all, in our accep-tation of the word. The modern essay, from Addison to Stevenson, derives from Montaigne; the Baconian essay derives from the epigram-matic aphorism of antiquity. "The Tatler" and all its successors, even to this latest day, conform in general to Dr. Johnson's definition,—"A loose sally of the mind; an irregular, indigested piece." So, wherever and whenever we encounter the typical essayist, he is found to be a tatler, a spectator, a rambler, a lounger, and, in the best sense, a citizen of the world. But Bacon's intention, so richly fulfilled, was "to write certain brief notes, set down rather significantly than curiously, which I have called Essays; the word is late, but the thing is ancient. For Seneca's Epistles to Lucilius, if one mark them well, are but Essays,—that is, dispersed Meditations."

What Bacon intended, that he did. The final result is the wisest book of its size in the world, in its form much closer kin to Pascal than to Montaigne. By it and it alone is Bacon, mighty philosopher and man of science though he was, a part of existing literature. Whatever he may mean to scholars and men of letters, to the general mind of man he is bound up in this one weighty little volume. "Significantly" set down, indeed, are those rounded thoughts, these close-set maxims,—significantly, and far more "curiously" (that is, carefully) than the author was willing to admit. *Curiosa felicitas,* in truth, is the sign manual of Bacon's Essays, as it is of almost every enduring masterpiece in any art. I do not mean that Bacon's style is external, or niggling, or precious. No, it is the terse finality of a determination to say the thing he meant, and none other, in the fewest, most precise, and most expressive words. Nor is rhetorical intention absent. Bacon was too much the orator celebrated by Ben Jonson not to have his audience in mind; and even a tyro can see that his beginnings, to speak of those alone, were intended to waylay and grip the reader. "Revenge is a kind of wild justice," "men fear death as children fear to go in the dark," "he that hath wife and children hath given hostages to fortune,"—these and at least a dozen other openings of essays are famous wherever English is spoken. They deserve their fame. Can any man believe that they came by chance?

Thus arresting attention in the sixteenth century, Bacon holds it in the twentieth. That is why you and I are here tonight. The little book is still current. We quote from it, not always knowing whom we quote. And many a golden phrase of Bacon's coinage still rings and shines in our dull, common speech.

How much the priceless volume contains! How much it lacks! There is no moral enthusiasm in the Essays, no passion or emotion of any kind. No laughter; no tears. None of the humor of the age Bacon lived in; none of its strongly marked melancholy. In Bacon's essays there is no imagination, and no religion save that of formal reverence. He quotes scripture for his purpose, to be sure, with all the skill attributed to a certain powerful personage. And yet his purpose is not of hell any more than it is of heaven. His purpose and his teaching are of this immediate world. Although Bacon has been truly called Machiavellian, he is without the diabolism of Machiavelli. But in reading the Essays we never feel that "God is come into the camp."

Yet how much the great little book contains! The keenest wit, which is often more than wit, keeps us frequently from noting the absence of humor. Better for his aim than the imagination that the essayist lacks, is the inexhaustible fancy that wings his meaning with unforgetable analogies and startling contrasts, drawn often from the life that every man knows. Cool, tolerant, loving nature—especially in Gardens —admiring and envying youth, almost pitying age, searching his own time and the whole past for examples, Bacon urges his seeing mind among the motives, and hopes, and fears of men, with a triumphant skill that makes us suspect him of white magic. Black magic he deals in only at such half-repented moments as when, for extreme exigencies, he excuses simulation. Dissimulation is for him a virtue.

A thinker, Bacon is also the occasion of thought in others. And although the remark has probably been made—I should give you the authority if I knew it—I should like, in closing, to remind you that for most of us, only two men equal Bacon as breeders of thought. These two are Socrates and Emerson. Far nobler than Bacon, the essayist, they are less acute and not more homely or plain. His worldliness is a complement to their other-worldliness. The dignity of his manner is an education for any world. It is a piece of good fortune for ours that he still lives and teaches.

NOT "POOR CHARLES LAMB."

Carlyle speaks of Lamb's "proclivity to gin." People used to try to get away from it, smooth it over. It is wiser now to admit not only that he drank gin but a great many other things, and that he drank too much. Therefore many persons refer to him as "Poor Charles Lamb." Call Byron poor, if you will, who ruined his own happiness and that of many other people; call Keats poor, who died of consumption before he could do what his genius meant him to do; call Coleridge poor, stupefied and befogged as he was with opium, content to live on charity and have his family supported by his friends; but never call Lamb poor. To begin with, he saved two thousand pounds out of his small salary and innumerable benevolences, to take care of his sister after he should be gone. He helped everybody about him. Fielding's earliest biographer says that Fielding's table was always open to those who had been his friends in youth and had impaired their fortunes. Lamb's table during the later years in the Inner Temple and afterwards in other lodgings, was open to those who had impaired their fortunes, whether or not they had been his friends in youth.

He allowed fifty pounds a year for years to an old schoolmistress of his; he helped not only with money, of which he had little, but with care and thought and painstaking, of which you may find a hundred traces in his letters. You won't find in his letters more than necessary mention of the money he gave and lent. Therefore not poor Charles Lamb, but rich Charles Lamb, saint Charles Lamb, as Thackeray called him, and none the less a saint upon earth because he could not help drinking too much. The failing never kept him from his life-long duty. We may be sorry for it. We must be endlessly sorry because it grieved him and his sister for years. But to blame him were absurd; to pity were profane. Lamb himself resented even a hint of patronage. Coleridge called him "gentle-hearted," in print. Lamb wrote to him in one of the best passages in all his letters: "Substitute drunken-dog; ragged-head; seld-shaven; odd-eyed; stuttering; or any other epithet which truly and properly belongs to the gentleman in question."

But Lamb was important not merely to the needy. His letters, virtually an autobiography, are a record of great friendships and friendships with great men. The fame of his talk with them will never die. "No one," says Hazlitt, "ever stammered out such fine, piquant, deep, eloquent things in half a dozen half-sentences as he does. His jests scald like tears; and he probes a question with a play upon words."

Moreover, one cannot well condescend to a man who, although he was full of whims and pranks, of melancholy, and wild gaiety, was in essence as sensible as Ben Franklin. And his letters run the whole gamut.

HAWTHORNE'S INHERITANCE AND HIS ART

Honest, hearty, external romance is not for Hawthorne. His heart is not with Nathan Hale, or with Paul Revere on his ride, or with Wolfe taking the Heights of Abraham, and conquering the foe who courted death with the high chivalry of Sidney. Incident is not unimportant with Hawthorne, but it is important chiefly as the outward, bodily sign of the inward and moral drama. And if young readers (and all other readers) of Hawthorne would grasp this cardinal fact of his genius, they would cease demanding from him "action," in the conventional sense, and several other elements, to be noted anon, which, though in themselves admirable and to be desired, the author of "The Scarlet Letter" has not found indispensable to his unique endeavor.

In apparent contradiction to what has just been said, Hawthorne is often spoken of as if he were the historical novelist of New England, annalist-in-ordinary to "the old thirteen." In letter, nothing could be more false: in spirit, nothing more true. All that most of us know of the life of our ancestors resolves itself into a kind of tableau, intermittently present to the inward eye, and moralized by what we remember of "The Scarlet Letter," and "Legends of the Province House," and certain portions of "The House of the Seven Gables." Our not too graphic historians coöperate with the word of mouth, spoken on from generation to generation, to outline a sketch of the bleak past.

A few legends soberly color this sketch. Old portraits, old teaspoons, old chairs, and beautiful old brass candlesticks, document and certify the partial portrait; and even the average young New Englander, incurious of his country's past, is always able to draw aside the curtain from some such latent tableau or series of tableaux as this. He sees a long, narrow, wind-swept strip of land between forest and shore,—between the Indian and the deep sea. If it is muster day in any village of the strip, all the ancestors above sixteen years old are marching about in armor. The officers wear swords, the men carry "match-locks" or ten-foot pikes. If it is town-meeting, the ancestors, clad now in the small-clothes, jerkins, ruffs, and steeple-crown hats of peace, discuss even the least affairs with the patience of their constitutional breeding, and gravely cast the affirmative corn or the negative bean. If it is no day in particular, the young New Englander may look through the leaded panes of a log house and see the ancestor—*his* ancestor, perhaps—reading the Bible aloud, or dozing before a mighty fire, or making ready his guns against the Indian enemy who neither slumbered nor slept. Winter, Sunday, the little fortified meeting-house, and the rote of a few doleful hymns, probably appear often indeed to our contemporary's vision of those strenuous beginnings. If the conception he has, the conception most of us have, of the intellectual and moral life of the people is as grim as the physical conditions under which they thought, prayed, worked, and fought, Hawthorne is probably responsible for it. Those brave, intelligent fanatics—always brave, and always intelligent where superstition was not concerned—were no doubt morbidly sensitive in both religion and morals. The early government of Massachusetts has rightly been called a theocracy. Although the church-members probably felt themselves nearer the Unseen than any like body of modern men except the Scottish Covenanters, yet the gist of all their praying was, in the words of the hymn, "for a closer walk with God."

The truth of this general statement cannot be denied. But it is an imperfect statement, too often left without the obvious and needful supplement.   In the Theocracy as such, in the preachings, prayings, and persecutions, we forget other quite as real aspects of these men.   We forget them as soldiers and sailors; as law-makers, town-makers, and state-builders; as subjects of James and Charles and Cromwell, and Charles again.   We lose sight of the secular man bound up with the consecrated man within the iron ribs of the Puritan.   It is as if one should say that Franklin never lived because Jonathan Edwards was so much alive.   And Hawthorne is to blame.   Innocently, even unconsciously; yet still to blame.   Other men have written about Puritans and their descendants; none other with Hawthorne's power, or with a tithe of his imagination.

People forget, too, how seldom that imagination exercises itself with simply historical subjects in dealing with New England life; and, although Hawthorne has unmistakably the historic consciousness, it might better be called the *frisson historique*.   For, however he starts with a subject taken from history, in nine cases out of ten he either gives it an eerie twist, or makes it a mere point of departure into conscience-land, where, as an artist, he is forever pondering, in his inherited preoccupation with sin, grim, dusky problems of good and evil.   The secular Puritan is nothing to him.   The sinning good men, the persecutor and the persecuted, the bewitched, and the hag-ridden, are the Puritans for him.   And this controlling bent of Hawthorne's mind, which shows itself first in tales of the early colonial time, still controls it in "The Blithedale Romance" and other stories of later New England life, as well as in "Rappacini's Daughter" and "Transformation."

At first, while Hawthorne was trying his hand at the external, the ethical preoccupation was probably unconscious.   In "Mosses from an Old Manse" and in "Blithedale," where he is of course conscious enough of the habitual direction of his art, there are some admirable words of his own that are directly in point.   "The Old Apple Dealer"—to be found in the "Mosses"—begins with the following sentence: "The lover of the moral picturesque may sometimes find what he seeks in a character which is nevertheless of too negative a description to be seized upon and represented to the imaginative vision by word painting."   The inveterate "lover of the moral picturesque" causes Miles Coverdale to say: "I had never before experienced a mood that so robbed the actual world of its solidity.   It nevertheless involved a charm, on which—a devoted epicure of my own emotions—I resolved to pause, and enjoy the moral sillabub until quite dissolved away."   Coverdale, whatever his habitual relation to his creator, is evidently Hawthorne during that pause. Hawthorne himself is never more quintessentially Hawthorne than in a passage of the "Italian Note-Books," which, during some comment on the confessional, includes the pregnant remark:—"It must be very tedious to listen, day after day, to the minute and commonplace iniquities of the multitude of penitents, and it cannot be often that these are redeemed by the treasure-trove of a great sin." Hawthorne's provinciality, so far as he was provincial—and in some directions this quality carried him a good way—was important in circumscribing the field of his imagination. It was still more important to a writer whose professional treasure-trove was sin, or rather the sense of sin, that there were few or no outward distractions to beguile him from the main tendency of his genius. Hawthorne's heart was with New England, and his treasure was in the consecrated, Calvinistic part of the Puritan tradition.

But the Puritan, *redivivus,* would have thought this treasure ill-gotten gain, a fortune with a curse on it. The Reverend John Cotton, minister of "New Boston," being asked why in his later days he indulged *nocturnal studies* more than formerly, . . . pleasantly replied, "Because I love to sweeten my mouth with a piece of Calvin before I go to sleep." Now Mr. Cotton, were he still with us, might find many a piece of Calvin in the works of Hawthorne, but so flavored, sauced, and garnished as to be no better than witches' broth in the mouth of a Puritan divine. Mr. Henry James, who first expressed in precise terms the truth about Hawthorne's use of his material, thereby did an immense service to criticism in relieving the world of the impression, on the one hand, that he was the *romancier pessimiste* of Montégut's essay, and of the impression, on the other hand, that he was a kind of Neo-Puritanic teacher, with a moral and a purpose. Nothing in criticism is more subtle, and nothing, I am persuaded, more just, than Mr. James's pages concerning this matter. I risk injustice to him for the pleasure of quoting here a word or two of that remarkable exposition. "Nothing is more curious and interesting," says Mr. James, "than this almost exclusively *imported* character of the sense of sin in Hawthorne's mind; it seems to exist there merely for an artistic or literary purpose. He had ample cognizance of the Puritan conscience; it was his natural heritage; it was reproduced in him; looking into his soul he found it there. But his relation to it was only, as one may say, intellectual: it was not moral and theological. He played with it, and used it as a pigment; he treated it, as the metaphysicians say, objectively." In less dignified language, he found a great lump of Puritan black lead, which, by some process he never explained, arrived upon his palette as the varying hues of fancy. Hawthorne, indeed, was a psychoanalyst ahead of time.

DICKENS: HIS BEST BOOK?

Centenaries do two things, among others. They expose the community—in the case of Dickens a widest commonalty of race and speech —to a good deal of ill-regulated sentiment. And they breed much quiet and refreshing talk among friends. You, I doubt not, in corners of this great house of friendship, have lately been comparing notes about Charles Dickens. When you began to read him, and where; how much you read him now, and with how much pleasure; what are his best books, what even his best book—these are some of the recollections and opinions that engage all of us as the hundredth birthday draws nigh.

Where novelists are concerned, because with lyric poets novelists are the most personal of writers, the question of the best book is likely to be as alluring as it is ultimately futile. If "The Antiquary" and "Guy Mannering" and "The Heart of Midlothian" are to be placed at the head of Scott's list by reason of their sheer creative power, unaided by history, what then becomes of "Old Mortality" and the superbly constructed "Quentin Durward"? And if a man of taste, condemned to a desert island, were allowed to take with him just one Waverley novel, he would scarcely choose "The Abbot," or "Redgauntlet," or "Rob Roy," or even "Waverley." Yet are The Queen of Scots and the Young Chevalier, with all their inalienable charm, to be left behind on the never-to-be-revisited mainland?

Nor are the Janites without excellent divergences. The young and lively always prefer "Pride and Prejudice." As to those who are not so young as they have been, "Emma" is the book for them. A few amateurs of the pensive are all for "Persuasion." I have long since cast my vote for "Emma," and I know I shall never change it. But what a suffrage, that must exclude Elizabeth and Anne!

Thackeray is easy. On "the big four," everyone, I should suppose, is agreed—"Vanity Fair," "Pendennis," "Henry Esmond," and "The Newcomes," in order of composition. "Vanity Fair" is the greatest of the four; "Esmond" the most beautiful. But, with all its beauty and fire, with its English that lives in the memory like music, "Esmond" is yet a tour de force, conditioned by the manners and speech of a day long dead. However inferior in form "Vanity Fair" may be to "Henry Esmond," it yet has method enough to serve its high satirical purpose, and to liberate the characters that work out this purpose in a book whose height Thackeray never reached again.

As to Dickens's achievements, which most concern us just now, there is an extraordinary difference of opinion. There is still a multitude, though a waning multitude, that, taking his novels in the gross, thanks its stars for all and each. God rest you merry, gentlemen, let nothing you dismay. A curious remnant, mainly devoid of humor, swear by Dickens's one humorless story, and maintain the primacy of "A Tale of Two Cities." By all academic standards, to be sure, its structure is uncommonly good, and gives it a notable place in that regard. For the rest, "A Tale of Two Cities" seems to most of us, in spite of some fine chapters, a fearsome blend of Carlyle's spirit and Dickens's least lovely mannerisms. Without humor, with few striking characters, this well-ordered tale is one of the author's very few least spontaneous productions. And spontaneity, like humor, is of his essence.

Another little committee, as the French say, are fondly attached to "Great Expectations," the title of which, by the way, like many another of Dickens's titles, is in itself a stroke of genius. The partisans of "Great Expectations" not only laud its construction, in which Dickens was uncommonly successful, but they hold that here the master is more constantly and consistently "real" than in any other of his novels. Well, reality—literal, not symbolic reality—is not Dickens's long suit. And, though the tone of this book is quieter than that of the others, Miss Havisham is of a ghastly artificiality, the melodrama is plentiful and dark and dour, and Joe Gargery and Trabb's boy save the book. Trabb's boy has all the bounce and salience of a social revolution. Joe is a triumph, and the best of all Dickens's workingmen.

To a far larger company, and with far more reason, "Martin Chuzzlewit" leads all the rest. Many of its pages are full of that dæmonic power, that hallucination more vivid than reality, which Dickens exercised in his early prime. And if half of "Chuzzlewit" were equal, or even half equal, to Mrs. Gamp, the great humorist's top achievement in humor, it would be such a book as the world has never seen. "Thou Manning-tree ox, with the pudding in thy belly," send Quickly and Doll Tearsheet packing. Gamp is thy true helpmeet. She has not thy forgetive brain, thy wit or thy marvellous humor. All her humor resides in her creator. But she is thy soulmate, thine affinity. Take her, she is thine. Alas for "Chuzzlewit," Mrs. Gamp glorifies and immortalizes only a few of its chapters. Its form is invertebrate, it is choked with impossible characters, its total effect is bewildering.

Two books give "A Tale of Two Cities," "Great Expectations," and "Chuzzlewit" and all the others, a very long lead in popularity. In fact, "The Pickwick Papers" and "David Copperfield" probably divide the suffrages of the vast majority of those that read Dickens. "Copperfield" must always be viewed tenderly. To the degree that it is autobiography, it is enchanting. As with "Pendennis," "The Mill on the Floss," "Redgauntlet"—as always when a great writer looks back on his childhood and youth—there is a golden mist over the early days of Dickens transmuted into those of Copperfield. If only we could have those magical pages, and David, and the Micawbers, without Agnes or Dora—poor things—or Mr. Dick, or Rosa Dartle, or little Em'ly, or so many donkeys on the green! Micawber alone could furnish forth a volume.

You will be perceiving, as the Scotch minister said after eliminating all other fish in favor of the whale—you will be perceiving that "The Pickwick Papers" is the book most after my own heart. In that book Dickens attacks no abuses. There can be nothing but praise for the reforms he so nobly initiated in schools and courts and prisons. But for every reform his art suffered. In "Pickwick" there are no dark emotions, except in the incidental stories, which don't count; no love making, save as burlesque; no wallowing in pathos, and, happily, no plot to speak of. Whenever Dickens made a poor plot it hurt his book; whenever he made a good one it hurt him.

The very era of "Pickwick," "the year one thousand eight hundred and twenty-seven," was one of its good fortunes. Close to us in spirit, it is incredibly far from us in time. As regards the material and mechanical side of life Mr. Pickwick is aeons from us and almost synchronous with Julius Caesar. Railroads not having come to spoil whatever of "Merry England" was left by the Protestant Reformation, Mr. Pickwick moved about the island as Caesar did, with horses and wheels. Compare Carker's frantic railway trip with the flight of the Muggleton coach and you will see that Dickens himself was a man of stage coaches, not a man of railroads. Franklin had played a Yankee Prometheus on the cowshed, but electricity was still mainly confined to lightning rods. You cannot "call up" the Pickwickians at their club, or even telegraph to them. Telepathy is your only hope. Railroads won't bring you to Dingley Dell—there's no station within a thousand miles of it. Nor murder-wagons—"automobiles not allowed on this estate." Write first, and seal your letter (wafers are vulgar); then follow it in the coach, or in a postchaise, or in your own curricle.

In truth, in glad truth, "modern inventions" help us only by contrast to savor "The Pickwick Papers," where these things have no more place than in a fairy-tale. The book is, to be sure, a kind of cockney fairy-tale, strongly dashed with "Don Quixote." Not a few critics have called Mr. Pickwick a middle-class Don Quixote, and Sam Weller a cockney Sancho Panza. Though the comparison is inexact, especially concerning Sam, Mr. Pickwick, nevertheless—like Colonel Newcome, and Parson Adams, and My Uncle Toby, and Sir Roger de Coverley—is of the seed and lineage of the Don. "Quelle composition défectueuse," cried Flaubert, on finishing "Pickwick." Right, Brigadier; but, oddly enough, the defect of the composition is its quality. And so it is, of course, in the far greater work of Cervantes, in "Roderick Random," and in those other picaresque exemplars that young Copperfield-Dickens's father left for him in "the little room."

The naïve plan of "Pickwick" came clearly from the books in the little room. Worked in with it are much coaching and "posting," fantastic comedy, old English fun, broad humor and good humor, happiness and—this above all—the perpetual spirit of youth. The innocence of Mr. Pickwick helps to endear him to us. The least worldly of readers feel that they know a thing or two unknown to Mr. Pickwick. From this book you learn as little of sex as from "Robinson Crusoe" or Emerson's Essays. Without the sense of religion, without poetry, without psychology, without Swiveller and Micawber, and Gamp, "Pickwick" yet prevails by its score of old inns, its happy journeys, its sunlight and hearth-light and what Lamb called "punch-light." In its mirth and youthful jollity a tormented modern may forget Nietzsche, Mr. Bernard Shaw, and Mr. H. G. Wells. On the title-page of "Pickwick" belongs the famous motto for a sun-dial, "Horas non numero nisi serenas."

Gentlemen, the hundredth birthday of Charles Dickens falls on February seventh. If midnight of the sixth find you drinking a tankard of purl to his memory, you will see a brave and genial ghost.

TENNYSON AND BROWNING

AS RELIGIOUS POETS

When one comes to them as religious poets the difference is sharp indeed. Tennyson mirrors his time; he was brought up as a boy in the Church of England, and there is a loving, lingering touch in whatever he writes of the parish church or church-yard, or the rubrics, or any beautiful ceremony or observance,—such a love, almost, as you might imagine the later Romans would have had for all the rites of the temple in the literal truth of which they had ceased to believe. Because Tennyson went so far from the words "Our Father which art in Heaven" as to come to expressing faith in these lines which everyone remembers,—"One far-off divine event, To which the whole creation moves." He often mirrored doubt as to individual existence beyond the grave, but he did for the most part contrive to cling to the belief in it, as to which he made the extraordinary remark more than once that if he did not believe in personal immortality he should commit suicide. And so one has the feeling, as one has in those vehement lines of his against free-thinkers, that if his faith had been more complete, more spontaneous, less checkered by constantly recurring doubt, he would have been less insistent in his statements of it, and less perturbed by any attacks of the atheists and free-thinkers. Towards the end, in his old age, he came into a much more serene and undoubting mood.

How far, however, can we accept the latest utterances of an old man to be characteristic utterances of the man in his strength? The doubting faith of "In Memoriam" seems to me to represent the true Tennyson, the Tennyson for the greater part of his career, far more truly than the lovely lines of "Crossing the Bar," written in the last five years of his life. "And may there be no moaning of the bar, when I put out to sea." At the end he appeared to have a complete faith that there would be no moaning of the bar, and that he should see his Pilot face to face. But there were doubts many and grave in the earlier years, and the middle and later middle years of his career.

Browning, on the other hand, is an out and out personal believer, an exception to the greater number of the able writers of our time. As you would scarcely gather from most of Browning's poetry that there was such a country as England—Italy would appear to be the principal spot on the map in by far the greater part of Browning's poetry—so you would not gather from the greater number of his poems that there had been any such thing in the world as a discovery that had revolutionized human thought, that had turned it upside down as nothing had before since the beginning. These men were born into a world which everybody believed to be six thousand years old,—just about that,—they spent their manhood and died in a world which all persons whether intelligent or not knew, if they cared to know, must have existed for millions of years. They were born when everybody, almost everybody, believed that God made the world in six days, in a world which contemplated no God but a personal God, who dealt in special providences and special penalties, who exercised an intimate supervision over individual affairs; they passed their manhood and died in a world in which the leading intellectual spirits of the day were disposed to find no evidence of personal supervision whatever; a world whose operation was regulated as almost an infinitesimal part of the circling worlds about us. They think, the leading spirits of the time, that this small planet and all others, revolve in obedience to laws that proceed from we know not where or whom. You might read Browning and scarcely surmise what you are constantly reminded of in Tennyson,—all the time you are reminded in Tennyson of what the intellectual life of the time means to him, how it has interested him and disquieted him. And that very same personal feeling of Browning's, the old-fashioned feeling that the matter of life is between a man and God or a woman and God, that very feeling of Browning's keeps him from having much sympathy, or showing any sign of what is Tennyson's chief enthusiasm, that is order, patriotic order, and a patriotism that is ready some day to extend to the parliament of man, the federation of the world. Tennyson everywhere, when he doubts and when he believes, and he believes oftener than he doubts, is forever telling us of eternal process, of sublime order, and of the fact that is to him fact, that God fulfills himself in many ways through the new order as through the old. When his friend dies in early youth, Arthur Hallam, young as he was, Tennyson writes of him:

> "The fame is quenched that I foresaw,
>   The head hath missed an earthly wreath;
>   I curse not nature, no, nor death;
> For nothing is that errs from law."

And of this life and another he writes:

> "Eternal process moving on,
>   From state to state the spirits walk;
>   And these are but the shattered stalk
> Or ruin'd chrysalis of one."

The same enthusiasm for order and obedience to law, and desire for the ultimate well-being of the race is what lifts the ideal dreamer of "Locksley Hall" into such lines as these:

> "Not in vain the distance beacons. Forward,
>   forward let us range,
> Let the great world spin forever down the
>   ringing grooves of change."

> "For all we thought and loved and did,
>   And hoped and suffer'd, is but seed
> Of what in them is flower and fruit."

This is the crowning race to be:

> "Whereof the man, that with me trod
>   This planet, was a noble type
>   Appearing ere the times were ripe,
> That friend of mine who lives in God.

> That God who ever lives and loves,
>   One God, one law, one element,
>   And one far-off divine event,
> To which the whole creation moves."

All that is out of Browning; socially dynamic a good deal of his poetry is, if one went literally by it. Tennyson is an optimist, but as you may see, an optimist once removed; that is, the world as Tennyson sees it is very far indeed from pleasing him; the world Browning sees pleases him because the very imperfection delights him as the best earnest and proof that we are to go on and advance, each man for himself, if you please, not the race, but the individual; after his death the imperfection is to be made perfect. And with Browning apparently a conclusive proof of a life to come is that this life must be, for every man, in a way frustrated and imperfect; whereas in Tennyson the hope of immortality is a hope based on the justice, the beneficence of the law which rules it all.

AS TO "MARGARET OGILVY"

Perhaps not every one remembers what Stevenson wrote to Mr. Barrie from Vailima in December, 1892. "There are two of us now," he said, writing of the "Window," "that the Shirra might have patted on the head. And please do not think that when I thus seem to bracket myself with you I am wholly blinded with vanity. Jess is beyond my frontier line; I could not touch her skirt; I have no such glamour on my pen. I am a capable artist, but it begins to look to me as if you were a man of genius."

Whether Scott, the Shirra, would have patted Barrie on the head for "Margaret Ogilvy" must ever remain doubtful. Like Carlyle and like Barrie, he made for himself the discovery never made by most people, and first expressed by Gray in the year 1766, "that in one's whole life one can never have more than a single mother." Yet Scott's deepest testimony to this truth was not discovered till after he was gone. Although all know the passage, still I will read it. What emotion throbs under Lockhart's formal phrase:

Perhaps the most touching evidence of the lasting tenderness of his early domestic feelings was exhibited to his executors when they opened his repositories in search of his testament the evening after his burial.

On lifting up his desk we found arranged in careful order a series of little objects, which had obviously been placed there so that his eye might rest on them every morning before he began his tasks. These were the old-fashioned boxes that had garnished his mother's toilet, when he, a sickly child, slept in her dressing room—a silver taper stand which the young advocate had bought her with his first five-guinea fee—a row of small packets inscribed with her hand and containing the hair of her off-spring that had died before her—his father's snuff box and etui case—and more things of the like sort recalling the "old familiar faces."

Can "Margaret Ogilvy" say more? Yes, one thing more, at least. We—I mean the public—then first learned explicitly from Mr. Barrie how very poor and lowly had been his beginnings. Most self-made men either qualify—"everybody was poor in those days, you know"—or boast or hide. Barrie—but if you would know how he does it, you must recall or read "Margaret Ogilvy." At first reading one is likely to be shocked at the intimacy of the book, and to think that it never should have been written. At a second reading not only do we know that literature should not have been deprived of a masterpiece, but we realize as from no other volume the whole truth of Gray's famous discovery. Let no one who has not read the strange book be afraid of it. "Margaret Ogilvy" is almost as full of humor as of pathos. And its English is only less beautiful than its lowland Scotch.

So much for set pieces *before* any projected reading. Whatever such pieces may do by way of information and stimulus, all good teachers are aware that what comes *after* the reading is of more importance. Extemporaneous talks, question and answer, free discussion, are of the essence in all such affairs of the class-room, whether literature or composition be concerned. In the case of "The Critic," Sheridan's glorious farce, printed in The Copeland Reader, by the way, I have found that young people are vastly interested in the stage history of the time, old customs of the theatre, players of the early casts, Sheridan's other plays, and—of course—Sheridan himself. Best of all, after a few needful explanations, they are delighted and, as Lamb would say, much arrided by the trenchant, never-failing wit of the farce. Except for the inevitable, disinherited few that have no sense of humor, I have always found that young men and women understand and fully enjoy the splendid ridicule so cunningly directed against plays, play-actors, playwrights, stage-managers, critics, and audiences. They also understand the audacious digs at Shakespeare in the madness of Tilburina and the last combat of Don Ferolo Whiskerandos. In view of "The Critic" and all its implications, it is almost incredible yet after all natural enough that, in his own theatrical practice, Sheridan himself should have been an arch-conservative. Nothing shows his proverbial timidity better than the well-worn anecdote of Mrs. Siddons, Sheridan, and the sleep-walking scene. In that incident, the lady prevailed and was proved to be right, but most often Sheridan was "monstrous witty" yet also wise in his generation. Mrs. Fiske's highly original (and triumphant) conception of Mrs. Malaprop would have given Sheridan a very bad turn. Who can say how the public of his day would have decided?

Similarly introduced, Shakespeare will always go with any class or audience that is worth reading to. He that would precipitate a discussion in his class-room has only to read, after illuminating preface, the account of the death of Falstaff, from "King Henry V," and follow it with the death of Socrates from the "Phaedo." I have chosen both scenes for the collection, though the chronological order keeps them far apart. Dr. Furness, who was a capital reader, gave the whole Falstaff scene as broad farce, in which I venture to think he was almost entirely wrong. But here beginneth new matter—for the class-room. Certain portions of the Bible provoke fine differences of opinion. A few among many such I have found to be the Book of Ruth, the Book of Ecclesiastes, the story of the Prodigal Son, the story of Naaman and Elisha and Gehazi. "Are not Abana and Pharpar, rivers of Damascus, better than all the waters of Israel? May I not wash in them and be clean?"

Here is a good place to say that I should not like to have the Bible as much dramatized in church as I incline to dramatize it. The clergy should, however, be audible. Not all of them are. The clergy should give us the meaning. Not all of them do. The theological schools send out many of them not even emphasizing the negative in the Ten Commandments. How then can the laity be expected to be good?

But let us go back to College. Much as I have read with comment, I have favored and often practised a method praised in a recent article in the Boston *Herald*. "The head of the English department in a state university," this editorial piece begins, "recently said in discussing his work that he rated no influence that he was able to bring to bear upon students higher than that of reading aloud to them masterpieces, and accompanying the exercise with a minimum of critical discussion. . . . A member of the Yale faculty, whose department is not English, feels that one of the best things that he can do for selected groups of students is to stir their interest and appreciation of great literature in evenings of reading aloud and free discussion." These words bring to the minds of old Harvard men Child and the ballads, Palmer and his own translation of Homer. The few persons privileged to hear Mr. Palmer read Shelley and other modern verse today note with delight that the charm and the spell are quite what they so famously were in that distant time. There never sounded in the voices of those great professors the didactic, almost hectoring tone that often ruins the effect of literature made audible.

To conclude, without sequence but very heartily, Harvard undergraduates have become even better to teach and to read to in the last few years,—the years during which the tutorial system has begun to make itself felt. And further, in conclusion, among my few best audiences for more than a generation have been those assembled at Radcliffe College, in Sever Hall, at the Harvard Union, and at the Harvard clubs of Chicago and Boston. But all my audiences are good, and therefore I sha'n't blame them when they begin to give me a good-natured signal to stop lecturing and talking and reading.

C. T. Copeland.

Cambridge,
October, 1926.

CONTENTS

CONTENTS

CONTENTS

CONTENTS

ILLUSTRATIONS

PUBLISHERS' NOTE

Professor Copeland says in his introduction to this Treasury, that "the selection includes only what I have read aloud during thirty-four years of teaching, lecturing, and reading." But as no panorama of English and American literature could be complete which omitted Chaucer and Spenser, Professor Copeland has included selections from these great English poets, even though he has not made use of them in his readings; and on the principle that the American historians William H. Prescott, John Lothrop Motley, and Francis Parkman should be represented to complete the Treasury, selections from them also are given.

Except for the selections referred to in this note, every passage in these five volumes has met the test of being read aloud by Professor Copeland to audiences or classes.

COPELAND'S
TREASURY FOR BOOKLOVERS

COPELAND'S
TREASURY FOR BOOKLOVERS

I. TRANSLATIONS

From THE BIBLE (KING JAMES VERSION)

Judges, IV; V, 19-31

IV

AND the children of Israel again did evil in the sight of the LORD, when Ehud was dead.

2 And the LORD sold them into the hand of Jabin king of Canaan, that reigned in Hazor; the captain of whose host *was* Sisera, which dwelt in Harosheth of the Gentiles.

3 And the children of Israel cried unto the LORD; for he had nine hundred chariots of iron; and twenty years he mightily oppressed the children of Israel.

4 And Deborah a prophetess, the wife of Lapidoth, she judged Israel at that time.

5 And she dwelt under the palm tree of Deborah, between Ramah and Bethel in mount Ephraim; and the children of Israel came up to her for judgment.

6 And she sent and called Barak, the son of Abinoam, out of Kedesh-naphtali, and said unto him, Hath not the LORD God of Israel commanded, *saying,* Go, and draw toward mount Tabor, and take with thee ten thousand men of the children of Naphtali and of the children of Zebulun?

7 And I will draw unto thee, to the river Kishon, Sisera, the captain of Jabin's army, with his chariots and his multitude; and I will deliver him into thine hand.

8 And Barak said unto her, If thou wilt go with me, then I will go; but if thou wilt not go with me, *then* I will not go.

9 And she said, I will surely go with thee: notwithstanding the journey that thou takest shall not be for thine honour; for the LORD

shall sell Sisera into the hand of a woman. And Deborah arose, and went with Barak to Kedesh.

10 And Barak called Zebulun and Naphtali to Kedesh; and he went up with ten thousand men at his feet: and Deborah went up with him.

11 Now Heber the Kenite, *which was* of the children of Hobab, the father in law of Moses, had severed himself from the Kenites, and pitched his tent unto the plain of Zaanaim, which *is* by Kedesh.

12 And they shewed Sisera that Barak the son of Abinoam was gone up to mount Tabor.

13 And Sisera gathered together all his chariots, *even* nine hundred chariots of iron, and all the people that *were* with him, from Harosheth of the Gentiles unto the river of Kishon.

14 And Deborah said unto Barak, Up; for this *is* the day in which the Lord hath delivered Sisera into thine hand: is not the Lord gone out before thee? So Barak went down from mount Tabor, and ten thousand men after him.

15 And the Lord discomfited Sisera, and all *his* chariots, and all *his* host, with the edge of the sword, before Barak; so that Sisera lighted down off *his* chariot, and fled away on his feet.

16 But Barak pursued after the chariots, and after the host, unto Harosheth of the Gentiles: and all the host of Sisera fell upon the edge of the sword; *and* there was not a man left.

17 Howbeit, Sisera fled away on his feet to the tent of Jael the wife of Heber the Kenite: for *there was* peace between Jabin the king of Hazor and the house of Heber the Kenite.

18 And Jael went out to meet Sisera, and said unto him, Turn in, my lord, turn in to me; fear not: and when he had turned in unto her into the tent, she covered him with a mantle.

19 And he said unto her, Give me, I pray thee, a little water to drink; for I am thirsty: and she opened a bottle of milk, and gave him drink, and covered him.

20 Again he said unto her, Stand in the door of the tent, and it shall be, when any man doth come and inquire of thee, and say, Is there any man here? that thou shalt say, No.

21 Then Jael, Heber's wife, took a nail of the tent, and took an hammer in her hand, and went softly unto him, and smote the nail into his temples, and fastened it into the ground; for he was fast asleep, and weary: so he died.

22 And, behold, as Barak pursued Sisera, Jael came out to meet him, and said unto him, Come, and I will shew thee the man whom thou

seekest. And when he came into her *tent,* behold, Sisera lay dead, and the nail *was* in his temples.

23 So God subdued on that day Jabin the king of Canaan before the children of Israel.

24 And the hand of the children of Israel prospered, and prevailed against Jabin the king of Canaan, until they had destroyed Jabin king of Canaan.

V

19 The kings came *and* fought; then fought the kings of Canaan in Taanach by the waters of Megiddo; they took no gain of money.

20 They fought from heaven; the stars in their courses fought against Sisera.

21 The river of Kishon swept them away, that ancient river, the river Kishon. O my soul, thou hast trodden down strength.

22 Then were the horsehoofs broken by the means of the pransings, the pransings of their mighty ones.

23 Curse ye Meroz, said the angel of the LORD; curse ye bitterly the inhabitants thereof; because they came not to the help of the LORD, to the help of the LORD against the mighty.

24 Blessed above women shall Jael the wife of Heber the Kenite be; blessed shall she be above women in the tent.

25 He asked water, *and* she gave *him* milk; she brought forth butter in a lordly dish.

26 She put her hand to the nail, and her right hand to the workmen's hammer; and with the hammer she smote Sisera; she smote off his head, when she had pierced and stricken through his temples.

27 At her feet he bowed, he fell, he lay down: at her feet he bowed, he fell; where he bowed there he fell down dead.

28 The mother of Sisera looked out at a window, and cried through the lattice, Why is his chariot *so* long in coming? why tarry the wheels of his chariots?

29 Her wise ladies answered her, yea, she returned answer to herself.

30 Have they not sped? have they *not* divided the prey; to every man a damsel *or* two? to Sisera a prey of divers colours, a prey of divers colours of needlework, of divers colours of needlework on both sides, *meet* for the necks of *them that take* the spoil?

31 So let all thine enemies perish, O LORD: but *let* them that love him *be* as the sun when he goeth forth in his might. And the land had rest forty years.

Ruth

I

Now it came to pass, in the days when the judges ruled, that there was a famine in the land. And a certain man of Beth-lehem-judah went to sojourn in the country of Moab, he, and his wife, and his two sons.

2 And the name of the man *was* Elimelech, and the name of his wife Naomi, and the name of his two sons, Mahlon and Chilion, Ephrathites of Beth-lehem-judah. And they came into the country of Moab, and continued there.

3 And Elimelech, Naomi's husband, died; and she was left, and her two sons.

4 And they took them wives of the women of Moab; the name of the one *was* Orpah, and the name of the other Ruth: and they dwelled there about ten years.

5 And Mahlon and Chilion died also both of them; and the woman was left of her two sons and her husband.

6 Then she arose, with her daughters in law, that she might return from the country of Moab: for she had heard in the country of Moab how that the LORD had visited his people in giving them bread.

7 Wherefore she went forth out of the place where she was, and her two daughters in law with her: and they went on the way to return unto the land of Judah.

8 And Naomi said unto her two daughters in law, Go, return each to her mother's house: the LORD deal kindly with you, as ye have dealt with the dead, and with me.

9 The LORD grant you that ye may find rest, each *of you* in the house of her husband. Then she kissed them; and they lifted up their voice, and wept.

10 And they said unto her, Surely we will return with thee unto thy people.

11 And Naomi said, Turn again, my daughters, why will ye go with me? *are* there yet *any more* sons in my womb, that they may be your husbands?

12 Turn again, my daughters, go *your way;* for I am too old to have an husband. If I should say, I have hope, *if* I should have an husband also to night, and should also bear sons;

13 Would ye tarry for them till they were grown? would ye stay for them from having husbands? nay, my daughters; for it grieveth me much, for your sakes, that the hand of the LORD is gone out against me.

14 And they lifted up their voice, and wept again: and Orpah kissed her mother in law, but Ruth clave unto her.

15 And she said, Behold, thy sister in law is gone back unto her people, and unto her gods; return thou after thy sister in law.

16 And Ruth said, Entreat me not to leave thee, *or* to return from following after thee: for whither thou goest, I will go; and where thou lodgest, I will lodge: thy people *shall be* my people, and thy God my God:

17 Where thou diest will I die, and there will I be buried: the LORD do so to me, and more also, *if ought* but death part thee and me.

18 When she saw that she was stedfastly minded to go with her, then she left speaking unto her.

19 So they two went until they came to Beth-lehem. And it came to pass, when they were come to Beth-lehem, that all the city was moved about them, and they said, *Is* this Naomi?

20 And she said unto them, Call me not Naomi, call me Mara: for the Almighty hath dealt very bitterly with me.

21 I went out full, and the LORD hath brought me home again empty: why *then* call ye me Naomi, seeing the LORD hath testified against me, and the Almighty hath afflicted me?

22 So Naomi returned, and Ruth the Moabitess, her daughter in law, with her, which returned out of the country of Moab: and they came to Beth-lehem in the beginning of barley harvest.

II

AND Naomi had a kinsman of her husband's, a mighty man of wealth of the family of Elimelech; and his name *was* Boaz.

2 And Ruth the Moabitess said unto Naomi, Let me now go to the field, and glean ears of corn after *him* in whose sight I shall find grace. And she said unto her, Go, my daughter.

3 And she went, and came, and gleaned in the field after the reapers: and her hap was to light on a part of the field *belonging* unto Boaz, who *was* of the kindred of Elimelech.

4 And, behold, Boaz came from Beth-lehem, and said unto the reapers, The LORD *be* with you. And they answered him, The LORD bless thee.

5 Then said Boaz unto his servant that was set over the reapers, Whose damsel *is* this?

6 And the servant that was set over the reapers answered and said, It *is* the Moabitish damsel that came back with Naomi out of the country of Moab:

7 And she said, I pray you, let me glean and gather after the reapers among the sheaves: so she came, and hath continued even from the morning until now, that she tarried a little in the house.

8 Then said Boaz unto Ruth, Hearest thou not, my daughter? Go not to glean in another field, neither go from hence, but abide here fast by my maidens:

9 *Let* thine eyes *be* on the field that they do reap, and go thou after them: have I not charged the young men that they shall not touch thee? and when thou art athirst, go unto the vessels, and drink of *that* which the young men have drawn.

10 Then she fell on her face, and bowed herself to the ground, and said unto him, Why have I found grace in thine eyes, that thou shouldest take knowledge of me, seeing I *am* a stranger?

11 And Boaz answered and said unto her, It hath fully been shewed me all that thou hast done unto thy mother in law since the death of thine husband; and *how* thou hast left thy father and thy mother, and the land of thy nativity, and art come unto a people which thou knewest not heretofore.

12 The LORD recompense thy work, and a full reward be given thee of the LORD God of Israel, under whose wings thou art come to trust.

13 Then she said, Let me find favour in thy sight, my lord; for that thou hast comforted me, and for that thou hast spoken friendly unto thine handmaid, though I be not like unto one of thine handmaidens.

14 And Boaz said unto her, At mealtime come thou hither, and eat of the bread, and dip thy morsel in the vinegar. And she sat beside the reapers: and he reached her parched *corn,* and she did eat, and was sufficed, and left.

15 And when she was risen up to glean, Boaz commanded his young men, saying, Let her glean even among the sheaves, and reproach her not:

16 And let fall also *some* of the handfuls of purpose for her, and leave *them,* that she may glean *them,* and rebuke her not.

17 So she gleaned in the field until even, and beat out that she had gleaned: and it was about an ephah of barley.

18 And she took *it* up, and went into the city; and her mother in law saw what she had gleaned; and she brought forth, and gave to her that she had reserved after she was sufficed.

19 And her mother in law said unto her, Where hast thou gleaned to day? and where wroughtest thou? blessed be he that did take knowledge of thee. And she shewed her mother in law with whom she had wrought, and said, The man's name with whom I wrought to day *is* Boaz.

20 And Naomi said unto her daughter in law, Blessed *be* he of the

LORD, who hath not left off his kindness to the living and to the dead. And Naomi said unto her, The man *is* near of kin unto us, one of our next kinsmen.

21 And Ruth the Moabitess said, He said unto me also, Thou shalt keep fast by my young men, until they have ended all my harvest.

22 And Naomi said unto Ruth her daughter in law, *It is* good, my daughter, that thou go out with his maidens, that they meet thee not in any other field.

23 So she kept fast by the maidens of Boaz to glean unto the end of barley harvest, and of wheat harvest; and dwelt with her mother in law.

III

THEN Naomi her mother in law said unto her, My daughter, shall I not seek rest for thee, that it may be well with thee?

2 And now *is* not Boaz of our kindred, with whose maidens thou wast? Behold, he winnoweth barley to night in the threshingfloor.

3 Wash thyself, therefore, and anoint thee, and put thy raiment upon thee, and get thee down to the floor: *but* make not thyself known unto the man, until he shall have done eating and drinking.

4 And it shall be, when he lieth down, that thou shalt mark the place where he shall lie, and thou shalt go in, and uncover his feet, and lay thee down; and he will tell thee what thou shalt do.

5 And she said unto her, All that thou sayest unto me I will do.

6 And she went down unto the floor, and did according to all that her mother in law bade her.

7 And when Boaz had eaten and drunk, and his heart was merry, he went to lie down at the end of the heap of corn: and she came softly, and uncovered his feet, and laid her down.

8 And it came to pass at midnight, that the man was afraid, and turned himself; and, behold, a woman lay at his feet.

9 And he said, Who *art* thou? And she answered, I *am* Ruth thine handmaid; spread therefore thy skirt over thine handmaid; for thou *art* a near kinsman.

10 And he said, Blessed *be* thou of the Lord, my daughter; *for* thou hast shewed more kindness in the latter end than at the beginning, inasmuch as thou followest not young men, whether poor or rich.

11 And now, my daughter, fear not; I will do to thee all that thou requirest: for all the city of my people doth know that thou *art* a virtuous woman.

12 And now, it is true that I *am thy* near kinsman: howbeit, there is a kinsman nearer than I.

13 Tarry this night, and it shall be in the morning, *that* if he will perform unto thee the part of a kinsman, well; let him do the kinsman's part: but if he will not do the part of a kinsman to thee, then will I do the part of a kinsman to thee, *as* the Lord liveth: lie down until the morning.

14 And she lay at his feet until the morning; and she rose up before one could know another. And he said, Let it not be known that a woman came into the floor.

15 Also he said, Bring the vail that *thou hast* upon thee, and hold it. And when she held it, he measured six *measures* of barley, and laid *it* on her: and she went into the city.

16 And when she came to her mother in law, she said, Who *art* thou, my daughter? And she told her all that the man had done to her.

17 And she said, These six *measures* of barley gave he me: for he said to me, Go not empty unto thy mother in law.

18 Then said she, Sit still, my daughter, until thou know how the matter will fall: for the man will not be in rest, until he have finished the thing this day.

IV

THEN went Boaz up to the gate, and sat him down there: and, behold, the kinsman of whom Boaz spake, came by: unto whom he said, Ho, such a one! turn aside, sit down here. And he turned aside, and sat down.

2 And he took ten men of the elders of the city, and said, Sit ye down here. And they sat down.

3 And he said unto the kinsman, Naomi, that is come again out of the country of Moab, selleth a parcel of land, which *was* our brother Elimelech's:

4 And I thought to advertise thee, saying, Buy *it* before the inhabitants, and before the elders of my people. If thou wilt redeem *it*, redeem *it;* but if thou wilt not redeem *it, then* tell me, that I may know: for *there is* none to redeem *it* beside thee; and I *am* after thee. And he said, I will redeem *it*.

5 Then said Boaz, What day thou buyest the field of the hand of Naomi, thou must buy *it* also of Ruth the Moabitess, the wife of the dead, to raise up the name of the dead upon his inheritance.

6 And the kinsman said, I cannot redeem *it* for myself, lest I mar

mine own inheritance: redeem thou my right to thyself: for I cannot redeem *it*.

7 Now this *was the manner* in former time in Israel, concerning redeeming, and concerning changing, for to confirm all things; A man plucked off his shoe, and gave *it* to his neighbour: and this *was* a testimony in Israel.

8 Therefore the kinsman said unto Boaz, Buy *it* for thee. So he drew off his shoe.

9 And Boaz said unto the elders, and *unto* all the people, Ye *are* witnesses this day, that I have bought all that *was* Elimelech's, and all that *was* Chilion's and Mahlon's, of the hand of Naomi.

10 Moreover, Ruth the Moabitess, the wife of Mahlon, have I purchased to be my wife, to raise up the name of the dead upon his inheritance, that the name of the dead be not cut off from among his brethren and from the gate of his place: ye *are* witnesses this day.

11 And all the people that *were* in the gate, and the elders, said, *We are* witnesses. The LORD make the woman that is come into thine house like Rachel and like Leah, which two did build the house of Israel: and do thou worthily in Ephratah, and be famous in Beth-lehem:

12 And let thy house be like the house of Pharez, whom Tamar bare unto Judah, of the seed which the LORD shall give thee of this young woman.

13 So Boaz took Ruth, and she was his wife: and when he went in unto her, the LORD gave her conception, and she bare a son.

14 And the women said unto Naomi, Blessed *be* the LORD, which hath not left thee this day without a kinsman, that his name may be famous in Israel.

15 And he shall be unto thee a restorer of *thy* life, and a nourisher of thine old age: for thy daughter in law, which loveth thee, which is better to thee than seven sons, hath born him.

16 And Naomi took the child, and laid it in her bosom, and became nurse unto it.

17 And the women her neighbours gave it a name, saying, There is a son born to Naomi; and they called his name Obed: he *is* the father of Jesse, the father of David.

18 Now these *are* the generations of Pharez: Pharez begat Hezron,

19 And Hezron begat Ram, and Ram begat Amminadab,

20 And Amminadab begat Nahshon, and Nahshon begat Salmon.

21 And Salmon begat Boaz, and Boaz begat Obed,

22 And Obed begat Jesse, and Jesse begat David.

II. Samuel, XVIII, 1 —XIX, 4

XVIII

AND David numbered the people that *were* with him, and set captains of thousands and captains of hundreds over them.

2 And David sent forth a third part of the people under the hand of Joab, and a third part under the hand of Abishai the son of Zeruiah, Joab's brother, and a third part under the hand of Ittai the Gittite. And the king said unto the people, I will surely go forth with you myself also.

3 But the people answered, Thou shalt not go forth: for if we flee away, they will not care for us; neither if half of us die, will they care for us: but now *thou art* worth ten thousand of us: therefore now *it is* better that thou succour us out of the city.

4 And the king said unto them, What seemeth you best I will do. And the king stood by the gate side, and all the people came out by hundreds and by thousands.

5 And the king commanded Joab and Abishai and Ittai, saying, *Deal* gently for my sake with the young man, *even* with Absalom. And all the people heard when the king gave all the captains charge concerning Absalom.

6 So the people went out into the field against Israel: and the battle was in the wood of Ephraim;

7 Where the people of Israel were slain before the servants of David; and there was there a great slaughter that day of twenty thousand *men*.

8 For the battle was there scattered over the face of all the country: and the wood devoured more people that day than the sword devoured.

9 And Absalom met the servants of David. And Absalom rode upon a mule, and the mule went under the thick boughs of a great oak, and his head caught hold of the oak, and he was taken up between the heaven and the earth; and the mule that *was* under him went away.

10 And a certain man saw *it,* and told Joab, and said, Behold, I saw Absalom hanged in an oak.

11 And Joab said unto the man that told him, And, behold, thou sawest *him,* and why didst thou not smite him there to the ground? and I would have given thee ten *shekels* of silver, and a girdle.

12 And the man said unto Joab, Though I should receive a thousand *shekels* of silver in mine hand, *yet* would I not put forth mine hand against the king's son: for in our hearing the king charged thee and

Abishai and Ittai, saying, Beware that none *touch* the young man Absalom.

13 Otherwise I should have wrought falsehood against mine own life: for there is no matter hid from the king, and thou thyself wouldest have set thyself against *me*.

14 Then said Joab, I may not tarry thus with thee. And he took three darts in his hand, and thrust them through the heart of Absalom, while he *was* yet alive in the midst of the oak.

15 And ten young men that bare Joab's armour compassed about and smote Absalom, and slew him.

16 And Joab blew the trumpet, and the people returned from pursuing after Israel: for Joab held back the people.

17 And they took Absalom, and cast him into a great pit in the wood, and laid a very great heap of stones upon him: and all Israel fled every one to his tent.

18 Now Absalom in his lifetime had taken and reared up for himself a pillar, which *is* in the king's dale: for he said, I have no son to keep my name in remembrance, and he called the pillar after his own name: and it is called unto this day, Absalom's place.

19 Then said Ahimaaz the son of Zadok, Let me now run, and bear the king tidings, how that the LORD hath avenged him of his enemies.

20 And Joab said unto him, Thou shalt not bear tidings this day, but thou shalt bear tidings another day; but this day thou shalt bear no tidings, because the king's son is dead.

21 Then said Joab to Cushi, Go tell the king what thou hast seen. And Cushi bowed himself unto Joab, and ran.

22 Then said Ahimaaz the son of Zadok yet again to Joab, but howsoever, let me, I pray thee, also run after Cushi. And Joab said, Wherefore wilt thou run, my son, seeing that thou hast no tidings ready?

23 But howsoever, *said he,* let me run. And he said unto him, Run. Then Ahimaaz ran by the way of the plain, and overran Cushi.

24 And David sat between the two gates: and the watchman went up to the roof over the gate unto the wall, and lifted up his eyes, and looked, and behold, a man running alone.

25 And the watchman cried, and told the king. And the king said, If he *be* alone, *there is* tidings in his mouth. And he came apace, and drew near.

26 And the watchman saw another man running, and the watchman called unto the porter, and said, Behold, *another* man running alone. And the king said, He also bringeth tidings.

27 And the watchman said, Me thinketh the running of the foremost is like the running of Ahimaaz the son of Zadok. And the king said, He *is* a good man, and cometh with good tidings.

28 And Ahimaaz called, and said unto the king, All is well. And he fell down to the earth upon his face before the king, and said, Blessed *be* the LORD thy God, which hath delivered up the men that lifted up their hand against my lord the king.

29 And the king said, Is the young man Absalom safe? And Ahimaaz answered, When Joab sent the king's servant, and *me* thy servant, I saw a great tumult, but I knew not what *it was*.

30 And the king said *unto him,* Turn aside, *and* stand here. And he turned aside, and stood still.

31 And, behold, Cushi came; and Cushi said, Tidings, my lord the king: for the LORD hath avenged thee this day of all them that rose up against thee.

32 And the king said unto Cushi, *Is* the young man Absalom safe? And Cushi answered, The enemies of my lord the king, and all that rise against thee to do *thee* hurt, be as *that* young man *is.*

33 And the king was much moved, and went up to the chamber over the gate, and wept; and as he went, thus he said, O my son Absalom! my son, my son Absalom! would God I had died for thee, O Absalom, my son, my son!

XIX

AND it was told Joab, Behold, the king weepeth and mourneth for Absalom.

2 And the victory that day was *turned* into mourning unto all the people: for the people heard say that day how the king was grieved for his son.

3 And the people gat them by stealth that day into the city, as people being ashamed steal away when they flee in battle.

4 But the king covered his face, and the king cried with a loud voice, O my son Absalom! O Absalom, my son, my son!

I. Kings, XVIII

AND it came to pass, *after* many days, that the word of the LORD came to Elijah in the third year, saying, Go, shew thyself unto Ahab; and I will send rain upon the earth.

2 And Elijah went to shew himself unto Ahab. And *there was* a sore famine in Samaria.

3 And Ahab called Obadiah, which *was* the governor of *his* house. (Now Obadiah feared the Lord greatly:

4 For it was *so,* when Jezebel cut off the prophets of the Lord, that Obadiah took an hundred prophets, and hid them by fifty in a cave, and fed them with bread and water.)

5 And Ahab said unto Obadiah, Go into the land, unto all fountains of water, and unto all brooks: peradventure we may find grass to save the horses and mules alive, that we lose not all the beasts.

6 So they divided the land between them, to pass throughout it: Ahab went one way by himself, and Obadiah went another way by himself.

7 And as Obadiah was in the way, behold, Elijah met him: and he knew him, and fell on his face, and said, *Art* thou that my lord Elijah?

8 And he answered him, I *am:* go, tell thy lord, Behold, Elijah *is here.*

9 And he said, What have I sinned, that thou wouldest deliver thy servant into the hand of Ahab, to slay me?

10 *As* the Lord thy God liveth, there is no nation or kingdom whither my lord hath not sent to seek thee: and when they said, *He is* not *there;* he took an oath of the kingdom and nation, that they found thee not.

11 And now thou sayest, Go, tell thy lord, Behold, Elijah *is here.*

12 And it shall come to pass, *as soon as* I am gone from thee, that the Spirit of the Lord shall carry thee whither I know not; and *so* when I come and tell Ahab, and he cannot find thee, he shall slay me: but I thy servant fear the Lord from my youth.

13 Was it not told my lord what I did when Jezebel slew the prophets of the Lord, how I hid an hundred men of the Lord's prophets by fifty in a cave, and fed them with bread and water?

14 And now thou sayest, Go, tell thy lord, Behold, Elijah *is here:* and he shall slay me.

15 And Elijah said, *As* the Lord of hosts liveth, before whom I stand, I will surely shew myself unto him to day.

16 So Obadiah went to meet Ahab, and told him: and Ahab went to meet Elijah.

17 And it came to pass, when Ahab saw Elijah, that Ahab said unto him, *Art* thou he that troubleth Israel?

18 And he answered, I have not troubled Israel; but thou and thy father's house, in that ye have forsaken the commandments of the Lord, and thou hast followed Baalim.

19 Now therefore send, *and* gather to me all Israel unto mount

Carmel, and the prophets of Baal four hundred and fifty, and the prophets of the groves four hundred, which eat at Jezebel's table.

20 So Ahab sent unto all the children of Israel, and gathered the prophets together unto mount Carmel.

21 And Elijah came unto all the people, and said, How long halt ye between two opinions? if the LORD *be* God, follow him: but if Baal, *then* follow him. And the people answered him not a word.

22 Then said Elijah unto the people, I, *even* I only, remain a prophet of the LORD; but Baal's prophets *are* four hundred and fifty men.

23 Let them therefore give us two bullocks; and let them choose one bullock for themselves, and cut it in pieces, and lay *it* on wood, and put no fire *under:* and I will dress the other bullock, and lay *it* on wood, and put no fire *under:*

24 And call ye on the name of your gods, and I will call on the name of the LORD: and the God that answereth by fire, let him be God. And all the people answered and said, It is well spoken.

25 And Elijah said unto the prophets of Baal, Choose you one bullock for yourselves, and dress *it* first; for ye *are* many: and call on the name of your gods, but put no fire *under.*

26 And they took the bullock which was given them, and they dressed *it,* and called on the name of Baal from morning even until noon, saying, O Baal, hear us. But *there was* no voice, nor any that answered. And they leaped upon the altar which was made.

27 And it came to pass at noon, that Elijah mocked them, and said, Cry aloud; for he *is* a god: either he is talking, or he is pursuing, or he is in a journey, *or* peradventure he sleepeth, and must be awaked.

28 And they cried aloud, and cut themselves, after their manner, with knives and lancets, till the blood gushed out upon them.

29 And it came to pass, when midday was past, and they prophesied until the *time* of the offering of the *evening* sacrifice, that *there was* neither voice, nor any to answer, nor any that regarded.

30 And Elijah said unto all the people, Come near unto me. And all the people came near unto him. And he repaired the altar of the LORD *that was* broken down.

31 And Elijah took twelve stones, according to the number of the tribes of the sons of Jacob, unto whom the word of the LORD came, saying, Israel shall be thy name:

32 And with the stones he built an altar in the name of the LORD: and he made a trench about the altar, as great as would contain two measures of seed.

33 And he put the wood in order, and cut the bullock in pieces, and laid *him* on the wood, and said, Fill four barrels with water, and pour *it* on the burnt sacrifice, and on the wood.

34 And he said, Do *it* the second time: and they did *it* the second time. And he said, Do *it* the third time: and they did *it* the third time.

35 And the water ran round about the altar; and he filled the trench also with water.

36 And it came to pass, at *the time of* the offering of the *evening's* sacrifice, that Elijah the prophet came near, and said, Lord God of Abraham, Isaac, and of Israel, let it be known this day that thou *art* God in Israel, and *that* I *am* thy servant, and *that* I have done all these things at thy word.

37 Hear me, O Lord, hear me; that this people may know that thou *art* the Lord God, and *that* thou hast turned their heart back again.

38 Then the fire of the Lord fell, and consumed the burnt sacrifice, and the wood, and the stones, and the dust, and licked up the water that *was* in the trench.

39 And when all the people saw *it,* they fell on their faces: and they said, The Lord, he *is* the God; the Lord, he *is* the God.

40 And Elijah said unto them, Take the prophets of Baal; let not one of them escape. And they took them: and Elijah brought them down to the brook Kishon, and slew them there.

41 And Elijah said unto Ahab, Get thee up, eat and drink; for *there is* a sound of abundance of rain.

42 So Ahab went up to eat and to drink. And Elijah went up to the top of Carmel; and he cast himself down upon the earth, and put his face between his knees,

43 And said to his servant, Go up now, look toward the sea. And he went up, and looked, and said, *There is* nothing. And he said, Go again seven times.

44 And it came to pass at the seventh time, that he said, Behold, there ariseth a little cloud out of the sea, like a man's hand. And he said, Go up, say unto Ahab, Prepare *thy chariot,* and get thee down, that the rain stop thee not.

45 And it came to pass in the mean while, that the heaven was black with clouds and wind, and there was a great rain. And Ahab rode, and went to Jezreel.

46 And the hand of the Lord was on Elijah: and he girded up his loins, and ran before Ahab to the entrance of Jezreel.

II. Kings, V

Now Naaman, captain of the host of the king of Syria, was a great man with his master, and honourable, because by him the LORD had given deliverance unto Syria: he was also a mighty man in valour; *but he was* a leper.

2 And the Syrians had gone out by companies, and had brought away captive out of the land of Israel a little maid; and she waited on Naaman's wife.

3 And she said unto her mistress, Would God my lord *were* with the prophet that *is* in Samaria! for he would recover him of his leprosy.

4 And *one* went in, and told his lord, saying, Thus and thus said the maid that *is* of the land of Israel.

5 And the king of Syria said, Go to, go, and I will send a letter unto the king of Israel.   And he departed, and took with him ten talents of silver, and six thousand *pieces* of gold, and ten changes of raiment.

6 And he brought the letter to the king of Israel, saying, Now, when this letter is come unto thee, behold, I have *therewith* sent Naaman my servant to thee, that thou mayest recover him of his leprosy.

7 And it came to pass, when the king of Israel had read the letter, that he rent his clothes, and said, *Am* I God, to kill and to make alive, that this man doth send unto me to recover a man of his leprosy? Wherefore consider, I pray you, and see how he seeketh a quarrel against me.

8 And it was *so,* when Elisha the man of God had heard that the king of Israel had rent his clothes, that he sent to the king, saying, Wherefore hast thou rent thy clothes? let him come now to me, and he shall know that there is a prophet in Israel.

9 So Naaman came with his horses and with his chariot, and stood at the door of the house of Elisha.

10 And Elisha sent a messenger unto him, saying, Go and wash in Jordan seven times, and thy flesh shall come again to thee, and thou shalt be clean.

11 But Naaman was wroth, and went away, and said, Behold, I thought, He will surely come out to me, and stand and call on the name of the LORD his God, and strike his hand over the place, and recover the leper.

12 *Are* not Abana and Pharpar, rivers of Damascus, better than all the waters of Israel? may I not wash in them, and be clean?   So he turned, and went away in a rage.

13 And his servants came near, and spake unto him, and said, My father, *if* the prophet had bid thee *do some* great thing, wouldest thou

not have done *it?* how much rather then, when he saith to thee, Wash, and be clean?

14 Then went he down, and dipped himself seven times in Jordan, according to the saying of the man of God: and his flesh came again like unto the flesh of a little child, and he was clean.

15 And he returned to the man of God, he and all his company, and came and stood before him: and he said, Behold, now I know that *there is* no God in all the earth, but in Israel: now therefore, I pray thee, take a blessing of thy servant.

16 But he said, *As* the LORD liveth, before whom I stand, I will receive none. And he urged him to take *it;* but he refused.

17 And Naaman said, Shall there not then, I pray thee, be given to thy servant two mules' burden of earth? for thy servant will hence-forth offer neither burnt offering nor sacrifice unto other gods, but unto the LORD.

18 In this thing the LORD pardon thy servant, *that* when my master goeth into the house of Rimmon to worship there, and he leaneth on my hand, and I bow myself in the house of Rimmon; when I bow down myself in the house of Rimmon, the LORD pardon thy servant in this thing.

19 And he said unto him, Go in peace. So he departed from him a little way.

20 But Gehazi, the servant of Elisha the man of God, said, Behold, my master hath spared Naaman this Syrian, in not receiving at his hands that which he brought: but, *as* the LORD liveth, I will run after him, and take somewhat of him.

21 So Gehazi followed after Naaman. And when Naaman saw *him* running after him, he lighted down from the chariot to meet him, and said, *Is* all well?

22 And he said, All *is* well. My master hath sent me, saying, Behold, even now there be come to me from mount Ephraim two young men of the sons of the prophets: give them, I pray thee, a talent of silver, and two changes of garments.

23 And Naaman said, Be content, take two talents. And he urged him, and bound two talents of silver in two bags, with two changes of garments, and laid *them* upon two of his servants; and they bare *them* before him.

24 And when he came to the tower, he took *them* from their hand, and bestowed *them* in the house: and he let the men go, and they departed.

25 But he went in, and stood before his master. And Elisha said unto him, Whence *comest thou,* Gehazi? And he said, Thy servant went no whither.

26 And he said unto him, Went not mine heart *with thee,* when the man turned again from his chariot to meet thee? *Is it* a time to receive money, and to receive garments, and oliveyards, and vineyards, and sheep, and oxen, and menservants, and maidservants?

27 The leprosy therefore of Naaman shall cleave unto thee, and unto thy seed for ever. And he went out from his presence a leper *as white* as snow.

Psalms, CXLVII; CXLVIII; CXLIX; CL

CXLVII

PRAISE ye the LORD: for *it is* good to sing praises unto our God; for *it is* pleasant; *and* praise is comely.

2 The LORD doth build up Jerusalem; he gathereth together the outcasts of Israel.

3 He healeth the broken in heart, and bindeth up their wounds.

4 He telleth the number of the stars; he calleth them all by *their* names.

5 Great *is* our Lord, and of great power: his understanding *is* infinite.

6 The LORD lifteth up the meek: he casteth the wicked down to the ground.

7 Sing unto the LORD with thanksgiving; sing praise upon the harp unto our God;

8 Who covereth the heaven with clouds, who prepareth rain for the earth, who maketh grass to grow upon the mountains.

9 He giveth to the beast his food, *and* to the young ravens which cry.

10 He delighteth not in the strength of the horse; he taketh not pleasure in the legs of a man.

11 The LORD taketh pleasure in them that fear him, in those that hope in his mercy.

12 Praise the LORD, O Jerusalem; praise thy God, O Zion.

13 For he hath strengthened the bars of thy gates; he hath blessed thy children within thee.

14 He maketh peace *in* thy borders, *and* filleth thee with the finest of the wheat.

15 He sendeth forth his commandment *upon* earth: his word runneth very swiftly.

16 He giveth snow like wool: he scattereth the hoarfrost like ashes.

17 He casteth forth his ice like morsels: who can stand before his cold?

18 He sendeth out his word, and melteth them: he causeth his wind to blow, *and* the waters flow.

19 He sheweth his word unto Jacob, his statutes and his judgments unto Israel.

20 He hath not dealt so with any nation; and *as for his* judgments, they have not known them. Praise ye the Lord.

CXLVIII

Praise ye the Lord. Praise ye the Lord from the heavens: praise him in the heights.

2 Praise ye him, all his angels: praise ye him, all his hosts.

3 Praise ye him, sun and moon: praise him, all ye stars of light.

4 Praise him, ye heavens of heavens, and ye waters that *be* above the heavens.

5 Let them praise the name of the Lord: for he commanded, and they were created.

6 He hath also stablished them for ever and ever: he hath made a decree which shall not pass.

7 Praise the Lord from the earth, ye dragons, and all deeps:

8 Fire, and hail; snow, and vapours; stormy wind fulfilling his word:

9 Mountains, and all hills; fruitful trees, and all cedars:

10 Beasts, and all cattle; creeping things, and flying fowl:

11 Kings of the earth, and all people; princes, and all judges of the earth:

12 Both young men and maidens; old men and children:

13 Let them praise the name of the Lord: for his name alone is excellent; his glory *is* above the earth and heaven.

14 He also exalteth the horn of his people, the praise of all his saints, *even* of the children of Israel, a people near unto him. Praise ye the Lord.

CXLIX

Praise ye the Lord. Sing unto the Lord a new song, *and* his praise in the congregation of saints.

2 Let Israel rejoice in him that made him; let the children of Zion be joyful in their King.

3 Let them praise his name in the dance: let them sing praises unto him with the timbrel and harp.

4 For the Lord taketh pleasure in his people: he will beautify the meek with salvation.

5 Let the saints be joyful in glory: let them sing aloud upon their beds.

6 *Let* the high *praises* of God *be* in their mouth, and a two edged sword in their hand;

7 To execute vengeance upon the heathen, *and* punishments upon the people;

8 To bind their kings with chains, and their nobles with fetters of iron;

9 To execute upon them the judgment written: this honour have all his saints. Praise ye the Lord.

CL

Praise ye the Lord. Praise God in his sanctuary: praise him in the firmament of his power.

2 Praise him for his mighty acts: praise him according to his excellent greatness.

3 Praise him with the sound of the trumpet: praise him with the psaltery and harp.

4 Praise him with the timbrel and dance: praise him with stringed instruments and organs.

5 Praise him upon the loud cymbals: praise him upon the high sounding cymbals.

6 Let every thing that hath breath praise the Lord. Praise ye the Lord.

Ecclesiastes, III; IV; XI; XII

III

To every *thing there is* a season, and a time to every purpose under the heaven.

2 A time to be born, and a time to die: a time to plant, and a time to pluck up *that which is* planted:

3 A time to kill, and a time to heal: a time to break down, and a time to build up:

4 A time to weep, and a time to laugh: a time to mourn, and a time to dance:

5 A time to cast away stones, and a time to gather stones together: a time to embrace, and a time to refrain from embracing:

6 A time to get, and a time to lose: a time to keep, and a time to cast away:

7 A time to rend, and a time to sew: a time to keep silence, and a time to speak:

8 A time to love, and a time to hate: a time of war, and a time of peace.

9 What profit hath he that worketh in that wherein he laboureth?

10 I have seen the travail, which God hath given to the sons of men to be exercised in it.

11 He hath made every *thing* beautiful in his time: also he hath set the world in their heart, so that no man can find out the work that God maketh from the beginning to the end.

12 I know that *there is* no good in them, but for *a man* to rejoice, and to do good in his life.

13 And also that every man should eat and drink, and enjoy the good of all his labour, it *is* the gift of God.

14 I know that whatsoever God doeth, it shall be for ever: nothing can be put to it, nor any thing taken from it: and God doeth *it* that *men* should fear before him.

15 That which hath been is now; and that which is to be hath already been; and God requireth that which is past.

16 And, moreover, I saw under the sun the place of judgment, *that* wickedness *was* there; and the place of righteousness, *that* iniquity *was* there.

17 I said in mine heart, God shall judge the righteous and the wicked: for *there is* a time there for every purpose, and for every work.

18 I said in mine heart concerning the estate of the sons of men, that God might manifest them, and that they might see that they themselves are beasts.

19 For that which befalleth the sons of men befalleth beasts; even one thing befalleth them: as the one dieth, so dieth the other; yea, they have all one breath; so that a man hath no preeminence above a beast: for all *is* vanity.

20 All go unto one place: all are of the dust, and all turn to dust again.

21 Who knoweth the spirit of man that goeth upward, and the spirit of the beast that goeth downward to the earth?

22 Wherefore I perceive that *there is* nothing better, than that a man should rejoice in his own works; for that *is* his portion: for who shall bring him to see what shall be after him?

IV

So I returned, and considered all the oppressions that are done under the sun; and, behold, the tears of *such as were* oppressed, and they had no comforter; and on the side of their oppressors *there was* power; but they had no comforter.

2 Wherefore I praised the dead which are already dead, more than the living which are yet alive.

3 Yea, better *is he* than both they, which hath not yet been, who hath not seen the evil work that is done under the sun.

4 Again, I considered all travail, and every right work, that for this a man is envied of his neighbour. This *is* also vanity and vexation of spirit.

5 The fool foldeth his hands together, and eateth his own flesh.

6 Better *is* an handful *with* quietness, than both the hands full *with* travail and vexation of spirit.

7 Then I returned, and I saw vanity under the sun.

8 There is one *alone,* and *there* is not a second; yea, he hath neither child nor brother: yet *is there* no end of all his labour; neither is his eye satisfied with riches; neither *saith he,* For whom do I labour, and bereave my soul of good? This *is* also vanity, yea, it *is* a sore travail.

9 Two *are* better than one; because they have a good reward for their labour.

10 For if they fall, the one will lift up his fellow: but woe to him *that is* alone when he falleth; for *he hath* not another to help him up.

11 Again, if two lie together, then they have heat: but how can one be warm *alone?*

12 And if one prevail against him, two shall withstand him; and a threefold cord is not quickly broken.

13 Better *is* a poor and a wise child than an old and foolish king, who will no more be admonished.

14 For out of prison he cometh to reign; where also *he that is* born in his kingdom becometh poor.

15 I considered all the living which walk under the sun, with the second child that shall stand up in his stead.

16 *There is* no end of all the people, *even* of all that have been before them: they also that come after shall not rejoice in him. Surely this also *is* vanity and vexation of spirit.

XI

Cast thy bread upon the waters: for thou shalt find it after many days.

2 Give a portion to seven, and also to eight; for thou knowest not what evil shall be upon the earth.

3 If the clouds be full of rain, they empty *themselves* upon the earth: and if the tree fall toward the south or toward the north, in the place where the tree falleth, there it shall be.

4 He that observeth the wind, shall not sow; and he that regardeth the clouds, shall not reap.

5 As thou knowest not what *is* the way of the spirit, *nor* how the bones *do grow* in the womb of her that is with child; even so thou knowest not the works of God who maketh all.

6 In the morning sow thy seed, and in the evening withhold not thine hand: for thou knowest not whether shall prosper, either this or that, or whether they both *shall be* alike good.

7 Truly the light *is* sweet, and a pleasant *thing it is* for the eyes to behold the sun:

8 But if a man live many years, *and* rejoice in them all; yet let him remember the days of darkness; for they shall be many. All that cometh *is* vanity.

9 Rejoice, O young man, in thy youth, and let thy heart cheer thee in the days of thy youth, and walk in the ways of thine heart, and in the sight of thine eyes: but know thou, that for all these *things* God will bring thee into judgment.

10 Therefore remove sorrow from thy heart, and put away evil from thy flesh: for childhood and youth *are* vanity.

XII

Remember now thy Creator in the days of thy youth, while the evil days come not, nor the years draw nigh, when thou shalt say, I have no pleasure in them;

2 While the sun, or the light, or the moon, or the stars, be not darkened; nor the clouds return after the rain:

3 In the day when the keepers of the house shall tremble, and the strong men shall bow themselves, and the grinders cease because they are few, and those that look out of the windows be darkened,

4 And the doors shall be shut in the streets, when the sound of the

grinding is low, and he shall rise up at the voice of the bird, and all the daughters of music shall be brought low:

5 Also *when* they shall be afraid of *that which is* high, and fears *shall be* in the way, and the almond tree shall flourish, and the grasshopper shall be a burden, and desire shall fail; because man goeth to his long home, and the mourners go about the streets:

6 Or ever the silver cord be loosed, or the golden bowl be broken, or the pitcher be broken at the fountain, or the wheel broken at the cistern.

7 Then shall the dust return to the earth as it was; and the spirit shall return unto God who gave it.

8 Vanity of vanities, saith the Preacher; all *is* vanity.

9 And, moreover, because the Preacher was wise, he still taught the people knowledge; yea, he gave good heed, and sought out, *and* set in order, many proverbs.

10 The Preacher sought to find out acceptable words: and *that which was* written *was* upright, *even* words of truth.

11 The words of the wise *are* as goads, and as nails fastened *by* the masters of assemblies, *which* are given from one shepherd.

12 And further, by these, my son, be admonished: of making many books *there is* no end; and much study *is* a weariness of the flesh.

13 Let us hear the conclusion of the whole matter: Fear God, and keep his commandments: for this *is* the whole *duty* of man.

14 For God shall bring every work into judgment, with every secret thing, whether *it be* good, or whether *it be* evil.

Ezekiel, XXXVII, 1-14

THE hand of the LORD was upon me, and carried me out in the spirit of the LORD, and set me down in the midst of the valley which *was* full of bones,

2 And caused me to pass by them round about: and, behold, *there were* very many in the open valley; and, lo, *they were* very dry.

3 And he said unto me, Son of man, can these bones live? And I answered, O LORD GOD, thou knowest.

4 And he said unto me, Prophesy upon these bones, and say unto them, O ye dry bones, hear the word of the LORD.

5 Thus saith the Lord GOD unto these bones, Behold, I will cause breath to enter into you, and ye shall live:

6 And I will lay sinews upon you, and will bring up flesh upon you,

and cover you with skin, and put breath in you, and ye shall live; and ye shall know that I *am* the LORD.

7 So I prophesied as I was commanded: and as I prophesied there was a noise, and, behold, a shaking, and the bones came together, bone to his bone.

8 And when I beheld, lo, the sinews and the flesh came up upon them, and the skin covered them above; but *there was* no breath in them.

9 Then said he unto me, Prophesy unto the wind, prophesy, son of man, and say to the wind, Thus saith the Lord GOD, Come from the four winds, O breath, and breathe upon these slain, that they may live.

10 So I prophesied as he commanded me, and the breath came into them, and they lived, and stood up upon their feet, an exceeding great army.

11 Then he said unto me, Son of man, these bones are the whole house of Israel: behold they say, Our bones are dried, and our hope is lost; we are cut off for our parts.

12 Therefore prophesy, and say unto them, Thus saith the Lord GOD, Behold, O my people, I will open your graves, and cause you to come up out of your graves, and bring you into the land of Israel.

13 And ye shall know that I *am* the LORD, when I have opened your graves, O my people, and brought you up out of your graves.

14 And shall put my spirit in you, and ye shall live; and I shall place you in your own land: then shall ye know that I the LORD have spoken *it,* and performed *it,* saith the LORD.

I. Esdras, III, 1 —IV, 42

III

Now when Darius reigned, he made a great feast unto all his subjects, and unto all his household, and unto all the princes of Media and Persia.

2 And to all the governors and captains and lieutenants that were under him, from India unto Ethiopia, of an hundred twenty and seven provinces.

3 And when they had eaten and drunken, and being satisfied were gone home, then Darius the king went into his bedchamber, and slept, and soon after awaked.

4 Then three young men, that were of the guard that kept the king's body, spake one to another;

5 Let every one of us speak a sentence: he that shall overcome, and

whose sentence shall seem wiser than the others, unto him shall the king Darius give great gifts, and great things in token of victory:

6 As, to be clothed in purple, to drink in gold, and to sleep upon gold, and a chariot with bridles of gold, and an headtire of fine linen, and a chain about his neck:

7 And he shall sit next to Darius because of his wisdom, and shall be called Darius his cousin.

8 And then every one wrote his sentence, sealed it, and laid it under king Darius his pillow;

9 And said that, when the king is risen, some will give him the writings; and of whose side the king and the three princes of Persia shall judge that his sentence is the wisest, to him shall the victory be given, as was appointed.

10 The first wrote, Wine is the strongest.

11 The second wrote, The King is strongest.

12 The third wrote, Women are strongest: but above all things Truth beareth away the victory.

13 ¶ Now when the king was risen up, they took their writings, and delivered them unto him, and so he read them:

14 And sending forth he called all the princes of Persia and Media, and the governors, and the captains, and the lieutenants, and the chief officers;

15 And sat him down in the royal seat of judgment; and the writings were read before them.

16 And he said, Call the young men, and they shall declare their own sentences. So they were called, and came in.

17 And he said unto them, Declare unto us your mind concerning the writings. Then began the first, who had spoken of the strength of wine;

18 And he said thus, O ye men, how exceeding strong is wine! it causeth all men to err that drink it:

19 It maketh the mind of the king and of the fatherless child to be all one; of the bondman and of the freeman, of the poor man and of the rich:

20 It turneth also every thought into jollity and mirth, so that a man remembereth neither sorrow nor debt:

21 And it maketh every heart rich, so that a man remembereth neither king nor governor; and it maketh to speak all things by talents:

22 And when they are in their cups, they forget their love both to friends and brethren, and a little after draw out swords:

23 But when they are from the wine, they remember not what they have done.

24 O ye men, is not wine the strongest, that enforceth to do thus?
And when he had so spoken, he held his peace

IV

THEN the second, that had spoken of the strength of the king, began
to say,

2 O ye men, do not men excel in strength, that bear rule over sea and
land, and all things in them?

3 But yet the king is more mighty: for he is lord of all these things,
and hath dominion over them; and whatsoever he commandeth them
they do.

4 If he bid them make war the one against the other, they do it: if
he send them out against the enemies, they go, and break down mountains,
walls, and towers.

5 They slay and are slain, and transgress not the king's commandment: if they get the victory, they bring all to the king, as well the spoil,
as all things else.

6 Likewise for those that are no soldiers, and have not to do with
wars, but use husbandry, when they have reaped again that which they
had sown, they bring it to the king, and compel one another to pay tribute
unto the king.

7 And yet he is but one man: if he command to kill, they kill; if he
command to spare, they spare;

8 If he command to smite, they smite; if he command to make
desolate, they make desolate; if he command to build, they build;

9 If he command to cut down, they cut down; if he command to plant,
they plant.

10 So all his people and his armies obey him: furthermore he lieth
down, he eateth and drinketh, and taketh his rest:

11 And these keep watch round about him, neither may any one
depart, and do his own business, neither disobey they him in any thing.

12 O ye men, how should not the king be mightiest, when in such sort
he is obeyed? And he held his tongue.

13 ¶ Then the third, who had spoken of women, and of the truth,
(this was Zorobabel,) began to speak.

14 O ye men, it is not the great king, nor the multitude of men,
neither is it wine, that excelleth; who is it then that ruleth them, or hath
the lordship over them? are they not women?

15 Women have borne the king and all the people that bear rule by
sea and land.

16 Even of them came they: and they nourished them up that planted the vineyards, from whence the wine cometh.

17 These also make garments for men; these bring glory unto men; and without women cannot men be.

18 Yea, and if men have gathered together gold and silver, or any other goodly thing, do they not love a woman which is comely in favour and beauty?

19 And letting all those things go, do they not gape, and even with open mouth fix their eyes fast on her; and have not all men more desire unto her than unto silver or gold, or any goodly thing whatsoever?

20 A man leaveth his own father that brought him up, and his own country, and cleaveth unto his wife.

21 He sticketh not to spend his life with his wife, and remembereth neither father, nor mother, nor country.

22 By this also ye must know that women have dominion over you: do ye not labour and toil, and give and bring all to the woman?

23 Yea, a man taketh his sword, and goeth his way to rob and to steal, to sail upon the sea and upon rivers;

24 And looketh upon a lion, and goeth in the darkness; and when he hath stolen, spoiled, and robbed, he bringeth it to his love.

25 Wherefore a man loveth his wife better than father or mother.

26 Yea, many there be that have run out of their wits for women, and become servants for their sakes.

27 Many also have perished, have erred, and sinned, for women.

28 And now do ye not believe me? is not the king great in his power? do not all regions fear to touch him?

29 Yet did I see him and Apame the king's concubine, the daughter of the admirable Bartacus, sitting at the right hand of the king,

30 And taking the crown from the king's head, and setting it upon her own head; she also struck the king with her left hand.

31 And yet for all this the king gaped and gazed upon her with open mouth: if she laughed upon him, he laughed also: but if she took any displeasure at him, the king was fain to flatter, that she might be reconciled to him again.

32 O ye men, how can it be but women should be strong, seeing they do thus?

33 Then the king and the princes looked one upon another: so he began to speak of the truth.

34 O ye men, are not women strong? great is the earth, high is the heaven, swift is the sun in his course, for he compasseth the heavens round about, and fetcheth his course again to his own place in one day.

35 Is he not great that maketh these things? therefore great is the truth, and stronger than all things.

36 All the earth calleth upon the truth, and the heaven blesseth it: all works shake and tremble at it, and with it is no unrighteous thing.

37 Wine is wicked, the king is wicked, women are wicked, all the children of men are wicked, and such are all their wicked works; and there is no truth in them; in their unrighteousness also they shall perish.

38 As for the truth, it endureth, and is always strong; it liveth and conquereth for evermore.

39 With her there is no accepting of persons or rewards; but she doeth the things that are just, and refraineth from all unjust and wicked things; and all men do well like of her works.

40 Neither in her judgment is any unrighteousness; and she is the strength, kingdom, power, and majesty, of all ages. Blessed be the God of truth.

41 And with that he held his peace. And all the people then shouted, and said, Great is Truth, and mighty above all things.

42 Then said the king unto him, Ask what thou wilt more than is appointed in the writing, and we will give it thee, because thou art found wisest; and thou shalt sit next me, and shalt be called my cousin.

Ecclesiasticus, XXXVIII

HONOUR a physician with the honour due unto him for the uses which ye may have of him: for the lord hath created him.

2 For of the most High cometh healing, and he shall receive honour of the king.

3 The skill of the physician shall lift up his head: and in the sight of great men he shall be in admiration.

4 The lord hath created medicines out of the earth; and he that is wise will not abhor them.

5 Was not the water made sweet with wood, that the virtue thereof might be known?

6 And he hath given men skill, that he might be honoured in his marvellous works.

7 With such doth he heal [men,] and taketh away their pains.

8 Of such doth the apothecary make a confection; and of his works there is no end; and from him is peace over all the earth.

9 My son, in thy sickness be not negligent: but pray unto the lord, and he will make thee whole.

10 Leave off from sin, and order thine hands aright, and cleanse thy heart from all wickedness,

11 Give a sweet savour, and a memorial of fine flour; and make a fat offering, as not being.

12 Then give place to the physician, for the lord hath created him: let him not go from thee, for thou hast need of him.

13 There is a time when in their hands there is good success.

14 For they shall also pray unto the lord, that he would prosper that which they give for ease and remedy to prolong life.

15 He that sinneth before his Maker, let him fall into the hand of the physician.

16 My son, let tears fall down over the dead, and begin to lament, as if thou hadst suffered great harm thyself; and then cover his body according to the custom, and neglect not his burial.

17 Weep bitterly, and make great moan, and use lamentation, as he is worthy, and that a day or two, lest thou be evil spoken of: and then comfort thyself for thy heaviness.

18 For of heaviness cometh death, and the heaviness of the heart breaketh strength.

19 In affliction also sorrow remaineth: and the life of the poor is the curse of the heart.

20 Take no heaviness to heart: drive it away, and remember the last end.

21 Forget it not, for there is no turning again: thou shalt not do him good, but hurt thyself.

22 Remember my judgment: for thine also shall be so; yesterday for me, and to day for thee.

23 When the dead is at rest, let his remembrance rest; and be comforted for him, when his spirit is departed from him.

24 The wisdom of a learned man cometh by opportunity of leisure: and he that hath little business shall become wise.

25 How can he get wisdom that holdeth the plough, and that glorieth in the goad, that driveth oxen, and is occupied in their labours, and whose talk is of bullocks?

26 He giveth his mind to make furrows; and is diligent to give the kine fodder.

27 So every carpenter and workmaster, that laboureth night and day: and they that cut and grave seals, and are diligent to make great variety, and give themselves to counterfeit imagery, and watch to finish a work:

28 The smith also sitting by the anvil, and considering the iron work, the vapour of the fire wasteth his flesh, and he fighteth with the heat of the

furnace: the noise of the hammer and the anvil is ever in his ears, and his eyes look still upon the pattern of the thing that he maketh; he setteth his mind to finish his work, and watcheth to polish it perfectly:

29 So doth the potter sitting at his work, and turning the wheel about with his feet, who is always carefully set at his work, and maketh all his work by number;

30 He fashioneth the clay with his arm, and boweth down his strength before his feet; he applieth himself to lead it over; and he is diligent to make clean the furnace:

31 All these trust to their hands: and every one is wise in his work.

32 Without these cannot a city be inhabited: and they shall not dwell where they will, nor go up and down:

33 They shall not be sought for in publick counsel, nor sit high in the congregation: they shall not sit on the judges' seat, nor understand the sentence of judgment: they cannot declare justice and judgment; and they shall not be found where parables are spoken.

34 But they will maintain the state of the world, and [all] their desire is in the work of their craft.

Luke, XV

THEN drew near unto him all the publicans and sinners for to hear him.

2 And the Pharisees and scribes murmured, saying, This man receiveth sinners, and eateth with them.

3 And he spake this parable unto them, saying,

4 What man of you, having an hundred sheep, if he lose one of them, doth not leave the ninety and nine in the wilderness, and go after that which is lost, until he find it?

5 And when he hath found *it,* he layeth *it* on his shoulders, rejoicing.

6 And when he cometh home, he calleth together *his* friends and neighbours, saying unto them, Rejoice with me; for I have found my sheep which was lost.

7 I say unto you, that likewise joy shall be in heaven over one sinner that repenteth, more than over ninety and nine just persons, which need no repentance.

8 Either what woman having ten pieces of silver, if she lose one piece, doth not light a candle, and sweep the house, and seek diligently till she find *it?*

9 And when she hath found *it,* she calleth *her* friends and *her*

neighbours together, saying, Rejoice with me; for I have found the piece which I had lost.

10 Likewise, I say unto you, there is joy in the presence of the angels of God over one sinner that repenteth.

11 And he said, A certain man had two sons:

12 And the younger of them said to *his* father, Father, give me the portion of goods that falleth *to me*. And he divided unto them *his* living.

13 And not many days after, the younger son gathered all together, and took his journey into a far country, and there wasted his substance with riotous living.

14 And when he had spent all, there arose a mighty famine in that land; and he began to be in want.

15 And he went and joined himself to a citizen of that country; and he sent him into his fields to feed swine.

16 And he would fain have filled his belly with the husks that the swine did eat: and no man gave unto him.

17 And when he came to himself, he said, How many hired servants of my father's have bread enough and to spare, and I perish with hunger!

18 I will arise and go to my father, and will say unto him, Father, I have sinned against heaven, and before thee,

19 And am no more worthy to be called thy son: make me as one of thy hired servants.

20 And he arose, and came to his father. But when he was yet a great way off, his father saw him, and had compassion, and ran, and fell on his neck, and kissed him.

21 And the son said unto him, Father, I have sinned against heaven, and in thy sight, and am no more worthy to be called thy son.

22 But the father said to his servants, Bring forth the best robe, and put *it* on him; and put a ring on his hand, and shoes on *his* feet:

23 And bring hither the fatted calf, and kill *it;* and let us eat, and be merry:

24 For this my son was dead, and is alive again; he was lost, and is found. And they began to be merry.

25 Now his elder son was in the field: and as he came and drew nigh to the house, he heard music and dancing.

26 And he called one of the servants, and asked what these things meant.

27 And he said unto him, Thy brother is come; and thy father hath killed the fatted calf, because he hath received him safe and sound.

28 And he was angry, and would not go in: therefore came his father out, and intreated him.

29 And he, answering, said to *his* father, Lo, these many years do I serve thee, neither transgressed I at any time thy commandment; and yet thou never gavest me a kid, that I might make merry with my friends:

30 But as soon as this thy son was come, which hath devoured thy living with harlots, thou hast killed for him the fatted calf.

31 And he said unto him, Son, thou art ever with me, and all that I have is thine.

32 It was meet that we should make merry, and be glad: for this thy brother was dead, and is alive again; and was lost, and is found.

General Epistle of James, III

My brethren, be not many masters, knowing that we shall receive the greater condemnation.

2 For in many things we offend all. If any man offend not in word, the same *is* a perfect man, *and* able also to bridle the whole body.

3 Behold, we put bits in the horses' mouths, that they may obey us; and we turn about their whole body.

4 Behold also the ships, which though *they be* so great, and *are* driven of fierce winds, yet are they turned about with a very small helm, whithersoever the governor listeth.

5 Even so the tongue is a little member, and boasteth great things. Behold, how great a matter a little fire kindleth!

6 And the tongue *is* a fire, a world of iniquity: so is the tongue among our members, that it defileth the whole body, and setteth on fire the course of nature; and it is set on fire of hell.

7 For every kind of beasts, and of birds, and of serpents, and of things in the sea, is tamed, and hath been tamed of mankind:

8 But the tongue can no man tame; *it is* an unruly evil, full of deadly poison.

9 Therewith bless we God, even the Father; and therewith curse we men, which are made after the similitude of God.

10 Out of the same mouth proceedeth blessing and cursing. My brethren, these things ought not so to be.

11 Doth a fountain send forth at the same place sweet *water* and bitter?

12 Can the fig tree, my brethren, bear olive berries? either a vine, figs? so *can* no fountain both yield salt water and fresh.

13 Who *is* a wise man and endued with knowledge among you? let him shew out of a good conversation his works with meekness of wisdom.

14 But if ye have bitter envying and strife in your hearts, glory not; and lie not against the truth.

15 This wisdom descendeth not from above, but *is* earthly, sensual, devilish.

16 For where envying and strife *is,* there *is* confusion and every evil work.

17 But the wisdom that is from above is first pure, then peaceable, gentle, *and* easy to be intreated, full of mercy and good fruits, without partiality, and without hypocrisy.

18 And the fruit of righteousness is sown in peace of them that make peace.

Revelation, VI; VII

VI

AND I saw when the Lamb opened one of the seals; and I heard, as it were the noise of thunder, one of the four beasts, saying, Come and see.

2 And I saw, and beheld a white horse: and he that sat on him had a bow; and a crown was given unto him: and he went forth conquering, and to conquer.

3 And when he had opened the second seal, I heard the second beast say, Come and see.

4 And there went out another horse *that was* red: and *power* was given to him that sat thereon to take peace from the earth, and that they should kill one another: and there was given unto him a great sword.

5 And when he had opened the third seal, I heard the third beast say, Come and see. And I beheld, and, lo, a black horse; and he that sat on him had a pair of balances in his hand.

6 And I heard a voice in the midst of the four beasts say, A measure of wheat for a penny, and three measures of barley for a penny; and *see* thou hurt not the oil and the wine.

7 And when he had opened the fourth seal, I heard the voice of the fourth beast say, Come and see.

8 And I looked, and behold a pale horse; and his name that sat on him was Death, and Hell followed with him. And power was given unto them over the fourth part of the earth, to kill with sword, and with hunger, and with death, and with the beasts of the earth.

9 And when he had opened the fifth seal, I saw under the altar the souls of them that were slain for the word of God, and for the testimony which they held:

THE FOUR HORSEMEN OF THE APOCALYPSE

From a woodcut by Albrecht Dürer

10 And they cried with a loud voice, saying, How long, O Lord, holy and true, dost thou not judge and avenge our blood on them that dwell on the earth?

11 And white robes were given unto every one of them; and it was said unto them, that they should rest yet for a little season, until their fellowservants also and their brethren, that should be killed as they *were,* should be fulfilled.

12 And I beheld when he had opened the sixth seal, and, lo, there was a great earthquake; and the sun became black as sackcloth of hair, and the moon became as blood;

13 And the stars of heaven fell unto the earth, even as a fig tree casteth her untimely figs, when she is shaken of a mighty wind.

14 And the heaven departed as a scroll when it is rolled together; and every mountain and island were moved out of their places.

15 And the kings of the earth, and the great men, and the rich men, and the chief captains, and the mighty men, and every bondman, and every free man, hid themselves in the dens and in the rocks of the mountains;

16 And said to the mountains and rocks, Fall on us, and hide us from the face of him that sitteth on the throne, and from the wrath of the Lamb:

17 For the great day of his wrath is come; and who shall be able to stand?

VII

AND after these things I saw four angels standing on the four corners of the earth, holding the four winds of the earth, that the wind should not blow on the earth, nor on the sea, nor on any tree.

2 And I saw another angel ascending from the east, having the seal of the living God: and he cried with a loud voice to the four angels, to whom it was given to hurt the earth and the sea,

3 Saying, Hurt not the earth, neither the sea, nor the trees, till we have sealed the servants of our God in their foreheads.

4 And I heard the number of them which were sealed: *and there were* sealed an hundred *and* forty *and* four thousand of all the tribes of the children of Israel.

5 Of the tribe of Juda *were* sealed twelve thousand. Of the tribe of Reuben *were* sealed twelve thousand. Of the tribe of Gad *were* sealed twelve thousand.

6 Of the tribe of Aser *were* sealed twelve thousand. Of the tribe of Nepthalim *were* sealed twelve thousand. Of the tribe of Manasses *were* sealed twelve thousand.

7 Of the tribe of Simeon *were* sealed twelve thousand. Of the tribe of Levi *were* sealed twelve thousand. Of the tribe of Issachar *were* sealed twelve thousand.

8 Of the tribe of Zabulon *were* sealed twelve thousand. Of the tribe of Joseph *were* sealed twelve thousand. Of the tribe of Benjamin *were* sealed twelve thousand.

9 After this I beheld, and, lo, a great multitude, which no man could number, of all nations, and kindreds, and people, and tongues, stood before the throne, and before the Lamb, clothed with white robes, and palms in their hands;

10 And cried with a loud voice, saying, Salvation to our God which sitteth upon the throne, and unto the Lamb.

11 And all the angels stood round about the throne, and *about* the elders and the four beasts, and fell before the throne on their faces, and worshipped God.

12 Saying, Amen: Blessing, and glory, and wisdom, and thanksgiving, and honour, and power, and might, *be* unto our God for ever and ever. Amen.

13 And one of the elders answered, saying unto me, What are these which are arrayed in white robes? and whence came they?

14 And I said unto him, Sir, thou knowest. And he said to me, These are they which came out of great tribulation, and have washed their robes, and made them white in the blood of the Lamb.

15 Therefore are they before the throne of God, and serve him day and night in his temple: and he that sitteth on the throne shall dwell among them.

16 They shall hunger no more, neither thirst any more; neither shall the sun light on them, nor any heat.

17 For the Lamb, which is in the midst of the throne, shall feed them, and shall lead them unto living fountains of waters: and God shall wipe away all tears from their eyes.

From HOMER'S ILIAD

The Grief of Achilles for the Slaying of Patroclus

(From Book XVIII; translated by George Chapman)

Angered against Agamemnon, the greatest king among the Achaeans besieging Troy, Achilles withdrew himself from battle. His mother Thetis secured from Zeus a pledge to honor her offended son at the expense of the Achaeans. With the Trojans gaining advantage, Agamemnon sent an embassage to Achilles, but Achilles denied him. The Trojans pressed hard upon the Achaeans, and broke within the wall that they had built to protect their ships. Patroclus, in the borrowed armor of Achilles, drove away the enemy from the ships; but he was slain at last by Hector. The grief of Achilles for the slaying of his comrade made him secure new armor from Hephaestus and go forth to battle. He wrought havoc among the men of Troy, driving them back within their gates, and finally slew Hector, and dragged his body to the ships.

THEY fought still like the rage of fire.
   And now Antilochus
Came to Æacides, whose mind was much
   solicitous
For that which, as he fear'd, was fall'n.
   He found him near the fleet
With upright sail-yards, uttering this to
   his heroic conceit:
"Ay me, why see the Greeks themselves,
   thus beaten from the field,
And routed headlong to their fleet? O
   let not heaven yield
Effect to what my sad soul fears, that,
   as I was foretold,
The strongest Myrmidon next me, when
   I should still behold
The sun's fair light, must part with it.
   Past doubt Menoetius' son
Is he on whom that fate is wrought. O
   wretch, to leave undone
What I commanded; that, the fleet once
   freed of hostile fire,
Not meeting Hector, instantly he should
   his powers retire."
   As thus his troubled mind discoursed,
   Antilochus appear'd,
And told with tears the sad news thus:
   "My lord, that must be heard

Which would to heaven I might not tell;
   Menoetius' son lies dead,
And for his naked corse (his arms
   already forfeited,
And worn by Hector) the debate is now
   most vehement."
   This said, grief darken'd all his powers.
   With both his hands he rent
The black mould from the forced earth,
   and pour'd it on his head,
Smear'd all his lovely face; his weeds,
   divinely fashioned,
All 'filed and mangled; and himself he
   threw upon the shore,
Lay, as laid out for funeral, then tumbled
   round, and tore
His gracious curls. His ecstasy he did
   so far extend,
That all the ladies won by him and his
   now slaughter'd friend,
Afflicted strangely for his plight, came
   shrieking from the tents,
And fell about him, beat their breasts,
   their tender lineaments
Dissolved with sorrow. And with them
   wept Nestor's warlike son,
Fell by him, holding his fair hands, in
   fear he would have done
His person violence; his heart, extremely
   straiten'd, burn'd,
Beat, swell'd, and sigh'd as it would
   burst. So terribly he mourn'd,
That Thetis, sitting in the deeps of her
   old father's seas,
Heard, and lamented.

From HOMER'S ODYSSEY

Hermes in Calypso's Island

(From Book V; translated by George Chapman.)

Odysseus, on his homeward voyage after the destruction of Troy, to resume his throne in the island kingdom of Ithaca, was pursued by the wrath of Poseidon. After three years of wanderings and adventures, he came shipwrecked and alone to Calypso's island, where for seven years he was held, an unwilling guest. At the instance of the goddess Athene, Zeus sent the messenger Hermes to Calypso with orders of release. Hermes delivered the message, and Calypso unwillingly consented to the departure of Odysseus. Freed from the toils of Calypso, he built a raft and again set sail for home. On the eighteenth day of his voyage, he was discovered by Poseidon, who wrecked him on the island of Phaeacia. Naked and fainting, he struggled ashore, and fell asleep under some shrubs, in a bed of leaves. Book VI begins at this point. Nausicaä, daughter of King Alcinoüs, aided Odysseus. At a banquet, on hearing a song of Troy, Odysseus could not keep back his tears. He disclosed his name, and recounted the marvels and the hardships of his experience. The Phaeacians bore him in one of their marvelous ships to the coast of Ithaca. After revealing himself to his son Telemachus, he slew the insolent suitors who for years had beset his loyal wife Penelope, and took her to his heart again. Finally, going to the farm of his father Laërtes, he reveals himself to the aged man. There is an insurrection of the kinsmen of the suitors; but Athene, in the guise of Mentor, makes peace.

———————

Thus charged he; nor Argicides denied,
But to his feet his fair wing'd shoes he tied,
Ambrosian, golden; that in his command
Put either sea, or the unmeasured land,
With pace as speedy as a puff of wind.
Then up his rod went, with which he declined
The eyes of any waker, when he pleased,
And any sleeper, when he wish'd, diseased.
　This took, he stoop'd Pieria, and thence
Glid through the air, and Neptune's confluence
Kiss'd as he flew, and check'd the waves as light
As any sea-mew in her fishing flight
Her thick wings sousing in the savoury seas;
Like her, he pass'd a world of wilderness;
But when the far-off isle he touch'd, he went
Up from the blue sea to the continent,
And reach'd the ample cavern of the Queen,
Whom he within found; without seldom seen.
A sun-like fire upon the hearth did flame;
The matter precious, and divine the frame;

Of cedar cleft and incense was the pile,
That breathed an odour round about the isle.
Herself was seated in an inner room,
Whom sweetly sing he heard, and at her loom,
About a curious web, whose yarn she threw
In with a golden shittle. A grove grew
In endless spring about her cavern round,
With odorous cypress, pines, and poplars crown'd,
Where hawks, sea-owls, and long-tongued bittours bred,
And other birds their shady pinions spread;
All fowls maritimal; none roosted there,
But those whose labours in the waters were.
A vine did all the hollow cave embrace,
Still green, yet still ripe bunches gave it grace.
Four fountains, one against another, pour'd
Their silver streams; and meadows all enflower'd
With sweet balm-gentle, and blue violets hid,
That deck'd the soft breasts of each fragrant mead.
Should any one, though he immortal were,
Arrive and see the sacred objects there,
He would admire them, and be overjoy'd;
And so stood Hermes' ravish'd powers employ'd.
　But having all admir'd, he enter'd on
The ample cave, nor could be seen unknown
Of great Calypso (for all Deities are
Prompt in each other's knowledge, though so far
Sever'd in dwellings) but he could not see
Ulysses there within; without was he
Set sad ashore, where 'twas his use to view
Th' unquiet sea, sigh'd, wept, and empty drew
His heart of comfort.

The Landing in Phaeacia (Book VI; translated by S. H. Butcher and A. Lang)

See the note prefixed to "Hermes in Calypso's Island," above.

So there he lay asleep, the steadfast goodly Odysseus, fordone with toil and drowsiness. Meanwhile Athene went to the land and the city of the Phæacians, who of old, upon a time, dwelt in spacious Hypereia; near the Cyclopes they dwelt, men exceeding proud, who harried them continually, being mightier than they. Thence the godlike Nausithous made them depart, and he carried them away, and planted them in Scheria, far off from men that live by bread. And he drew a wall around the town, and builded houses and made temples for the gods and meted out the fields. Howbeit ere this had he been stricken by fate, and had gone down to the house of Hades, and now Alcinous was reigning, with wisdom granted by the gods. To his house went the goddess, grey-eyed Athene, devising a return for the great-hearted Odysseus. She betook her to the rich-wrought bower, wherein was sleeping a maiden like to the gods in form and comeliness, Nausicaa, the daughter of Alcinous, high of heart. Beside her on either hand of the pillars of the door were two handmaids, dowered with beauty from the Graces, and the shining doors were shut.

But the goddess, fleet as the breath of the wind, swept towards the couch of the maiden, and stood above her head, and spake to her in the semblance of the daughter of a famous seafarer, Dymas, a girl of like age with Nausicaa, who had found grace in her sight. In her shape the grey-eyed Athene spake to the princess, saying:

"Nausicaa, how hath thy mother so heedless a maiden to her daughter? Lo, thou hast shining raiment that lies by thee uncared for, and thy marriage-day is near at hand, when thou thyself must needs go beautifully clad, and have garments to give to them who shall lead thee to the house of the bridegroom! And, behold, these are the things whence a good report goes abroad among men, wherein a father and lady mother take delight. But come, let us arise and go a-washing with the breaking of the day, and I will follow with thee to be thy mate in the toil, that without delay thou mayst get thee ready, since truly thou art not long to be a maiden. Lo, already they are wooing thee, the noblest youths of all the Phæacians, among that people whence thou thyself dost draw thy lineage. So come, beseech thy noble father betimes in the morning to furnish thee with mules and a wain to carry the men's raiment, and the robes, and the shining coverlets. Yea and for thyself it is seernlier far to go thus than on foot, for the places where we must wash are a great way off the town."

So spake the grey-eyed Athene, and departed to Olympus, where, as they say, is the seat of the gods that standeth fast for ever. Not by winds is it shaken, nor ever wet with rain, nor doth the snow come nigh thereto, but most clear air is spread about it cloudless, and the white light floats over it. Therein the blessed gods are glad for all their days, and thither Athene went when she had shown forth all to the maiden.

Anon came the throned Dawn, and awakened Nausicaa of the fair robes, who straightway marvelled on the dream, and went through the halls to tell her parents, her father dear and her mother. And she found them within, her mother sitting by the hearth with the women her hand-maids, spinning yarn of sea-purple stain, but her father she met as he was going forth to the renowned kings in their council, whither the noble Phæacians called him. Standing close by her dear father she spake, saying: "Father, dear, couldst thou not lend me a high waggon with strong wheels, that I may take the goodly raiment to the river to wash, so much as I have lying soiled? Yea and it is seemly that thou thyself, when thou art with the princes in council, shouldest have fresh raiment to wear. Also, there are five dear sons of thine in the halls, two married, but three are lusty bachelors, and these are always eager for new-washen garments wherein to go to the dances; for all these things have I taken thought."

This she said, because she was ashamed to speak of glad marriage to her father; but he saw all and answered, saying:

"Neither the mules nor aught else do I grudge thee, my child. Go thy ways, and the thralls shall get thee ready a high waggon with good wheels, and fitted with an upper frame."

Therewith he called to his men, and they gave ear, and without the palace they made ready the smooth-running mule-wain, and led the mules beneath the yoke, and harnessed them under the car, while the maiden brought forth from her bower the shining raiment. This she stored in the polished car, and her mother filled a basket with all manner of food to the heart's desire, dainties too she set therein, and she poured wine into a goat-skin bottle, while Nausicaa climbed into the wain. And her mother gave her soft olive oil also in a golden cruse, that she and her maidens might anoint themselves after the bath. Then Nausicaa took the whip and the shining reins, and touched the mules to start them; then there was a clatter of hoofs, and on they strained without flagging, with their load of the raiment and the maiden. Not alone did she go, for her attendants followed with her.

Now when they were come to the beautiful stream of the river, where truly were the unfailing cisterns, and bright water welled up free from beneath, and flowed past, enough to wash the foulest garments clean, there the girls unharnessed the mules from under the chariot, and turning them loose they drove them along the banks of the eddying river to graze on the honey-sweet clover. Then they took the garments from the wain, in their hands, and bore them to the black water, and briskly trod them down in the trenches, in busy rivalry. Now when they had washed and cleansed all the stains, they spread all out in order along the shore of the deep, even where the sea, in beating on the coast, washed the pebbles clean. Then having bathed and anointed them well with olive oil, they took their mid-day meal on the river's banks, waiting till the clothes should dry in the brightness of the sun. Anon, when they were satisfied with food, the maidens and the princess, they fell to playing at ball, casting away their tires, and among them Nausicaa of the white arms began the song. And even as Artemis, the archer, moveth down the mountain, either along the ridges of lofty Taygetus or Erymanthus, taking her pastime in the chase of boars and swift deer, and with her the wild wood-nymphs disport them, the daughters of Zeus, lord of the ægis, and Leto is glad at heart, while high over all she rears her head and brows, and easily may she be known,—but all are fair; even so the girl unwed outshone her maiden company.

But when now she was about going homewards, after yoking the mules and folding up the goodly raiment, then grey-eyed Athene turned to other thoughts, that so Odysseus might awake, and see the lovely maiden, who should be his guide to the city of the Phæacian men. So then the princess threw the ball at one of her company; she missed the girl, and cast the ball into the deep eddying current, whereat they all raised a piercing cry. Then the goodly Odysseus awoke and sat up, pondering in his heart and spirit:

"Woe is me! to what men's land am I come now? say, are they froward, and wild, and unjust, or are they hospitable, and of God-fearing mind? How shrill a cry of maidens rings round me, of the nymphs that hold the steep hill-tops, and the river-springs, and the grassy water meadows! It must be, methinks, that I am near men of human speech. Go to, I myself will make trial and see."

Therewith the goodly Odysseus crept out from under the coppice, having broken with his strong hand a leafy bough from the thick wood, to hold athwart his body, that it might hide his nakedness withal. And forth he sallied like a lion mountain-bred, trusting in his strength, who fares out blown and rained upon, with flaming eyes; amid the kine he goes or amid the sheep or in the track of the wild deer; yea, his belly bids him go even to the good homestead to make assay upon the flocks. Even so Odysseus was fain to draw nigh to the fair-tressed maidens, all naked as he was, such need had come upon him. But he was terrible in their eyes, being marred with the salt sea foam, and they fled cowering here and there about the jutting spits of shore. And the daughter of Alcinous alone stood firm, for Athene gave her courage of heart, and took all trembling from her limbs. So she halted and stood over against him, and Odysseus considered whether he should clasp the knees of the lovely maiden, and so make his prayer, or should stand as he was, apart, and beseech her with smooth words, if haply she might show him the town, and give him raiment. And as he thought within himself, it seemed better to stand apart, and beseech her with smooth words, lest the maiden should be angered with him if he touched her knees: so straightway he spake a sweet and cunning word:

"I supplicate thee, O queen, whether thou art a goddess or a mortal! If indeed thou art a goddess of them that keep the wide heaven; to Artemis, then, the daughter of great Zeus, I mainly liken thee, for beauty and stature and shapeliness. But if thou art one of the daughters of men who dwell on earth, thrice blessed are thy father and thy lady mother, and thrice blessed thy brethren. Surely their souls ever glow with gladness for thy sake, each time they see thee entering the dance, so fair a flower of maidens. But he is of heart the most blessed beyond all other who shall prevail with gifts of wooing, and lead thee to his home. Never have mine eyes beheld such an one among mortals, neither man nor woman; great awe comes upon me as I look on thee. Yet in Delos once I saw as goodly a thing: a young sapling of a palm tree springing by the altar of Apollo. For thither too I went, and much people with me, on that path where my sore troubles were to be. Yea, and when I looked thereupon, long time I marvelled in spirit,—for never grew there yet so goodly a shoot from ground,—even in such wise as I wonder at thee, lady, and am astonied and do greatly fear to touch thy knees, though grievous sorrow is upon me. Yesterday, on the twentieth day, I escaped from the wine-dark deep, but all that time continually the wave bare me, and the vehement winds drave, from the isle Ogygia. And now some god has cast me on this shore, that here too, methinks, some evil may betide me; for I trow not that trouble will cease; the gods ere that time will yet bring many a thing to pass. But, queen, have pity on me, for after many trials and sore to thee first of all am I come, and of the other folk, who hold this city and land, I know no man. Nay show me the town, give me an old garment to cast about me, if thou hadst, when thou camest here, any wrap for the linen. And may the gods grant thee all thy heart's desire: a husband and a home, and a mind at one with his may they give—a good gift, for there is nothing mightier and nobler than when man and wife are of one heart and mind in a house, a grief to their foes, and to their friends great joy, but their own hearts know it best."

Then Nausicaa of the white arms answered him, and said: "Stranger, forasmuch as thou seemest no evil man nor foolish—and it is Olympian Zeus himself that giveth weal to men, to the good and to the evil, to each one as he will, and this thy lot doubtless is of him, and so thou must in anywise endure it:—and now, since thou hast come to our city and our land, thou shalt not lack raiment, nor aught else that is the due of a hapless suppliant, when he has met them who can befriend him. And I will show thee the town, and name the name of the people. The Phæacians hold this city and land, and I am the daughter of Alcinous, great of heart, on whom all the might and force of the Phæacians depend."

Thus she spake, and called to her maidens of the fair tresses: "Halt, my maidens, whither flee ye at the sight of a man? Ye surely do not take him for an enemy? That mortal breathes not, and never will be born, who shall come with war to the land of the Phæacians, for they are very dear to the gods. Far apart we live in the wash of the waves, the outermost of men, and no other mortals are conversant with us. Nay, but this man is some helpless one come hither in his wanderings, whom now we must kindly entreat, for all strangers and beggars are from Zeus, and a little gift is dear. So, my maidens, give the stranger meat and drink, and bathe him in the river, where withal is a shelter from the winds."

So she spake, but they had halted and called each to the other, and they brought Odysseus to the sheltered place, and made him sit down, as Nausicaa bade them, the daughter of Alcinous, high of heart. Beside him they laid a mantle, and doublet for raiment, and gave him soft olive oil in the golden cruse, and bade him wash in the streams of the river. Then goodly Odysseus spake among the maidens, saying: "I pray you stand thus apart, while I myself wash the brine from my shoulders, and anoint me with olive oil, for truly oil is long a stranger to my skin. But in your sight I will not bathe, for I am ashamed to make me naked in the company of fair-tressed maidens."

Then they went apart and told all to their lady. But with the river water the goodly Odysseus washed from his skin the salt scurf that covered his back and broad shoulders, and from his head he wiped the crusted brine of the barren sea. But when he had washed his whole body, and anointed him with olive oil, and had clad himself in the raiment that the unwedded maiden gave him, then Athene, the daughter of Zeus, made him greater and more mighty to behold, and from his head caused deep curling locks to flow, like the hyacinth flower. And as when some skillful man overlays gold upon silver—one that Hephæstus and Pallas Athene have taught all manner of craft, and full of grace is his handiwork—even so did Athene shed grace about his head and shoulders.

Then to the shore of the sea went Odysseus apart, and sat down, glowing in beauty and grace, and the princess marvelled at him, and spake among her fair-tressed maidens, saying:

"Listen, my white-armed maidens, and I will say somewhat. Not without the will of all the gods who hold Olympus hath this man come among the godlike Phæacians. Erewhile he seemed to me uncomely, but now he is like the gods that keep the wide heaven. Would that such an one might be called my husband, dwelling here, and that it might please him here to abide! But come, my maidens, give the stranger meat and drink."

Thus she spake, and they gave ready ear and hearkened, and set beside Odysseus meat and drink, and the steadfast goodly Odysseus did eat and drink eagerly, for it was long since he had tasted food.

Now Nausicaa of the white arms had another thought. She folded the raiment and stored it in the goodly wain, and yoked the mules strong of hoof, and herself climbed into the car. Then she called on Odysseus, and spake and hailed him: "Up now, stranger, and rouse thee to go to the city, that I may convey thee to the house of my wise father, where, I promise thee, thou shalt get knowledge of all the noblest of the Phæacians. But do thou even as I tell thee, and thou seemest a discreet man enough. So long as we are passing along the fields and farms of men, do thou fare quickly with the maidens behind the mules and the chariot, and I will lead the way. But when we set foot within the city, —whereby goes a high wall with towers; and there is a fair haven on either side of the town, and narrow is the entrance, and curved ships are drawn up on either hand of the mole, for all the folk have stations for their vessels, each man one for himself. And there is the place of assembly about the goodly temple of Poseidon, furnished with heavy stones, deep bedded in the earth. There men look to the gear of the black ships, hawsers and sails, and there they fine down the oars. For the Phæacians care not for bow nor quiver, but for masts, and oars of ships, and gallant barques, wherein rejoicing they cross the grey sea.

Their ungracious speech it is that I would avoid, lest some man afterward rebuke me, and there are but too many insolent folk among the people. And some one of the baser sort might meet me and say: "Who is this that goes with Nausicaa, this tall and goodly stranger? Where found she him? Her husband he will be, her very own. Either she has taken in some shipwrecked wanderer of strange men,—for no men dwell near us; or some god has come in answer to her instant prayer; from heaven has he descended, and will have her to wife for evermore. Better so, if herself she has ranged abroad and found a lord from a strange land, for verily she holds in no regard the Phæacians here in this country, the many men and noble who are her wooers." So will they speak, and this would turn to my reproach. Yea, and I myself would think it blame of another maiden who did such things in despite of her friends, her father and mother being still alive, and was conversant with men before the day of open wedlock. But, stranger, heed well what I say, that as soon as may be thou mayest gain at my father's hands an escort and a safe return. Thou shalt find a fair grove of Athene, a poplar grove near the road, and a spring wells forth therein, and a meadow lies all around. There is my father's demesne, and his fruitful close, within the sound of a man's shout from the city. Sit thee down there and wait until such time as we may have come into the city, and reached the house of my father. But when thou deemest that we are got to the palace, then go up to the city of the Phæacians, and ask for the house of my father Alcinous, high of heart. It is easily known, and a young child could be thy guide, for nowise like it are builded the houses of the Phæacians, so goodly is the palace of the hero Alcinous. But when thou art within the shadow of the halls and the court, pass quickly through the great chamber, till thou comest to my mother, who sits at the hearth in the light of the fire, weaving yarn of sea-purple stain, a wonder to behold. Her chair is leaned against a pillar, and her maidens sit behind her. And there my father's throne leans close to hers, wherein he sits and drinks his wine, like an immortal. Pass thou by him, and cast thy hands about my mother's knees, that thou mayest see quickly and with joy the day of thy returning, even if thou art from a very far country. If but her heart be kindly disposed toward thee, then is there hope that thou shalt see thy friends, and come to thy well-builded house, and to thine own country."

She spake, and smote the mules with the shining whip, and quickly they left behind them the streams of the river. And well they trotted and well they paced, and she took heed to drive in such wise that the maidens and Odysseus might follow on foot, and cunningly she plied the lash. Then the sun set, and they came to the famous grove, the sacred place of Athene; so there the goodly Odysseus sat him down. Then straightway he prayed to the daughter of mighty Zeus: "Listen to me, child of Zeus, lord of the ægis, unwearied maiden; hear me even now, since before thou heardest not when I was smitten on the sea, when the renowned Earth-shaker smote me. Grant me to come to the Phæacians as one dear, and worthy of pity."

So he spake in prayer, and Pallas Athene heard him; but she did not yet appear to him face to face, for she had regard unto her father's brother, who furiously raged against the godlike Odysseus, till he should come to his own country.

Odysseus Reveals Himself to His Father

(From Book XXIV; translated by George Chapman)

See the note prefixed to "The Landing in Phaeacia," above.

ALL this haste made not his staid faith
so free
To trust his words; who said: "If you
are he,
Approve it by some sign." "This scar
then see,"
Replied Ulysses, "given me by the boar
Slain in Parnassus; I being sent before
By yours and by my honour'd mother's
will,
To see your sire Autolycus fulfil
The gifts he vow'd at giving of my name.
I'll tell you, too, the trees, in goodly
frame
Of this fair orchard, that I ask'd of you
Being yet a child, and follow'd for your
show,
And name of every tree. You gave me
then
Of fig-trees forty, apple-bearers ten,
Pear-trees thirteen, and fifty ranks of
vine;
Each one of which a season did confine
For his best eating. Not a grape did
grow
That grew not there, and had his heavy
brow

When Jove's fair daughters, the all-
ripening Hours,
Gave timely date to it." This charged
the powers
Both of his knees and heart with such
impression
Of sudden comfort, that it gave posses-
sion
Of all to trance; the signs were all so
true;
And did the love that gave them so renew.
He cast his arms about his son and
sunk,
The circle slipping to his feet; so shrunk
Were all his age's forces with the fire
Of his young love rekindled. The old sire
The son took up quite lifeless. But his
breath
Again respiring, and his soul from death
His body's powers recovering, out he
cried,
And said: "O Jupiter! I now have tried
That still there live in heaven remember-
ing Gods
Of men that serve them; though the
periods
They set on their appearances are long
In best men's sufferings, yet as sure as
strong
They are in comforts; be their strange
delays
Extended never so from days to days.
Yet see the short joys or the soon-fix'd
fears

Of helps withheld by them so many
years:
For if the wooers now have paid the
pain
Due to their impious pleasures, now
again

Extreme fear takes me, lest we straight
shall see
The Ithacensians here in mutiny;
Their messengers dispatch'd to win to
friend
The Cephallenian cities."

From PLATO'S PHAEDO

The Death of Socrates (Translated by Benjamin Jowett)

When Socrates drank the hemlock, in B. C. 399, he was in his seventieth
year. His life had been spent in the effort to awaken moral consciousness and
consideration of the eternal, in the minds of all who heard him. The charges of
corrupting the youth and despising the gods, on which he had been condemned,
had been dictated by political enemies. Though Socrates was allied to no party,
these men hated him, as their predecessors in power had done, for his unsparing
attacks on injustice and the false pretense of knowledge.

During the voyage of the sacred ship to Delos on the Theoric mission, which
occupied thirty days, the execution was deferred. Socrates spent the time in
daily conversations with a company of friends and disciples. At the beginning
of the *Phædo,* the holy season is over, and the company come earlier than usual,
to converse with him for the last time. Almost as soon as they enter the prison,
Xanthippe and her children are sent home in the care of a servant of Crito's.
The philosopher has just been released from chains. He explains why he
welcomes death, and why he holds the immutable conviction that the soul is immortal. Then follows the last scene of all.

WHEN he had done speaking, Crito said: And have you any commands for us, Socrates—anything to say about your children, or any
other matter in which we can serve you?

Nothing particular, Crito, he replied: only, as I have always told you,
take care of yourselves; that is a service which you may be ever rendering
to me and mine and to all of us, whether you promise to do so or not.
But if you have no thought for yourselves, and care not to walk according
to the rule which I have prescribed for you, not now for the first time,
however much you may profess or promise at the moment, it will be of
no avail.

We will do our best, said Crito: And in what way shall we bury you?

In any way that you like; but you must get hold of me, and take care
that I do not run away from you. Then he turned to us, and added with
a smile:—I cannot make Crito believe that I am the same Socrates who
have been talking and conducting the argument; he fancies that I am the
other Socrates whom he will soon see, a dead body—and he asks, How
shall he bury me? And though I have spoken many words in the
endeavour to show that when I have drunk the poison I shall leave you
and go to the joys of the blessed,—these words of mine, with which I

was comforting you and myself, have had, as I perceive, no effect upon Crito. And therefore I want you to be surety for me to him now, as at the trial he was surety to the judges for me: but let the promise be of another sort; for he was surety for me to the judges that I would remain, and you must be my surety to him that I shall not remain, but go away and depart; and then he will suffer less at my death, and not be grieved when he sees my body being burned or buried. I would not have him sorrow at my hard lot, or say at the burial, Thus we lay out Socrates, or, Thus we follow him to the grave or bury him; for false words are not only evil in themselves, but they infect the soul with evil. Be of good cheer then, my dear Crito, and say that you are burying my body only, and do with that whatever is usual, and what you think best.

When he had spoken these words, he arose and went into a chamber to bathe; Crito followed him and told us to wait. So we remained behind, talking and thinking of the subject of discourse, and also of the greatness of our sorrow; he was like a father of whom we were being bereaved, and we were about to pass the rest of our lives as orphans. When he had taken the bath his children were brought to him—(he had two young sons and an elder one); and the women of his family also came, and he talked to them and gave them a few directions in the presence of Crito; then he dismissed them and returned to us.

Now the hour of sunset was near, for a good deal of time had passed while he was within. When he came out, he sat down with us again after his bath, but not much was said. Soon the jailer, who was the servant of the Eleven, entered and stood by him, saying:—To you, Socrates, whom I know to be the noblest and gentlest and best of all who ever came to this place, I will not impute the angry feelings of other men, who rage and swear at me, when, in obedience to the authorities, I bid them drink the poison—indeed, I am sure that you will not be angry with me; for others, as you are aware, and not I, are to blame. And so fare you well, and try to bear lightly what must needs be—you know my errand. Then bursting into tears he turned away and went out.

Socrates looked at him and said: I return your good wishes, and will do as you bid. Then turning to us, he said, How charming the man is: since I have been in prison he has always been coming to see me, and at times he would talk to me, and was as good to me as could be, and now see how generously he sorrows on my account. We must do as he says, Crito; and therefore let the cup be brought, if the poison is prepared; if not, let the attendant prepare some.

Yet, said Crito, the sun is still upon the hill-tops, and I know that many a one has taken the draught late, and after the announcement has been made to him, he has eaten and drunk, and enjoyed the society of his beloved; do not hurry—there is time enough.

Socrates said: Yes, Crito, and they of whom you speak are right in so acting, for they think that they will be gainers by the delay; but I am right in not following their example, for I do not think that I should gain anything by drinking the poison a little later; I should only be ridiculous in my own eyes for sparing and saving a life which is already forfeit. Please then to do as I say, and not to refuse me.

Crito made a sign to the servant, who was standing by; and he went out, and having been absent for some time, returned with the jailer carrying the cup of poison. Socrates said: You, my good friend, who are experienced in these matters, shall give me directions how I am to proceed. The man answered: You have only to walk about until your legs are heavy, and then to lie down, and the poison will act. At the same time he handed the cup to Socrates, who in the easiest and gentlest manner, without the least fear or change of colour or feature, looking at the man with all his eyes, Echecrates, as his manner was, took the cup and said: What do you say about making a libation out of this cup to any god? May I, or not? The man answered: We only prepare, Socrates, just so much as we deem enough. I understand, he said: but I may and must ask the gods to prosper my journey from this to the other world—even so—and so be it according to my prayer. Then raising the cup to his lips, quite readily and cheerfully he drank off the poison. And hitherto most of us had been able to control our sorrow; but now when we saw him drinking, and saw too that he had finished the draught, we could no longer forbear, and in spite of myself my own tears were flowing fast; so that I covered my face and wept, not for him, but at the thought of my own calamity in having to part from such a friend. Nor was I the first; for Crito, when he found himself unable to restrain his tears, had got up, and I followed; and at that moment, Apollodorus, who had been weeping all the time, broke out in a loud and passionate cry which made cowards of us all. Socrates alone retained his calmness: What is this strange outcry? he said. I sent away the women mainly in order that they might not misbehave in this way, for I have been told that a man should die in peace. Be quiet then, and have patience. When we heard his words we were ashamed, and refrained our tears; and he walked about until, as he said, his legs began to fail, and then he lay on his back, according to the directions, and the man who gave him the poison now and then looked at his feet and legs; and after a while he pressed his foot hard, and asked him if he could feel; and he saïd, No; and then his leg, and so upwards and upwards, and showed us that he was cold and stiff. And he felt them himself, and said: When the poison reaches the heart, that will be the end. He was beginning to grow cold about the groin, when he uncovered his face, for he had covered himself up, and said—they were his last words—he said: Crito, I owe a cock to Æsculapius; will you remember to pay the debt? The debt shall be paid, said Crito; is there anything else? There was no answer to this question; but in a minute or two a movement was heard, and the attendants uncovered him; his eyes were set, and Crito closed his eyes and mouth.

Such was the end, Echecrates, of our friend; concerning whom I may truly say, that of all the men of his time whom I have known, he was the wisest and justest and best.

II. ENGLISH SELECTIONS

BALLADS

Sir Patrick Spens

The king sits in Dumferling toune,
  Drinking the blude-reid wine:
"O whar will I get guid sailor,
  To sail this schip of mine?"

Up and spak an eldern knicht,
  Sat at the kings richt kne:
"Sir Patrick Spence is the best sailor
  That sails upon the se."

The king has written a braid letter,
  And signd it wi his hand,
And sent it to Sir Patrick Spence,
  Was walking on the sand.

The first line that Sir Patrick red,
  A loud lauch lauched he;
The next line that Sir Patrick red,
  The teir blinded his ee.

"O wha is this has don this deid,
  This ill deid don to me,
To send me out this time o' the yeir,
  To sail upon the se!

"Mak hast, mak haste, my mirry men all,
  Our guid schip sails the morne:"
"O say na sae, my master deir,
  For I feir a deadlie storme.

"Late late yestreen I saw the new moone,
  Wi the auld moone in hir arme,
And I feir, I feir, my deir master,
  That we will cum to harme."

O our Scots nobles wer richt laith
  To weet their cork-heild schoone;
Bot lang owre a' the play wer playd,
  Thair hats they swam aboone.

O lang, lang may their ladies sit,
  Wi thair fans into their hand,
Or eir they se Sir Patrick Spence
  Cum sailing to the land.

O lang, lang may the ladies stand,
  Wi thair gold kems in their hair,
Waiting for thair ain deir lords,
  For they'll se thame na mair.

Haf owre, haf owre to Aberdour,
  It's fiftie fadom deip,
And thair lies guid Sir Patrick Spence,
  Wi the Scots lords at his feit.

Clerk Saunders

Clark Sanders and May Margret
  Walkt ower yon graveld green,
And sad and heavy was the love,
  I wat, it fell this twa between.

"A bed, a bed," Clark Sanders said,
  "A bed, a bed for you and I;"
"Fye no, fye no," the lady said
  "Until the day we married be.

"For in it will come my seven brothers,
  And a' their torches burning bright;
They'll say, We hae but ae sister,
  And here her lying wi a knight."

"Ye'l take the sourde fray my scabbord,
  And lowly, lowly lift the gin,
And you may say, your oth to save,
  You never let Clark Sanders in.

"Yele take a napken in your hand,
  And ye'l ty up baith your een,
And ye may say, your oth to save,
  That ye saw na Sandy sen late yestreen."

"Yele take me in your armes twa,
  Yele carrey me ben into your bed,
And ye may say, your oth to save,
  In your bower-floor I never tread."

She has taen the sourde fray his scab-
      bord,
  And lowly, lowly lifted the gin;
She was to swear, her oth to save,
  She never let Clerk Sanders in.

She has tain a napkin in her hand,
  And she ty'd up baith her eeen;
She was to swear, her oth to save,
  She say na him sene late yestreen.

She has taen him in her armes twa,
  And carried him ben into her bed;
She was to swear, her oth to save,
  He never in her bower-floor tread.

In and came her seven brothers,
  And all their torches burning bright;
Says thay, We hae but ae sister,
  And see there her lying wi a knight.

Out and speaks the first of them,
  "A wat they hay been lovers dear;"
Out an speaks the next of them,
  "They hay been in love this many a
      year."

Out an speaks the third of them,
  "It wear great sin this twa to twain;"
Out an speaks the fourth of them,
  "It wear a sin to kill a sleeping man."

Out an speaks the fifth of them,
  "A wat they'll near be twained by me;"
Out an speaks the sixt of them,
  "We'l tak our leave an gae our way."

Out an speaks the seventh of them,
  "Altho there wear no a man but me,
· · · · · · · · · · ·
  I bear the brand, I'le gar him die."

Out he has taen a bright long brand,
  And he has striped it throw the straw,
And throw and throw Clarke Sanders'
      body
  A wat he has gard cold iron gae.

Sanders he started, an Margret she lapt,
  Intill his arms whare she lay,
And well and wellsome was the night,
  A wat it was between these twa.

And they lay still, and sleeped sound,
  Untill the day began to daw;
And kindly till him she did say
  "It's time, trew-love, ye wear awa."

They lay still, and sleeped sound,
  Untill the sun began to shine;
She lookt between her and the wa,
  And dull and heavy was his eeen.

She thought it had been a loathsome
      sweat,
  A wat it had fallen this twa between;
But it was the blood of his fair body,
  A wat his life days wair na lang.

"O Sanders, I'le do for your sake
  What other ladys would na thoule;
When seven years is come and gone,
  There's near a shoe go on my sole.

"O Sanders, I'le do for your sake
  What other ladies would think mare;
When seven years is come an gone,
  Ther's nere a comb go in my hair.

"O Sanders, I'le do for your sake
  What other ladies would think lack;
When seven years is come an gone,
  I'le wear nought but dowy black."

The bells gaed clinking throw the towne,
  To carry the dead corps to the clay,
An sighing says her May Margret,
  "A wat I bide a doulfou day."

In an come her father dear,
  Stout steping on the floor;
· · · · · · · · · · ·
· · · · · · · · · · ·

"Hold your toung, my doughter dear,
  Let all your mourning a bee;
I'le carry the dead corps to the clay,
  An I'le come back an comfort thee."

"Comfort well your seven sons,
  For comforted will I never bee;
For it was neither lord nor loune
  That was in bower last night wi mee."

Johnie Armstrong

Is there never a man in all Scotland,
  From the highest state to the lowest
    degree,
That can shew himself now before the
    king?
  Scotland is so full of their traitery.

Yes, there is a man in Westmerland,
  And John Armstrong some do him
    call;
He has no lands nor rents coming in,
  Yet he keeps eightscore men within
    his hall.

He has horse and harness for them all,
  And goodly steeds that be milk-white,
With their goodly belts about their necks,
  With hats and feathers all alike.

The king he writ a lovely letter,
  With his own hand so tenderly,
And has sent it unto John Armstrong,
  To come and speak with him speedily.

When John he looked the letter upon,
  Then, Lord! he was as blithe as a bird
    in a tree:
"I was never before no king in my life,
  My father, my grandfather, nor none
    of us three.

"But seeing we must [go] before the
    king,
  Lord! we will go most valiantly;
You shall every one have a velvet coat,
  Laid down with golden laces three.

"And you shall every one have a scarlet
    cloak,
  Laid down with silver laces five,
With your golden belts about your necks,
  With hats [and] brave feathers all
    alike."

But when John he went from Guilt-
    knock Hall!
  The wind it blew hard, and full sore
    it did rain:
"Now fare you well, brave Guiltknock
    Hall!
  I fear I shall never see thee again."

Now John he is to Edenborough gone,
  And his eightscore men so gallantly,
And every one of them on a milk-white
    steed,
  With their bucklers and swords hang-
    ing down to the knee.

But when John he came the king before,
  With his eightscore men so gallant to
    see,
The king he moved his bonnet to him;
  He thought he had been a king as well
    as he.

"O pardon, pardon, my soveraign leige,
  Pardon for my eightscore men and me!
For my name it is John Armstrong,
  And a subject of yours, my leige," said
    he.

"Away with thee, thou false traitor!
  No pardon I will grant to thee,
But, to-morrow before eight of the clock,
  I will hang thy eightscore men and
    thee."

O how John looked over his left
    shoulder!
  And to his merry men thus said he:
I have asked grace of a graceless face,
  No pardon here is for you nor me.

Then John pulld out a nut-brown sword,
  And it was made of mettle so free;
Had not the king moved his foot as he
    did,
  John had taken his head from his
    body.

"Come, follow me, my merry men all,
  We will scorn one foot away to fly;

It never shall be said we were hung like
    doggs;
  No, wee'l fight it out most manfully."

Then they fought on like champions
    bold—
  For their hearts was sturdy, stout, and
    free—
Till they had killed all the kings good
    guard;
  There was none left alive but onely
    three.

But then rise up all Edenborough,
  They rise up by thousands three;
Then a cowardly Scot came John behind,
  And run him thorow the fair body.

Said John, Fight on, my merry men all,
  I am a little hurt, but I am not slain;
I will lay me down for to bleed a while,
  Then I'le rise and fight with you
    again.

Then they fought on like mad men all,
  Till many a man lay dead on the plain;
For they were resolved, before they
    would yield,
That every man would there be slain.

So there they fought couragiously,
  'Till most of them lay dead there and
    slain,

But little Musgrave, that was his foot-
    page,
  With his bonny grissell got away un-
    tain.

But when he came up to Guiltknock
    Hall,
  The lady spyed him presently:
"What news, what news, thou little foot-
    page?
  What news from thy master and his
    company?"

"My news is bad, lady," he said,
  "Which I do bring, as you may see;
My master, John Armstrong, he is
    slain,
  And all his gallant company.

"Yet thou are welcome home, my bonny
    grisel!
  Full oft thou hast fed at the corn and
    hay,
But now thou shalt be fed with bread
    and wine,
  And thy sides shall be spurred no more,
    I say."

O then bespoke his little son,
  Ae he was set on his nurses knee:
"If ever I live for to be a man,
  My fathers blood revenged shall be."

GEOFFREY CHAUCER
(1340-1400)

From THE CANTERBURY TALES

The Prologue

WHAN that Aprille with his schowres
  swoote
The drought of Marche hath perced to the
  roote,
And bathud every veyne in swich licour,
Of which vertue engendred is the flour;
Whan Zephirus eek with his swete breeth
Enspirud hath in every holte and heeth
The tendre croppes, and the yonge sonne

Hath in the Ram his halfe cours i-ronne,
And smale fowles maken melodie,
That slepen al the night with open yhe,
So priketh hem nature in here corages:—
Thanne longen folk to gon on pilgrimages,
And palmers for to seeken straunge
  strondes.
To ferne halwes, kouthe in sondry londes;
And specially, from every schires ende
Of Engelond, to Canturbury they wende,
The holy blisful martir for to seeke,

That hem hath holpen whan that they
   were seeke.
  Byfel that, in that sesoun on a day,
In Southwerk at the Tabbard as I lay,
Redy to wenden on my pilgrimage
To Canturbury with ful devout corage,
At night was come into that hostelrie
Wel nyne and twenty in a companye,
Of sondry folk, by aventure i-falle
In felawschipe, and pilgryms were thei
   alle,
That toward Canturbury wolden ryde.
The chambres and the stables weren
   wyde,
And wel we weren esud atte beste.
And schortly, whan the sonne was to
   reste,
So hadde I spoken with hem everychon,
That I was of here felawschipe anon,
And made forward erly to aryse,
To take oure weye ther as I yow devyse.
But natheles, whiles I have tyme and
   space,
Or that I ferthere in this tale pace,
Me thinketh it acordant to resoun,
To telle yow alle the condicioun
Of eche of hem, so as it semed me,
And which they weren, and of what degre;
And eek in what array that they were inne:
And at a knight than wol I first bygynne.
  A KNIGHT ther was, and that a worthy
   man,
That from the tyme that he first bigan
To ryden out, he lovede chyvalrye,
Trouthe and honour, fredom and curtesie.
Ful worthi was he in his lordes werre,
And thereto hadde he riden, noman ferre,
As wel in Cristendom as in hethenesse,
And evere honoured for his worthinesse.
At Alisandre he was whan it was wonne,
Ful ofte tyme he hadde the bord bygonne
Aboven alle naciouns in Pruce.
In Lettowe hadde reyced and in Ruce,
No cristen man so ofte of his degre.
In Gernade atte siege hadde he be
Of Algesir, and riden in Belmarie.
At Lieys was he, and at Satalie,
Whan they were wonne; and in the Greete
   see

At many a noble arive hadde he be.
At mortal batailles hadde he ben fitene,
And foughten for our feith at Tramassene
In lystes thries, and ay slayn his foo.
This ilke worthi knight hadde ben also
Somtyme with the lord of Palatye,
Ageyn another hethene in Turkye:
And everemore he hadde a sovereyn prys.
And though that he was worthy he was
   wys,
And of his port as meke as is a mayde.
He never yit no vilonye ne sayde
In al his lyf, unto no maner wight.
He was a verray perfight gentil knight.
But for to telle you of his aray,
His hors was good, but he ne was nought
   gay.
Of fustyan he wered a gepoun
Al bysmoterud with his haburgeoun.
For he was late comen from his viage,
And wente for to doon his pilgrimage.
  With him ther was his sone, a yong
   SQUYER,
A lovyer, and a lusty bacheler,
With lokkes crulle as they were layde in
   presse.
Of twenty yeer he was of age I gesse.
Of his stature he was of evene lengthe,
And wondurly delyver, and gret of
   strengthe.
And he hadde ben somtyme in chivachie,
In Flaundres, in Artoys, and in Picardie,
And born him wel, as in so litel space,
In hope to stonden in his lady grace.
Embrowdid was he, as it were a mede
Al ful of fresshe floures, white and reede.
Syngynge he was, or flowtynge, al the
   day;
He was as fressh as is the moneth of May.
Schort was his goune, with sleeves long
   and wyde.
Wel cowde he sitte on hors, and faire
   ryde.
He cowde songes wel make and endite,
Justne and eek daunce, and wel purtray
   and write.
So hote he lovede, that by nightertale
He sleep nomore than doth a nightyn-
   gale.

Curteys he was, lowly, and servysable,
And carf byforn his fadur at the table.
   A YEMAN had he, and servantes nomoo
At that tyme, for him lust ryde soo;
And he was clad in coote and hood of
      grene.
A shef of pocok arwes bright and kene
Under his belte he bar full thriftily.
Wel cowde he dresse his takel yomanly;
His arwes drowpud nought with fetheres
      lowe.
And in his hond he bar a mighty bowe.
A not-heed hadde he with a broun visage.
Of woode-craft cowde he wel al the usage.
Upon his arme he bar a gay bracer,
And by his side a swerd and a bokeler,
And on that other side a gay daggere,
Harneysed wel, and scharp as poynt of
      spere;
A Cristofre on his brest of silver schene.
An horn he bar, the bawdrik was of grene;
A forster was he sothely, as I gesse.
   Ther was also a Nonne, a PRIORESSE,
That of hire smylyng was ful symple and
      coy;
Hire grettest ooth nas but by seynt Loy;
And sche was clept madame Englentyne.
Ful wel sche sang the servise devyne,
Entuned in hire nose ful semyly;
And Frensch sche spak ful faire and fety-
      sly,
Aftur the scole of Stratford atte Bowe,
For Frensch of Parys was to hire un-
      knowe.
At mete wel i-taught was sche withalle;
Sche leet no morsel from hire lippes falle,
Ne wette hire fyngres in hire sauce deepe.
Wel cowde sche carie a morsel, and wel
      keepe,
That no drope fil uppon hire brest.
In curtesie was sett al hire lest.
Hire overlippe wypud sche so clene,
That in hire cuppe was no ferthing sene
Of grees, whan sche dronken hadde hire
      draught.
Ful semely aftur hire mete sche raught.
And sikurly sche was of gret disport,
And ful plesant, and amyable of port,
And peyned hire to counterfete cheere

Of court, and ben estatlich of manere,
And to ben holden digne of reverence.
But for to speken of hire conscience,
Sche was so charitable and so pitous,
Sche wolde weepe if that sche sawe a
      mous
Caught in a trappe, if it were deed or
      bledde.
Of smale houndes hadde sche, that sche
      fedde
With rostud fleissh and mylk and wastel
      breed.
But sore wepte sche if oon of hem were
      deed,
Or if men smot it with a yerde smerte:
And al was conscience and tendre herte.
Ful semely hire wymple i-pynched was;
Hire nose streight; hire eyen grey as glas;
Hire mouth ful smal, and therto softe and
      reed;
But sikurly sche hadde a fair forheed.
It was almost a spanne brood, I trowe;
For hardily sche was not undurgrowe.
Ful fetys was hire cloke, as I was waar.
Of smal coral aboute hire arme sche baar
A peire of bedes gaudid al with grene;
And theron heng a broch of gold ful
      schene,
On which was first i-writen a crowned A,
And after that, *Amor vincit omnia.*
Anothur NONNE also with hire hadde sche,
That was hire chapelleyn, and PRESTES
      thre.
   A MONK ther was, a fair for the mais-
      trie,
An out-rydere, that loved venerye;
A manly man, to ben an abbot able.
Full many a deynte hors hadde he in
      stable:
And whan he rood, men might his bridel
      heere
Gyngle in a whistlyng wynd so cleere,
And eek as lowde as doth the chapel belle.
Ther as this lord was keper of the selle,
The reule of seynt Maure or of seint
      Beneyt,
Bycause that it was old and somdel
      streyt,
This ilke monk leet forby hem pace,

And helde aftur the newe world the space.
He gaf nat of that text a pulled hen,
That seith, that hunters been noon holy
    men;
Ne that a monk, whan he is cloysterles,
Is likned to a fissche that is watirles;
This is to seyn, a monk out of his cloystre.
But thilke text hild he not worth an
    oystre.
And I seide his opinioun was good.
What schulde he studie, and make him-
    selven wood,
Uppon a book in cloystre alway to powre,
Or swynke with his handes, and laboure,
As Austyn byt?   How schal the world be
    served?
Lat Austyn have his swynk to him re-
    served.
Therfore he was a pricasour aright;
Greyhoundes he hadde as swifte as fowel
    in flight;
Of prikyng and of huntyng for the hare
Was al his lust, for no cost wolde he spare.
I saugh his sleves purfiled atte hond
With grys, and that the fynest of a lond.
And for to festne his hood undur his
    chyn
He hadde of gold y-wrought a curious pyn:
A love-knotte in the gretter ende ther was.
His heed was ballid, and schon as eny glas,
And eek his face as he hadde be anoynt.
He was a lord ful fat and in good poynt;
His eyen steep, and rollyng in his heed,
That stemed as a forneys of a leed;
His bootes souple, his hors in gret estat.
Now certeinly he was a fair prelat;
He was not pale as a for-pyned goost.
A fat swan loved he best of eny roost.
His palfray was as broun as eny berye.
    A FRERE ther was a wantoun and a
        merye,
A lymytour, a ful solempne man.
In alle the ordres foure is noon that can
So noche of daliaunce and fair langage.
He hadde i-made many a fair mariage
Of yonge wymmen, at his owne cost.
Unto his ordre he was a noble post.
Ful wel biloved and famulier was he
With frankeleyns over al in his cuntre,

And eek with worthi wommen of the toun:
For he hadde power of confessioun,
As seyde himself, more than a curat,
For of his ordre he was licenciat.
Ful sweetly herde he confessioun,
And plesaunt was his absolucioun;
He was an esy man to geve penance
Ther as he wiste to han a good pitance:
For unto a povre ordre for to geve
Is signe that a man is wel i-schreve.
For if he gaf, he dorste make avaunt,
He wiste that a man was repentaunt.
For many a man so hard is of his herte,
He may not wepe though him sore smerte.
Therfore in stede of wepyng and prayeres,
Men mooten given silver to the pore
    freres.
His typet was ay farsud ful of knyfes
And pynnes, for to give faire wyfes.
And certayn he hadde a mery noote.
Wel couthe he synge and pleye on a rote.
Of yeddynges he bar utterly the prys.
His nekke whit was as the flour-de-lys.
Therto he strong was as a champioun.
He knew wel the tavernes in every toun,
And every ostiller or gay tapstere,
Bet than a lazer, or a beggere,
For unto such a worthi man as he
Acorded not, as by his faculté,
To have with sike lazars aqueyntaunce.
It is not honest, it may not avaunce,
For to delen with such poraile,
But al with riche and sellers of vitaille.
And over al, ther eny profyt schulde arise,
Curteys he was, and lowe of servyse.
Ther was no man nowher so vertuous.
He was the beste begger in al his hous,
For though a widewe hadde but oo schoo,
So plesaunt was his *In principio*,
Yet wolde he have a ferthing or he wente.
His purchace was bettur than his rente.
And rage he couthe and pleye as a whelpe,
In love-days ther couthe he mochil helpe.
For ther was he not like a cloysterer,
With a thredbare cope as a pore scoler,
But he was like a maister or a pope.
Of double worstede was his semy-cope,
That rounded was as a belle out of presse.
Somwhat he lipsede, for wantounesse,

To make his Englissch swete upon his
  tunge;
And in his harpyng, whan that he hadde
  sunge,
His eyghen twynkeled in his heed aright,
As don the sterres in the frosty night.
This worthi lymytour was called Huberd.
   A MARCHAUNT was ther with a forked
  berd,
In motteleye, and high on horse he sat,
Uppon his heed a Flaundrisch bever hat;
His botus clapsud faire and fetously.
His resons he spak ful solempnely,
Sownynge alway the encres of his wyn-
  nyng.
He wolde the see were kepud for eny thinge
Betwixe Middulburgh and Orewelle.
Wel couthe he in eschange scheeldes selle.
This worthi man ful wel his witte bisette;
Ther wiste no man that he was in dette,
So estately was he of governaunce,
With his bargayns, and with his chevy-
  saunce
For sothe he was a worthi man withalle,
But soth to say, I not what men him calle.
   A CLERK ther was of Oxenford also,
That unto logik hadde longe i-go.
Al so lene was his hors as is a rake,
And he was not right fat, I undertake;
But lokede holwe, and therto soburly.
Ful thredbare was his overest courtepy,
For he hadde nought geten him yit a
  benefice,
Ne was not worthy to haven an office.
For him was lever have at his beddes heed
Twenty bookes, clothed in blak and reed,
Of Aristotil, and of his philosophie,
Then robus riche, or fithul, or sawtrie.
But al though he were a philosophre,
Yet hadde he but litul gold in cofre;
But al that he might of his frendes hente,
On bookes and his lernyng he it spente,
And busily gan for the soules pray
Of hem that gaf him wherwith to scolay.
Of studie tooke he most cure and heede.
Not oo word spak he more than was neede;
Al that he spak it was of heye prudence,
And schort and quyk, and ful of gret sen-
  tence.

Sownynge in moral manere was his speche,
And gladly wolde he lerne, and gladly
  teche.
   A SERGEANT OF LAWE, war and wys,
That often hadde ben atte parvys,
Ther was also, ful riche of excellence.
Discret he was, and of gret reverence:
He semed such, his wordes were so wise,
Justice he was ful often in assise,
By patent, and by pleyn commissioun;
For his science, and for his heih renoun,
Of fees and robes had he many oon.
So gret a purchasour was ther nowher
  noon.
Al was fee symple to him in effecte,
His purchasyng might nought ben to him
  suspecte.
Nowher so besy a man as he ther nas,
And yit he semed besier than he was.
In termes hadde caas and domes alle,
That fro the tyme of kyng Will were falle.
Therto he couthe endite, and make a
  thing,
Ther couthe no man pynche at his writ-
  yng.
And every statute couthe he pleyn by
  roote.
He rood but hoomly in a medled coote,
Gird with a seynt of silk, with barres
  smale;
Of his array telle I no lenger tale.
   A FRANKELEYN ther was in his com-
  panye;
Whit was his berde, as the dayesye.
Of his complexioun he was sangwyn.
Wel loved he in the morn a sop of wyn.
To lyve in delite was al his wone,
For he was Epicurius owne sone,
That heeld opynyoun that pleyn delyt
Was verraily felicite perfyt.
An househaldere, and that a gret, was he;
Seynt Julian he was in his countré.
His breed, his ale, was alway after oon;
A bettre envyned man was nowher noon.
Withoute bake mete was never his hous,
Of fleissch and fissch, and that so plenty-
  vous,
It snewed in his hous of mete and drynk,
Of alle deyntees that men cowde thynke.

Aftur the sondry sesouns of the yeer,
He chaunged hem at mete and at soper.
Ful many a fat partrich had he in mewe,
And many a brem and many a luce in
 stewe.
Woo was his cook, but if his sauce were
Poynant and scharp, and redy al his gere.
His table dormant in his halle alway
Stood redy covered al the longe day.
At sessions ther was he lord and sire.
Ful ofte tyme he was knight of the schire.
An anlas and a gipser al of silk
Heng at his gerdul, whit as morne mylk.
A schirreve hadde he ben, and a counter;
Was nowher such a worthi vavaser.

 An HABURDASSHER and a CARPENTER,
A WEBBE, a DEYER, and a TAPICER,
Weren with us eeke, clothed in oo lyveré,
Of a solempne and gret fraternite.
Ful freissh and newe here gere piked was;
Here knyfes were i-chapud nat with bras,
But al with silver wrought ful clene and wel,
Here gurdles and here pouches every del.
Wel semed eche of hem a fair burgeys,
To sitten in a geldehalle on the deys.
Every man for the wisdom that he can,
Was schaply for to ben an aldurman.
For catel hadde they inough and rente,
And eek here wyfes wolde it wel assente;
And elles certeyn hadde thei ben to blame.
It is right fair for to be clept *madame*,
And for to go to vigilies al byfore,
And han a mantel rially i-bore.

 A COOK thei hadde with hem for the
 nones,
To boyle chyknes and the mary bones,
And poudre marchant, tart, and galyn-
 gale.
Wel cowde he knowe a draught of Lon-
 done ale.
He cowde roste, sethe, broille, and frie,
Make mortreux, and wel bake a pye.
But gret harm was it, as it semede me,
That on his schyne a mormal hadde he;
For blankmanger he made with the beste.

 A SCHIPMAN was ther, wonyng fer by
 weste:
For ought I woot, he was of Dertemouthe.
He rood upon a rouncy, as he couthe,

In a gowne of faldyng to the kne.
A dagger hangyng on a laas hadde he
Aboute his nekke under his arm adoun.
The hoote somer had maad his hew al
 broun,
And certeinly he was a good felawe.
Ful many a draught of wyn had he drawe
From Burdeux-ward, whil that the chap-
 man sleep.
Of nyce conscience took he no keep.
If that he foughte, and hadde the heigher
 hand,
By water he sente hem hoom to every
 land.
But of his craft to rikne wel the tydes,
His stremes and his dangers him bisides,
His herbergh and his mone, his lodeme-
 nage,
Ther was non such from Hulle to Cartage.
Hardy he was, and wys to undertake;
With many a tempest hadde his berd ben
 schake.
He knew wel alle the havenes, as thei
 were,
From Scotlond to the cape of Fynestere,
And every cryk in Bretayne and in
 Spayne;
His barge y-clepud was the Magdelayne.

 Ther was also a DOCTOUR OF PHISIK,
In al this world ne was ther non him lyk
To speke of phisik and of surgerye;
For he was groundud in astronomye.
He kepte his pacient wondurly wel
In houres by his magik naturel.
Wel cowde he fortune the ascendent
Of his ymages for his pacient.
He knew the cause of every maladye,
Were it of cold, or hete, or moyst, or drye,
And where thei engendrid, and of what
 humour;
He was a verrey parfight practisour.
The cause i-knowe, and of his harm the
 roote,
Anon he gaf the syke man his boote.
Ful redy hadde he his apotecaries,
To sende him dragges, and his letuaries,
For eche of hem made othur for to wynne;
Here friendschipe was not newe to be-
 gynne.

Wel knew he the olde Esculapius,
And Deiscorides, and eeke Rufus;
Old Ypocras, Haly, and Galien;
Serapyon, Razis, and Avycen;
Averrois, Damescen, and Constantyn;
Bernard, and Gatisden, and Gilbertyn.
Of his diete mesurable was he,
For it was of no superfluité,
But of gret norisching and digestible.
His studie was but litel on the Bible.
In sangwin and in pers he clad was al,
Lined with taffata and with sendal.
And yit he was but esy in dispence;
He kepte that he wan in pestilence.
For gold in phisik is a cordial;
Therfore he lovede gold in special.

A good WIF was ther of byside BATHE,
But sche was somdel deef, and that was
    skathe.
Of cloth-makyng she hadde such an haunt,
Sche passed hem of Ypris and of Gaunt.
In al the parisshe wyf ne was ther noon
That to the offryng byforn hire schulde
    goon,
And if ther dide, certeyn so wroth was
    sche,
That sche was thanne out of alle charité.
Hire keverchefs weren ful fyne of grounde;
I durste swere they weyghede ten pounde
That on the Sonday were upon hire heed.
Hir hosen were of fyn scarlett reed,
Ful streyte y-teyed, and schoos ful moyste
    and newe.
Bold was hir face, and fair, and reed of
    hewe.
Sche was a worthy womman al hire lyfe,
Housbondes atte chirche dore hadde sche
    fyfe,
    Withouten othur companye in youthe;
But thereof needeth nought to speke as
    nouthe.
And thries hadde sche ben at Jerusalem;
Sche hadde passed many a straunge
    streem;
At Rome sche hadde ben, and at Boloyne,
In Galice at seynt Jame, and at Coloyne.
Sche cowde moche of wandryng by the
    weye.
Gattothud was sche, sothly for to seye.

Uppon an amblere esely sche sat,
Wymplid ful wel, and on hire heed an hat
As brood as is a bocler or a targe;
A foot-mantel aboute hire hupes large,
And on hire feet a paire of spores scharpe.
In felawschipe wel cowde lawghe and
    carpe.
Of remedyes of love sche knew par-
    chaunce,
For of that art sche knew the olde daunce.
    A good man was ther of religioun,
And was a pore PERSOUN of a toun;
But riche he was of holy thought and
    werk.
He was also a lerned man, a clerk
That Cristes gospel gladly wolde preche;
His parischens devoutly wolde he teche.
Benigne he was, and wonder diligent,
And in adversite ful pacient;
And such he was i-proved ofte sithes.
Ful loth were him to curse for his tythes,
But rather wolde he geven out of dowte,
Unto his pore parisschens aboute,
Of his offrynge, and eek of his substaunce.
He cowde in litel thing han suffisance.
Wyd was his parisch, and houses fer ason-
    dur,
But he ne lafte not for reyne ne thondur,
In siknesse ne in meschief to visite
The ferrets in his parissche, moche and
    lite,
Uppon his feet, and in his hond a staf.
This noble ensample unto his scheep he
    gaf,
That ferst he wroughte, and after that he
    taughte,
Out of the gospel he tho wordes caughte,
And this figure he addid yit therto,
That if gold ruste, what schulde yren doo?
For if a prest be foul, on whom we truste,
No wondur is a lewid man to ruste;
And schame it is, if that a prest take kepe,
A schiten schepperd and a clene schepe;
Wel oughte a prest ensample for to give,
By his clennesse, how that his scheep
    schulde lyve.
He sette not his benefice to huyre,
And lefte his scheep encombred in the
    myre,

And ran to Londone, unto seynte Poules,
To seeken him a chaunterie for soules,
Or with a brethurhede be withholde;
But dwelte at hoom, and kepte wel his
    folde,
So that the wolfe ne made it not myscarye.
He was a schepperde and no mercenarie;
And though he holy were, and vertuous,
He was to senful man nought dispitous,
Ne of his speche daungerous ne digne,
But in his teching discret and benigne.
To drawe folk to heven by fairnesse,
By good ensample, was his busynesse:
But it were eny persone obstinat,
What so he were of high or lowe estat,
Him wolde he snybbe scharply for the
    nones.
A bettre preest I trowe ther nowher non
    is.
He waytud after no pompe ne reverence,
Ne maked him a spiced conscience,
But Cristes lore, and his apostles twelve,
He taught, and ferst he folwed it him-
    selve.
    With him ther was a PLOUGHMAN, his
        brothur,
That hadde i lad of dong ful many a
    fothur.
A trewe swynker and a good was hee,
Lyvynge in pees and parfight charitee.
God loved he best with al his trewe herte
At alle tymes, though him gained or
    smerte,
And thanne his neighebour right as him-
    selve.
He wolde threisshe, and therto dyke and
    delve,
For Cristes sake, with every pore wight,
Withouten huyre, if it laye in his might.
His tythes payede he ful faire and wel,
Bathe of his owne swynk and his catel.
In a tabbard he rood upon a mere.
    Ther was also a reeve and a mellere,
A sompnour and a pardoner also,
A maunciple, and my self, ther was no mo.
    The MELLERE was a stout carl for the
        nones,
Ful big he was of braun, and eek of
    boones;

That prevede wel, for over al ther he cam,
At wrastlynge he wolde bere away the
    ram.
He was schort schuldred, broode, a thikke
    knarre,
Ther nas no dore that he nold heve of
    harre,
Or breke it with a rennyng with his heed.
His berd as ony sowe or fox was reed,
And therto brood, as though it were a
    spade.
Upon the cop right of his nose he hade
A werte, and theron stood a tuft of heres,
Reede as the berstles of a souwes eeres.
His nose-thurles blake were and wyde.
A swerd and a bocler baar he by his side,
His mouth as wyde was as a gret forneys.
He was a jangler, and a golyardeys,
And that was most of synne and harlo-
    tries.
Wel cowde he stele corn, and tollen thries;
And yet he had a thombe of gold pardé.
A whight cote and blewe hood wered he.
A baggepipe cowde he blowe and sowne,
And therwithal he brought us out of
    towne.
    A gentil MAUNCIPLE was ther of a
        temple,
Of which achatours mighten take exemple
For to be wys in beyying of vitaille.
For whethur that he payde, or took by
    taille,
Algate he wayted so in his acate,
That he was ay biforn and in good state.
Now is not that of God a ful fair grace,
That such a lewed mannes wit schal pace
The wisdom of an heep of lernede men?
Of maystres hadde moo than thries ten,
That were of lawe expert and curious;
Of which ther were a doseyn in an house,
Worthi to be stiwardes of rente and lond
Of any lord that is in Engelond,
To make him lyve by his propre good,
In honour detteles, but if he were wood,
Or lyve as scarsly as he can desire;
And able for to helpen al a schire
In any caas that mighte falle or happe;
And yit this maunciple sette here aller
    cappe.

The REEVE was a sklendre colerik man,
His berd was schave as neigh as ever he
can.
His heer was by his eres neighe i-shorn.
His top was dockud lyk a preest biforn.
Ful longe wern his leggus, and ful lene,
Al like a staff, ther was no calf y-sene.
Wel cowde he kepe a gerner and a bynne;
Ther was non auditour cowde on him
wynne.
Wel wist he by the drought, and by the
reyn,
The yeeldyng of his seed, and of his greyn.
His lordes scheep, his nete, and his day-
erie,
His swyn, his hors, his stoor, and his pul-
trie,
Was holly in this reeves governynge,
And by his covenaunt gaf the rekenynge,
Syn that his lord was twenti yeer of age;
Ther couthe noman bringe him in arrer-
age.
Ther nas ballif, ne herde, ne other hyne,
That they ne knewe his sleight and his
covyne;
They were adrad of him, as of the deth.
His wonyng was ful fair upon an heth,
With grene trees i-schadewed was his
place.
He cowde bettre than his lord purchace.
Ful riche he was i-stored prively,
His lord wel couthe he plese subtilly,
To geve and lene him of his owne good,
And have a thank, a cote, and eek an
hood.
In youthe he lerned hadde a good mester;
He was a wel good wright, a carpenter.
This reeve sat upon a wel good stot,
That was a pomely gray, and highte Scot.
A long surcote of pers uppon he hadde,
And by his side he bar a rusty bladde.
Of Northfolk was this reeve of which I
telle,
Byside a toun men callen Baldeswelle.
Tukkud he was, as is a frere, aboute,
And ever he rood the hynderest of the
route.
  A SOMPNOUR was ther with us in that
place,

That hadde a fyr-reed cherubynes face,
For sawceflem he was, with eyghen narwe.
As hoot he was, and leccherous, as a
sparwe,
With skalled browes blak, and piled berd;
Of his visage children weren sore aferd.
Ther nas quyksilver, litarge, ne brimstone,
Boras, ceruce, ne oille of tartre noon,
Ne oynement that wolde clense and byte,
That him might helpen of his whelkes
white,
Ne of the knobbes sittyng on his cheekes.
Wel loved he garleek, oynouns, and ek
leekes,
And for to drinke strong wyn reed as
blood.
Thanne wolde he speke, and crye as he
were wood.
And whan that he wel dronken hadde the
wyn,
Than wolde he speke no word but Latyn.
A fewe termes hadde he, tuo or thre,
That he hadde lerned out of som decree;
No wondur is, he herde it al the day;
And eek ye knowe wel, how that a jay
Can clepe Watte, as wel as can the pope.
But who so wolde in othur thing him
grope,
Thanne hadde he spent al his philosophie,
Ay, *Questio quid juris*, wolde he crye,
He was a gentil harlot and a kynde;
A bettre felaw schulde men nowher fynde.
He wolde suffre for a quart of wyn
A good felawe to han his concubyn
A twelve moneth, and excuse him atte
fulle.
And prively a fynch eek cowde he pulle.
And if he fond owher a good felawe,
He wolde teche him to have non awe
In such a caas of the archedecknes curs,
But if a mannes sole were in his purs;
For in his purs he scholde punyssched be.
'Purs is the ercedeknes helle,' quod he.
But well I woot he lyeth right in dede;
Of cursyng oweth ech gulty man to drede;
For curs wol slee right as assoillyng sav-
eth;
And also ware of him a *significavit*.
In daunger he hadde at his own assise

The yonge gurles of the diocise,
And knew here counseil, and was al here
red.
A garland had he set upon his heed,
As gret as it were for an ale-stake;
A bokeler had he maad him of a cake.
  With him ther rood a gentil PARDONER
Of Rouncival, his frend and his comper,
That streyt was comen from the court of
Rome.
Ful lowde he sang, Come hider, love, to
me.
This sompnour bar to him a stif burdoun,
Was nevere trompe of half so gret a soun.
This pardoner hadde heer as yelwe as wex,
But smothe it heng, as doth a strike of
flex;
By unces hynge his lokkes that he hadde,
And therwith he his schuldres over-
spradde.
Ful thenne it lay, by culpons on and oon,
But hood, for jolitee, ne wered he noon,
For it was trussud up in his walet.
Him thought he rood al of the newe get,
Dischevele, sauf his cappe, he rood al bare.
Suche glaryng eyghen hadde he as an hare.
A vernicle hadde he sowed on his cappe.
His walet lay byforn him in his lappe,
Bret ful of pardoun come from Rome al
hoot.
A voys he hadde as smale as eny goot.
No berd ne hadde he, ne never scholde
have,
As smothe it was as it ware late i-schave;
I trowe he were a geldyng or a mare.
But of his craft, fro Berwyk unto Ware,
Ne was ther such another pardoner.
For in his male he hadde a pilwebeer,
Which, that he saide, was oure lady veyl:
He seide, he hadde a gobet of the seyl
That seynt Petur hadde, whan that he
wente
Uppon the see, till Jhesu Crist him hente.
He hadde a cros of latoun ful of stones,
And in a glas he hadde pigges bones.
But with thise reliques, whanne that he
fand
A pore persoun dwellyng uppon land,
Upon a day he gat him more moneye

Than that the persoun gat in monthes
tweye.
And thus with feyned flaterie and japes,
He made the persoun and the people his
apes.
But trewely to tellen atte laste,
He was in churche a noble ecclesiaste.
Wel cowde he rede a lessoun or a storye,
But altherbest he sang an offertorie;
For wel wyst he, whan that song was
songe,
He moste preche, and wel affyle his tunge,
To wynne silver, as he right wel cowde;
Therefore he sang ful meriely and lowde.
  Now have I told you schortly in a
clause
Thestat, tharray, the nombre, and eek the
cause
Why that assembled was this companye
In Southwerk at this gentil ostelrie,
That highte the Tabbard, faste by the
Belle.
But now is tyme to yow for to telle
How that we bare us in that ilke night,
Whan we were in that ostelrie alight;
And aftur wol I telle of oure viage,
And al the remenaunt of oure pilgrimage.
But ferst I pray you of your curtesie,
That ye ne rette it nat my vilanye,
Though that I speke al pleyn in this
matere,
To telle you here wordes and here cheere;
Ne though I speke here wordes propurly.
For this ye knowen al so wel as I,
Who so schal telle a tale aftur a man,
He moste reherce, as neigh as ever he can,
Every word, if it be in his charge,
Al speke he never so rudely ne large;
Or elles he moot telle his tale untrewe,
Or feyne thing, or fynde wordes newe.
He may not spare, though he were his
brothur;
He moste as wel sey oo word as anothur.
Crist spak himself ful broode in holy writ,
And wel ye woot no vilanye is it.
Eke Plato seith, who so that can him rede,
The wordes mot be cosyn to the dede.
Also I pray you to forgeve it me,
Al have I folk nat set in here degre

Here in this tale, as that thei schulde
 stonde;
My witt is schorte, ye may wel undur-
 stonde.
 Greet cheere made oure ost us everichon
And to the souper sette he us anon;
And served us with vitaille atte beste.
Strong was the wyn, and wel to drynke
 us leste.
A semely man oure ooste was withalle
For to han been a marchal in an halle;
A large man was he with eyghen stepe,
A fairere burgeys is ther noon in Chepe:
Bold of his speche, and wys and well
 i-taught,
And of manhede lakkede he right naught.
Eke therto he was right a mery man,
And after soper playen he bygan,
And spak of myrthe among othur thinges,
Whan that we hadde maad our reken-
 ynges;
And sayde thus: 'Lo, lordynges, trewely
Ye ben to me right welcome hertily:
For by my trouthe, if that I schal not lye,
I ne saugh this yeer so mery a companye
At oones in this herbergh as is now.
Fayn wold I do yow merthe, wiste I how.
And of a merthe I am right now by-
 thought,
To doon you eese, and it schal coste
 nought.
Ye goon to Caunturbury; God you
 speede,
The blisful martir quyte you youre
 meede!
And wel I woot, as ye gon by the weye,
Ye schapen yow to talken and to pleye;
For trewely comfort ne merthe is noon
To ryde by the weye domb as a stoon;
And therfore wol I make you disport,
As I seyde erst, and do you som confort.
And if yow liketh alle by oon assent
Now for to standen at my juggement;
And for to werken as I schal you seye,
To morwe, whan ye riden by the weye,
Now by my fadres soule that is deed,
But ye be merye, smyteth of myn heed.
Hold up youre hond withoute more
 speche.'

Oure counseil was not longe for to seche;
Us thought it was not worth to make it
 wys,
And graunted him withoute more avys,
And bad him seie his verdite, as him leste.
'Lordynges,' quoth he, 'now herkeneth
 for the beste!
But taketh not, I pray you, in disdayn;
This is the poynt, to speken schort and
 playn,
That ech of yow to schorte with youre
 weie,
In this viage, schal telle tales tweye,
To Caunturburi-ward, I mene it so,
And hom-ward he schal tellen othur tuo,
Of aventures that ther han bifalle.
And which of yow that bereth him best of
 alle,
That is to seye, that telleth in this caas
Tales of best sentence and of solas,
Schal han a soper at your alther cost
Here in this place sittynge by this post,
Whan that we comen ageyn from Cantur-
 bery.
And for to make you the more mery,
I wol myselven gladly with you ryde,
Right at myn owen cost, and be youre
 gyde.
And whoso wole my juggement withseie
Schal paye for al we spenden by the weye.
And if ye vouchesauf that it be so,
Telle me anoon, withouten wordes moo,
And I wole erely schappe me therfore.'
This thing was graunted, and oure othus
 swore
With ful glad herte, and prayden him also
That he would vouchesauf for to doon so,
And that he wolde ben oure governour,
And of our tales jugge and reportour,
And sette a souper at a certeyn prys;
And we wolde rewled be at his devys,
In heygh and lowe; and thus by oon as-
 sent
We been acorded to his juggement.
And therupon the wyn was fet anoon;
We dronken, and to reste wente echoon,
Withouten eny lengere taryinge.
A morwe whan that the day bigan to
 sprynge,

Up roos oure ost, and was oure althur cok,
And gaderud us togider all in a flok,
And forth we riden a litel more than paas,
Unto the waterynge of seint Thomas.
And there oure ost bigan his hors areste,
And seyde; 'Lordus, herkeneth if yow
    leste.
Ye woot youre forward, and I it you re-
    corde.
If eve-song and morwe-song accorde,
Let se now who schal telle ferst a tale.
As evere I moote drinke wyn or ale,
Who so be rebel to my juggement
Schal paye for al that by the weye is spent.
Now draweth cut, er that we forther
    twynne;
Which that hath the schortest schal by-
    gynne.'
'Sire knight,' quoth he, 'maister and my
    lord
Now draweth cut, for that is myn acord.
Cometh ner,' quoth he, 'my lady prior-
    esse;
And ye, sir clerk, lat be your schamfast-
    nesse,
Ne studieth nat; ley hand to, every man.'
  Anon to drawen every wight bigan,
And schortly for to tellen as it was,
Were it by aventure, or sort, or cas,
The soth is this, the cut fil to the knight,
Of which full glad and blithe was every
    wight;
And telle he moste his tale as was resoun,
By forward and by composicioun,
As ye han herd; what needeth wordes
    moo?
And whan this goode man seigh that it
    was so,
As he that wys was and obedient
To kepe his forward by his fre assent,
He seyde: 'Syn I schal bygynne the game,
What, welcome be thou cut, a Goddus
    name!
Now lat us ryde, and herkneth what I
    seye.'
  And with that word we ridden forth
    oure weye;
And he bigan with right a merie chere
His tale, and seide right in this manere.

The Tale of the Doctor of Phisik

THER was, as telleth Titus Lyvius,
A knight, that cleped was Virginius,
Fulfild of honours and of worthines.
And strong of frendes, and of gret riches.
This knight a doughter hadde by his wyf,
And never ne hadde he mo in al his lyf.
Fair was this mayde in excellent beaute
Above every wight that men may se;
For Nature hath with sovereyn diligence
I-formed hir in so gret excellence,
As though sche wolde say, 'Lo, I, Nature,
Thus can I forme and peynte a creature,
Whan that me lust; who can me counter-
    fete?
Pigmalion? nought, though he alwey
    forge and bete,
Or grave, or peynte; for I dar wel sayn,
Apelles, Zeuxis, schulde wirche in vayn,
Other to grave, or paynte, or forge or bete,
If thay presumed me to counterfete.
For He that is the Former principal
Hath maad me his viker general,
To forme and peynte erthely creature
Right as me lust, al thing is in my cure
Under the moone that may wane and
    waxe,
And for my werke no thing wol I axe;
My lord and I ben fully at accord.
I made hir to the worschip of my Lord;
So do I alle myn other creatures,
What colour that thay been, or what
    figures.'
Thus semeth me that Nature wolde say.
  This mayde was of age twelf yer and
    tway,
In which that nature hath suche delite.
For right as sche can peynte a lili white
And rody a rose, right with such peynture
Sche peynted hath this noble creature
Er sche was born, upon her limes fre,
Wheras by right such colours schulde be;
And Phebus deyed hadde hire tresses
    grete,
I-lyk to the stremes of his borned hete.
And if that excellent was hir beaute,
A thousand fold more vertuous was sche.
In hire ne lakketh no condicioun,

That is to preyse, as by discrecioun.
As wel in body as goost chaste was sche;
For which sche floured in virginite,
With alle humilite and abstinence,
With alle attemperaunce and pacience,
With mesure eek of beryng and array.
Discret sche was in answeryng alway,
Though sche were wis as Pallas, dar I
  sayn.
Hir facound eek ful wommanly and playn;
Noon countrefeted termes hadde sche
To seme wys; but after hir degre
Sche spak, and alle hire wordes more or
  lesse
Sounyng in vertu and in gentilesse.
Schamefast sche was in maydenes scham-
  fastnesse,
Constant in hert, and ever in besynesse,
To dryve hire out of idel slogardye.
Bachus had of hir mouth no maistrye;
For wyn and thought doon Venus encrece,
As men in fuyr wil caste oyle or grece.
And of hir oughne vertu unconstreigned,
Sche hath ful ofte tyme hire seek y-feyned,
For that sche wolde fleen the companye,
Wher likly was to treten of folye,
As is at festes, reveles, and at daunces,
That ben occasiouns of daliaunces.
Such thinges maken children for to be
To soone rype and bold, as men may se,
Which is ful perilous, and hath ben yore;
For al to soone may sche lerne lore
Of boldenesse, whan sche is a wyf.
And ye maystresses in youre olde lyf
That lordes doughtres han in governaunce,
Ne taketh of my word no displesaunce;
Thinketh that ye ben set in governynges
Of lordes doughtres, oonly for tuo thinges;
Outher for ye han kept your honeste,
Other elles for ye han falle in frelete,
And knowe wel y-nough the olde daunce,
And conne forsake fully such meschaunce
For evermo; therfore, for Cristes sake,
Kepeth wel tho that ye undertake.
A theof of venisoun, that hath for-laft
His licorousnesse, and al his theves craft,
Can kepe a forest best of every man.
Now kepe hem wel, for and ye wil ye can;
Loke wel, that ye unto no vice assent,

Lest ye be dampned for your wikked en-
  tent,
For who so doth, a traytour is certayn;
And taketh keep of that that I schal sayn;
Of al tresoun sovereyn pestilence
Is, whan a wight bytrayeth innocence.
Ye fadres, and ye modres eek also,
Though ye han children, be it oon or mo,
Youre is the charge of al her sufferaunce,
Whiles thay be under your governaunce.
Beth war, that by ensample of youre
  lyvynge,
Outher by necgligence in chastisynge,
That thay ne perische; for I dar wel seye,
If that thay doon, ye schul ful sore abeye.
Under a schepherd softe and necligent,
The wolf hath many a schep and lamb to-
  rent.
Sufficeth oon ensample now as here,
For I moot turne agein to my matiere.
  This mayde, of which I telle my tale
    expresse,
So kept hir self, hir neded no maystresse;
For in hir lyvyng maydens might rede,
As in a book, every good word and dede,
That longeth unto a mayden vertuous;
Sche was so prudent and so bounteous.
For which the fame outsprong on every
  syde
Bothe of hir beaute and hir bounte wyde;
That thurgh the lond thay praysed hir
  ilkoone,
That lovede vertu, save envye alloone,
That sory is of other mennes wele,
And glad is of his sorwe and unhele.
The doctor made this descripcioun.
This mayde wente on a day into the toun
Toward the temple, with hir moder deere,
As is of yonge maydenes the manere.
  Now was ther than a justice in the toun,
That governour was of that regioun.
And so bifel, this juge his eyghen cast
Upon this mayde, avysing hir ful fast,
As sche cam forby ther the juge stood.
Anoon his herte chaunged and his mood,
So was he caught with beaute of this
  mayde,
And to him self ful prively he sayde,
'This mayde schal be myn for any man.'

Anoon the feend into his herte ran,
And taughte him sodeinly, that he by
　slighte
This mayde to his purpos wynne mighte.
For certes, by no fors, ne by no mede,
Him thought he was not able for to
　speede;
For sche was strong of frendes, and eek
　sche
Confermed was in such soverayne bounte
That wel he wist he might hir never
　wynne,
As for to make hir with hir body synne.
For which with gret deliberacioun
He sent after a clerk was in the toun,
The which he knew for subtil and for bold.
This juge unto the clerk his tale hath told
In secre wyse, and made him to assure,
He schulde telle it to no creature;
And if he dede he schulde lese his heed.
Whan that assented was this cursed reed,
Glad was the juge, and made him gret
　cheere,
And gaf him giftes precious and deere.

　Whan schapen was al this conspiracye
Fro poynt to poynt, how that his lecherie
Parformed scholde be ful subtilly,
As ye schul here after-ward openly,
Hom goth this clerk, that highte Claudius.
This false juge, that highte Apius,—
(So was his name, for it is no fable,
But knowen for a storial thing notable;
The sentence of it soth is out of doubte),—
This false jugge goth now fast aboute
To hasten his delit al that he may.
And so bifel, soone after on a day
This false juge, as telleth us the story,
As he was wont, sat in his consistory,
And gaf his domes upon sondry caas;
This false clerk com forth a ful good paas,
And saide, 'Lord, if that it be your wille,
As doth me right upon this pitous bille,
In which I pleyne upon Virginius.
And if he wile seyn it is nought thus,
I wil it prove, and fynde good witnesse,
That soth is that my bille wol expresse.'
The juge answerd, 'Of this in his absence
I may not give diffinityf sentence.
Let do him calle, and I wol gladly hiere;

Thou schalt have alle right, and no wrong
　heere.
Virginius com to wite the jugges wille,
And right anoon was red this cursed bille;
The sentence of it was as ye schul heere.
　'To yow, my lord sire Apius so deere,
Scheweth youre pore servaunt Claudius,
How that a knight called Virginius,
Ageins the lawe, agens alle equyte,
Holdeth, expresse ageinst the wille of me,
My servaunt, which that my thral is by
　right,
Which fro myn hous was stolen on a night
Whiles sche was ful yong, that wol I preve
By witnesse, lord, so that ye yow not
　greve:
Sche is nought his doughter, what so he
　say,
Wherfore to yow, my lord the jugge, I
　pray,
Yelde me my thralle, if that it be your
　wille.'
Lo, this was al the sentence of the bille.
　Virginius gan upon the clerk byholde;
But hastily, er he his tale tolde,
And wolde have proved it, as schold a
　knight,
And eek by witnessyng of many a wight,
That al was fals that sayde his adversarie,
This cursed juge wold no lenger tarye,
Ne heere a word more of Virginius,
But gaf his jugement, and saide thus;
'I deme anoon this clerk his servaunt
　have.
Thou schalt no lengur in thin hous hir
　save.
Go bringe hir forth, and put hir in oure
　warde.
This clerk schal have his thral; thus I
　awarde.'
　And whan this worthy knight Virginius,
Thurgh thassent of this juge Apius,
Moste by force his deere doughter given
Unto the juge, in lecchery to lyven,
He goth him hom, and sette him in his
　halle,
And leet anoon his deere doughter calle;
And with a face deed as aisshen colde,
Upon hir humble face he gan byholde,

With fadres pite stiking thorugh his herte,
Al wolde he from his purpos not converte.
'Doughter,' quod he, 'Virginia by name,
Ther ben tuo weyes, eyther deth or schame,
That thou most suffre, allas that I was bore!
For never thou deservedest wherfore
To deyen with a swerd or with a knyf.
O deere doughter, ender of my lyf,
Which I have fostred up with such plesaunce,
That thou nere never oute of my remembraunce;
O doughter, which that art my laste wo,
And in this lif my laste joye also,
O gemme of chastite, in pacience
Tak thou thy deth, for this is my sentence;
For love and not for hate thou must be deed,
My pitous hond mot smyten of thin heed.
Allas that ever Apius the say!
Thus hath he falsly jugged the to day.'
And told hir al the caas, as ye bifore
Han herd, it needeth nought to telle it more.
  'Mercy, deere fader,' quod this mayde.
And with that word sche bothe hir armes layde
Aboute his nekke, as sche was want to doo,
(The teeres brast out of hir eyghen tuo),
And sayde: 'Goode fader, schal I dye?
Is ther no grace? is ther no remedye?'
'No, certeyn, deere doughter myn,' quod he.
'Than geve me leve, fader myn,' quod sche,
'My deth for to compleyne a litel space;
For pardy Jepte gaf his doughter grace
For to compleyne, er he hir slough, allas!
And God it woot, no thing was hir trespas,
But that sche ran hir fader first to se,
To welcome him with gret solempnite.'
And with that word aswoun sche fel anoon,
And after, whan hir swownyng was agoon,

Sche riseth up, and to hir fader sayde;
'Blessed be God, that I schal deye a mayde.
Geve me my deth, er that I have a schame.
Do with your child your wille, a goddes name!'
And with that word sche prayed him ful ofte,
That with his swerd he schulde smyte hir softe;
And with that word on swoune doun sche fel.
Hir fader, with ful sorwful hert and fel,
Hir heed of smoot, and by the top it hente,
And to the juge bigan it to presente,
As he sat in his doom in consistory.
And whan the juge it say, as saith the story,
He bad to take him, and honge him faste.
But right anoon alle the poeple in thraste
To save the knight, for routhe and for pite,
For knowen was the fals iniquite.
The poeple anoon had suspect in this thing,
By maner of this clerkes chalengyng,
That it was by thassent of Apius;
They wiste wel that he was leccherous.
For which unto this Apius thay goon,
And casten him in prisoun right anoon,
Wher as he slough him self; and Claudius,
That servaunt was unto this Apius,
Was demed for to honge upon a tree;
But Virginius of his gret pite
Prayde for him, that he was exiled,
And elles certes he had ben bigiled.
The remenaunt were anhanged, more and lesse,
That were consented to this cursednesse.
  Her may men se how synne hath his merite;
Be war, for no man woot how God wol smyte
In no degre, ne in which maner wise
The worm of conscience wol agrise
Of wicked lyf, though it so pryve be,
That no man woot of it but God and he;
Whether that he be lewed man or lered,

He not how soone that he may be afered.
Therfore I rede yow this counseil take,
Forsakith synne, er synne yow forsake.

The Compleynte of Chaucer to his Purse.

To yow my purse and to noon other
      wighte
Complayne I, for ye be my lady dere!
I am so sory now that ye been lyghte,
For, certes yf ye make me hevy chere,
Me were as leef be layde upon my bere.
For whiche unto your mercy thus I crye,
Beeth hevy ageyne, or elles mote I die!

Now voucheth sauf this day, or hyt be
      nyghte,
That I of yow the blissful soune may here,
Or see your colour lyke the sunne bryghte,
That of yelownesse hadde never pere.

Ye be my lyf! ye be myn hertys stere!
Quene of comfort and good companye!
Beth hevy ayeyne, or elles moote I dye!

Now, purse! that ben to me my lyves
      lyghte,
And saveour as doune in this worlde here,
Oute of this toune helpe me thurgh your
      myghte,
Syn that you wole not bene my tresorere;
For I am shave as nye as is a frere.
But I pray unto your curtesye,
Bethe hevy ayeyne, or elles moote I dye!

L'ENVOY DE CHAUCER.

O conquerour of Brutes Albyon,
Whiche that by lygne and free election,
Been verray Kynge, this song to yow I
      sende,
And ye that mowen alle myn harme
      amende,
Have mynde upon my supplicacion.

SIR THOMAS MALORY (Fifteenth Century)

From LE MORTE D'ARTHUR

The Last Battle and the Passing of Arthur

THEN were they condescended that King Arthur and Sir Mordred
should meet betwixt both their hosts, and every each of them should
bring fourteen persons; and they came with this word unto Arthur.
Then said he: I am glad that this is done: and so he went into the field.
And when Arthur should depart, he warned all his host that an they see
any sword drawn: Look ye come on fiercely, and slay that traitor, Sir
Mordred, for I in no wise trust him. In likewise Sir Mordred warned
his host that: An ye see any sword drawn, look that ye come on fiercely,

and so slay all that ever before you standeth; for in no wise I will not trust for this treaty, for I know well my father will be avenged on me. And so they met as their appointment was, and so they were agreed and accorded thoroughly; and wine was fetched, and they drank. Right soon came an adder out of a little heath bush, and it stung a knight on the foot. And when the knight felt him stung, he looked down and saw the adder, and then he drew his sword to slay the adder, and thought of none other harm. And when the host on both parties saw that sword drawn, then they blew beamous, trumpets, and horns, and shouted grimly. And so both hosts dressed them together. And King Arthur took his horse, and said: Alas this unhappy day! and so rode to his party. And Sir Mordred in likewise. And never was there seen a more dolefuller battle in no Christian land; for there was but rushing and riding, foining and striking, and many a grim word was there spoken either to other, and many a deadly stroke. But ever King Arthur rode throughout the battle of Sir Mordred many times, and did full nobly as a noble king should, and at all times he fainted never; and Sir Mordred that day put him in devoir, and in great peril. And thus they fought all the long day, and never stinted till the noble knights were laid to the cold earth; and ever they fought still till it was near night, and by that time was there an hundred thousand laid dead upon the down. Then was Arthur wood wroth out of measure, when he saw his people so slain from him. Then the king looked about him, and then was he ware, of all his host and of all his good knights, were left no more on live but two knights; that one was Sir Lucan the Butler, and his brother Sir Bedivere, and they were full sore wounded. Jesu mercy, said the king, where are all my noble knights become? Alas that ever I should see this doleful day, for now, said Arthur, I am come to mine end. But would to God that I wist where were that traitor Sir Mordred, that hath caused all this mischief. Then was King Arthur ware where Sir Mordred leaned upon his sword among a great heap of dead men. Now give me my spear, said Arthur unto Sir Lucan, for yonder I have espied the traitor that all this woe hath wrought. Sir, let him be, said Sir Lucan, for he is unhappy; and if ye pass this unhappy day ye shall be right well revenged upon him. Good lord, remember ye of your night's dream, and what the spirit of Sir Gawaine told you this night, yet God of his great goodness hath preserved you hitherto. Therefore, for God's sake, my lord, leave off by this, for blessed be God ye have won the field, for here we be three on live, and with Sir Mordred is none on live; and if ye leave off now this wicked day of destiny is past. Tide me death, betide me life, saith the king, now I see him yonder alone he shall never escape mine hands, for at a better avail shall I never have him. God speed you well, said Sir Bedivere. Then the king gat his spear in both his hands, and ran toward Sir Mordred, crying: Traitor, now is thy death day come. And when Sir Mordred heard Sir Arthur, he ran until him with his sword drawn in his hand. And there King Arthur smote Sir Mordred under the shield, with a foin of his spear, throughout the body, more than a fathom. And when Sir Mordred felt that he had his death wound he thrust himself with the might that he had up to the bur of King Arthur's spear. And right so he smote his father Arthur, with his sword holden in both his hands, on the side of the head, that the sword pierced the helmet and the brain pan, and therewithal Sir Mordred fell stark dead to the earth; and the noble Arthur fell in a swoon to the earth, and there he swooned ofttimes. And Sir Lucan the Butler and Sir Bedivere ofttimes heave him up. And so weakly they led him betwixt them both, to a little chapel not far from the seaside. And when the king was there he thought him well eased. Then heard they people cry in the field. Now go thou, Sir Lucan, said the king, and do me to wit what betokens that noise in the field. So Sir Lucan departed, for he was grievously wounded in many places. And so as he yede, he saw and hearkened by the moonlight, how that pillers and robbers were come into the field, to pill and to rob many a full noble knight of brooches, and beads, of many a good ring, and of many a rich jewel; and who that were not dead all out, there they slew them for their harness and their riches. When Sir Lucan understood this work, he came to the king as soon as he might, and told him all what he had heard and seen. Therefore by my rede, said Sir Lucan, it is best that we bring you to some town. I would it were so, said the king.

But I may not stand, mine head works so. Ah Sir Launcelot, said King Arthur, this day have I sore missed thee: alas, that ever I was against thee, for now have I my death, whereof Sir Gawaine me warned in my dream. Then Sir Lucan took up the king the one part, and Sir Bedivere the other part, and in the lifting the king swooned; and Sir Lucan fell in a swoon with the lift, that the part of his guts fell out of his body, and therewith the noble knight's heart brast. And when the king awoke, he beheld Sir Lucan, how he lay foaming at the mouth, and part of his guts lay at his feet. Alas, said the king, this is to me a full heavy sight, to see this noble duke so die for my sake, for he would have holpen me, that had more need of help than I. Alas, he would not complain him, his heart was so set to help me: now Jesu have mercy upon his soul! Then Sir Bedivere wept for the death of his brother. Leave this mourning and weeping, said the king, for all this

will not avail me, for wit thou well an I might live myself, the death of
Sir Lucan would grieve me evermore; but my time hieth fast, said the
king. Therefore, said Arthur unto Sir Bedivere, take thou Excalibur,
my good sword, and go with it to yonder water side, and when thou
comest there I charge thee throw my sword in that water, and come
again and tell me what thou there seest. My lord, said Bedivere, your
commandment shall be done, and lightly bring you word again. So Sir
Bedivere departed, and by the way he beheld that noble sword, that the
pommel and the haft was all of precious stones; and then he said to
himself: If I throw this rich sword in the water, thereof shall never
come good, but harm and loss. And then Sir Bedivere hid Excalibur
under a tree. And so, as soon as he might, he came again unto the king,
and said he had been at the water, and had thrown the sword in the
water. What saw thou there? said the king. Sir, he said, I saw nothing
but waves and winds. That is untruly said of thee, said the king, therefore go thou lightly again, and do my commandment; as thou art to me
lief and dear, spare not, but throw it in. Then Sir Bedivere returned
again, and took the sword in his hand; and then him thought sin and
shame to throw away that noble sword, and so efte he hid the sword,
and returned again, and told to the king that he had been at the water,
and done his commandment. What saw thou there? said the king. Sir,
he said, I saw nothing but the waters wappe and waves wanne. Ah,
traitor untrue, said King Arthur, now hast thou betrayed me twice.
Who would have weened that, thou that has been to me so lief and dear?
and thou art named a noble knight, and would betray me for the richness of the sword. But now go again lightly, for thy long tarrying put-
teth me in great jeopardy of my life, for I have taken cold. And but
if thou do now as I bid thee, if ever I may see thee, I shall slay thee with
mine own hands; for thou wouldst for my rich sword see me dead. Then
Sir Bedivere departed, and went to the sword, and lightly took it up, and
went to the water side; and there he bound the girdle about the hilts,
and then he threw the sword as far into the water, as he might; and
there came an arm and an hand above the water and met it, and caught
it, and so shook it thrice and brandished, and then vanished away the
hand with the sword in the water. So Sir Bedivere came again to the
king, and told him what he saw. Alas, said the king, help me hence,
for I dread me I have tarried over long. Then Sir Bedivere took the
king upon his back, and so went with him to that water side. And when
they were at the water side, even fast by the bank hoved a little barge
with many fair ladies in it, and among them all was a queen, and all
they had black hoods, and all they wept and shrieked when they saw

King Arthur. Now put me into the barge, said the king. And so he did softly; and there received him three queens with great mourning; and so they set them down, and in one of their laps King Arthur laid his head. And then that queen said: Ah, dear brother, why have ye tarried so long from me? alas, this wound on your head hath caught over-much cold. And so then they rowed from the land, and Sir Bedivere beheld all those ladies go from him. Then Sir Bedivere cried: Ah my lord Arthur, what shall become of me, now ye go from me and leave me here alone among mine enemies? Comfort thyself, said the king, and do as well as thou mayest, for in me is no trust for to trust in; for I will into the vale of Avilion to heal me of my grievous wound: and if thou hear never more of me, pray for my soul.

CHRISTOPHER MARLOWE
[1564-1593]

The Passionate Shepherd to his Love

COME live with me and be my Love,
And we will all the pleasures prove
That valleys, groves, hills and fields,
Woods or steepy mountain yields.

And we will sit upon the rocks
Seeing the shepherds feed their flocks,
By shallow rivers, to whose falls
Melodious birds sing madrigals.

And I will make thee beds of roses
And a thousand fragrant posies,
A cap of flowers, and a kirtle
Embroidered all with leaves of myrtle.

A gown made of the finest wool,
Which from our pretty lambs we pull,
Fair linèd slippers for the cold,
With buckles of the purest gold.

A belt of straw and ivy buds,
With coral clasps and amber studs:
And if these pleasures may thee move,
Come live with me and be my Love.

The shepherd swains shall dance and sing
For thy delight each May-morning:
If these delights thy mind may move,
Then live with me and be my Love.

SIR WALTER RALEIGH
[1552?-1618]

The Nymph's Reply to the Shepherd

IF all the world and love were young,
And truth in every shepherd's tongue,
These pretty pleasures might me move
To live with thee and be thy love.

But time drives flocks from field to fold,
When rivers rage and rocks grow cold;
And Philomel becometh dumb;
The rest complains of cares to come.

The flowers do fade, and wanton fields
To wayward winter reckoning yields:
A honey tongue, a heart of gall,
Is fancy's spring, but sorrow's fall.

Thy gowns, thy shoes, thy beds of roses,
Thy cap, thy kirtle, and thy posies,
Soon break, soon wither, soon for-
gotten,—
In folly ripe, in reason rotten.

Thy belt of straw and ivy buds,
Thy coral clasps and amber studs,—
All those in me no means can move
To come to thee and be thy love.

But could youth last, and love still breed;
Had joys no date, nor age no need;
Then those delights my mind might move
To live with thee and be thy love.

A Vision upon this Conceit of the Fairy Queen

This sonnet was appended to Spenser's *Faerie Queene,* Books i.-iii., published in 1590.

METHOUGHT I saw the grave where
    Laura lay,
Within that temple where the vestal
    flame
Was wont to burn: and, passing by that
    way,
To see that buried dust of living fame,
Whose tomb fair Love and fairer Virtue
    kept,
All suddenly I saw the Fairy Queen;
At whose approach the soul of Petrarch
    wept,
And from thenceforth those graces were
    not seen,
For they this Queen attended; in whose
    stead
Oblivion laid him down on Laura's
    hearse.
Hereat the hardest stones were seen to
    bleed,
And groans of buried ghosts the heavens
    did pierce:
    Where Homer's spright did tremble all
      for grief,
    And cursed the access of that celestial
      thief.

His Pilgrimage

GIVE me my scallop-shell of quiet,
    My staff of faith to walk upon,
My scrip of joy, immortal diet,
    My bottle of salvation,
My gown of glory, hope's true gage;
And thus I'll take my pilgrimage.

Blood must be my body's balmer;
    No other balm will there be given;
Whilst my soul, like quiet palmer,
    Travelleth towards the land of
      heaven;

Over the silver mountains,
Where spring the nectar fountains:
    There will I kiss
    The bowl of bliss;
And drink mine everlasting fill
Upon every milken hill.
My soul will be a-dry before;
But after, it will thirst no more.

Then by that happy blissful day,
    More peaceful pilgrims I shall see,
That have cast off their rags of clay,
    And walk apparell'd fresh like me.
    I'll take them first
    To quench their thirst
    And taste of nectar suckets,
      At those clear wells
      Where sweetness dwells,
    Drawn up by saints in crystal buckets.

And when our bottles and all we
Are fill'd with immortality,
Then the blessed paths we'll travel,
Strow'd with rubies thick as gravel;
Ceilings of diamonds, sapphire floors,
High walls of coral and pearly bowers.
From thence to heaven's bribeless hall,
Where no corrupted voices brawl;
No conscience molten into gold,
No forg'd accuser bought or sold,
No cause deferr'd, no vain-spent jour-
    ney,
For there Christ is the king's Attorney,
Who pleads for all without degrees,
And He hath angels, but no fees.
And when the grand twelve-million jury
Of our sins, with direful fury,
Against our souls black verdicts give,
Christ pleads His death, and then we
    live.

    Be Thou my speaker, taintless
      pleader,
    Unblotted lawyer, true proceeder!
    Thou givest salvation even for alms;
    Not with a bribed lawyer's palms.
    And this is mine eternal plea
    To Him that made heaven, earth,
      and sea,

That, since my flesh must die so soon,
And want a head to dine next noon,
Just at the stroke, when my veins start and spread,
Set on my soul an everlasting head!
Then am I ready, like a palmer fit,
To tread those blest paths which before I writ.

Of death and judgment, heaven and hell,
Who oft doth think, must needs die well.

Verses found in his Bible in the Gate-House at Westminster

These verses were printed in *Reliquiae Wottonianae*, 1651, &c., with the title "Sir Walter Raleigh the night before his death." He was executed on October 29, 1618, in Old Palace Yard, Westminster.

EVEN such is time, that takes in trust
Our youth, our joys, our all we have,
And pays us but with earth and dust;
Who, in the dark and silent grave,
When we have wandered all our ways,
Shuts up the story of our days;
But from this earth, this grave, this dust,
My God shall raise me up, I trust!

From THE HISTORY OF THE WORLD
The Conqueror Death

These concluding paragraphs of Raleigh's *History of the World* suggest to readers acquainted with the facts of Raleigh's life and death a picture of the great courtier, poet, and warrior of earlier days, confined in the Bloody Tower under sentence of death for thirteen years, from 1603 to 1616. The *History* was written in the Tower, 1607-1614.

FOR the rest, if we seek a reason of the succession and continuance of this boundless ambition in mortal men, we may add to that which hath been already said, that the kings and princes of the world have always laid before them the actions, but not the ends, of those great ones which preceded them. They are always transported with the glory of the one, but they never mind the misery of the other, till they find the experience in themselves. They neglect the advice of God, while they enjoy life, or hope it; but they follow the counsel of Death upon his first approach. It is he that puts into man all the wisdom of the world, without speaking a word, which God, with all the words of his law, promises, or threats, doth not infuse. Death, which hateth and destroyeth man, is believed; God, which hath made him and loves him, is always deferred; *I have considered*, saith Solomon, *all the works that are under the sun, and, behold, all is vanity and vexation of spirit;* but who believes it, till Death tells it us? It was Death, which opening the conscience of Charles the Fifth, made him enjoin his son Philip to restore Navarre; and king Francis the First of France, to command that justice should be done upon the murderers of the protestants in Merindol and Cabrieres, which till then he neglected. It is therefore Death alone that can suddenly make a man to know himself. He tells the proud and insolent, that they are but abjects, and humbles them at the instant, makes them cry, complain, and repent, yea, even to hate their forepast happiness. He takes the account of the rich, and proves him a beggar, a naked beggar, which hath interest in nothing but in the gravel that fills his mouth. He holds a glass before the eyes of the most beautiful, and makes them see therein their deformity and rottenness, and they acknowledge it.

O eloquent, just, and mighty Death! whom none can advise, thou hast persuaded; what none hath dared, thou hast done; and whom all the world hath flattered, thou only hast cast out of the world and despised; thou hast drawn together all the far-stretched greatness, all the pride, cruelty, and ambition of man, and covered it all over with these two narrow words, *Hic jacet!*

From THE DISCOVERY OF GUIANA

Description of the Orinoco Country

I HAVE therefore laboured all my life, both according to my small power and persuasion, to advance all those attempts that might either promise return of profit to ourselves, or at least be a let and impeachment to the quiet course and plentiful trades of the Spanish nation; who, in my weak judgment, by such a war were as easily endangered and brought from his powerfulness as any prince in Europe, if it be considered from how many kingdoms and nations his revenues are gathered, and those so weak in their own beings and so far severed from mutual succour. But because such a preparation and resolution is not to be hoped for in haste, and that the time which our enemies embrace cannot be had again to advantage, I will hope that these provinces, and that empire now by me discovered, shall suffice to enable her Majesty and the whole kingdom with no less quantities of treasure than the king of Spain hath in all the Indies, East and West, which he possesseth; which if the same be considered and followed, ere the Spaniards enforce the same, and if her Majesty will undertake it, I will be contented to lose her Highness' favour and good opinion forever, and my life withal, if the same be not found to exceed than to equal whatsoever is in this discourse promised and declared.

. . . .

The empire of Guiana is directly east from Peru towards the sea, and lieth under the equinoctial line; and it hath more abundance of gold than any part of Peru, and as many or more great cities than ever Peru had when it flourished most. It is governed by the same laws, and the emperor and people observe the same religion, and the same form and policies in government as were used in Peru, not differing in any part. And I have been assured by such of the Spaniards as have seen Manoa, the imperial city of Guiana, which the Spaniards call El Dorado, that for the greatness, for the richness, and for the excellent seat, it far exceedeth any of the world, at least of so much of the world as is known to the Spanish nation. It is founded upon a lake of salt water of 200 leagues long, like unto Mare Caspium. And if we compare it to that of Peru, and but read the report of Francisco Lopez and others, it will seem more than credible; and because we may judge of the one by the other, I thought good to insert part of the 120. chapter of Lopez in his *General History of the Indies,* wherein he describeth the court and magnificence of Guayna Capac, ancestor to the emperor of Guiana, whose very words are these:

"All the vessels of his house, table, and kitchen, were of gold and silver, and the meanest of silver and copper for strength and hardness of metal. He had in his wardrobe hollow statues of gold which seemed giants, and the figures in proportion and bigness of all the beasts, birds, trees, and herbs, that the earth bringeth forth; and of all the fishes that the sea or waters of his kingdom breedeth. He had also ropes, budgets, chests, and troughs of gold and silver, heaps of billets of gold, that seemed wood marked out to burn. Finally, there was nothing in his country whereof he had not the counterfeit in gold. Yea, and they say, the Ingas had a garden of pleasure in an island near Puna, where they went to recreate themselves, when they would take the air of the sea, which had all kinds of garden-herbs, flowers, and trees of gold and silver; an invention and magnificence till then never seen. Besides all this, he had an infinite quantity of silver and gold unwrought in Cuzco, which was lost by the death of Guascar, for the Indians hid it, seeing that the Spaniards took it, and sent it into Spain."

. . . .

As we abode here awhile, our Indian pilot, called Ferdinando, would needs go ashore to their village to fetch some fruits and to drink of their artificial wines, and also to see the place and know the lord of it against another time, and took with him a brother of his which he had with him in the journey. When they came to the village of these people the lord of the islands offered to lay hands on them, purposing to have slain them both; yielding for reason that this Indian of ours had brought a strange nation into their territory to spoil and destroy them. But the pilot being quick and of a disposed body, slipt their fingers and ran into the woods, and his brother, being the better footman of the two, recovered the creek's mouth, where we stayed in our barge, crying out that his brother was slain. With that we set hands on one of them that was next us, a very old man, and brought him into the barge, assuring him that if we had not our pilot again we would presently cut off his head. This old man, being resolved that he should pay the loss of the other, cried out to those in the woods to save Ferdinando, our pilot; but they followed him notwithstanding, and hunted after him upon the foot with their deer-dogs, and with so main a cry that all the woods echoed with the shout they made. But at the last this poor chased Indian recovered the river side and got upon a tree, and, as we were coasting, leaped down and swam to the barge half dead with fear. But our good hap was that we kept the other old Indian, which we handfasted to redeem our pilot withal; for, being natural of those rivers, we assured ourselves that he knew the way better than any stranger could. And, indeed, but for this chance, I think we had never found the way either to Guiana or back to our ships; for Ferdinando after a few days knew nothing at all, nor which way to turn; yea, and many times the old man himself was in great doubt which river to take.

. . . .

On the banks of these rivers were divers sorts of fruits good to eat, flowers and trees of such variety as were sufficient to make ten volumes of *Herbals;* we relieved ourselves many times with the fruits of the country, and sometimes with fowl and fish. We saw birds of all colours, some carnation, some crimson, orange-tawny, purple, watchet, and of all other sorts, both simple and mixed, and it was unto us a great goodpassing of the time to behold them, besides the relief we found by killing some store of them with our fowling-pieces; without which, having little or no bread, and less drink, but only the thick and troubled water of the river, we had been in a very hard case.

. . . .

When we were come to the tops of the first hills of the plains adjoining to the river, we beheld that wonderful breach of waters which ran down Caroli; and might from that mountain see the river how it ran in three parts, above twenty miles off, and there appeared some ten or twelve overfalls in sight, every one as high over the other as a church tower, which fell with that fury, that the rebound of water made it seem as if it had been all covered over with a great shower of rain; and in some places we took it at the first for a smoke that had risen over some great town. For mine own part I was well persuaded from thence to have returned, being a very ill footman; but the rest were all so desirous to go near the said strange thunder of waters, as they drew me on by little and little, till we came into the next valley, where we might better discern the same. I never saw a more beautiful country, nor more lively prospects; hills so raised here and there over the valleys; the river winding into divers branches; the plains adjoining without bush or stubble, all fair green grass; the ground of hard sand, easy to march on, either for horse or foot; the deer crossing in every path; the birds towards the evening singing on every tree with a thousand several tunes; cranes and herons of white, crimson, and carnation, perching in the river's side; the air fresh with a gentle easterly wind; and every stone that we stooped to take up promised either gold or silver by his complexion.

. . . .

Next unto Arui there are two rivers Atoica and Caura, and on that branch which is called Caura are a nation of people whose heads appear not above their shoulders; which though it may be thought a mere fable, yet for mine own part I am resolved it is true, because every child in the provinces of Aromaia and Canuri affirm the same. They are called Ewaipanoma; they are reported to have their eyes in their shoulders, and their mouths in the middle of their breasts, and that a long train of hair groweth backward between their shoulders. The son of Topiawari, which I brought with me into England, told me that they were the most mighty men of all the land, and use bows, arrows, and clubs twice as big as any of Guiana, or of the Orenoqueponi.

. . . .

When it grew towards sunset, we entered a branch of a river that fell into Orenoque, called Winicapora; where I was informed of the mountain of crystal, to which in truth for the length of the way, and the evil season of the year, I was not able to march, nor abide any longer upon the journey. We saw it afar off; and it appeared like a white church-tower of an exceeding height. There falleth over it a mighty river which toucheth no part of the side of the mountain, but rusheth over the top of it, and falleth to the ground with so terrible a noise and clamour, as if a thousand great bells were knocked one against another. I think there is not in the world so strange an overfall, nor so wonderful to behold. Berreo told me that there were diamonds and other precious stones on it, and that they shined very far off; but what it hath I know not, neither durst he or any of his men ascend to the top of the said mountain, those people adjoining being his enemies, as they were, and the way to it so impassable.

Dying Speech on the Scaffold

(*From Oldys*)

THE next morning, being Thursday, the 29th of October (1618), Sir Walter Ralegh was conducted, by the sheriffs of Middlesex, to the Old Palace Yard in Westminster, where there was a large scaffold erected before the parliament-house for his execution. He had on a wrought nightcap under his hat; a ruff band; a black wrought velvet nightgown over a hair-coloured satin doublet, and a black wrought waistcoat; a pair of black cut taffeta breeches, and ash-coloured silk stockings. He mounted the scaffold with a cheerful countenance, and saluted the lords, knights, and gentlemen of his acquaintance there present. Then proclamation being made by an officer for silence, he began his speech as follows:

" I thank God, that he has sent me to die in the light, and not in darkness. I likewise thank God that he has suffered me to die before such an assembly of honourable witnesses, and not obscurely in the Tower; where, for the space of thirteen years together, I have been oppressed with many miseries. And I return him thanks, that my fever hath not taken me at this time, as I prayed to him it might not, that I might clear myself of some accusations unjustly laid to my charge, and leave behind me the testimony of a true heart both to my king and country.

" There are two main points of suspicion that his Majesty hath conceived against me, and which, I conceive, have specially hastened my coming hither; therefore I desire to clear them to your lordships, and resolve you in the truth thereof. The first is, that his Majesty hath been informed, I have had some plot or confederacy with France, for which he had some reasons, though grounded upon a weak foundation. One was, that when I returned to Plymouth, I endeavoured to go to Rochel, which was because I would fain have made my peace before I returned to England. Another reason was, that again I would have bent my course to France, upon my last intended escape from London, being the place where I might have the best means of making such peace, and the best safeguard during that terror from above. These, joined with the coming of the French agent to my house here in London, only to confer about my said voyage, together with the report of my having a commission from the king of France, might occasion my being so suspected in this particular, and his Majesty to be so displeased with me. But this I say; for a man to call God to witness at any time to a falsehood, is a grievous sin. To call him as witness to a falsehood at the point of death, when there is no time for repentance, is a crime far more impious and desperate; therefore, for me to call that Majesty to witness an untruth, before whose tribunal I am instantly to appear, were beyond measure sinful, and without hope of pardon. I do yet call that great God to witness, that, as I hope to see him, to be saved by him, and live in the world to come, I never had any plot or intelligence with the French king; never had any commission from him, nor saw his hand or seal; that I never had any practice or combination with the French agent, nor ever knew or saw such a person, till I met him in my gallery unlooked for. If I speak not true, O Lord, let me never enter into thy kingdom.

" The second suspicion or imputation was, that his Majesty had been informed I had spoken disloyally of him. The only witness of this was a base Frenchman, a runagate, a chymical fellow, whom I soon knew to be perfidious; for being drawn by him into the action of freeing myself at Winchester, in which I confess my hand was touched, he, being sworn to secrecy overnight, revealed it the next morning. It is strange, that so mean a fellow could so far encroach himself into the favour of the lords; and, gaping after some great reward, could so falsely accuse me of seditious speeches against his Majesty, and be so credited. But this I here speak, it is no time for me to flatter or to fear princes, I, who am subject only unto death: and for me, who have now to do with God alone, to tell a lie to get the favour of the king were in vain: and yet, if ever I spake disloyally or dishonestly of the king, either to this Frenchman or any other; ever intimated the least thought hurtful or prejudicial of him, the Lord blot me out of the book of life.

" I confess, I did attempt to escape, and it was only to save my life. I likewise confess, that I feigned myself to be indisposed at Salisbury, but I hope it was no sin; for the prophet David did make himself a fool, and suffer spittal to fall upon his beard to escape from the hands of his enemies, and it was not imputed unto him as a sin: what I did was only to prolong time, till his Majesty came, in hopes of some commiseration from him.

" But I forgive that Frenchman, and likewise Sir Lewis Stucley the wrongs he hath done me, with all my heart; for I received the sacrament this morning of Mr. Dean, and I have forgiven all men; but, in charity to others, am bound to caution them against him, and such as he is. For Sir Lewis Stucley, my keeper and kinsman, hath affirmed, that I should tell him, my lord Carew and my lord of Doncaster here, did advise me to escape; but I protest before God I never told him any such thing; neither did these lords advise me to any such matter. It is not likely that I should acquaint two privy-counsellors of my escape; nor that I should tell him, my keeper, it was their advice; neither was there any reason to tell it him, or he to report it; for it is well known he left me six, eight, or ten days together alone, to go whither I listed, while he rode about the country. He further accused me, that I should shew him a letter, whereby I did signify that I would give him ten thousand pounds to escape; but God cast my soul into everlasting fire if ever I made such proffer of ten thousand pounds, or one thousand pounds; but indeed I shewed him a letter, that if he would go with me, there should be order taken for the discharge of his debts when he was gone; neither had I one thousand pounds, for, if I had, I could have made my peace better with it otherwise than by giving it Stucley. Further, he gave out, when I came to Sir Edward Parham's house, who had been a follower of mine, and gave me good entertainment, I had there received some dram of poison. When I answered, that I feared no such thing, for I was well-assured of those in the house; and therefore wished him to have no such thought. Now I will not only say, that God is the God of revenge, but also of mercy; and I desire God to forgive him, as I hope to be forgiven." Then casting his eye upon his note of remembrance, he went on thus:

" It was told the king, that I was brought perforce into England; and that I did not intend to return again: whereas Captain Charles Parker, Mr. Tresham, Mr. Leak, and divers others, that knew how I was dealt withal by the common soldiers, will witness to the contrary. They were an hundred and fifty of them who mutinied against me, and sent for me to come to them; for unto me they would not come. They kept me close prisoner in my cabin, and forced me to take an oath, that I would not go into England without their consent, otherwise they would have cast me into the sea. After I had taken this oath, I did, by wine, gifts, and fair words, so work upon the master-gunner, and ten or twelve of the faction, that I won them to desist from their purposes, and intended, when I returned home, to procure their pardon; in the mean while proposed, that I would dispose of some of them in Ireland; to which they agreed, and would have gone into the north parts, from which I dissuaded them, and told them, they were red-shanks who inhabited there, so drew them to the south; and the better to clear myself of them, was forced to get them a hundred and fifty pounds at Kingsale, otherwise I had never got from them.

"There was a report also, that I meant not to go to Guiana at all; and that I knew not of any mine, nor intended any such matter, but only to get my liberty, which I had not the wit to keep. But it was my full intent to go for gold, for the benefit of his Majesty, myself, and those who went with me, with the rest of my countrymen: though he that knew the head of the mine would not discover it when he saw my son was slain, but made himself away." Then turning to the earl of Arundel, he said, " My lord, you being in the gallery of my ship at my departure, I remember you took me by the hand, and said, you would request one thing of me; which was, whether I made a good voyage or a bad, that I would return again into England; which I then promised, and gave you my faith I would." " So you did," said his lordship; " it is true, and they were the last words I said to you." " Another slander was raised of

me, that I should have gone away from them, and have left them at
Guiana; but there were a great many worthy men, who accompanied me
always, as my sergeant-major, and divers other (whom he named), that
knew it was none of my intention.   Also it hath been said, that I stinted
them of fresh water; to which I answer, every one was, as they must
be in a ship, furnished by measure, and not according to their appetites.
This course all seamen know must be used among them, and to this strait
were we driven.   Another opinion was held, that I carried with me
sixteen thousand pieces of gold; and that all the voyage I intended, was
but to gain my liberty and this money into my hands: but, as I shall
answer it before God, I had no more in all the world, directly or indirectly,
than one hundred pounds; whereof I gave about forty-five pounds to
my wife.   But the ground of this false report was, that twenty thousand pounds being adventured, and but four thousand appearing in the
surveyor's books, the rest had my hand to the bills for divers adventures;
but, as I hope to be saved, I had not a penny more than one hundred
pounds.   These are the material points I thought good to speak of; I am
at this instant to render my account to God, and I protest, as I shall
appear before him, this that I have spoken is true.

   " I will borrow but a little time more of Mr. Sheriff, that I may not
detain him too long; and herein I shall speak of the imputation laid upon
me through the jealousy of the people, that I had been a persecutor of
my lord of Essex; that I rejoiced in his death, and stood in a window
over-against him when he suffered, and puffed out tobacco in defiance
of him; when as, God is my witness, that I shed tears for him when he
died; and, as I hope to look God in the face hereafter, my lord of Essex
did not see my face at the time of his death; for I was far off, in the
armoury, where I saw him, but he saw not me.   It is true, I was of a
contrary faction; but I take the same God to witness, that I had no hand
in his death, nor bear him any ill affection, but always believed it would
be better for me that his life had been preserved; for after his fall, I
got the hatred of those who wished me well before: and those who set
me against him, set themselves afterwards against me, and were my
greatest enemies: and my soul hath many times been grieved, that I was
not nearer to him when he died; because, as I understood afterwards,
he asked for me at his death, and desired to have been reconciled to me.

   " And now I entreat, that you all will join with me in prayer to that
great God of heaven whom I have grievously offended, being a man full
of all vanity, who has lived a sinful life in such callings as have been
most inducing to it; for I have been a soldier, a sailor, and a courtier,
which are courses of wickedness and vice; that his almighty goodness

will forgive me; that he will cast away my sins from me; and that he will receive me into everlasting life: so I take my leave of you all, making my peace with God."

Then proclamation being made, that all men should depart the scaffold, he prepared himself for death, giving away his hat and cap and money to some attendants who stood near him. When he took leave of the lords and other gentlemen, he entreated the lord Arundel to desire the king, that no scandalous writings to defame him might be published after his death; concluding, "I have a long journey to go, therefore must take my leave." Then having put off his gown and doublet, he called to the headsman to shew him the axe, which not being suddenly done, he said, "I prithee, let me see it. Dost thou think that I am afraid of it?" Having fingered the edge of it a little, he returned it, and said, smiling, to the sheriff, "This is a sharp medicine, but it is a sound cure for all diseases"; and having entreated the company to pray to God to assist and strengthen him, the executioner kneeled down and asked him forgiveness; which Ralegh, laying his hand upon his shoulder, granted. Then being asked which way he would lay himself on the block, he answered, "So the heart be right, it is no matter which way the head lies." As he stooped to lay himself along, and reclined his head, his face being towards the east, the headsman spread his own cloak under him. After a little pause, he gave the sign that he was ready for the stroke by lifting up his hand, and his head was struck off at two blows, his body never shrinking or moving. His head was shewed on each side of the scaffold, and then put into a red leather bag, and, with his velvet nightgown thrown over it, was afterwards conveyed away in a mourning coach of his lady's. His body, as we are told, was buried hard by, in the chancel of St. Margaret's church, near the altar; but his head was long preserved in a case by his widow, for she survived him twenty-nine years, as I have found by some anecdotes remaining in the family; and after her death it was kept also by her son Carew, with whom it is said to have been buried.

SIR PHILIP SIDNEY (1554-1586)

From ASTROPHEL AND STELLA

His Lady's Cruelty

(Sonnet XXXI. With how sad steps, O Moon, thou climb'st the skies!)

WITH how sad steps, O Moon, thou
    climb'st the skies!
How silently, and with how wan a face!

What! may it be that even in heavenly
    place
That busy archer his sharp arrows
    tries?
Sure, if that long-with-love-acquainted
    eyes
Can judge of love, thou feel'st a lover's
    case:
I read it in thy looks; thy languish'd
    grace

To me, that feel the like, thy state
descries.
Then, even of fellowship, O Moon, tell
me,
Is constant love deem'd there but want
of wit?
Are beauties there as proud as here they
be?
Do they above love to be loved, and yet
Those lovers scorn whom that love
doth possess?
Do they call "virtue" there—ungrate-
fulness?

Sleep

(Sonnet XXXIX. Come, Sleep; O
Sleep! the certain knot of peace)

COME, Sleep; O Sleep! the certain knot
of peace.
The baiting-place of wit, the balm of
woe,
The poor man's wealth, the prisoner's
release,
Th' indifferent judge between the high
and low;
With shield of proof shield me from out
the prease
Of those fierce darts Despair at me doth
throw:
O make in me those civil wars to cease;
I will good tribute pay, if thou do so.
Take thou of me smooth pillows, sweetest
bed,
A chamber deaf to noise and blind of
light,
A rosy garland and a weary head;
And if these things, as being thine by
right,
Move not thy heavy grace, thou shalt
in me,
Livelier than elsewhere, Stella's image
see.

Song. Absence

(Tenth Song)

O DEAR life, when shall it be
That mine eyes thine eyes shall see,

And in them thy mind discover
Whether absence have had force
Thy remembrance to divorce
From the image of thy lover?

Or if I myself find not,
After parting, aught forgot,
Nor debarred from Beauty's treasure,
Let not tongue aspire to tell
In what high joys I shall dwell;
Only thought aims at the pleasure.

Thought, therefore, I will send thee
To take up the place for me:
Long I will not after tarry,
There, unseen, thou mayst be bold,
Those fair wonders to behold,
Which in them my hopes do carry.

Thought, see thou no place forbear,
Enter bravely everywhere,
Seize on all to her belonging;
But if thou wouldst guarded be,
Fearing her beams, take with thee
Strength of liking, rage of longing.

Think of that most grateful time
When my leaping heart will climb,
In my lips to have his biding,
There those roses for to kiss,
Which do breathe a sugared bliss,
Opening rubies, pearls dividing.

* * * * *

Think, think of those dallyings,
When with dove-like murmurings,
With glad moaning, passèd anguish,
We change eyes, and heart for heart,
Each to other do depart,
Joying til'. joy makes us languish.

O my thought, my thoughts surcease,
Thy delights my woes increase,
My life melts with too much thinking;
Think no more, but die in me,
Till thou shalt revivèd be,
At her lips my nectar drinking.

SIR FRANCIS BACON (1561-1626)

Of Friendship

IT had been hard for him that spake it to have put more truth and untruth together in few words, than in that speech, *Whosoever is delighted in solitude is either a wild beast or a god.* For it is most true that a natural and secret hatred and aversation towards society in any man, hath somewhat of the savage beast; but it is most untrue that it should have any character at all of the divine nature; except it proceed, not out of a pleasure in solitude, but out of a love and desire to sequester a man's self for a higher conversation: such as is found to have been falsely and feignedly in some of the heathen; as Epimenides the Candian, Numa the Roman, Empedocles the Sicilian, and Apollonius of Tyana; and truly and really in divers of the ancient hermits and holy fathers of the church. But little do men perceive what solitude is, and how far it extendeth. For a crowd is not company; and faces are but a gallery of pictures; and talk but a tinkling cymbal, where there is no love. The Latin adage meeteth with it a little: *Magna civitas, magna solitudo,* because in a great town friends are scattered; so that there is not that fellowship, for the most part, which is in less neighbourhoods. But we may go further, and affirm most truly that it is a mere and miserable solitude to want true friends; without which the world is but a wilderness; and even in this sense also of solitude, whosoever in the frame of his nature and affections is unfit for friendship, he taketh it of the beast, and not from humanity.

A principal fruit of friendship is the ease and discharge of the fulness and swellings of the heart, which passions of all kinds do cause and induce. We know diseases of stoppings and suffocations are the most dangerous in the body; and it is not much otherwise in the mind; you may take sarza to open the liver, steel to open the spleen, flower of sulphur for the lungs, castoreum for the brain; but no receipt openeth the heart, but a true friend; to whom you may impart griefs, joys, fears, hopes, suspicions, counsels, and whatsoever lieth upon the heart to oppress it, in a kind of civil shrift or confession.

It is a strange thing to observe how high a rate great kings and monarchs do set upon this fruit of friendship whereof we speak: so great, as they purchase it many times at the hazard of their own safety and greatness. For princes, in regard of the distance of their fortune from that of their subjects and servants, cannot gather this fruit, except (to make themselves capable thereof) they raise some persons to be as

it were companions and almost equals to themselves, which many times
sorteth to inconvenience. The modern languages give unto such persons
the name of favourites, or privadoes; as if it were matter of grace, or
conversation. But the Roman name attaineth the true use and cause
thereof, naming them *participes curarum;* for it is that which tieth the
knot. And we see plainly that this hath been done, not by weak and passionate princes only, but by the wisest and most politic that ever reigned;
who have oftentimes joined to themselves some of their servants; whom
both themselves have called friends, and allowed others likewise to call
them in the same manner; using the word which is received between
private men.

L. Sylla, when he commanded Rome, raised Pompey (after sur-
named the Great) to that height, that Pompey vaunted himself for
Sylla's over-match. For when he had carried the consulship for a friend
of his, against the pursuit of Sylla, and that Sylla did a little resent
thereat, and began to speak great, Pompey turned upon him again, and
in effect bade him be quiet; *for that more men adored the sun rising than
the sun setting.* With Julius Cæsar, Decimus Brutus had obtained that
interest, as he set him down in his testament for heir in remainder after
his nephew. And this was the man that had power with him to draw him
forth to his death. For when Cæsar would have discharged the senate,
in regard of some ill presages, and specially a dream of Calpurnia; this
man lifted him gently by the arm out of his chair, telling him he hoped
he would not dismiss the senate till his wife had dreamt a better dream.
And it seemeth his favour was so great, as Antonius, in a letter which
is recited *verbatim* in one of Cicero's Philippics, calleth him *venefica,
witch;* as if he had enchanted Cæsar. Augustus raised Agrippa (though
of mean birth) to that height, as when he consulted with Mæcenas about
the marriage of his daughter Julia, Mæcenas took the liberty to tell him,
*that he must either marry his daughter to Agrippa, or take away his life:
there was no third way, he had made him so great.* With Tiberius
Cæsar, Sejanus had ascended to that height, as they two were termed
and reckoned as a pair of friends. Tiberius in a letter to him saith, *hæc
pro amicitiâ nostrâ non occultavi;* and the whole senate dedicated an
altar to Friendship, as to a goddess, in respect of the great dearness of
friendship between them two. The like or more was between Septimius
Severus and Plautianus. For he forced his eldest son to marry the
daughter of Plautianus; and would often maintain Plautianus in doing
affronts to his son; and did write also in a letter to the senate, by these
words: *I love the man so well, as I wish he may over-live me.* Now if
these princes had been as a Trajan or a Marcus Aurelius, a man might

have thought that this had proceeded of an abundant goodness of nature; but being men so wise, of such strength and severity of mind, and so extreme lovers of themselves, as all these were, it proveth most plainly that they found their own felicity (though as great as ever happened to mortal men) but as an half piece, except they mought have a friend to make it entire; and yet, which is more, they were princes that had wives, sons, nephews; and yet all these could not supply the comfort of friendship.

It is not to be forgotten what Comineus observeth of his first master, Duke Charles the Hardy; namely, that he would communicate his secrets with none; and least of all, those secrets which troubled him most. Whereupon he goeth on and saith that towards his latter time *that closeness did impair and a little perish his understanding.* Surely Comineus mought have made the same judgment also, if it had pleased him, of his second master Lewis the Eleventh, whose closeness was indeed his tormentor. That parable of Pythagoras is dark, but true; *Cor ne edito: Eat not the heart.* Certainly, if a man would give it a hard phrase, those that want friends to open themselves unto are cannibals of their own hearts. But one thing is most admirable (wherewith I will conclude this first fruit of friendship), which is, that this communicating of a man's self to his friend works two contrary effects; for it redoubleth joys, and cutteth griefs in halfs. For there is no man that imparteth his joys to his friend, but he joyeth the more: and no man that imparteth his griefs to his friend, but he grieveth the less. So that it is in truth of operation upon a man's mind, of like virtue as the alchymists use to attribute to their stone for man's body; that it worketh all contrary effects, but still to the good and benefit of nature. But yet without praying in aid of alchymists, there is a manifest image of this in the ordinary course of nature. For in bodies, union strengtheneth and cherisheth any natural action; and on the other side weakeneth and dulleth any violent impression: and even so it is of minds.

The second fruit of friendship is healthful and sovereign for the understanding, as the first is for the affections. For friendship maketh indeed a fair day in the affections, from storm and tempest; but it maketh daylight in the understanding, out of darkness and confusion of thoughts. Neither is this to be understood only of faithful counsel, which a man receiveth from his friend; but before you come to that, certain it is that whosoever hath his mind fraught with many thoughts, his wits and understanding do clarify and break up, in the communicating and discoursing with another; he tosseth his thoughts more easily; he marshalleth them more orderly; he seeth how they look when they are turned into words: finally, he waxeth wiser than himself; and that more by an hour's discourse than by a day's meditation. It was well said by Themistocles to the king of Persia, *That speech was like cloth of Arras, opened and put abroad; whereby the imagery doth appear in figure; whereas in thoughts they lie but as in packs.* Neither is the second fruit of friendship, in opening the understanding, restrained only to such friends as are able to give a man counsel; (they indeed are best;) but even without that, a man learneth of himself, and bringeth his own thoughts to light, and whetteth his wits as against a stone, which itself cuts not. In a word, a man were better relate himself to a statua or picture, than to suffer his thoughts to pass in smother.

Add now, to make this second fruit of friendship complete, that other point which lieth more open and falleth within vulgar observation; which is faithful counsel from a friend. Heraclitus saith well in one of his enigmas, *Dry light is ever the best.* And certain it is, that the light that a man receiveth by counsel from another, is drier and purer than that which cometh from his own understanding and judgment; which is ever infused and drenched in his affections and customs. So as there is as much difference between the counsel that a friend giveth, and that a man giveth himself, as there is between the counsel of a friend and of a flatterer. For there is no such flatterer as is a man's self; and there is no such remedy against flattery of a man's self, as the liberty of a friend. Counsel is of two sorts: the one concerning manners, the other concerning business. For the first, the best preservative to keep the mind in health is the faithful admonition of a friend. The calling of a man's self to a strict account is a medicine, sometime, too piercing and corrosive. Reading good books of morality is a little flat and dead. Observing our faults in others is sometimes improper for our case. But the best receipt (best, I say, to work, and best to take) is the admonition of a friend. It is a strange thing to behold what gross errors and extreme absurdities many (especially of the greater sort) do commit, for want of a friend to tell them of them; to the great damage both of their fame and fortune: for, as St. James saith, they are as men *that look sometimes into a glass, and presently forget their own shape and favour.* As for business, a man may think, if he will, that two eyes see no more than one; or that a gamester seeth always more than a looker-on; or that a man in anger is as wise as he that hath said over the four and twenty letters; or that a musket may be shot off as well upon the arm as upon a rest; and such other fond and high imaginations, to think himself all in all. But when all is done, the help of good counsel is that which setteth business straight. And if any man think that he will take counsel, but it shall be by pieces; asking counsel in one business of one man, and in another business of another man; it is well, (that is to say, better perhaps than if he asked none at all;) but he runneth two dangers: one, that he shall not be faithfully counselled; for it is a rare thing, except it be from a perfect and entire friend, to have counsel given, but such as shall be bowed and crooked to some ends which he hath that giveth it. The other, that he shall have counsel given, hurtful and unsafe, (though with good meaning,) and mixed partly of mischief and partly of remedy; even as if you would call a physician that is thought good for the cure of the disease you complain of, but is unacquainted with your body; and therefore may put you in way for a present cure, but overthroweth your health in some other kind; and so cure the disease and kill the patient. But a friend that is wholly acquainted with a man's estate will beware, by furthering any present business, how he dasheth upon other inconvenience. And therefore rest not upon scattered counsels; they will rather distract and mislead, than settle and direct.

After these two noble fruits of friendship, (peace in the affections, and support of the judgment,) followeth the last fruit; which is like the pomegranate, full of many kernels; I mean aid and bearing a part in all actions and occasions. Here the best way to represent to life the manifold use of friendship, is to cast and see how many things there are which a man cannot do himself; and then it will appear that it was a sparing speech of the ancients, to say, *that a friend is another himself;* for that a friend is far more than himself. Men have their time, and die many times in desire of some things which they principally take to heart; the bestowing of a child, the finishing of a work, or the like. If a man have a true friend, he may rest almost secure that the care of those things will continue after him. So that a man hath, as it were, two lives in his desires. A man hath a body, and that body is confined to a place; but where friendship is, all offices of life are as it were granted to him and his deputy. For he may exercise them by his friend. How many things are there which a man cannot, with any face or comeliness, say or do himself? A man can scarce allege his own merits with modesty, much less extol them; a man cannot sometimes brook to supplicate or beg; and a number of the like. But all these things are graceful in a friend's mouth, which are blushing in a man's own. So again, a man's person hath many proper relations which he cannot put off. A man cannot speak to his son but as a father; to his wife but as a husband; to his enemy but upon terms: whereas a friend may speak as the case requires, and not as it sorteth with the person. But to enumerate these things were endless; I have given the rule, where a man cannot fitly play his own part: if he have not a friend, he may quit the stage.

Of Studies

STUDIES serve for delight, for ornament, and for ability. Their chief use for delight, is in privateness and retiring; for ornament, is in discourse; and for ability, is in the judgment and disposition of business. For expert men can execute, and perhaps judge of particulars, one by one; but the general counsels, and the plots and marshalling of affairs, come best from those that are learned. To spend too much time in studies is sloth; to use them too much for ornament, is affectation; to make judgment wholly by their rules, is the humour of a scholar. They perfect nature, and are perfected by experience: for natural abilities are like natural plants, that need proyning by study; and studies themselves do give forth directions too much at large, except they be bounded in by experience. Crafty men contemn studies, simple men admire them, and wise men use them, for they teach not their own use; but that is a wisdom without them, and above them, won by observation. Read not to contradict and confute; nor to believe and take for granted; nor to find talk and discourse; but to weigh and consider. Some books are to be tasted, others to be swallowed, and some few to be chewed and digested; that is, some books are to be read only in parts; others to be read, but not curiously; and some few to be read wholly, and with diligence and attention. Some books also may be read by deputy, and extracts made of them by others; but that would be only in the less important arguments, and the meaner sort of books; else distilled books are like common distilled waters, flashy things. Reading maketh a full man; conference a ready man; and writing an exact man. And therefore, if a man write little, he had need have a great memory; if he confer little, he had need have a present wit: and if he read little, he had need have much cunning, to seem to know that he doth not. Histories make men wise; poets witty; the mathematics subtile; natural philosophy deep; moral grave; logic and rhetoric able to contend. *Abeunt studia in mores.* Nay there is no stond or impediment in the wit, but may be wrought out by fit studies: like as diseases of the body may have appropriate exercises. Bowling is good for the stone and reins; shooting for the lungs and breast; gentle walking for the stomach; riding for head; and the like. So if a man's wit be wandering, let him study the mathematics; for in demonstrations, if his wit be called away never so little, he must begin again. If his wit be not apt to distinguish or find differences, let him study the schoolmen; for they are *cymini sectores*. If he be not apt to beat over matters, and to call up one thing to prove and illustrate another, let him study the lawyer's cases. So every defect of the mind may have a special receipt.

EDMUND SPENSER (1552–1599)

From THE FAERIE QUEENE

Canto XI

The knight with that old Dragon fights
Two dayes incessantly:
The third, him overthrowes, and gayns
Most glorious victory.

HIGH time now gan it wex for Una fayre
To thinke of those her captive parents
    deare,
And their forwasted kingdom to repayre:
Whereto whenas they now approched
    neare,
With hartie wordes her knight she gan to
    cheare,
And in her modest maner thus bespake:
'Deare knight, as deare as ever knight
    was deare,
That all these sorrowes suffer for my sake,
High heven behold the tedious toyle, ye
    for me take.

'Now are we come unto my native soyle,
And to the place, where all our perilles
    dwell;
Here hauntes that feend, and does his
    dayly spoyle;
Therefore henceforth bee at your keep-
    ing well,
And ever ready for your foeman fell.
The sparke of noble corage now awake,
And strive your excellent selfe to excell;
That shall ye evermore renowmed make
Above all knights on earth, that batteill
    undertake.'

And pointing forth, 'Lo! yonder is,' said
    she,
'The brasen towre, in which my parents
    deare
For dread of that huge feend emprisond
    be;
Whom I from far see on the walles ap-
    peare,
Whose sight my feeble soule doth greatly
    cheare:
And on the top of all I do espye
The watchman wayting tydings glad to
    heare;

That, O my parents, might I happily
Unto you bring, to ease you of your mis-
    ery!'

With that they heard a roaring hideous
    sownd,
That all the ayre with terror filled wyde,
And seemd uneath to shake the stedfast
    ground.
Eftsoones that dreadfull dragon they
    espyde,
Where stretcht he lay upon the sunny side
Of a great hill, himselfe like a great hill.
But all so soone as he from far descryde
Those glistring armes, that heven with
    light did fill,
He rousd himselfe full blyth, and hastned
    them untill.

Then badd the knight his lady yede aloof,
And to an hill her selfe withdraw asyde,
From whence she might behold that bat-
    tailles proof,
And eke be safe from daunger far de-
    scryde:
She him obayd, and turnd a litle wyde.
Now, O thou sacred Muse, most learned
    dame,
Fayre ympe of Phœbus, and his aged
    bryde,
The nourse of time and everlasting fame,
That warlike handes ennoblest with im-
    mortall name;

O gently come into my feeble brest,
Come gently, but not with that mightie
    rage,
Wherewith the martiall troupes thou doest
    infest,
And hartes of great heroës doest enrage,
That nought their kindled corage may
    aswage:
Soone as thy dreadfull trompe begins to
    sownd,
The god of warre with his fiers equipage
Thou doest awake, sleepe never he so
    sownd,
And scared nations doest with horror
    sterne astownd.

Fayre goddesse, lay that furious fitt asyde,
Till I of warres and bloody Mars doe sing,
And Bryton fieldes with Sarazin blood
  bedyde,
Twixt that great Faery Queene and Pay-
  nim King,
That with their horror heven and earth
  did ring,
A worke of labour long, and endlesse
  prayse:
But now a while lett downe that haughtie
  string,
And to my tunes thy second tenor rayse,
That I this man of God his godly armes
  may blaze.

By this the dreadfull beast drew nigh to
  hand,
Halfe flying and halfe footing in his haste,
That with his largenesse measured much
  land,
And made wide shadow under his huge
  waste;
As mountaine doth the valley overcaste.
Approaching nigh, he reared high afore
His body monstrous, horrible, and vaste,
Which, to increase his wondrous greatnes
  more,
Was swoln with wrath, and poyson, and
  with bloody gore.

And over, all with brasen scales was armd,
Like plated cote of steele, so couched
  neare,
That nought mote perce, ne might his
  corse bee harmd
With dint of swerd, nor push of pointed
  speare:
Which as an eagle, seeing pray appeare,
His aery plumes doth rouze, full rudely
  dight,
So shaked he, that horror was to heare:
For as the clashing of an armor bright,
Such noyse his rouzed scales did send unto
  the knight.

His flaggy winges, when forth he did display,
Were like two sayles, in which the hollow
  wynd

Is gathered full, and worketh speedy
  way:
And eke the pennes, that did his pineons
  bynd,
Were like mayne-yardes, with flying canvas lynd,
With which whenas him list the ayre to
  beat,
And there by force unwonted passage
  fynd,
The clowdes before him fledd for terror
  great,
And all the hevens stood still, amazed
  with his threat.

His huge long tayle, wownd up in hun-
  dred foldes,
Does overspred his long bras-scaly back,
Whose wreathed boughtes when ever he
  unfoldes,
And thick entangled knots adown does
  slack,
Bespotted as with shields of red and
  blacke,
It sweepeth all the land behind him farre,
And of three furlongs does but litle lacke;
And at the point two stinges in fixed arre,
Both deadly sharp, that sharpest steele
  exceeden farr.

But stinges and sharpest steele did far
  exceed
The sharpnesse of his cruel rending
  clawes:
Dead was it sure, as sure as death in deed,
What ever thing does touch his ravenous
  pawes,
Or what within his reach he ever drawes.
But his most hideous head my tongue to
  tell
Does tremble; for his deepe devouring
  jawes
Wyde gaped, like the griesly mouth of
  hell,
Through which into his darke abysse all
  ravin fell.

And, that more wondrous was, in either
  jaw

Threeranckes of yron teeth enraunged were,
In which yett trickling blood and gobbets raw
Of late devoured bodies did appeare,
That sight thereof bredd cold congealed feare:
Which to increase, and all atonce to kill,
A cloud of smoothering smoke and sulphure seare
Out of his stinking gorge forth steemed still,
That all the ayre about with smoke and stench did fill.

His blazing eyes, like two bright shining shieldes,
Did burne with wrath, and sparkled living fyre;
As two broad beacons, sett in open fieldes,
Send forth their flames far of to every shyre,
And warning give, that enimies conspyre
With fire and sword the region to invade;
So flam'd his eyne with rage and rancorous yre:
But far within, as in a hollow glade,
Those glaring lampes were sett, that made a dreadfull shade.

So dreadfully he towardes him did pas,
Forelifting up a loft his speckled brest,
And often bounding on the brused gras,
As for great joyaunce of his newcome guest.
Eftsoones he gan advaunce his haughty crest,
As chauffed bore his bristles doth upreare,
And shoke his scales to battaile ready drest,
That made the Redcrosse Knight nigh quake for feare,
As bidding bold defyaunce to his foeman neare.

The knight gan fayrely couch his steady speare,
And fiersely ran at him with rigorous might:

The pointed steele, arriving rudely theare,
His harder hyde would nether perce nor bight,
But, glauncing by, foorth passed forward right:
Yet, sore amoved with so puissaunt push,
The wrathful beast about him turned light,
And him so rudely, passing by, did brush
With his long tayle, that horse and man to ground did rush.

Both horse and man up lightly rose againe,
And fresh encounter towardes him addrest:
But th' ydle stroke yet backe recoyld in vaine,
And found no place his deadly point to rest.
Exceeding rage enflam'd the furious beast,
To be avenged of so great despight;
For never felt his imperceable brest
So wondrous force from hand of living wight;
Yet had he prov'd the powre of many a puissant knight.

Then, with his waving wings displayed wyde,
Himselfe up high he lifted from the ground,
And with strong flight did forcibly divyde
The yielding ayre, which nigh too feeble found
Her flitting parts, and element unsound,
To beare so great a weight: he, cutting way
With his broad sayles, about him soared round;
At last, low stouping with unweldy sway,
Snatcht up both horse and man, to beare them quite away.

Long he them bore above the subject plaine,
So far as ewghen bow a shaft may send,
Till struggling strong did him at last constraine

To let them downe before his flightes end:
As hagard hauke, presuming to contend
With hardy fowle, above his hable might,
His wearie pounces all in vaine doth spend
To trusse the pray too heavy for his flight;
Which, comming down to ground, does free it selfe by fight.

He so disseized of his gryping grosse,
The knight his thrillant speare againe assayd
In his bras-plated body to embosse,
And three mens strength unto the stroake he layd;
Wherewith the stiffe beame quaked, as affrayd,
And glauncing from his scaly necke, did glyde
Close under his left wing, then broad displayd.
The percing steele there wrought a wound full wyde,
That with the uncouth smart the monster lowdly cryde.

He cryde, as raging seas are wont to rore,
When wintry storme his wrathful wreck does threat;
The rolling billowes beat the ragged shore,
As they the earth would shoulder from her seat,
And greedy gulfe does gape, as he would eat
His neighbour element in his revenge:
Then gin the blustring brethren boldly threat,
To move the world from off his stedfast henge,
And boystrous battaile make, each other to avenge.

The steely head stuck fast still in his flesh,
Till with his cruell clawes he snatcht the wood,
And quite a sunder broke.   Forth flowed fresh
A gushing river of blacke gory blood,
That drowned all the land, whereon he stood:

The streame thereof would drive a water-mill.
Trebly augmented was his furious mood
With bitter sence of his deepe rooted ill,
That flames of fire he threw forth from his large nosethril.

His hideous tayle then hurled he about,
And therewith all enwrapt the nimble thyes
Of his froth-fomy steed, whose courage stout
Striving to loose the knott, that fast him tyes,
Himselfe in streighter bandes too rash implyes,
That to the ground he is perforce constraynd
To throw his ryder: who can quickly ryse
From of the earth, with durty blood distaynd,
For that reprochfull fall right fowly he disdaynd.

And fercely tooke his trenchand blade in hand,
With which he stroke so furious and so fell,
That nothing seemd the puissaunce could withstand:
Upon his crest the hardned yron fell;
But his more hardned crest was armd so well,
That deeper dint therein it would not make;
Yet so extremely did the buffe him quell,
That from thenceforth he shund the like to take,
But, when he saw them come, he did them still forsake.

The knight was wroth to see his stroke beguyld,
And smot againe with more outrageous might;
But backe againe the sparcling steele recoyld,
And left not any marke where it did light,
As if in adamant rocke it had beene pight.

The beast, impatient of his smarting
wound,
And of so fierce and forcible despight,
Thought with his winges to stye above
the ground;
But his late wounded wing unserviceable
found.

Then, full of griefe and anguish vehement,
He lowdly brayd, that like was never
heard,
And from his wide devouring oven sent
A flake of fire, that, flashing in his beard,
Him all amazd, and almost made afeard:
The scorching flame sore swinged all his
face,
And through his armour all his body
seard,
That he could not endure so cruell cace,
But thought his armes to leave, and hel-
met to unlace.

Not that great champion of the antique
world,
Whom famous poetes verse so much doth
vaunt,
And hath for twelve huge labours high ex-
told,
So many furies and sharpe fits did haunt,
When him the poysoned garment did en-
chaunt,
With Centaures blood and bloody verses
charmd,
As did this knight twelve thousand do-
lours daunt,
Whom fyrie steele now burnt, that erst
him armd,
That erst him goodly armd, now most of
all him harmd.

Faynt, wearie, sore, emboyled, grieved,
brent
With heat, toyle, wounds, armes, smart,
and inward fire,
That never man such mischiefes did tor-
ment;
Death better were, death did he oft desire,
But death will never come, when needes
require.

Whom so dismayd when that his foe be-
held,
He cast to suffer him no more respire,
But gan his sturdy sterne about to weld,
And him so strongly stroke, that to the
ground him feld.

It fortuned (as fayre it then befell,)
Behynd his backe, unweeting, where he
stood,
Of auncient time there was a springing
well,
From which fast trickled forth a silver
flood,
Full of great vertues, and for med'cine
good.
Whylome, before that cursed dragon got
That happy land, and all with innocent
blood
Defyld those sacred waves, it rightly hot
The Well of Life, ne yet his vertues had
forgot.

For unto life the dead it could restore,
And guilt of sinfull crimes cleane wash
away;
Those that with sicknesse were infected
sore
It could recure, and aged long decay
Renew, as one were borne that very day.
Both Silo this, and Jordan, did excell,
And th' English Bath, and eke the Ger-
man Spau,
Ne can Cephise, nor Hebrus match this
well:
Into the same the knight back over-
thrown fell.

Now gan the golden Phœbus for to steepe
His fierie face in billowes of the west,
And his faint steedes watred in ocean
deepe,
Whiles from their journall labours they
did rest,
When that infernall monster, having kest
His wearie foe into that living well,
Can high advaunce his broad discoloured
brest

Above his wonted pitch, with countenance
   fell,
And clapt his yron wings, as victor he did
   dwell.

Which when his pensive lady saw from
   farre,
Great woe and sorrow did her soule assay,
As weening that the sad end of the warre,
And gan to highest God entirely pray,
That feared chaunce from her to turne
   away:
With folded hands, and knees full lowly
   bent,
All night shee watcht, ne once adowne
   would lay
Her dainty limbs in her sad dreriment,
But praying still did wake, and waking
   did lament.

The morrow next gan earely to appeare,
That Titan rose to runne his daily race;
But earely, ere the morrow next gan reare
Out of the sea faire Titans deawy face,
Up rose the gentle virgin from her place,
And looked all about, if she might spy
Her loved knight to move his manly pace:
For she had great doubt of his safety,
Since late she saw him fall before his
   enimy.

At last she saw, where he upstarted brave
Out of the well, wherein he drenched lay:
As eagle fresh out of the ocean wave,
Where he hath lefte his plumes all hory
   gray,
And deckt himselfe with fethers youthly
   gay,
Like eyas hauke up mounts unto the skies,
His newly budded pineons to assay,
And merveiles at him selfe, stil as he flies:
So new this new-borne knight to battell
   new did rise.

Whom when the damned feend so fresh
   did spy,
No wonder if he wondred at the sight,
And doubted, whether his late enimy

It were, or other new supplied knight.
He, now to prove his late renewed might,
High brandishing his bright deaw-burning
   blade,
Upon his crested scalp so sore did smite,
That to the scull a yawning wound it
   made:
The deadly dint his dulled sences all dis-
   maid.

I wote not whether the revenging steele
Were hardned with that holy water dew,
Wherein he fell, or sharper edge did feele,
Or his baptized hands now greater grew,
Or other secret vertue did ensew;
Els never could the force of fleshly arme,
Ne molten mettall, in his blood embrew:
For till that stownd could never wight him
   harme,
By subtilty, nor slight, nor might, nor
   mighty charme.

The cruell wound enraged him so sore,
That loud he yelled for exceeding paine;
As hundred ramping lions seemed to rore,
Whom ravenous hunger did thereto con-
   straine:
Then gan he tosse aloft his stretched
   traine,
And therewith scourge the buxome aire so
   sore,
That to his force to yielden it was faine;
Ne ought his sturdy strokes might stand
   afore,
That high trees overthrew, and rocks in
   peeces tore.

The same advauncing high above his head,
With sharpe intended sting so rude him
   smott,
That to the earth him drove, as stricken
   dead,
Ne living wight would have him life be-
   hott:
The mortall sting his angry needle shott
Quite through his shield, and in his
   shoulder seasd,
Where fast it stucke, ne would thereout
   be gott:

The griefe thereof him wondrous sore dis-
easd,
Ne might his rancling paine with patience
be appeasd.

But yet more mindfull of his honour deare
Then of the grievous smart, which him did
wring,
From loathed soile he can him lightly
reare,
And strove to loose the far in fixed sting:
Which when in vaine he tryde with strug-
geling,
Inflam'd with wrath, his raging blade he
hefte,
And strooke so strongly, that the knotty
string
Of his huge taile he quite a sonder clefte;
Five joints thereof he hewd, and but the
stump him lefte.

Hart cannot thinke, what outrage and
what cries,
With fowle enfouldred smoake and flash-
ing fire,
The hell-bred beast threw forth unto the
skies,
That all was covered with darknesse dire:
Then fraught with rancour, and engorged
yre,
He cast at once him to avenge for all,
And gathering up himselfe out of the mire
With his uneven wings, did fiercely fall
Upon his sunne-bright shield, and grypt it
fast withall.

Much was the man encombred with his
hold,
In feare to lose his weapon in his paw,
Ne wist yett how his talaunts to unfold;
For harder was from Cerberus greedy jaw
To plucke a bone, then from his cruell
claw
To reave by strength the griped gage
away:
Thrise he assayd it from his foote to draw,
And thrise in vaine to draw it did assay;
It booted nought to thinke to robbe him
of his pray.

Tho, when he saw no power might pre-
vaile,
His trusty sword he cald to his last aid,
Wherewith he fiersly did his foe assaile,
And double blowes about him stoutly laid,
That glauncing fire out of the yron plaid,
As sparckles from the andvile use to fly,
When heavy hammers on the wedg are
swaid;
Therewith at last he forst him to unty
One of his grasping feete, him to defend
thereby.

The other foote, fast fixed on his shield,
Whenas no strength nor stroks mote him
constraine
To loose, ne yet the warlike pledg to yield,
He smott thereat with all his might and
maine,
That nought so wondrous puissaunce
might sustaine:
Upon the joint the lucky steele did light,
And made such way, that hewd it quite in
twaine:
The paw yett missed not his minisht
might,
But hong still on the shield, as it at first
was pight.

For griefe thereof, and divelish despight,
From his infernall fournace forth he threw
Huge flames, that dimmed all the hevens
light,
Enrold in duskish smoke and brimstone
blew;
As burning Aetna from his boyling stew
Doth belch out flames, and rockes in
peeces broke,
And ragged ribs of mountaines molten
new,
Enwrapt in coleblacke clowds and filthy
smoke,
That al the land with stench, and heven
with horror choke.

The heate whereof, and harmefull pesti-
lence,
So sore him noyd, that forst him to retire
A litle backeward for his best defence,

To save his body from the scorching fire,
Which he from hellish entrailes did expire.
It chaunst (Eternall God that chaunce did
    guide)
As he recoiled backeward, in the mire
His nigh foreweried feeble feet did slide,
And downe he fell, with dread of shame
    sore terrifide.

There grew a goodly tree him faire beside,
Loaden with fruit and apples rosy redd,
As they in pure vermilion had beene dide,
Whereof great vertues over all were redd:
For happy life to all which thereon fedd,
And life eke everlasting did befall:
Great God it planted in that blessed stedd
With his Almighty hand, and did it call
The Tree of Life, the crime of our first
    fathers fall.

In all the world like was not to be fownd,
Save in that soile, where all good things
    did grow,
And freely sprong out of the fruitfull
    grownd,
As incorrupted Nature did them sow,
Till that dredd dragon all did overthrow.
Another like faire tree eke grew thereby,
Whereof who so did eat, eftsoones did
    know
Both good and ill: O mournfull memory!
That tree through one mans fault hath
    doen us all to dy.

From that first tree forth flowd, as from
    a well,
A trickling streame of balme, most sover-
    aine
And dainty deare, which on the ground
    still fell,
And overflowed all the fertile plaine,
As it had deawed bene with timely raine:
Life and long health that gracious oint-
    ment gave,
And deadly wounds could heale, and reare
    againe
The sencelesse corse appointed for the
    grave.
Into that same he fell: which did from
    death him save.

For nigh thereto the ever damned beast
Durst not approch, for he was deadly
    made,
And al that life preserved did detest:
Yet he it oft adventur'd to invade.
By this the drouping day-light gan to
    fade,
And yield his rowme to sad succeeding
    night,
Who with her sable mantle gan to shade
The face of earth, and wayes of living
    wight,
And high her burning torch set up in
    heaven bright.

When gentle Una saw the second fall
Of her deare knight, who, weary of long
    fight,
And faint through losse of blood, moov'd
    not at all,
But lay as in a dreame of deepe delight,
Besmeared with pretious balme, whose
    vertuous might
Did heale his woundes, and scorching heat
    alay,
Againe she stricken was with sore affright,
And for his safetie gan devoutly pray,
And watch the noyous night, and wait for
    joyous day.

The joyous day gan early to appeare,
And fayre Aurora from the deawy bed
Of aged Tithone gan her selfe to reare,
With rosy cheekes, for shame as blushing
    red;
Her golden locks for hast were loosely
    shed
About her eares, when Una her did marke
Clymbe to her charet, all with flowers
    spred,
From heven high to chace the chearelesse
    darke;
With mery note her lowd salutes the
    mounting larke.

Then freshly up arose the doughty knight,
All healed of his hurts and woundes wide,
And did himselfe to battaile ready dight;
Whose early foe awaiting him beside

To have devourd, so soone as day he
spyde,
When now he saw himselfe so freshly
reare,
As if late fight had nought him damni-
fyde,
He woxe dismaid, and gan his fate to
feare;
Nathlesse with wonted rage he him ad-
vaunced neare.

And in his first encounter, gaping wyde,
He thought attonce him to have swal-
lowd quight,
And rusht upon him with outragious
pryde;
Who him rencountring fierce, as hauke in
flight,
Perforce rebutted backe. The weapon
bright,
Taking advantage of his open jaw,
Ran through his mouth with so importune
might,
That deepe emperst his darksom hollow
maw,
And, back retyrd, his life blood forth with
all did draw.

So downe he fell, and forth his life did
breath,
That vanisht into smoke and cloudes
swift;
So downe he fell, that th' earth him under-
neath
Did grone, as feeble so great load to lift;
So downe he fell, as an huge rocky clift,
Whose false foundacion waves have washt
away,
With dreadful poyse is from the mayne-
land rift,
And, rolling downe, great Neptune doth
dismay;
So downe he fell, and like an heaped
mountaine lay.

The knight him selfe even trembled at his
fall,
So huge and horrible a masse it seemd;
And his deare lady, that beheld it all,

Durst not approch for dread which she
misdeemd;
But yet at last, whenas the direfull feend
She saw not stirre, of-shaking vaine af-
fright,
She nigher drew, and saw that joyous end:
Then God she praysd, and thankt her
faithfull knight,
That had atchievde so great a conquest by
his might.

Canto XII

Fayre Una to the Redcrosse Knight
Betrouthed is with joy:
Though false Duessa, it to barre,
Her false sleightes doe imploy.

BEHOLD! I see the haven nigh at hand,
To which I meane my wearie course to
bend;
Vere the maine shete, and beare up with
the land,
The which afore is fayrly to be kend,
And seemeth safe from storms that may
offend:
There this fayre virgin, wearie of her way,
Must landed bee, now at her journeyes
end;
There eke my feeble barke a while may
stay,
Till mery wynd and weather call her
thence away.

Scarsely had Phœbus in the glooming east
Yett harnessed his fyrie-footed teeme,
Ne reard above the earth his flaming
creast,
When the last deadly smoke aloft did
steeme,
That signe of last outbreathed life did
seeme
Unto the watchman on the castle wall;
Who thereby dead that balefull beast did
deeme,
And to his lord and lady lowd gan call,
To tell, how he had seene the dragons
fatall fall.

Uprose with hasty joy, and feeble speed,
That aged syre, the lord of all that land,

And looked forth, to weet if trew indeed
Those tydinges were, as he did under-
stand:
Which whenas trew by tryall he out fond,
He badd to open wyde his brasen gate,
Which long time had beene shut, and out
of hond.
Proclaymed joy and peace through all his
state;
For dead now was their foe, which them
forrayed late.

Then gan triumphant trompets sownd on
hye,
That sent to heven the ecchoed report
Of their new joy, and happie victory
Gainst him, that had them long opprest
with tort,
And fast imprisoned in sieged fort.
Then all the people, as in solemne feast,
To him assembled with one full consort,
Rejoycing at the fall of that great beast,
From whose eternall bondage now they
were releast.

Forth came that auncient lord and aged
queene,
Arayd in antique robes downe to the
grownd,
And sad habiliments right well beseene:
A noble crew about them waited rownd
Of sage and sober peres, all gravely
gownd;
Whom far before did march a goodly band
Of tall young men, all hable armes to
sownd;
But now they laurell braunches bore in
hand,
Glad signe of victory and peace in all their
land.

Unto that doughtie conquerour they came,
And him before themselves prostrating
low,
Their lord and patrone loud did him pro-
clame,
And at his feet their lawrell boughes did
throw.
Soone after them, all dauncing on a row,

The comely virgins came, with girlands
dight,
As fresh as flowres in medow greene doe
grow,
When morning deaw upon their leaves
doth light:
And in their handes sweet timbrels all up-
held on hight.

And them before, the fry of children yong
Their wanton sportes and childish mirth
did play,
And to the maydens sownding tymbrels
song,
In well attuned notes, a joyous lay,
And made delightfull musick all the way,
Untill they came where that faire virgin
stood.
As fayre Diana, in fresh sommers day,
Beholdes her nymphes enraung'd in shady
wood,
Some wrestle, some do run, some bathe in
christall flood;

So she beheld those maydens meriment
With chearefull vew; who, when to her
they came,
Themselves to ground with gracious hum-
blesse bent,
And her ador'd by honorable name,
Lifting to heven her everlasting fame:
Then on her head they sett a girlond
greene,
And crowned her twixt earnest and twixt
game;
Who, in her self-resemblance well beseene,
Did seeme, such as she was, a goodly
maiden queene.

And after all the raskall many ran,
Heaped together in rude rablement,
To see the face of that victorious man;
Whom all admired, as from heaven sent,
And gazd upon with gaping wonderment.
But when they came where that dead
dragon lay,
Stretcht on the ground in monstrous large
extent,

The sight with ydle feare did them dismay,
Ne durst approch him nigh, to touch, or
  once assay.

Some feard and fledd; some feard, and well
  it faynd;
One, that would wiser seeme then all the
  rest,
Warnd him not touch, for yet perhaps re-
  maynd
Some lingring life within his hollow brest,
Or in his wombe might lurke some hidden
  nest
Of many dragonettes, his fruitfull seede;
Another saide, that in his eyes did rest
Yet sparckling fyre, and badd thereof take
  heed;
Another said, he saw him move his eyes
  indeed.

One mother, whenas her foolehardy chyld
Did come to neare, and with his talants
  play,
Halfe dead through feare, her litle babe
  revyld,
And to her gossibs gan in counsell say:
'How can I tell, but that his talants may
Yet scratch my sonne, or rend his tender
  hand?'
So diversly them selves in vaine they fray;
Whiles some more bold, to measure him
  nigh stand,
To prove how many acres he did spred of
  land.

Thus flocked all the folke him rownd
  about,
The whiles that hoarie king, with all his
  traine,
Being arrived where that champion stout
After his foes defeasaunce did remaine,
Him goodly greetes, and fayre does enter-
  tayne
With princely gifts of yvory and gold,
And thousand thankes him yeeldes for all
  his paine:
Then when his daughter deare he does be-
  hold,

Her dearely doth imbrace, and kisseth
  manifold.

And after to his pallace he them bringes,
With shaumes, and trompets, and with
  clarions sweet;
And all the way the joyous people singes,
And with their garments strowes the
  paved street;
Whence mounting up, they fynd purvey-
  aunce meet
Of all that royall princes court became,
And all the floore was underneath their feet
Bespredd with costly scarlott of great
  name,
On which they lowly sitt, and fitting pur-
  pose frame.

What needes me tell their feast and goodly
  guize,
In which was nothing riotous nor vaine?
What needes of dainty dishes to devize,
Of comely services, or courtly trayne?
My narrow leaves cannot in them con-
  tayne
The large discourse of roiall princes state.
Yet was their manner then but bare and
  playne:
For th' antique world excesse and pryde
  did hate;
Such proud luxurious pompe is swollen up
  but late.

Then, when with meates and drinkes of
  every kinde
Their fervent appetites they quenched had,
That auncient lord gan fit occasion finde,
Of straunge adventures, and of perils sad,
Which in his travell him befallen had,
For to demaund of his renowmed guest:
Who then with utt'rance grave, and coun-
  t'nance sad,
From poynt to poynt, as is before exprest,
Discourst his voyage long, according his
  request.

Great pleasure, mixt with pittifull regard,
That godly king and queene did passionate,

Whyles they his pittifull adventures
   heard,
That oft they did lament his lucklesse
   state,
And often blame the too importune fate,
That heapd on him so many wrathfull
   wreakes;
For never gentle knight, as he of late,
So tossed was in Fortunes cruell freakes;
And all the while salt teares bedeawd the
   hearers cheaks.

Then sayd the royall pere in sober wise:
'Deare sonne, great beene the evils which
   ye bore
From first to last in your late enterprise,
That I note whether praise or pitty more:
For never living man, I weene, so sore
In sea of deadly daungers was distrest;
But since now safe ye seised have the
   shore,
And well arrived are, (High God be blest!)
Let us devize of ease and everlasting rest.'

'Ah! dearest lord,' said then that doughty
   knight,
'Of ease or rest I may not yet devize;
For by the faith which I to armes have
   plight,
I bownden am streight after this emprize,
As that your daughter can ye well advize,
Backe to retourne to that great Faery
   Queene,
And her to serve six yeares in warlike
   wize,
Gainst that proud Paynim King that
   works her teene:
Therefore I ought crave pardon, till I
   there have beene.'

'Unhappy falls that hard necessity,'
Quoth he, 'the troubler of my happy
   peace,
And vowed foe of my felicity;
Ne I against the same can justly preace:
But since that band ye cannot now re-
   lease,
Nor doen undoe, (for vowes may not be
   vayne)

Soone as the terme of those six yeares
   shall cease,
Ye then shall hether backe retourne
   agayne,
The marriage to accomplish vowd betwixt
   you twayn.

Which, for my part, I covet to performe,
In sort as through the world I did pro-
   clame,
That who so kild that monster most de-
   forme,
And him in hardy battayle overcame,
Should have mine onely daughter to his
   dame,
And of my kingdome heyre apparaunt
   bee:
Therefore since now to thee perteynes the
   same,
By dew desert of noble chevalree,
Both daughter and eke kingdome, lo! I
   yield to thee.'

Then forth he called that his daughter
   fayre,
The fairest Un', his onely daughter deare,
His onely daughter and his only hayre;
Who forth proceeding with sad sober
   cheare,
As bright as doth the morning starre ap-
   peare
Out of the east, with flaming lockes be-
   dight,
To tell that dawning day is drawing neare,
And to the world does bring long wished
   light;
So faire and fresh that lady shewd her
   selfe in sight:

So faire and fresh, as freshest flowre in
   May;
For she had layd her mournefull stole
   aside,
And widow-like sad wimple throwne away,
Wherewith her heavenly beautie she did
   hide,
Whiles on her wearie journey she did ride;
And on her now a garment she did weare
All lilly white, withoutten spot or pride,

That seemd like silke and silver woven
neare,
But neither silke nor silver therein did
appeare.

The blazing brightnesse of her beauties
beame,
And glorious light of her sunshyny face,
To tell, were as to strive against the
streame:
My ragged rimes are all too rude and bace,
Her heavenly lineaments for to enchace.
Ne wonder; for her own deare loved
knight,
All were she daily with himselfe in place,
Did wonder much at her celestiall sight:
Oft had he seene her faire, but never so
faire dight.

So fairely dight, when she in presence
came,
She to her syre made humble reverence,
And bowed low, that her right well be-
came,
And added grace unto her excellence:
Who with great wisedome and grave elo-
quence
Thus gan to say— But eare he thus had
sayd,
With flying speede, and seeming great pre-
tence,
Came running in, much like a man dis-
mayd,
A messenger with letters, which his mes-
sage sayd.

All in the open hall amazed stood
At suddeinnesse of that unwary sight,
And wondred at his breathlesse hasty
mood.
But he for nought would stay his passage
right,
Till fast before the king he did alight;
Where falling flat, great humblesse he did
make,
And kist the ground whereon his foot was
pight;
Then to his handes that writt he did be-
take,

Which he disclosing, read thus, as the paper spake:

'To thee, most mighty king of Eden fayre,
Her greeting sends in these sad lines ad-
drest
The wofull daughter and forsaken heyre
Of that great Emperour of all the West;
And bids thee be advized for the best,
Ere thou thy daughter linck in holy band
Of wedlocke to that new unknowen guest:
For he already plighted his right hand
Unto another love, and to another land.

'To me, sad mayd, or rather widow sad,
He was affyaunced long time before,
And sacred pledges he both gave, and had,
False erraunt knight, infamous, and for-
swore!
Witnesse the burning altars, which he
swore,
And guilty heavens of his bold perjury,
Which though he hath polluted oft of yore,
Yet I to them for judgement just doe fly,
And them conjure t' avenge this shamefull
injury.

'Therefore since mine he is, or free or
bond,
Or false or trew, or living or else dead,
Withhold, O soverayne prince, your hasty
hond
From knitting league with him, I you
aread;
Ne weene my right with strength adowne
to tread,
Through weakenesse of my widowhed or
woe:
For Truth is strong, her rightfull cause to
plead,
And shall finde friends, if need requireth
soe.
So bids thee well to fare, thy neither friend
nor foe,   FIDESSA.'

When he these bitter byting wordes had
red,
The tydings straunge did him abashed
make,

That still he sate long time astonished,
As in great muse, ne word to creature
spake.
At last his solemne silence thus he brake,
With doubtfull eyes fast fixed on his
guest:
'Redoubted knight, that for myne only
sake
Thy life and honor late adventurest,
Let nought be hid from me, that ought to
be exprest.

'What meane these bloody vowes and idle
threats,
Throwne out from womanish impatient
mynd?
What hevens? what altars? what enraged
heates,
Here heaped up with termes of love un-
kynd,
My conscience cleare with guilty bands
would bynd?
High God be witnesse, that I guiltlesse
ame!
But if your selfe, sir knight, ye faulty
fynd,
Or wrapped be in loves of former dame,
With cryme doe not it cover, but disclose
the same.'

To whom the Redcrosse Knight this an-
swere sent:
'My lord, my king, be nought hereat dis-
mayd,
Till well ye wote by grave intendiment,
What woman, and wherefore, doth me up-
brayd
With breach of love and loialty betrayd.
It was in my mishaps, as hitherward
I lately traveild, that unwares I strayd
Out of my way, through perils straunge
and hard;
That day should faile me ere I had them
all declard.

'There did I find, or rather I was fownd
Of this false woman, that Fidessa hight;
Fidessa hight the falsest dame on grownd,
Most false Duessa, royall richly dight,

That easy was t' inveigle weaker sight:
Who by her wicked arts and wiely skill,
Too false and strong for earthly skill or
might,
Unwares me wrought unto her wicked
will,
And to my foe betrayd, when least I
feared ill.'

Then stepped forth the goodly royall
mayd,
And on the ground her selfe prostrating
low,
With sober countenaunce thus to him
sayd:
'O pardon me, my soveraine lord, to
sheow
The secret treasons, which of late I know
To have bene wrought by that false sor-
ceresse.
Shee, onely she, it is, that earst did throw
This gentle knight into so great distresse,
That death him did awaite in daily
wretchednesse.

'And now it seemes, that she suborned
hath
This crafty messenger with letters vaine,
To worke new woe and improvided scath,
By breaking of the band betwixt us twaine;
Wherein she used hath the practicke paine
Of this false footman, clokt with simple-
nesse,
Whome if ye please for to discover plaine,
Ye shall him Archimago find, I ghesse,
The falsest man alive; who tries, shall find
no lesse.'

The king was greatly moved at her speach,
And, all with suddein indignation fraight,
Bad on that messenger rude hands to
reach.
Eftsoones the gard, which on his state did
wait,
Attacht that faytor false, and bound him
strait:
Who, seeming sorely chauffed at his band,
As chained beare, whom cruell dogs doe
bait,

With ydle force did faine them to withstand,
And often semblaunce made to scape out
of their hand.

But they him layd full low in dungeon
deepe,
And bound him hand and foote with yron
chains,
And with continual watch did warely
keepe:
Who then would thinke, that by his subtile trains
He could escape fowle death or deadly
pains?
Thus when that princes wrath was paci-
fide,
He gan renew the late forbidden bains,
And to the knight his daughter deare he
tyde,
With sacred rites and vowes for ever to
abyde.

His owne two hands the holy knotts did
knitt,
That none but death for ever can divide;
His owne two hands, for such a turne
most fitt,
The housling fire did kindle and provide,
And holy water thereon sprinckled wide;
At which the bushy teade a groome did
light,
And sacred lamp in secret chamber hide,
Where it should not be quenched day nor
night,
For feare of evill fates, but burnen ever
bright.

Then gan they sprinckle all the posts with
wine,
And made great feast to solemnize that
day:
They all perfumde with frankincense divine,
And precious odours fetcht from far away,
That all the house did sweat with great
aray:
And all the while sweete musicke did apply

Her curious skill, the warbling notes to
play,
To drive away the dull melancholy;
The whiles one sung a song of love and
jollity.

During the which there was an heavenly
noise
Heard sownd through all the pallace
pleasantly,
Like as it had bene many an angels voice
Singing before th' Eternall Majesty,
In their trinall triplicities on hye;
Yett wist no creature, whence that hev-
enly sweet
Proceeded, yet each one felt secretly,
Himselfe thereby refte of his sences meet,
And ravished with rare impression in his
sprite.

Great joy was made that day of young
and old,
And solemne feast proclaymd throughout
the land,
That their exceeding merth may not be told:
Suffice it heare by signes to understand
The usuall joyes at knitting of loves band.
Thrise happy man the knight himselfe
did hold,
Possessed of his ladies hart and hand,
And ever, when his eie did her behold,
His heart did seeme to melt in pleasures
manifold.

Her joyous presence and sweet company
In full content he there did long enjoy,
Ne wicked envy, ne vile gealosy,
His deare delights were hable to annoy:
Yet, swimming in that sea of blisfull joy,
He nought forgott, how he whilome had
sworne,
In case he could that monstrous beast de-
stroy,
Unto his Faery Queene backe to retourne:
The which he shortly did, and Una left to
mourne.

Now strike your sailes, yee jolly mari-
ners,

For we be come unto a quiet rode,
Where we must land some of our passen-
gers,
And light this weary vessell of her lode.
Here she a while may make her safe
abode,
Till she repaired have her tackles spent,
And wants supplide; and then againe
abroad
On the long voiage whereto she is bent:
Well may she speede, and fairely finish her
intent.

Muiopotmos: or
The Fate of the Butterflie

I SING of deadly dolorous debate,
Stir'd up through wrathfull Nemesis de-
spight,
Betwixt two mightie ones of great estate,
Drawne into armes, and proofe of mortall
fight,
Through prowd ambition and hartswell-
ing hate,
Whilest neither could the others greater
might
And sdeignfull scorne endure; that from
small jarre
Their wraths at length broke into open
warre.

The roote whereof and tragicall effect,
Vouchsafe, O thou the mournfulst Muse
of nyne,
That wontst the tragick stage for to di-
rect,
In funerall complaints and waylfull tyne,
Reveale to me, and all the meanes detect
Through which sad Clarion did at last
declyne
To lowest wretchednes: And is there then
Such rancour in the harts of mightie
men?

Of all the race of silver-winged flies
Which doo possesse the empire of the
aire,
Betwixt the centred earth and azure
skies,

Was none more favourable, nor more faire,
Whilst heaven did favour his felicities,
Then Clarion, the eldest sonne and haire
Of Muscaroll, and in his fathers sight
Of all alive did seeme the fairest wight.

With fruitfull hope his aged breast he fed
Of future good, which his yong toward
yeares,
Full of brave courage and bold hardyhed,
Above th' ensample of his equall peares,
Did largely promise, and to him forered
(Whilst oft his heart did melt in tender
teares)
That he in time would sure prove such an
one,
As should be worthie of his fathers throne.

The fresh yong flie, in whom the kindly
fire
Of lustfull yongth began to kindle fast,
Did much disdaine to subject his desire
To loathsome sloth, or houres in ease to
wast,
But joy'd to range abroad in fresh attire,
Through the wide compas of the ayrie
coast,
And with unwearied wings each part t' in-
quire
Of the wide rule of his renowned sire.

For he so swift and nimble was of flight,
That from this lower tract he dar'd to stie
Up to the clowdes, and thence, with pin-
eons light,
To mount aloft unto the christall skie,
To vew the workmanship of heavens
hight:
Whence downe descending he along would
flie
Upon the streaming rivers, sport to finde;
And oft would dare to tempt the trou-
blous winde.

So on a summers day, when season milde
With gentle calme the world had quieted,
And high in heaven Hyperions fierie
childe
Ascending, did his beames abroad dispred,

Whiles all the heavens on lower creatures
smilde,
Yong Clarion, with vauntfull lustiehead,
After his guize did cast abroad to fare,
And theretoo gan his furnitures prepare.

His breastplate first, that was of substance
pure,
Before his noble heart he firmely bound,
That mought his life from yron death as-
sure,
And ward his gentle corpes from cruell
wound:
For it by arte was framed to endure
The bit of balefull steele and bitter
stownd,
No lesse than that which Vulcane made
to sheild
Achilles life from fate of Troyan field.

And then about his shoulders broad he
threw
An hairie hide some of wilde beast, whom
hee
In salvage forrest by adventure slew,
And reft the spoyle his ornament to bee:
Which, spredding all his backe with dread-
full vew,
Made all that him so horrible did see
Thinke him Alcides with the lyons skin,
When the Næmean conquest he did win.

Upon his head, his glistering burganet,
The which was wrought by wonderous de-
vice,
And curiously engraven, he did set:
The mettall was of rare and passing price;
Not Bilbo steele, nor brasse from Corinth
fet,
Nor costly oricalche from strange Phœ-
nice;
But such as could both Phœbus arrowes
ward,
And th' hayling darts of heaven beating
hard.

Therein two deadly weapons fixt he bore,
Strongly outlaunced towards either side,
Like two sharpe speares, his enemies to
gore:

Like as a warlike brigandine, applyde
To fight, layes forth her threatfull pikes
afore,
The engines which in them sad death doo
hyde:
So did this flie outstretch his fearefull
hornes,
Yet so as him their terrour more adornes.

Lastly his shinie wings, as silver bright,
Painted with thousand colours, passing
farre
All painters skill, he did about him dight:
Not halfe so manie sundrie colours arre
In Iris bowe, ne heaven doth shine so
bright,
Distinguished with manie a twinckling
starre,
Nor Junoes bird in her ey-spotted traine
So manie goodly colours doth containe.

Ne (may it be withouten perill spoken)
The Archer god, the sonne of Cytheree,
That joyes on wretched lovers to be
wroken,
And heaped spoyles of bleeding harts to
see,
Beares in his wings so manie a changefull
token.
Ah! my liege lord, forgive it unto mee,
If ought against thine honour I have tolde;
Yet sure those wings were fairer mani-
folde.

Full manie a ladie faire, in court full oft
Beholding them, him secretly envide,
And wisht that two such fannes, so silken
soft
And golden faire, her love would her pro-
vide;
Or that, when them the gorgeous flie had
doft,
Some one, that would with grace be grati-
fide,
From him would steale them privily away,
And bring to her so precious a pray.

Report is that Dame Venus on a day,
In spring when flowres doo clothe the
fruitful ground,

Walking abroad with all her nymphes to
    play,
Bad her faire damzels, flocking her
    arownd,
To gather flowres, her forhead to array.
Emongst the rest a gentle nymph was
    found,
Hight Astery, excelling all the crewe
In curteous usage and unstained hewe.

Who, being nimbler joynted than the rest,
And more industrious, gathered more
    store
Of the fields honour than the others best;
Which they in secret harts envying sore,
Tolde Venus, when her as the worthiest
She praisd, that Cupide (as they heard
    before)
Did lend her secret aide in gathering
Into her lap the children of the Spring.

Whereof the goddesse gathering jealous
    feare,
Not yet unmindfull how not long agoe
Her sonne to Psyche secrete love did
    beare,
And long it close conceal'd, till mickle woe
Thereof arose, and manie a rufull teare,
Reason with sudden rage did overgoe,
And giving hastie credit to th' accuser,
Was led away of them that did abuse her.

Eftsoones that damzel, by her heavenly
    might,
She turn'd into a winged butterflie,
In the wide aire to make her wandring
    flight;
And all those flowres, with which so plen-
    teouslie
Her lap she filled had, that bred her spight,
She placed in her wings, for memorie
Of her pretended crime, though crime
    none were:
Since which that flie them in her wings
    doth beare.

Thus the fresh Clarion, being readie dight,
Unto his journey did himselfe addresse,
And with good speed began to take his
    flight:

Over the fields, in his franke lustinesse,
And all the champion he soared light,
And all the countrey wide he did possesse,
Feeding upon their pleasures bounteouslie,
That none gainsaid, nor none did him
    envie.

The woods, the rivers, and the medowes
    green,
With his aire-cutting wings he measured
    wide,
Ne did he leave the mountaines bare un-
    seene,
Nor the ranke grassie fennes delights un-
    tride,
But none of these, how ever sweete they
    beene,
Mote please his fancie, nor him cause t'
    abide:
His choicefull sense with everie change
    doth flit;
No common things may please a wavering
    wit.

To the gay gardins his unstaid desire
Him wholly caried, to refresh his sprights:
There lavish Nature, in her best attire,
Powres forth sweete odors, and alluring
    sights;
And Arte, with her contending, doth
    aspire
T' excell the naturall with made delights:
And all that faire or pleasant may be
    found
In riotous excesse doth there abound.

There he arriving, round about doth flie,
From bed to bed, from one to other bor-
    der,
And takes survey, with curious busie eye,
Of everie flowre and herbe there set in
    order;
Now this, now that, he tasteth tenderly,
Yet none of them he rudely doth disorder,
Ne with his feete their silken leaves de-
    face;
But pastures on the pleasures of each
    place.

And evermore with most varietie,
And change of sweetnesse (for all change
　　is sweete)
He casts his glutton sense to satisfie;
Now sucking of the sap of herbe most
　　meete,
Or of the deaw, which yet on them does
　　lie,
Now in the same bathing his tender feete:
And then he pearcheth on some braunch
　　thereby,
To weather him, and his moyst wings to
　　dry.

And then againe he turneth to his play,
To spoyle the pleasures of that paradise:
The wholsome saulge, and lavender still
　　gray,
Ranke smelling rue, and cummin good for
　　eyes,
The roses raigning in the pride of May,
Sharpe isope, good for greene wounds rem-
　　edies,
Faire marigoldes, and bees-alluring thime,
Sweete marjoram, and daysies decking
　　prime:

Coole violets, and orpine growing still,
Embathed balme, and chearfull galingale,
Fresh costmarie, and breathfull camomill,
Dull poppie, and drink-quickning setuale,
Veyne-healing verven, and hed-purging
　　dill,
Sound savorie, and bazill hartie-hale,
Fat colworts, and comforting perseline,
Colde lettuce, and refreshing rosmarine.

And whatso else of vertue good or ill
Grewe in this gardin, fetcht from farre
　　away,
Of everie one he takes, and tastes at will,
And on their pleasures greedily doth pray.
Then, when he hath both plaid, and fed
　　his fill,
In the warme sunne he doth himselfe em-
　　bay,
And there him rests in riotous suffisaunce
Of all his gladfulnes and kingly joyaunce.

What more felicitie can fall to creature
Than to enjoy delight with libertie,
And to be lord of all the workes of Nature,
To raine in th' aire from earth to highest
　　skie,
To feed on flowres and weeds of glorious
　　feature,
To take what ever thing doth please the
　　eie?
Who rests not pleased with such happines,
Well worthie he to taste of wretchednes.

But what on earth can long abide in state,
Or who can him assure of happie day;
Sith morning faire may bring fowle eve-
　　ning late,
And least mishap the most blisse alter
　　may?
For thousand perills lie in close awaite
About us daylie, to worke our decay;
That none, except a God, or God him
　　guide,
May them avoyde, or remedie provide.

And whatso heavens in their secret doome
Ordained have, how can fraile fleshly
　　wight
Forecast, but it must needs to issue come?
The sea, the aire, the fire, the day, the
　　night,
And th' armies of their creatures all and
　　some
Do serve to them, and with importune
　　might
Warre against us, the vassals of their will.
Who then can save what they dispose to
　　spill?

Not thou, O Clarion, though fairest thou
Of all thy kinde, unhappie happie flie,
Whose cruell fate is woven even now
Of Joves owne hand, to worke thy miserie:
Ne may thee helpe the manie hartie vow,
Which thy olde sire with sacred pietie
Hath powred forth for thee, and th' altars
　　sprent:
Nought may thee save from heavens
　　avengement.

It fortuned (as heavens had behight)
That in this gardin, where yong Clarion
Was wont to solace him, a wicked wight,
The foe of faire things, th' author of con-
    fusion,
The shame of Nature, the bondslave of
    spight,
Had lately built his hatefull mansion,
And, lurking closely, in awayte now lay,
How he might anie in his trap betray.

But when he spide the joyous butterflie
In this faire plot dispacing too and fro,
Fearles of foes and hidden jeopardie,
Lord! how he gan for to bestirre him tho,
And to his wicked worke each part applie!
His heart did earne against his hated foe,
And bowels so with ranckling poyson
    swelde,
That scarce the skin the strong contagion
    helde.

The cause why he this flie so maliced
Was (as in stories it is written found)
For that his mother which him bore and
    bred,
The most fine-fingred workwoman on
    ground,
Arachne, by his meanes was vanquished
Of Pallas, and in her owne skill confound,
When she with her for excellence con-
    tended,
That wrought her shame, and sorrow
    never ended.

For the Tritonian goddesse, having hard
Her blazed fame, which all the world had
    fil'd,
Came downe to prove the truth, and due
    reward
For her prais-worthie workmanship to
    yeild:
But the presumptuous damzel rashly dar'd
The goddesse selfe to chalenge to the field,
And to compare with her in curious skill
Of workes with loome, with needle, and
    with quill.

Minerva did the chalenge not refuse,
But deign'd with her the paragon to make:
So to their worke they sit, and each doth
    chuse
What storie she will for her tapet take.
Arachne figur'd how Jove did abuse
Europa like a bull, and on his backe
Her through the sea did beare; so lively
    seene,
That it true sea and true bull ye would
    weene.

She seem'd still backe unto the land to
    looke,
And her play-fellowes aide to call, and
    feare
The dashing of the waves, that up she
    tooke
Her daintie feete, and garments gathered
    neare:
But (Lord!) how she in everie member
    shooke,
When as the land she saw no more ap-
    peare,
But a wilde wildernes of waters deepe!
Then gan she greatly to lament and weepe.

Before the bull she pictur'd winged Love,
With his yong brother Sport, light fluttering
Upon the waves, as each had been a dove;
The one his bowe and shafts, the other
    spring
A burning teade about his head did move,
As in their syres new love both triumphing:
And manie Nymphes about them flocking
    round,
And manie Tritons, which their hornes did
    sound.

And round about, her worke she did em-
    pale
With a faire border wrought of sundrie
    flowres,
Enwoven with an yvie winding trayle:
A goodly worke, full fit for kingly bowres,
Such as Dame Pallas, such as Envie pale,
That al good things with venemous tooth
    devowres,
Could not accuse. Then gan the god-
    desse bright
Her selfe likewise unto her worke to dight.

She made the storie of the olde debate,
Which she with Neptune did for Athens
    trie:
Twelve gods doo sit around in royall state,
And Jove in midst with awfull majestie,
To judge the strife betweene them stirred
    late:
Each of the gods by his like visnomie
Eathe to be knowen; but Jove above them
    all,
By his great lookes and power imperiall.

Before them stands the god of seas in place,
Clayming that sea-coast citie as his right,
And strikes the rockes with his three-
    forked mace;
Whenceforth issues a warlike steed in
    sight,
The signe by which he chalengeth the place;
That all the gods, which saw his wondrous
    might,
Did surely deeme the victorie his due:
But seldome seene, forejudgement prov-
    eth true.

Then to her selfe she gives her Aegide
    shield,
And steelhed speare, and morion on her
    hedd,
Such as she oft is seene in warlicke field:
Then sets she forth, how with her weapon
    dredd
She smote the ground, the which streight
    foorth did yield
A fruitfull olyve tree, with berries spredd,
That all the gods admir'd; then all the
    storie
She compast with a wreathe of olyves
    hoarie.

Emongst those leaves she made a butterflie,
With excellent device and wondrous slight,
Fluttring among the olives wantonly,
That seem'd to live, so like it was in sight:
The velvet nap which on his wings doth lie,
The silken downe with which his backe is
    dight,
His broad outstretched hornes, his hayrie
    thies,
His glorious colours, and his glistering eies.

Which when Arachne saw, as overlaid
And mastered with workmanship so rare,
She stood astonied long, ne ought gaine-
    said,
And with fast fixed eyes on her did stare,
And by her silence, signe of one dismaid,
The victorie did yeeld her as her share:
Yet did she inly fret, and felly burne,
And all her blood to poysonous rancor
    turne:

That shortly from the shape of woman-
    hed,
Such as she was, when Pallas she at-
    tempted,
She grew to hideous shape of dryrihed,
Pined with griefe of follie late repented:
Eftsoones her white streight legs were al-
    tered
To crooked crawling shankes, of marrowe
    empted,
And her faire face to fowle and loathsome
    hewe,
And her fine corpes to a bag of venim
    grewe.

This cursed creature, mindfull of that olde
Enfested grudge, the which his mother
    felt,
So soone as Clarion he did beholde,
His heart with vengefull malice inly swelt;
And weaving straight a net with manie a
    folde
About the cave in which he lurking dwelt,
With fine small cords about it stretched
    wide,
So finely sponne that scarce they could be
    spide.

Not anie damzell, which her vaunteth
    most
In skilfull knitting of soft silken twyne;
Nor anie weaver, which his worke doth
    boast
In dieper, in damaske, or in lyne;
Nor anie skil'd in workmanship embost;
Nor anie skil'd in loupes of fingring fine,
Might in their divers cunning ever dare,
With this so curious networke to compare.

Ne doo I thinke that that same subtil gin,
The which the Lemnian god framde craf-
　　tilie,
Mars sleeping with his wife to compasse
　　in,
That all the gods with common mockerie
Might laugh at them, and scorne their
　　shamefull sin,
Was like to this.　This same he did applie
For to entrap the careles Clarion,
That rang'd each where without suspition.

Suspition of friend, nor feare of foe,
That hazarded his health, had he at all,
But walkt at will, and wandred too and
　　fro,
In the pride of his freedome principall:
Litle wist he his fatall future woe,
But was secure; the liker he to fall.
He likest is to fall into mischaunce,
That is regardles of his governaunce.

Yet still Aragnoll (so his foe was hight)
Lay lurking covertly him to surprise,
And all his gins, that him entangle might,
Drest in good order as he could devise.
At length the foolish flie, without fore-
　　sight,
As he that did all daunger quite despise,
Toward those parts came flying careleslie,
Where hidden was his hatefull enemie.

Who, seeing him, with secrete joy there-
　　fore
Did tickle inwardly in everie vaine,
And his false hart, fraught with all trea-
　　sons store,
Was fil'd with hope his purpose to obtaine:
Himselfe he close upgathered more and
　　more
Into his den, that his deceiptfull traine
By his there being might not be bewraid,
Ne anie noyse, ne anie motion made.

Like as a wily foxe, that, having spide
Where on a sunnie banke the lambes doo
　　play,
Full closely creeping by the hinder side,
Lyes in ambushment of his hoped pray,

Ne stirreth limbe, till, seeing readie tide,
He rusheth forth, and snatcheth quite
　　away
One of the litle yonglings unawares:
So to his worke Aragnoll him prepares.

Who now shall give unto my heavie eyes
A well of teares, that all may overflow?
Or where shall I finde lamentable cryes,
And mournfull tunes enough my griefe to
　　show?
Helpe, O thou Tragick Muse, me to devise
Notes sad enough, t' expresse this bitter
　　throw:
For loe! the drerie stownd is now arrived,
That of all happines hath us deprived.

The luckles Clarion, whether cruell Fate
Or wicked Fortune faultles him misled,
Or some ungracious blast out of the gate
Of Aeoles raine perforce him drove on hed,
Was (O sad hap and howre unfortunate!)
With violent swift flight forth caried
Into the cursed cobweb, which his foe
Had framed for his finall overthroe.

There the fond flie, entangled, strugled
　　long,
Himselfe to free thereout; but all in vaine.
For, striving more, the more in laces
　　strong
Himselfe he tide, and wrapt his winges
　　twaine
In lymie snares the subtill loupes among;
That in the ende he breathelesse did re-
　　maine,
And all his youthly forces idly spent
Him to the mercie of th' avenger lent.

Which when the greisly tyrant did espie,
Like a grimme lyon rushing with fierce
　　might
Out of his den, he seized greedelie
On the resistles pray, and with fell spight,
Under the left wing stroke his weapon slie
Into his heart, that his deepe groning
　　spright
In bloodie streames foorth fled into the
　　aire,
His bodie left the spectacle of care.

MICHAEL DRAYTON
(1563-1632)

To the Cambro-Britons and their Harp, his Ballad of Agincourt

FAIR stood the wind for France,
When we our sails advance,
Nor now to prove our chance
    Longer will tarry;
But putting to the main,
At Caux, the mouth of Seine,
With all his martial train,
    Landed King Harry.

And taking many a fort,
Furnished in warlike sort,
Marcheth tow'rds Agincourt
    In happy hour;
Skirmishing day by day,
With those that stopp'd his way,
Where the French gen'ral lay
    With all his power.

Which in his height of pride,
King Henry to deride,
His ransom to provide,
    To the king sending.
Which he neglects the while,
As from a nation vile,
Yet with an angry smile
    Their fall portending.

And turning to his men,
Quoth our brave Henry then,
Though they to one be ten,
    Be not amazed.
Yet have we well begun,
Battles so bravely won,
Have ever to the sun
    By fame been raised.

And for myself (quoth he),
This my full rest shall be,
England ne'er mourn for me,
    Nor more esteem me.
Victor I will remain,
Or on this earth lie slain,
Never shall she sustain
    Loss to redeem me.

Poitiers and Cressy tell,
When most their pride did swell,
Under our swords they fell,
    No less our skill is,
Than when our grandsire-great,
Claiming the regal seat,
By many a warlike feat
    Lopp'd the French lilies.

The Duke of York so dread
The eager vaward led,
With the main, Henry sped,
    Amongst his hench-men.
Exeter had the rear,
A braver man not there,
O Lord, how hot they were,
    On the false Frenchmen!

They now to fight are gone,
Armour on armour shone,
Drum now to drum did groan,
    To hear, was wonder;
That with the cries they make,
The very earth did shake,
Trumpet to trumpet spake,
    Thunder to thunder.

Well it thine age became,
O noble Erpingham,
Which didst the signal aim
    To our hid forces;
When from a meadow by,
Like a storm suddenly,
The English archery
    Stuck the French horses.

With Spanish yew so strong,
Arrows a cloth-yard long,
That like to serpents stung,
    Piercing the weather;
None from his fellow starts,
But playing manly parts,
And like true English hearts,
    Stuck close together.

When down their bows they threw,
And forth their bilbos drew,
And on the French they flew,
    Not one was tardy;

Arms were from shoulders sent,
Scalps to the teeth were rent,
Down the French peasants went,
    Our men were hardy.

This while our noble king,
His broad sword brandishing,
Down the French host did ding,
    As to o'erwhelm it,
And many a deep wound lent,
His arms with blood besprent,
And many a cruel dent
    Bruised his helmet.

Gloucester, that duke so good,
Next of the royal blood,
For famous England stood,
    With his brave brother;
Clarence, in steel so bright,
Though but a maiden knight,
Yet in that furious fight
    Scarce such another.

Warwick in blood did wade,
Oxford the foe invade,
And cruel slaughter made,
    Still as they ran up;
Suffolk his axe did ply,
Beaumont and Willoughby,
Bare them right doughtily,
    Ferrers and Fanhope.

Upon Saint Crispin's day
Fought was this noble fray,
Which fame did not delay
    To England to carry;
O when shall English men
With such acts fill a pen,
Or England breed again
    Such a King Harry?

WILLIAM SHAKESPEARE
(1564-1616)

Under the Greenwood Tree

UNDER the greenwood tree
Who loves to lie with me,
And turn his merry note
Unto the sweet bird's throat,
Come hither, come hither, come hither!
    Here shall he see
        No enemy
But winter and rough weather.

Who doth ambition shun,
And loves to live i' the sun,
Seeking the food he eats,
And pleased with what he gets,
Come hither, come hither, come hither!
    Here shall he see
        No enemy
But winter and rough weather.

If it do come to pass
That any man turn ass,
Leaving his wealth and ease
A stubborn will to please,
Ducdame, ducdame, ducdame!
    Here shall he see
        Gross fools as he,
An if he will come to me.

Hark, Hark! the Lark

HARK, hark! the lark at heaven's gate
    sings,
    And Phœbus gins arise
His steeds to water at those springs
    On chalic'd flowers that lies;
And winking Mary-buds begin
    To ope their golden eyes;
With every thing that pretty is,
    My lady sweet, arise,
        Arise, arise.

Full Fathom Five

FULL fathom five thy father lies;
    Of his bones are coral made;
Those are pearls that were his eyes:
    Nothing of him that doth fade
But doth suffer a sea-change
Into something rich and strange.
Sea-nymphs hourly ring his knell:
    Ding-dong.
    Hark! now I hear them,—ding-dong,
    bell.

Hamlet

Act II, Scene II

A room in the castle

Flourish. Enter KING, QUEEN, ROSEN-
CRANTZ, GUILDENSTERN, *with others.*

King. Welcome, dear Rosencrantz and
Guildenstern!
Moreover that we much did long to see
you,
The need we have to use you did provoke
Our hasty sending. Something have you
heard
Of Hamlet's transformation; so I call it,
Since not the exterior nor the inward man
Resembles that it was. What it should
be,
More than his father's death, that thus
hath put him
So much from the understanding of him-
self,
I cannot dream of. I entreat you both,
That, being of so young days brought up
with him
And since so neighbour'd to his youth and
humour,
That you vouchsafe your rest here in
our court
Some little time; so by your companies
To draw him on to pleasures, and to
gather
So much as from occasions you may
glean,
[Whether aught, to us unknown, afflicts
him thus,]
That, open'd, lies within our remedy.

Queen. Good gentlemen, he hath much
talk'd of you;
And sure I am two men there are not
living
To whom he more adheres. If it will
please you
To show us so much gentry and good
will
As to expend your time with us a while
For the supply and profit of our hope,
Your visitation shall receive such thanks
As fits a king's remembrance.

Ros. Both your Majesties
Might, by the sovereign power you have
of us,
Put your dread pleasures more into com-
mand
Than to entreaty.

Guil. We both obey,
And here give up ourselves, in the full
bent
To lay our services freely at your feet,
To be commanded.

King. Thanks, Rosencrantz and gentle
Guildenstern.

Queen. Thanks, Guildenstern and
gentle Rosencrantz,
And I beseech you instantly to visit
My too much changed son. Go, some of
ye,
And bring the gentlemen where Hamlet
is.

Guil. Heavens make our presence and
our practices
Pleasant and helpful to him!

Queen. Amen!
[*Exeunt Rosencrantz, Guildenstern, and some Attendants*].

Enter POLONIUS.

Pol. The ambassadors from Norway,
my good lord,
Are joyfully return'd.

King. Thou still hast been the father
of good news.

Pol. Have I, my lord? Assure you,
my good liege,
I hold my duty as I hold my soul,
Both to my God and to my gracious king.
And I do think, or else this brain of mine
Hunts not the trail of policy so sure
As it hath us'd to do, that I have found
The very cause of Hamlet's lunacy.

King. O, speak of that; that I do long
to hear.

Pol. Give first admittance to the ambassadors.
My news shall be the fruit to that great
feast.

King. Thyself do grace to them, and
bring them in. [*Exit Polonius.*

He tells me, my sweet queen, that he
    hath found
The head and source of all your son's
    distemper.
  Queen. I doubt it is no other but the
    main,
His father's death and our o'erhasty
    marriage.

Re-enter POLONIUS, *with* VOLTIMAND
and CORNELIUS.

  King. Well, we shall sift him.—Wel-
    come, my good friends!
Say, Voltimand, what from our brother
    Norway?
  Volt. Most fair return of greetings
    and desires.
Upon our first, he sent out to suppress
His nephew's levies, which to him
    appear'd
To be a preparation 'gainst the Polack,
But, better look'd into, he truly found
It was against your Highness. Whereat
    grieved,
That so his sickness, age, and impotence
Was falsely borne in hand, sends out
    arrests
On Fortinbras; which he, in brief, obeys,
Receives rebuke from Norway, and in
    fine
Makes vow before his uncle never more
To give the assay of arms against your
    Majesty.
Whereon old Norway, overcome with
    joy,
Gives him three thousand crowns in an-
    nual fee,
And his commission to employ those
    soldiers,
So levied as before, against the Polack;
With an entreaty, herein further shown,
             [Giving a paper.]
That it might please you to give quiet
    pass
Through your dominions for his enter-
    prise,
On such regards of safety and allowance
As therein are set down.
  King.   It likes us well;

And at our more consider'd time we 'll
    read,
Answer, and think upon this business.
Meantime we thank you for your well-
    took labour.
Go to your rest; at night we 'll feast
    together.
Most welcome home!
    [Exeunt Voltimand and Cornelius.]
  Pol.   This business is well ended.
My liege, and madam, to expostulate
What majesty should be, what duty is,
Why day is day, night night, and time is
    time,
Were nothing but to waste night, day,
    and time;
Therefore, since brevity is the soul of wit
And tediousness the limbs and outward
    flourishes,
I will be brief. Your noble son is mad.
Mad call I it; for, to define true madness,
What is 't but to be nothing else but mad?
But let that go.
  Queen.   More matter, with less art.
  Pol. Madam, I swear I use no art at
    all.
That he is mad, 't is true; 't is true 't is
    pity,
And pity 't is 't is true. A foolish figure!
But farewell it, for I will use no art.
Mad let us grant him then; and now
    remains
That we find out the cause of this effect,
Or rather say, the cause of this defect,
For this effect defective comes by cause.
Thus it remains, and the remainder thus.
Perpend.
I have a daughter—have whilst she is
    mine—
Who, in her duty and obedience, mark,
Hath given me this. Now gather, and
  surmise.
               [Reads the letter.]
"To the celestial and my soul's idol, the
most beautified Ophelia,"—
That 's an ill phrase, a vile phrase;
"beautified" is a vile phrase. But you
shall hear. Thus:
"In her excellent white bosom, these."

Queen. Came this from Hamlet to
her?

Pol. Good madam, stay a while. I
will be faithful.   [*Reads.*]

"Doubt thou the stars are fire,
    Doubt that the sun doth move,
Doubt truth to be a liar,
    But never doubt I love.

"O dear Ophelia, I am ill at these numbers. I have not art to reckon my
groans; but that I love thee best, O most
best, believe it. Adieu.

    Thine evermore, most dear lady,
        Whilst this machine is to him,
                        HAMLET."

This in obedience hath my daughter
    show'd me,
And more above, hath his solicitings,
As they fell out by time, by means, and
    place,
All given to mine ear.

King.   But how hath she
Receiv'd his love?

Pol.   What do you think of me?

King. As of a man faithful and honourable.

Pol. I would fain prove so. But what
might you think,
When I had seen this hot love on the
    wing,—
As I perceiv'd it, I must tell you that,
Before my daughter told me,—what
    might you,
Or my dear Majesty your queen here,
    think,
If I had play'd the desk or table-book,
Or given my heart a winking, mute and
    dumb,
Or look'd upon this love with idle sight,
What might you think? No, I went
    round to work,
And my young mistress thus I did be-
    speak:
"Lord Hamlet is a prince, out of thy star.
This must not be;" and then I precepts
    gave her,
That she should lock herself from his
    resort,
Admit no messengers, receive no tokens.

Which done, she took the fruits of my
    advice;
And he, repulsed—a short tale to make—
Fell into a sadness, then into a fast,
Thence to a watch, thence into a weak-
    ness,
Thence to a lightness, and, by this de-
    clension,
Into the madness whereon now he raves,
And all we wail for.

King.   Do you think 't is this?

Queen. It may be, very likely.

Pol. Hath there been such a time—I'd
fain know that—
That I have positively said, "'T is so,"
When it prov'd otherwise?

King.   Not that I know.

Pol. Take this from this, if this be
otherwise.
If circumstances lead me, I will find
Where truth is hid, though it were hid
    indeed
Within the centre.

King.   How may we try it further?

Pol. You know, sometimes he walks
four hours together
Here in the lobby.

Queen.   So he has, indeed.

Pol. At such a time I 'll loose my
daughter to him.
Be you and I behind an arras then;
Mark the encounter. If he love her not
And be not from his reason fallen
    thereon,
Let me be no assistant for a state,
But keep a farm and carters.

King.   We will try it.

Enter HAMLET, *reading on a book.*

Queen. But look where sadly the poor
wretch comes reading.

Pol. Away, I do beseech you, both
away.
I 'll board him presently.
    [*Exeunt King, Queen and Atten-
    dants.*]
                    O, give me leave,
How does my good Lord Hamlet?

Ham: Well, God-a-mercy.

Pol. Do you know me, my lord?

Ham. Excellent well; you are a fish-monger.

Pol. Not I, my lord.

Ham. Then I would you were so honest a man.

Pol. Honest, my lord!

Ham. Ay, sir. To be honest, as this world goes, is to be one man pick'd out of ten thousand.

Pol. That 's very true, my lord.

Ham. For if the sun breed maggots in a dead dog, being a good kissing carrion, —Have you a daughter?

Pol. I have, my lord.

Ham. Let her not walk i' the sun. Conception is a blessing, but not as your daughter may conceive. Friend, look to 't.

Pol. [*Aside.*] How say you by that? Still harping on my daughter. Yet he knew me not at first; he said I was a fish-monger. He is far gone, far gone. And truly in my youth I suff'red much extremity for love; very near this. I 'll speak to him again.—What do you read, my lord?

Ham. Words, words, words.

Pol. What is the matter, my lord?

Ham. Between who?

Pol. I mean, the matter you read, my lord.

Ham. Slanders, sir; for the satirical slave says here that old men have grey beards, that their faces are wrinkled, their eyes purging thick amber or plum-tree gum, and that they have a plentiful lack of wit, together with weak hams; all which, sir, though I most powerfully and potently believe, yet I hold it not honesty to have it thus set down; for you yourself, sir, should be old as I am, if like a crab you could go backward.

Pol. [*Aside.*] Though this be madness, yet there is method in 't.—Will you walk out of the air, my lord?

Ham. Into my grave?

Pol. Indeed, that is out o' the air. [*Aside.*] How pregnant sometimes his replies are! a happiness that often mad-ness hits on, which reason and sanity could not so prosperously be deliver'd of. I will leave him, and suddenly contrive the means of meeting between him and my daughter.—My honourable lord, I will most humbly take my leave of you.

Ham. You cannot, sir, take from me anything that I will more willingly part withal,—[*Aside*] except my life, my life.

Pol. Fare you well, my lord.

Ham. These tedious old fools!

Enter ROSENCRANTZ *and* GUILDENSTERN.

Pol. You go to seek my Lord Hamlet? There he is.

Ros. [*To Polonius.*] God save you, sir!

[*Exit Polonius.*]

Guil. Mine honour'd lord!

Ros. My most dear lord!

Ham. My excellent good friends! How dost thou, Guildenstern? Oh, Rosencrantz! Good lads, how do ye both?

Ros. As the indifferent children of the earth.

Guil. Happy, in that we are not over-happy.

On Fortune's cap we are not the very button.

Ham. Nor the soles of her shoe?

Ros. Neither, my lord.

Ham. Then you live about her waist, or in the middle of her favour?

Guil. Faith, her privates we.

Ham. In the secret parts of Fortune? Oh, most true; she is a strumpet. What 's the news?

Ros. None, my lord, but that the world 's grown honest.

Ham. Then is doomsday near. But your news is not true. Let me question more in particular. What have you, my good friends, deserved at the hands of Fortune, that she sends you to prison hither?

Guil. Prison, my lord?

Ham. Denmark 's a prison.

Ros. Then is the world one.

Ham. A goodly one, in which there are many confines, wards, and dungeons, Denmark being one o' the worst.

Ros. We think not so, my lord.

Ham. Why, then, 't is none to you; for there is nothing either good or bad, but thinking makes it so. To me it is a prison.

Ros. Why, then, your ambition makes it one. 'T is too narrow for your mind.

Ham. O God, I could be bounded in a nutshell and count myself a king of infinite space, were it not that I have bad dreams.

Guil. Which dreams indeed are ambition, for the very substance of the ambitious is merely the shadow of a dream.

Ham. A dream itself is but a shadow.

Ros. Truly, and I hold ambition of so airy and light a quality that it is but a shadow's shadow.

Ham. Then are our beggars bodies, and our monarchs and outstretch'd heroes the beggars' shadows. Shall we to the court? for, by my fay, I cannot reason.

Ros. }
Guil. } We 'll wait upon you.

Ham. No such matter. I will not sort you with the rest of my servants, for, to speak to you like an honest man, I am most dreadfully attended. But in the beaten way of friendship, what make you at Elsinore?

Ros. To visit you, my lord; no other occasion.

Ham. Beggar that I am, I am even poor in thanks, but I thank you; and sure, dear friends, my thanks are too dear a halfpenny. Were you not sent for? Is it your own inclining? Is it a free visitation? Come, deal justly with me. Come, come. Nay, speak.

Guil. What should we say, my lord?

Ham. Why, anything, but to the purpose. You were sent for; and there is a kind of confession in your looks which your modesties have not craft enough to colour. I know the good king and queen have sent for you.

Ros. To what end, my lord?

Ham. That you must teach me. But let me conjure you, by the rights of our fellowship, by the consonancy of our youth, by the obligation of our ever-preserved love, and by what more dear a better proposer could charge you withal, be even and direct with me, whether you were sent for or no!

Ros. [*Aside to Guil.*] What say you?

Ham. [*Aside.*] Nay, then, I have an eye of you.—If you love me, hold not off.

Guil. My lord, we were sent for.

Ham. I will tell you why; so shall my anticipation prevent your discovery, and your secrecy to the King and Queen moult no feather. I have of late—but wherefore I know not—lost all my mirth, forgone all custom of exercise; and indeed it goes so heavily with my disposition that this goodly frame, the earth, seems to me a sterile promontory, this most excellent canopy, the air, look you, this brave o'erhanging firmament, this majestical roof fretted with golden fire, why, it appears no other thing to me than a foul and pestilent congregation of vapours. What a piece of work is a man! How noble in reason! How infinite in faculty! In form and moving how express and admirable! In action how like an angel! In apprehension how like a god! The beauty of the world! The paragon of animals! And yet, to me, what is this quintessence of dust? Man delights not me,—no, nor woman neither, though by your smiling you seem to say so.

Ros. My lord, there was no such stuff in my thoughts.

Ham. Why did you laugh then, when I said, "Man delights not me"?

Ros. To think, my lord, if you delight not in man, what lenten entertainment the players shall receive from you. We coted them on the way, and hither are they coming to offer you service.

Ham. He that plays the king shall be welcome; his majesty shall have tribute of me; the adventurous knight shall use his foil and target; the lover shall not sigh gratis; the humorous man shall end his part in peace; the clown shall make those laugh whose lungs are tickle o' the sere; and the lady shall say her mind freely, or the blank verse shall halt for 't. What players are they?

Ros. Even those you were wont to take delight in, the tragedians of the city.

Ham. How chances it they travel? Their residence, both in reputation and profit, was better both ways.

Ros. I think their inhibition comes by the means of the late innovation.

Ham. Do they hold the same estimation they did when I was in the city? Are they so follow'd?

Ros. No, indeed, they are not.

Ham. How comes it? Do they grow rusty?

Ros. Nay, their endeavour keeps in the wonted pace; but there is, sir, an aery of children, little eyases, that cry out on the top of question, and are most tyrannically clapp'd for 't. These are now the fashion, and so berattle the common stages—so they call them—that many wearing rapiers are afraid of goose-quills and dare scarce come thither.

Ham. What, are they children? Who maintains 'em? How are they escoted? Will they pursue the quality no longer than they can sing? Will they not say afterwards, if they should grow themselves to common players,—as it is most like, if their means are no better—their writers do them wrong, to make them exclaim against their own succession?

Ros. Faith, there has been much to do on both sides, and the nation holds it no sin to tarre them to controversy. There was for a while no money bid for argument unless the poet and the player went to cuffs in the question.

Ham. Is 't possible?

Guil. O, there has been much throwing about of brains.

Ham. Do the boys carry it away?

Ros. Ay, that they do, my lord; Hercules and his load too.

Ham. It is not strange; for mine uncle is King of Denmark, and those that would make mows at him while my father lived, give twenty, forty, [fifty,] an hundred ducats apiece for his picture in little. ['Sblood,] there is something in this more than natural, if philosophy could find it out.

[Flourish for the Players.

Guil. There are the players.

Ham. Gentlemen, you are welcome to Elsinore. Your hands, come. The appurtenance of welcome is fashion and ceremony. Let me comply with you in the garb, lest my extent to the players, which, I tell you, must show fairly outward, should more appear like entertainment than yours. You are welcome; but my uncle-father and aunt-mother are deceiv'd.

Guil. In what, my dear lord?

Ham. I am but mad north-north-west. When the wind is southerly I know a hawk from a handsaw.

Enter POLONIUS.

Pol. Well be with you, gentlemen!

Ham. [*Aside to them.*] Hark you, Guildenstern, and you too, at each ear a hearer: that great baby you see there is not yet out of his swathing-clouts.

Ros. Happily he is the second time come to them, for they say an old man is twice a child.

Ham. I will prophesy he comes to tell me of the players; mark it. [*Aloud.*] You say right, sir; for o' Monday morning 't was so indeed.

Pol. My lord, I have news to tell you.

Ham. My lord, I have news to tell you. When Roscius was an actor in Rome,—

Pol. The actors are come hither, my lord.

Ham. Buzz, buzz!

Pol. Upon mine honour,—

Ham. "Then came each actor on his ass,"—

Pol. The best actors in the world, either for tragedy, comedy, history, pastoral, pastoral-comical, historical-pastoral, tragical-historical, tragical-comical-historical-pastoral, scene individable, or poem unlimited; Seneca cannot be too heavy, nor Plautus too light. For the law of writ and the liberty, these are the only men.

Ham. O Jephthah, judge of Israel, what a treasure hadst thou!

Pol. What a treasure had he, my lord?

Ham. Why,
"One fair daughter, and no more,
    The which he loved passing well."

Pol. [*Aside.*] Still on my daughter.

Ham. Am I not i' the right, old Jephthah?

Pol. If you call me Jephthah, my lord, I have a daughter that I love passing well.

Ham. Nay, that follows not.

Pol. What follows, then, my lord?

Ham. Why.
    "As by lot, God wot,"
and then, you know,
"It came to pass, as most like it was,"—The first row of the pious chanson will show you more, for look where my abridgements come.

Enter four or five PLAYERS.

You 're welcome, masters, welcome all. I am glad to see thee well. Welcome, good friends. O, my old friend! Thy face is valanc'd since I saw thee last; com'st thou to beard me in Denmark? What, my young lady and mistress! By 'r lady, your ladyship is nearer heaven than when I saw you last, by the altitude of a chopine. Pray God, your voice, like a piece of uncurrent gold, be not crack'd within the ring. Masters, you are all welcome. We 'll e'en to 't like French falconers—fly at anything we see; we 'll have a speech straight. Come, give us a taste of your quality; come, a passionate speech.

1. Play. What speech, my lord?

Ham. I heard thee speak me a speech once, but it was never acted; or, if it was, not above once. For the play, I remember, pleas'd not the million; 't was caviare to the general; but it was—as I receiv'd it, and others, whose judgment in such matters cried in the top of mine —an excellent play, well digested in the scenes, set down with as much modesty as cunning. I remember, one said there were no sallets in the lines to make the matter savoury, nor no matter in the phrase that might indict the author of affectation; but call'd it an honest method, [as wholesome as sweet, and by very much more handsome than fine.] One speech in it I chiefly lov'd; 't was Æneas' tale to Dido, and thereabout of it especially where he speaks of Priam's slaughter. If it live in your memory, begin at this line: let me see, let me see—
"The rugged Pyrrhus, like the Hyrcanian
    beast,"
—It is not so. It begins with Pyrrhus:—
"The rugged Pyrrhus, he whose sable
    arms,
Black as his purpose, did the night resemble
When he lay couched in the ominous
    horse,
Hath now this dread and black complexion smear'd
With heraldry more dismal. Head to
    foot
Now is he total gules, horribly trick'd
With blood of fathers, mothers, daughters, sons,
Bak'd and impasted with the parching
    streets,
That lend a tyrannous and damned light
To their vile murders. Roasted in
    wrath and fire,
And thus o'er-sized with coagulate gore,
With eyes like carbuncles, the hellish
    Pyrrhus

Old grandsire Priam seeks."
[So, proceed you.]

Pol. 'Fore God, my lord, well spoken, with good accent and good discretion.

1. Play.   "Anon he finds him
Striking too short at Greeks. His antique sword,
Rebellious to his arm, lies where it falls,
Repugnant to command. Unequal match,
Pyrrhus at Priam drives, in rage strikes wide,
But with the whiff and wind of his fell sword
The unnerved father falls. Then senseless Ilium,
Seeming to feel his blow, with flaming top
Stoops to his base, and with a hideous crash
Takes prisoner Pyrrhus' ear; for, lo! his sword,
Which was declining on the milky head
Of reverend Priam, seem'd i' the air to stick.
So, as a painted tyrant, Pyrrhus stood
And like a neutral to his will and matter,
Did nothing.
But, as we often see, against some storm,
A silence in the heavens, the rack stand still,
The bold winds speechless and the orb below
As hush as death, anon the dreadful thunder
Doth rend the region; so, after Pyrrhus' pause,
Aroused vengeance sets him new a-work;
And never did the Cyclops' hammers fall
On Mars his armour forg'd for proof eterne
With less remorse than Pyrrhus' bleeding sword
Now falls on Priam.
Out, out, thou strumpet Fortune! All you gods,
In general synod take away her power!
Break all the spokes and fellies from her wheel,
And bowl the round nave down the hill

of heaven
As low as to the fiends!"

Pol. This is too long.

Ham. It shall to the barber's, with your beard. Prithee, say on; he's for a jig or a tale of bawdry, or he sleeps. Say on; come to Hecuba.

1. Play. "But who, O, who had seen the mobled queen"—

Ham. "The mobled queen"?

Pol. That's good; "mobled queen" is good.

1. Play. "Run barefoot up and down, threat'ning the flame
With bisson rheum, a clout about that head
Where late the diadem stood, and for a robe,
About her lank and all o'er-teemed loins,
A blanket, in the alarm of fear caught up;—
Who this had seen, with tongue in venom steep'd,
'Gainst Fortune's state would treason have pronounc'd.
But if the gods themselves did see her then,
When she saw Pyrrhus make malicious sport
In mincing with his sword her husband's limbs,
The instant burst of clamour that she made,
Unless things mortal move them not at all,
Would have made milch the burning eyes of heaven,
And passion in the gods."

Pol. Look, whe'er he has not turn'd his colour and has tears in 's eyes. Pray you, no more.

Ham. 'Tis well; I'll have thee speak out the rest soon. Good my lord, will you see the players well bestow'd? Do ye hear? Let them be well us'd, for they are the abstracts and brief chronicles of the time; after your death you were better have a bad epitaph than their ill report while you lived.

Pol. My lord, I will use them according to their desert.

Ham. God's bodykins, man, better. Use every man after his desert, and who should scape whipping? Use them after your own honour and dignity. The less they deserve, the more merit is in your bounty. Take them in.

Pol. Come, sirs. [*Exit.*

Ham. Follow him, friends; we'll hear a play to-morrow. [*Exeunt all the Players but the First.*] Dost thou hear me, old friend? Can you play "The Murder of Gonzago"?

1. Play. Ay, my lord.

Ham. We'll ha 't to-morrow night. You could, for a need, study a speech of some dozen or sixteen lines, which I would set down and insert in 't, could ye not?

1. Play. Ay, my lord.

Ham. Very well. Follow that lord,— and look you mock him not. [*Exit 1. Player.*] My good friends, I'll leave you till night. You are welcome to Elsinore.

Ros. Good my lord!

[*Exeunt Rosencrantz and Guildenstern.*]

Ham. Ay, so, God buy ye.—Now I am alone.

O, what a rogue and peasant slave am I!
Is it not monstrous that this player here,
But in a fiction, in a dream of passion,
Could force his soul so to his own conceit
That from her working all his visage wann'd,
Tears in his eyes, distraction in 's aspect,
A broken voice, and his whole function suiting
With forms to his conceit? And all for nothing!
For Hecuba!
What's Hecuba to him, or he to Hecuba,
That he should weep for her? What would he do,
Had he the motive and the cue for passion

That I have? He would drown the stage with tears
And cleave the general ear with horrid speech,
Make mad the guilty and appall the free,
Confound the ignorant, and amaze indeed
The very faculty of eyes and ears.
Yet I,
A dull and muddy-mettled rascal, peak
Like John-a-dreams, unpregnant of my cause,
And can say nothing; no, not for a king,
Upon whose property and most dear life
A damn'd defeat was made. Am I a coward?
Who calls me villain, breaks my pate across,
Plucks off my beard and blows it in my face,
Tweaks me by the nose, gives me the lie i' the throat
As deep as to the lungs, who does me this?
Ha!
['Swounds,] I should take it; for it cannot be
But I am pigeon-liver'd and lack gall
To make oppression bitter, or ere this
I should have fatted all the region kites
With this slave's offal. Bloody, bawdy villain!
Remorseless, treacherous, lecherous, kindless villain!
O, vengeance!
Why, what an ass am I! Sure, this is most brave,
That I, the son of a dear father murdered,
Prompted to my revenge by heaven and hell,
Must, like a whore, unpack my heart with words,
And fall a-cursing, like a very drab,
A scullion!
Fie upon 't! Foh! About, my brain! I have heard
That guilty creatures sitting at a play
Have by the very cunning of the scene

Been struck so to the soul that presently
They have proclaim'd their malefactions;
For murder, though it have no tongue,
will speak
With most miraculous organ. I'll have
these players
Play something like the murder of my
father
Before mine uncle. I'll observe his looks;
I'll tent him to the quick. If he but
blench,
I know my course. The spirit that I
have seen
May be the devil; and the devil hath
power
To assume a pleasing shape; yea, and
perhaps
Out of my weakness and my melancholy,
As he is very potent with such spirits,
Abuses me to damn me. I'll have
grounds
More relative than this. The play's the
thing
Wherein I'll catch the conscience of the
King.   [*Exit.*

Act III

SCENE I. *A room in the castle.*

Enter KING, QUEEN, POLONIUS,
OPHELIA, ROSENCRANTZ, *and*
GUILDENSTERN.

King. And can you, by no drift of cir-
cumstance,
Get from him why he puts on this con-
fusion,
Grating so harshly all his days of quiet
With turbulent and dangerous lunacy?
Ros. He does confess he feels himself
distracted;
But from what cause he will by no means
speak.
Guil. Nor do we find him forward to
be sounded,
But, with a crafty madness, keeps aloof
When we would bring him on to some
confession
Of his true state.

Queen. Did he receive you well?
Ros. Most like a gentleman.
Guil. But with much forcing of his
disposition.
Ros. Niggard of question; but, of our
demands,
Most free in his reply.
Queen.   Did you assay him
To any pastime?
Ros. Madam, it so fell out, that cer-
tain players
We o'er-raught on the way; of these we
told him,
And there did seem in him a kind of joy
To hear of it. They are about the court,
And, as I think, they have already order
This night to play before him.
Pol.   'T is most true.
And he beseech'd me to entreat your
Majesties
To hear and see the matter.
King. With all my heart; and it doth
much content me
To hear him so inclin'd.
Good gentlemen, give him a further edge,
And drive his purpose on to these de-
lights.
Ros. We shall, my lord.
        [*Exeunt Rosencrantz and
            Guildenstern.*]
King. Sweet Gertrude, leave us too,
For we have closely sent for Hamlet
hither,
That he, as 't were by accident, may here
Affront Ophelia.
Her father and myself, lawful espials,
Will so bestow ourselves that, seeing
unseen,
We may of their encounter frankly
judge,
And gather by him, as he is behaved,
If 't be the affliction of his love or no
That thus he suffers for.
Queen.   I shall obey you.
And for your part, Ophelia, I do wish
That your good beauties be the happy
cause
Of Hamlet's wildness. So shall I hope
your virtues

Will bring him to his wonted way again,
To both your honours.

    Oph.   Madam, I wish it may.
                    [*Exit Queen.*]

    Pol. Ophelia, walk you here. Gracious, so please ye,
We will bestow ourselves. [*To Ophelia.*]
    Read on this book,
That show of such an exercise may
    colour
Your loneliness. We are oft to blame in
    this,—
'T is too much prov'd—that with devotion's visage
And pious action we do sugar o'er
The devil himself.

    King.   O, 't is true!
[*Aside.*] How smart a lash that speech
    doth give my conscience!
The harlot's cheek, beautied with plast'ring art,
Is not more ugly to the thing that helps it
Than is my deed to my most painted
    word.
O heavy burden!

    Pol. I hear him coming. Let's withdraw, my lord. [*Exeunt King and Polonius*].

    Enter HAMLET.

    Ham. To be, or not to be: that is the
    question.
Whether 't is nobler in the mind to suffer
The slings and arrows of outrageous fortune,
Or to take arms against a sea of troubles,
And by opposing end them. To die; to
    sleep;
No more; and by a sleep to say we end
The heart-ache and the thousand natural
    shocks
That flesh is heir to. 'T is a consummation
Devoutly to be wish'd. To die; to
    sleep;—
To sleep? Perchance to dream! Ay,
    there's the rub;
For in that sleep of death what dreams
    may come,

When we have shuffl'd off this mortal
    coil,
Must give us pause. There's the respect
That makes calamity of so long life.
For who would bear the whips and
    scorns of time,
The oppressor's wrong, the proud man's
    contumely,
The pangs of dispriz'd love, the law's
    delay,
The insolence of office, and the spurns
That patient merit of the unworthy takes,
When he himself might his quietus make
With a bare bodkin? Who would fardels bear,
To grunt and sweat under a weary life,
But that the dread of something after
    death,
The undiscovered country from whose
    bourn
No traveller returns, puzzles the will
And makes us rather bear those ills we
    have
Than fly to others that we know not
    of?
Thus conscience does make cowards of
    us all;
And thus the native hue of resolution
Is sicklied o'er with the pale cast of
    thought,
And enterprises of great pith and moment
With this regard their currents turn
    awry,
And lose the name of action.—Soft you
    now!
The fair Ophelia! Nymph, in thy orisons
Be all my sins rememb'red.

    Oph.   Good my lord,
How does your honour for this many a
    day?

    Ham. I humbly thank you, well, well,
    well.

    Oph. My lord, I have remembrances
    of yours
That I have longed long to re-deliver.
I pray you, now receive them.

    Ham.   No, no;
I never gave you aught.

Oph. My honour'd lord, I know right
well you did,
And, with them, words of so sweet breath
compos'd
As made the things more rich. Their
perfume lost,
Take these again; for to the noble
mind
Rich gifts wax poor when givers prove
unkind.
There, my lord.

Ham. Ha, ha! are you honest?

Oph. My lord!

Ham. Are you fair?

Oph. What means your lordship?

Ham. That if you be honest and fair,
your honesty should admit no discourse
to your beauty.

Oph. Could beauty, my lord, have
better commerce than with honesty?

Ham. Ay, truly; for the power of
beauty will sooner transform honesty
from what it is to a bawd than the force
of honesty can translate beauty into his
likeness. This was sometime a paradox,
but now the time gives it proof. I did
love you once.

Oph. Indeed, my lord, you made me
believe so.

Ham. You should not have believ'd
me, for virtue cannot so inoculate our old
stock but we shall relish of it. I loved
you not.

Oph. I was the more deceived.

Ham. Get thee to a nunnery; why
wouldst thou be a breeder of sinners? I
am myself indifferent honest, but yet I
could accuse me of such things that it
were better my mother had not borne
me. I am very proud, revengeful, ambitious, with more offences at my beck
than I have thoughts to put them in, imagination to give them shape, or time to
act them in. What should such fellows
as I do crawling between heaven and
earth? We are arrant knaves all; believe none of us. Go thy ways to a
nunnery. Where's your father?

Oph. At home, my lord.

Ham. Let the doors be shut upon him,
that he may play the fool nowhere but in
's own house. Farewell!

Oph.. O, help him, you sweet
heavens!

Ham. If thou dost marry, I 'll give
thee this plague for thy dowry: be thou
as chaste as ice, as pure as snow, thou
shalt not escape calumny. Get thee to a
nunnery, go. Farewell! Or, if thou wilt
needs marry, marry a fool; for wise men
know well enough what monsters you
make of them. To a nunnery, go, and
quickly too. Farewell!

Oph. O heavenly powers, restore him!

Ham. I have heard of your paintings
too, well enough. God has given you
one face, and you make yourselves
another. You jig, you amble, and you
lisp and nick-name God's creatures and
make your wantonness your ignorance.
Go to, I 'll no more on 't; it hath made
me mad. I say, we will have no more
marriages. Those that are married
already, all but one, shall live; the rest
shall keep as they are. To a nunnery,
go.   [*Exit.*

Oph. O, what a noble mind is here
o'erthrown!
The courtier's, soldier's, scholar's, eye,
tongue, sword;
The expectancy and rose of the fair state,
The glass of fashion and the mould of
form,
The observ'd of all observers, quite,
quite down!
And I, of ladies most deject and
wretched,
That suck'd the honey of his music
vows,
Now see that noble and most sovereign
reason,
Like sweet bells jangled out of tune and
harsh;
That unmatch'd form and feature of
blown youth
Blasted with ecstasy. O, woe is me,
To have seen what I have seen, see what
I see!

Re-enter KING *and* POLONIUS.

King. Love! his affections do not that
way tend;
Nor what he spake, though it lack'd form
a little,
Was not like madness. There's some-
thing in his soul
O'er which his melancholy sits on brood,
And I do doubt the hatch and the disclose
Will be some danger; which for to pre-
vent,
I have in quick determination
Thus set it down: he shall with speed to
England
For the demand of our neglected tribute.
Haply the seas and countries different
With variable objects shall expel
This something-settled matter in his
heart,
Whereon his brains still beating puts him
thus
From fashion of himself. What think
you on 't?
Pol. It shall do well; but yet do I
believe
The origin and commencement of this
grief
Sprung from neglected love. How now,
Ophelia!
You need not tell us what Lord Hamlet
said;
We heard it all. My lord, do as you
please,
But, if you hold it fit, after the play
Let his queen mother all alone entreat
him
To show his griefs. Let her be round
with him,
And I'll be plac'd, so please you, in the
ear
Of all their conference. If she find him
not,
To England send him, or confine him
where
Your wisdom best shall think.
King.   It shall be so.
Madness in great ones must not un-
watch'd go.   [*Exeunt.*

SCENE II. *A hall in the castle.*

Enter HAMLET *and* PLAYERS

Ham. Speak the speech, I pray you, as
I pronounc'd it to you, trippingly on the
tongue; but if you mouth it, as many of
your players do, I had as lief the town-
crier spoke my lines. Nor do not saw
the air too much with your hand, thus,
but use all gently; for in the very torrent,
tempest, and, as I may say, the whirl-
wind of passion, you must acquire and
beget a temperance that may give it
smoothness. O, it offends me to the soul
to see a robustious periwig-pated fellow
tear a passion to tatters, to very rags, to
split the ears of the groundlings, who for
the most part are capable of nothing but
inexplicable dumb-shows and noise. I
could have such a fellow whipp'd for
o'erdoing Termagant. It out-herods
Herod. Pray you, avoid it.
1. Play. I warrant your honour.
Ham. Be not too tame neither, but
let your own discretion be your tutor.
Suit the action to the word, the word
to the action; with this special observance, that you o'erstep not the modesty
of nature. For anything so overdone is
from the purpose of playing, whose end,
both at the first and now, was and is,
to hold, as 't were, the mirror up to
nature; to show virtue her own feature,
scorn her own image, and the very age
and body of the time his form and pressure. Now this overdone, or come tardy
off, though it make the unskilful laugh,
cannot but make the judicious grieve;
the censure of the which one must, in
your allowance, o'erweigh a whole theatre of others. O, there be players that
I have seen play, and heard others praise,
and that highly, not to speak it pro-
fanely, that, neither having the accent of
Christians nor the gait of Christian,
pagan, nor man, have so strutted and
bellowed that I have thought some of
Nature's journeymen had made men and

not made them well, they imitated humanity so abominably.

1. Play. I hope we have reform'd that indifferently with us, sir.

Ham. O, reform it altogether. And let those that play your clowns speak no more than is set down for them; for there be of them that will themselves laugh to set on some quantity of barren spectators to laugh too, though in the mean time some necessary question of the play be then to be considered. That's villainous, and shows a most pitiful ambition in the Fool that uses it. Go, make you ready. [*Exeunt Players.*

Enter POLONIUS, ROSENCRANTZ, *and* GUILDENSTERN.

How now, my Lord! Will the King hear this piece of work?

Pol. And the Queen too, and that presently.

Ham. Bid the players make haste.
[*Exit Polonius.*

Will you two help to hasten them?

Ros. } We will, my lord.
Guil. }

[*Exeunt Rosencrantz and Guildenstern.*

Ham. What ho! Horatio.

Enter HORATIO.

Hor. Here, sweet lord, at your service.

Ham. Horatio, thou art e'en as just a man
As e'er my conversation cop'd withal.

Hor. O, my dear lord,—

Ham. Nay, do not think I flatter,
For what advancement may I hope from thee
That no revenue hast but thy good spirits
To feed and clothe thee? Why should the poor be flatter'd?
No, let the candied tongue lick absurd pomp,
And crook the pregnant hinges of the knee
Where thrift may follow fawning. Dost thou hear?
Since my dear soul was mistress of my choice
And could of men distinguish, her election
Hath seal'd thee for herself; for thou hast been
As one, in suffering all, that suffers nothing,
A man that Fortune's buffets and rewards
Hath ta'en with equal thanks; and blest are those
Whose blood and judgement are so well commingled,
That they are not a pipe for Fortune's finger
To sound what stop she please. Give me that man
That is not passion's slave, and I will wear him
In my heart's core, ay, in my heart of heart,
As I do thee.—Something too much of this.—
There is a play to-night before the King.
One scene of it comes near the circumstance
Which I have told thee of my father's death.
I prithee, when thou seest that act a-foot,
Even with the very comment of thy soul
Observe mine uncle. If his occulted guilt
Do not itself unkennel in one speech,
It is a damned ghost that we have seen,
And my imaginations are as foul
As Vulcan's stithy. Give him heedful note;
For I mine eyes will rivet to his face,
And after we will both our judgements join
To censure of his seeming.

Hor. Well, my lord.
If he steal aught the whilst this play is playing,
And scape detecting, I will pay the theft.

Danish march. A flourish. Enter KING, QUEEN, POLONIUS, OPHELIA, ROSEN-CRANTZ, GUILDENSTERN, *and other Lords attendant, with the guard carrying torches.*

Ham. They are coming to the play; I must be idle.
Get you a place.
King. How fares our cousin Hamlet?
Ham. Excellent, i' faith,—of the chameleon's dish. I eat the air, promise-cramm'd. You cannot feed capons so.
King. I have nothing with this answer, Hamlet; these words are not mine.
Ham. No, nor mine now. [*To Polonius.*] My lord, you play'd once i' the university, you say?
Pol. That I did, my lord, and was accounted a good actor.
Ham. And what did you enact?
Pol. I did enact Julius Cæsar. I was kill'd i' the Capitol; Brutus kill'd me.
Ham. It was a brute part of him to kill so capital a calf there. Be the players ready?
Ros. Ay, my lord, they stay upon your patience.
Queen. Come hither, my good Hamlet, sit by me.
Ham. No, good mother, here's metal more attractive.
　　　[*Lying down at Ophelia's feet.*]
Pol. [*To the King.*] O, ho! do you mark that?
Ham. Lady, shall I lie in your lap?
Oph. No, my lord.
Ham. I mean, my head upon your lap?
Oph. Ay, my lord.
Ham. Do you think I meant country matters?
Oph. I think nothing, my lord.
Ham. That's a fair thought to lie between maid's legs.
Oph. What is, my lord?
Ham. Nothing.
Oph. You are merry, my lord.
Ham. Who, I?

Oph. Ay, my lord.
Ham. O God, your only jig-maker. What should a man do but be merry? For, look you, how cheerfully my mother looks, and my father died within 's two hours.
Oph. Nay, 't is twice two months, my lord.
Ham. So long? Nay then, let the devil wear black, for I 'll have a suit of sables. O heavens! die two months ago, and not forgotten yet? Then there's hope a great man's memory may outlive his life half a year; but, by 'r lady, he must build churches then, or else shall he suffer not thinking on, with the hobby-horse, whose epitaph is, "For, O, for, O, the hobby-horse is forgot."

Hautboys play. The dumb-show enters.

Enter a King and Queen very lovingly, the Queen embracing him. She kneels and makes show of protestation unto him. He takes her up and declines his head upon her neck; lays him down upon a bank of flowers. She, seeing him asleep, leaves him. Anon comes in a fellow, takes off his crown, kisses it, and pours poison in the King's ears, and exit. The Queen returns, finds the King dead, and makes passionate action. The poisoner, with some two or three Mutes, comes in again, seeming to lament with her. The dead body is carried away. The poisoner woos the Queen with gifts; she seems loath and unwilling a while, but in the end accepts his love. [*Exeunt.*

Oph. What means this, my lord?
Ham. Marry, this is miching mallecho; that means mischief.
Oph. Belike this show imports the argument of the play?

Enter PROLOGUE.

Ham. We shall know by this fellow. The players cannot keep counsel, they 'll tell all.

Oph. Will they tell us what this show meant?

Ham. Ay, or any show that you'll show him. Be not you asham'd to show, he 'll not shame to tell you what it means.

Oph. You are naught, you are naught. I 'll mark the play.

Pro. For us, and for our tragedy,
Here stooping to your clemency,
We beg your hearing patiently.
[*Exit.*]

Ham. Is this a prologue, or the posy of a ring?

Oph. 'Tis brief, my lord.

Ham. As woman's love.

Enter [two Players,] KING *and his*
QUEEN.

P. King. Full thirty times hath Phœbus' cart gone round
Neptune's salt wash and Tellus' orbed ground,
And thirty dozen moons with borrowed sheen
About the world have times twelve thirties been,
Since love our hearts and Hymen did our hands
Unite commutual in most sacred bands.

P. Queen. So many journeys may the sun and moon
Make us again count o'er ere love be done!
But, woe is me, you are so sick of late,
So far from cheer and from your former state,
That I distrust you. Yet, though I distrust,
Discomfort you, my lord, it nothing must;
For women's fear and love holds quantity,
In neither aught, or in extremity.
Now, what my love is, proof hath made you know;
And as my love is siz'd my fear is so.
[Where love is great, the littlest doubts are fear;

Where little fears grow great, great love grows there.]

P. King. Faith, I must leave thee, love, and shortly too.
My operant powers their functions leave to do;
And thou shalt live in this fair world behind,
Honour'd, belov'd; and haply one as kind
For husband shalt thou—

P. Queen. O, confound the rest!
Such love must needs be treason in my breast!
In second husband let me be accurst!
None wed the second but who kill'd the first.

Ham. [*Aside.*] Wormwood, wormwood!

P. Queen. The instances that second marriage move
Are base respects of thrift, but none of love.
A second time I kill my husband dead,
When second husband kisses me in bed.

P. King. I do believe you think what now you speak,
But what we do determine oft we break.
Purpose is but the slave to memory,
Of violent birth, but poor validity;
Which now, like fruit unripe, sticks on the tree,
But fall unshaken when they mellow be.
Most necessary 't is that we forget
To pay ourselves what to ourselves is debt.
What to ourselves in passion we propose,
The passion ending, doth the purpose lose.
The violence of either grief or joy
Their own enactures with themselves destroy.
Where joy most revels, grief doth most lament;
Grief joys, joy grieves, on slender accident.
This world is not for aye, nor 't is not strange
That even our loves should with our fortunes change,

For 't is a question left us yet to prove,

Whether love lead fortune, or else fortune love.

The great man down, you mark his favourite flies;

The poor advanc'd makes friends of enemies.

And hitherto doth love on fortune tend,

For who not needs shall never lack a friend;

And who in want a hollow friend doth try,

Directly seasons him his enemy.

But, orderly to end where I begun,

Our wills and fates do so contrary run

That our devices still are overthrown;

Our thoughts are ours, their ends none of our own.

So think thou wilt no second husband wed;

But die thy thoughts when thy first lord is dead.

P. Queen. Nor earth to me give food, nor heaven light!

Sport and repose lock from me day and night!

[To desperation turn my trust and hope!

An anchor's cheer in prison be my scope!]

Each opposite that blanks the face of joy

Meet what I would have well and it destroy!

Both here and hence pursue me lasting strife,

If, once a widow, ever I be wife!

Ham. If she should break it now!

P. King. 'T is deeply sworn. Sweet, leave me here a while.

My spirits grow dull, and fain I would beguile

The tedious day with sleep.   [*Sleeps.*

P. Queen.   Sleep rock thy brain,

And never come mischance between us twain!   [*Exit.*

Ham. Madam, how like you this play?

Queen. The lady protests too much, methinks.

Ham. O, but she 'll keep her word.

King. Have you heard the argument? Is there no offence in 't?

Ham. No, no, they do but jest, poison in jest. No offence i' the world.

King. What do you call the play?

Ham. The Mouse-trap. Marry, how? Tropically. This play is the image of a murder done in Vienna. Gonzago is the duke's name; his wife, Baptista. You shall see anon. 'T is a knavish piece of work, but what o' that? Your Majesty and we that have free souls, it touches us not. Let the gall'd jade wince, our withers are unwrung.

Enter LUCIANUS.

This is one Lucianus, nephew to the king.

Oph. You are a good chorus, my lord.

Ham. I could interpret between you and your love, if I could see the puppets dallying.

Oph. You are keen, my lord, you are keen.

Ham. It would cost you a groaning to take off my edge.

Oph. Still better, and worse.

Ham. So you mistake your husbands. Begin, murderer; pox, leave thy damnable faces and begin. Come, "the croaking raven doth bellow for revenge."

Luc. Thoughts black, hands apt, drugs fit, and time agreeing;

Confederate season, else no creature seeing.

Thou mixture rank, of midnight weeds collected,

With Hecate's ban thrice blasted, thrice infected,

Thy natural magic and dire property

On wholesome life usurp immediately.

[*Pours the poison in* [*to the sleeper's*] *ears.*

Ham. He poisons him i' the garden for 's estate. His name's Gonzago; the story is extant, and writ in choice Italian. You shall see anon how the murderer gets the love of Gonzago's wife.

Oph. The King rises.

Ham. What, frighted with false fire?

Queen. How fares my lord?

Pol. Give o'er the play.

King. Give me some light. Away!

All. Lights, lights, lights!

> [*Exeunt all but Hamlet and
> Horatio.*

Ham. Why, let the strucken deer go
weep,

> The hart ungalled play;
> For some must watch, while
> some must sleep,—
> So runs the world away.

Would not this, sir, and a forest of
feathers—if the rest of my fortunes turn
Turk with me—with two Provincial
roses on my raz'd shoes, get me a fellowship in a cry of players, sir?

Hor. Half a share.

Ham. A whole one, I.

> For thou dost know, O Damon dear,
> This realm dismantled was
> Of Jove himself; and now reigns
> here
> A very, very—pajock.

Hor. You might have rhym'd.

Ham. O good Horatio, I'll take the
ghost's word for a thousand pound.
Didst perceive?

Hor. Very well, my lord.

Ham. Upon the talk of the poisoning?

Hor. I did very well note him.

Re-enter ROSENCRANTZ *and* GUILDEN-
STERN.

Ham. Ah, ha! Come, some music!
Come, the recorders!

> For if the King like not the comedy,
> Why then, belike, he likes it not, perdy.

Come, some music!

Guil. Good my lord, vouchsafe me a
word with you.

Ham. Sir, a whole history.

Guil. The King, sir,—

Ham. Ay, sir, what of him?

Guil. Is in his retirement marvellous
distemper'd.

Ham. With drink, sir?

Guil. No, my lord, rather with choler.

Ham. Your wisdom should show itself more richer to signify this to his
doctor; for, for me to put him to his
purgation would perhaps plunge him into
far more choler.

Guil. Good my lord, put your discourse into some frame, and start not so
wildly from my affair.

Ham. I am tame, sir; pronounce.

Guil. The Queen, your mother, in
most great affliction of spirit, hath sent
me to you.

Ham. You are welcome.

Guil. Nay, good my lord, this courtesy is not of the right breed. If it shall
please you to make me a wholesome
answer I will do your mother's commandment; if not, your pardon and my
return shall be the end of my business.

Ham. Sir, I cannot.

Guil. What, my lord?

Ham. Make you a wholesome answer.
My wit 's diseas'd. But, sir, such an-
swers as I can make, you shall command,
or, rather, as you say, my mother.
Therefore no more, but to the matter.
My mother, you say,—

Ros. Then thus she says: your behaviour hath struck her into amazement
and admiration.

Ham. O wonderful son, that can so
astonish a mother! But is there no
sequel at the heels of this mother's admiration? [Impart.]

Ros. She desires to speak with you
in her closet ere you go to bed.

Ham. We shall obey, were she ten
times our mother. Have you any further
trade with us?

Ros. My lord, you once did love me.

Ham. So I do still, by these pickers
and stealers.

Ros. Good my lord, what is your
cause of distemper? You do surely bar
the door upon your own liberty if you
deny your griefs to your friend.

Ham. Sir, I lack advancement.

Ros. How can that be, when you have
the voice of the King himself for your
succession in Denmark?

Ham. Ay, but "While the grass grows,"—the proverb is something musty.

Re-enter one with a recorder.

O, the recorder! Let me see.—To withdraw with you:—why do you go about to recover the wind of me, as if you would drive me into a toil?

Guil. O, my lord, if my duty be too bold, my love is too unmannerly.

Ham. I do not well understand that. Will you play upon this pipe?

Guil. My lord, I cannot.

Ham. I pray you.

Guil. Believe me, I cannot.

Ham. I do beseech you.

Guil. I know no touch of it, my lord.

Ham. 'T is as easy as lying. Govern these ventages with your finger and thumb, give it breath with your mouth, and it will discourse most excellent music. Look you, these are the stops.

Guil. But these cannot I command to any utterance of harmony. I have not the skill.

Ham. Why, look you now, how unworthy a thing you make of me! You would play upon me, you would seem to know my stops, you would pluck out the heart of my mystery, you would sound me from my lowest note to the top of my compass; and there is much music, excellent voice, in this little organ, yet cannot you make it [speak. 'Sblood,] do you think that I am easier to be play'd on than a pipe? Call me what instrument you will, though you can fret me, you cannot play upon me.

Enter POLONIUS.

God bless you, sir.

Pol. My lord, the Queen would speak with you, and presently.

Ham. Do you see that cloud that 's almost in shape like a camel?

Pol. By the mass, and it 's like a camel, indeed.

Ham. Methinks it is like a weasel.

Pol. It is back'd like a weasel.

Ham. Or like a whale?

Pol. Very like a whale.

Ham. Then will I come to my mother by and by. [*Aside.*] They fool me to the top of my bent.—I will come by and by.

Pol. I will say so. [*Exit.*

Ham. "By and by" is easily said. Leave me, friends.

[*Exeunt all but Hamlet.*]

'T is now the very witching time of night
When churchyards yawn and hell itself breathes out
Contagion to this world. Now could I drink hot blood,
And do such bitter business as the day
Would quake to look on. Soft! now to my mother.
O heart, lose not thy nature! Let not ever
The soul of Nero enter this firm bosom;
Let me be cruel, not unnatural.
I will speak daggers to her, but use none.
My tongue and soul in this be hypocrites;
How in my word soever she be shent
To give them seals never, my soul consent! [*Exit.*

SCENE III. *A room in the castle.*

Enter KING, ROSENCRANTZ, *and* GUILDENSTERN.

King. I like him not, nor stands it safe with us
To let his madness range. Therefore prepare you.
I your commission will forthwith dispatch,
And he to England shall along with you.
The terms of our estate may not endure
Hazard so dangerous as doth hourly grow
Out of his lunacies.

Guil. We will ourselves provide.
Most holy and religious fear it is
To keep those many many bodies safe
That live and feed upon your Majesty.

Ros. The single and peculiar life is
bound
With all the strength and armour of the
mind
To keep itself from noyance, but much
more
That spirit upon whose weal depends and
rests
The lives of many. The cease of majesty
Dies not alone, but, like a gulf, doth
draw
What 's near it with it. It is a massy
wheel,
Fixed on the summit of the highest
mount,
To whose huge spokes ten thousand
lesser things
Are mortis'd and adjoin'd; which, when
it falls,
Each small annexment, petty consequence,
Attends the boisterous ruin. Never alone
Did the King sigh, but with a general
groan.
  King. Arm you, I pray you, to this
speedy voyage,
For we will fetters put upon this fear,
Which now goes too free-footed.
  Ros. ⎱
  Guil. ⎰   We will haste us.

    [*Exeunt Rosencrantz and
      Guildenstern.*

    Enter POLONIUS.

  Pol. My lord, he 's going to his
mother's closet.
Behind the arras I 'll convey myself,
To hear the process. I 'll warrant she'll
tax him home;
And, as you said, and wisely was it said,
'Tis meet that some more audience than
a mother,
Since nature makes them partial, should
o'erhear
The speech, of vantage. Fare you well,
my liege.
I 'll call upon you ere you go to bed,
And tell you what I know.
  King.   Thanks, dear my lord.
               [*Exit Polonius.*]

O, my offence is rank, it smells to
heaven;
It hath the primal eldest curse upon 't,
A brother's murder. Pray can I not,
Though inclination be as sharp as will.
My stronger guilt defeats my strong in-
tent,
And, like a man to double business bound,
I stand in pause where I shall first begin,
And both neglect. What if this cursed
hand
Were thicker than itself with brother's
blood,
Is there not rain enough in the sweet
heavens
To wash it white as snow? Whereto
serves mercy
But to confront the visage of offence?
And what 's in prayer but this twofold
force,
To be forestalled ere we come to fall,
Or pardon'd being down? Then I'll look
up;
My fault is past. But, O, what form of
prayer
Can serve my turn? "Forgive me my
foul murder"?
That cannot be; since I am still pos-
sess'd
Of those effects for which I did the
murder,
My crown, mine own ambition, and my
queen.
May one be pardon'd and retain the
offence?
In the corrupted currents of this world
Offence's gilded hand may shove by
justice,
And oft 't is seen the wicked prize itself
Buys out the law. But 't is not so above.
There is no shuffling, there the action lies
In his true nature; and we ourselves
compell'd,
Even to the teeth and forehead of our
faults,
To give in evidence. What then? What
rests?
Try what repentance can. What can it
not?

Yet what can it when one cannot repent?
O wretched state! O bosom black as
  death!
O limed soul, that, struggling to be free,
Art more engag'd! Help, angels! Make
  assay!
Bow, stubborn knees, and, heart with
  strings of steel,
Be soft as sinews of the new-born babe!
All may be well. [*Retires and kneels.*

Enter HAMLET.

Ham. Now might I do it pat, now he
  is praying.
And now I 'll do 't.—And so he goes to
  heaven;
And so am I reveng'd. That would be
  scann'd.
A villain kills my father, and for that,
I, his sole son, do this same villain send
To heaven.
Oh, this is hire and salary, not revenge.
He took my father grossly, full of bread,
With all his crimes broad blown, as flush
  as May;
And how his audit stands who knows
  save Heaven?
But in our circumstance and course of
  thought
'Tis heavy with him. And am I then re-
  veng'd,
To take him in the purging of his soul,
When he is fit and season'd for his pas-
  sage?
No!
Up, sword, and know thou a more horrid
  hent.
When he is drunk asleep, or in his rage,
Or in the incestuous pleasure of his bed,
At gaming, swearing, or about some act
That has no relish of salvation in 't,—
Then trip him, that his heels may kick
  at heaven,
And that his soul may be as damn'd and
  black
As hell, whereto it goes. My mother
  stays.
This physic but prolongs thy sickly days.
                          [*Exit.*

King. [*Rising.*] My words fly up, my
  thoughts remain below.
Words without thoughts never to heaven
  go.   [*Exit.*

SCENE IV. *The Queen's closet.*

Enter QUEEN *and* POLONIUS.

Pol. He will come straight. Look
  you lay home to him.
Tell him his pranks have been too broad
  to bear with,
And that your Grace hath screen'd and
  stood between
Much heat and him. I 'll silence me e'en
  here.
Pray you, be round with him.
Ham. (*Within.*) Mother, mother,
mother!
Queen. I 'll warrant you, fear me
  not.
Withdraw, I hear him coming.
  [*Polonius hides behind the arras.*]

Enter HAMLET.

Ham. Now, mother, what's the
  matter?
Queen. Hamlet, thou hast thy father
  much offended.
Ham. Mother, you have my father
  much offended.
Queen. Come, come, you answer with
  an idle tongue.
Ham. Go, go, you question with a
  wicked tongue.
Queen. Why, how now, Hamlet!
Ham.   What 's the matter now?
Queen. Have you forgot me?
Ham.   No, by the rood, not so.
You are the Queen, your husband's
  brother's wife;
But would you were not so! You are
  my mother.
Queen. Nay, then, I 'll set those to
  you that can speak.
Ham. Come, come, and sit you down.
  You shall not budge.

You go not till I set you up a glass
Where you may see the inmost part of
you.
    Queen. What wilt thou do? Thou
    wilt not murder me?
Help, help, ho!
    Pol. [*Behind.*] What, ho! help, help,
    help!
    Ham. [*Drawing.*] How now! A
    rat? Dead, for a ducat, dead!
        [*Kills Polonius through the
        arras.*]
    Pol. [*Behind.*] O, I am slain!
    Queen. O me, what hast thou done?
    Ham.   Nay, I know not.
Is it the King?
    Queen. O, what a rash and bloody
    deed is this!
    Ham. A bloody deed! Almost as bad,
    good mother,
As kill a king, and marry with his
    brother.
    Queen. As kill a king!
    Ham.   Ay, lady, 't was my word.
        [*Lifts up the arras and dis-
        covers Polonius.*]
Thou wretched, rash, intruding fool,
    farewell!
I took thee for thy better. Take thy
    fortune.
Thou find'st to be too busy is some
    danger.
—Leave wringing of your hands. Peace!
    Sit you down,
And let me wring your heart; for so I
    shall,
If it be made of penetrable stuff,
If damned custom have not braz'd it so
That it is proof and bulwark against
    sense.
    Queen. What have I done, that thou
    dar'st wag thy tongue
In noise so rude against me?
    Ham.   Such an act
That blurs the grace and blush of
    modesty,
Calls virtue hypocrite, takes off the rose
From the fair forehead of an innocent
    love

And sets a blister there, makes marriage-
    vows
As false as dicers' oaths; O, such a deed
As from the body of contraction plucks
The very soul, and sweet religion makes
A rhapsody of words. Heaven's face
    doth glow,
Yea, this solidity and compound mass,
With tristful visage, as against the doom,
Is thought-sick at the act.
    Queen.   Ay me, what act,
That roars so loud and thunders in the
    index?
    Ham. Look here, upon this picture,
    and on this,
The counterfeit presentment of two
    brothers.
See, what a grace was seated on this
    brow:
Hyperion's curls, the front of Jove him-
    self,
An eye like Mars, to threaten or com-
    mand,
A station like the herald Mercury
New-lighted on a heaven-kissing hill,
A combination and a form indeed,
Where every god did seem to set his seal,
To give the world assurance of a man.
This was your husband. Look you now
    what follows:
Here is your husband, like a mildew'd
    ear,
Blasting his wholesome brother. Have
    you eyes?
Could you on this fair mountain leave to
    feed,
And batten on this moor? Ha! have you
    eyes?
You cannot call it love, for at your age
The hey-day in the blood is tame, it 's
    humble,
And waits upon the judgement; and what
    judgement
Would step from this to this? [Sense
    sure you have,
Else could you not have motion; but sure,
    that sense
Is apoplex'd; for madness would not err,
Nor sense to ecstasy was ne'er so thrall'd

But it reserv'd some quantity of choice,
To serve in such a difference.] What
devil was 't
That thus hath cozen'd you at hoodman-
blind?
[Eyes without feeling, feeling without
sight,
Ears without hands or eyes, smelling sans
all,
Or but a sickly part of one true sense
Could not so mope.]
O shame! where is thy blush? Rebel-
lious hell,
If thou canst mutine in a matron's bones,
To flaming youth let virtue be as wax,
And melt in her own fire. Proclaim no
shame
When the compulsive ardour gives the
charge,
Since frost itself as actively doth burn
And reason panders will.
   Queen.   O Hamlet, speak no more!
Thou turn'st mine eyes into my very soul,
And there I see such black and grained
spots
As will not leave their tinct.
   Ham.   Nay, but to live
In the rank sweat of an enseamed bed,
Stew'd in corruption, honeying and mak-
ing love
Over the nasty sty,—
   Queen.   O, speak to me no more!
These words like daggers enter in mine
ears.
No more, sweet Hamlet!
   Ham.   A murderer and a villain!
A slave that is not twentieth part the
tithe
Of your precedent lord! A vice of kings!
A cutpurse of the empire and the rule,
That from a shelf the precious diadem
stole,
And put it in his pocket!
   Queen.   No more!

Enter GHOST.

   Ham. A king of shreds and patches,—
Save me, and hover o'er me with your
wings,

You heavenly guards! What would
your gracious figure?
   Queen. Alas, he 's mad!
   Ham. Do you not come your tardy
son to chide,
That, laps'd in time and passion, lets go
by
The important acting of your dread com-
mand?
O, say!
   Ghost. Do not forget! This visita-
tion
Is but to whet thy almost blunted pur-
pose.
But, look, amazement on thy mother sits.
O, step between her and her fighting soul.
Conceit in weakest bodies strongest
works.
Speak to her, Hamlet.
   Ham.   How is it with you, lady?
   Queen. Alas, how is 't with you,
That you do bend your eye on vacancy
And with the incorporal air do hold dis-
course?
Forth at your eyes your spirits wildly
peep,
And, as the sleeping soldiers in the alarm,
Your bedded hair, like life in excrements,
Start up and stand on end. O gentle son,
Upon the heat and flame of thy distemper
Sprinkle cool patience. Whereon do you
look?
   Ham. On him, on him! Look you,
how pale he glares!
His form and cause conjoin'd, preaching
to stones,
Would make them capable. Do not look
upon me,
Lest with this piteous action you convert
My stern effects; then what I have to
do
Will want true colour, tears perchance
for blood.
   Queen. To whom do you speak this?
   Ham.   Do you see nothing there?
   Queen. Nothing at all, yet all that is
I see.
   Ham. Nor did you nothing hear?
   Queen.   No, nothing but ourselves.

Ham. Why, look you there! Look,
how it steals away!
My father, in his habit as he lived!
Look, where he goes, even now, out at
the portal!   [*Exit Ghost.*
Queen. This is the very coinage of
your brain.
This bodiless creation ecstasy
Is very cunning in.
Ham.   Ecstasy!
My pulse, as yours, doth temperately
keep time,
And makes as healthful music. It is not
madness
That I have uttered. Bring me to the
test,
And I the matter will re-word, which
madness
Would gambol from. Mother, for love
of grace,
Lay not that flattering unction to your
soul,
That not your trespass, but my madness
speaks.
It will but skin and film the ulcerous
place,
Whilst rank corruption, mining all
within,
Infects unseen. Confess yourself to
Heaven;
Repent what's past, avoid what is to
come,
And do not spread the compost on the
weeds,
To make them rank. Forgive me this
my virtue
For in the fatness of these pursy times
Virtue itself of vice must pardon beg,
Yea, curb and woo for leave to do him
good.
Queen. O Hamlet, thou hast cleft my
heart in twain.
Ham. O, throw away the worser part
of it,
And live the purer with the other
half.
Good-night; but go not to mine uncle's
bed.
Assume a virtue, if you have it not.

[That monster, custom, who all sense
doth eat,
Of habits devil, is angel yet in this,
That to the use of actions fair and good
He likewise gives a frock or livery,
That aptly is put on.] Refrain to-night,
And that shall lend a kind of easiness
To the next abstinence; [the next more
easy;
For use almost can change the stamp of
nature,
And either master the devil or throw him
out,
With wondrous potency.] Once more,
good-night;
And when you are desirous to be blest,
I 'll blessing beg of you. For this same
lord,   [*Pointing to Polonius.*]
I do repent; but Heaven hath pleas'd it
so,
To punish me with this and this with
me,
That I must be their scourge and min-
ister.
I will bestow him, and will answer well
The death I gave him. So, again, good-
night.
I must be cruel, only to be kind.
Thus bad begins and worse remains
behind.
[One word more, good lady.]
Queen.   What shall I do?
Ham. Not this, by no means, that I
bid you do:
Let the bloat king tempt you again to
bed,
Pinch wanton on your cheek, call you his
mouse,
And let him, for a pair of reechy kisses,
Or paddling in your neck with his
damn'd fingers,
Make you to ravel all this matter out,
That I essentially am not in madness,
But mad in craft. 'T were good you let
him know;
For who, that 's but a queen, fair,
sober, wise,
Would from a paddock, from a bat, a
gib,

Such dear concernings hide? Who would
do so?
No, in despite of sense and secrecy,
Unpeg the basket on the house's top,
Let the birds fly, and like the famous ape,
To try conclusions, in the basket creep,
And break your own neck down.

    Queen. Be thou assur'd, if words be
made of breath,
And breath of life, I have no life to breathe
What thou hast said to me.

    Ham. I must to England; you know
that?

    Queen. Alack,
I had forgot. 'T is so concluded on.

    Ham. [There's letters sealed, and my
two school-fellows,
Whom I will trust as I will adders fang'd,
They bear the mandate. They must
sweep my way,
And marshal me to knavery. Let it
work;
For 't is the sport to have the enginer
Hoist with his own petar; and 't shall go
hard
But I will delve one yard below their
mines,
And blow them at the moon. O, 't is
most sweet,
When in one line two crafts directly meet.]
This man shall set me packing.
I 'll lug the guts into the neighbour room.
Mother, good-night. Indeed this coun-
sellor
Is now most still, most secret, and most
grave,
Who was in life a foolish prating knave.
Come, sir, to draw toward an end with
you.
Good-night, mother.

        [*Exeunt, severally, Hamlet
tugging in Polonius.*

Henry V

ACT II, SCENE III.

London.   Before a tavern.

Enter PISTOL, NYM, BARDOLPH, BOY, *and*
HOSTESS.

    Host. Prithee honey, sweet husband,
let me bring thee to Staines.

    Pist. No; for my manly heart doth
yearn.
Bardolph, be blithe; Nym, rouse thy
vaunting veins;
Boy, bristle thy courage up; for Falstaff
he is dead,
And we must yearn therefore.

    Bard. Would I were with him, where-
some'er he is, either in heaven or in hell!

    Host. Nay, sure, he 's not in hell.
He 's in Arthur's bosom, if ever man went
to Arthur's bosom. 'A made a finer end
and went away an it had been any chris-
tom child. 'A parted even just between
twelve and one, even at the turning o' the
tide: for after I saw him fumble with the
sheets, and play with flowers, and smile
upon his fingers' ends, I knew there was
but one way; for his nose was as sharp as
a pen, and 'a babbled of green fields.
"How now, Sir John!" quoth I; "what,
man! be o' good cheer." So 'a cried out,
"God, God, God!" three or four times.
Now I, to comfort him, bid him 'a should
not think of God; I hop'd there was no
need to trouble himself with any such
thoughts yet. So 'a bade me lay more
clothes on his feet. I put my hand into
the bed and felt them, and they were as
cold as any stone; then I felt to his knees,
[and they were as cold as any stone;] and
so upward and upward, and all was as
cold as any stone.

Nym. They say he cried out of sack.

Host. Ay, that 'a did.

Bard. And of women.

Host. Nay, that 'a did not.

Boy. Yes, that 'a did; and said they were devils incarnate.

Host. 'A could never abide carnation; 't was a colour he never lik'd.

Boy. 'A said once, the devil would have him about women.

Host. 'A did in some sort, indeed, handle women; but then he was rheumatic, and talk'd of the whore of Babylon.

Boy. Do you not remember, 'a saw a flea stick upon Bardolph's nose, and 'a said it was a black soul burning in hell-fire?

Bard. Well, the fuel is gone that maintain'd that fire. That's all the riches I got in his service.

Nym. Shall we shog? The King will be gone from Southampton.

Pist. Come, let's away. My love, give me thy lips.

Look to my chattels and my movables.

Let senses rule; the word is "Pitch and Pay."

Trust none;

For oaths are straws, men's faiths are wafer-cakes,

And hold-fast is the only dog, my duck;

Therefore, *Caveto* be thy counsellor.

Go, clear thy crystals. Yoke-fellows in arms,

Let us to France; like horse-leeches, my boys,

To suck, to suck, the very blood to suck!

Boy. And that's but unwholesome food, they say.

Pist. Touch her soft mouth, and march.

Bard. Farewell, hostess. [*Kissing her.*

Nym. I cannot kiss; that is the humour of it; but, adieu.

Pist. Let housewifery appear. Keep close, I thee command.

Host. Farewell; adieu.   [*Exeunt.*

Act III, Scene I.

France.   Before Harfleur.

Alarm.   Enter King Henry, Exeter, Bedford, Gloucester, [*and Soldiers, with*] *scaling-ladders.*

K. Hen. Once more unto the breach, dear friends, once more,

Or close the wall up with our English dead.

In peace there 's nothing so becomes a man

As modest stillness and humility;

But when the blast of war blows in our ears,

Then imitate the action of the tiger;

Stiffen the sinews, summon up the blood,

Disguise fair nature with hard-favour'd rage;

Then lend the eye a terrible aspect;

Let it pry through the portage of the head

Like the brass cannon; let the brow o'er-whelm it

As fearfully as doth a galled rock

O'erhang and jutty his confounded base,

Swill'd with the wild and wasteful ocean.

Now set the teeth and stretch the nostril wide,

Hold hard the breath, and bend up every spirit

To his full height. On, on, you noblest English,

Whose blood is fet from fathers of war-proof!

Fathers that, like so many Alexanders,
Have in these parts from morn till even
    fought,
And sheath'd their swords for lack of ar-
    gument.
Dishonour not your mothers; now attest
That those whom you call'd fathers did
    beget you.
Be copy now to men of grosser blood,
And teach them how to war. And you,
    good yeomen,
Whose limbs were made in England, show
    us here
The mettle of your pasture; let us swear
That you are worth your breeding, which
    I doubt not;
For there is none of you so mean and base,
That hath not noble lustre in your eyes.
I see you stand like greyhounds in the
    slips,
Straining upon the start. The game 's
    afoot!
Follow your spirit, and upon this charge
Cry, "God for Harry! England and
    Saint George!"

Act IV, Scene III.

The English camp.

Enter Gloucester, Bedford, Exeter,
Erpingham, *with all his host:* Salisbury *and* Westmoreland.

Glou. Where is the King?
Bed. The King himself is rode to view
    their battle.
West. Of fighting men they have full
    three-score thousand.
Exe. There 's five to one; besides, they
    all are fresh.
Sal. God's arm strike with us! 't is
    a fearful odds.
God be wi' you, princes all; I 'll to my
    charge.
If we no more meet till we meet in heaven,
Then, joyfully, my noble Lord of Bedford,
My dear Lord Gloucester, and my good
    Lord Exeter,

And my kind kinsman, warriors all, adieu!
Bed. Farewell, good Salisbury, and
    good luck go with thee!
Exe. Farewell, kind lord; fight val-
    iantly to-day!
And yet I do thee wrong to mind thee of
    it,
For thou art fram'd of the firm truth of
    valour.   [*Exit Salisbury.*
Bed. He is as full of valour as of kind-
    ness,
Princely in both.

Enter the King.

West.   O that we now had here
But one ten thousand of those men in
    England
That do no work to-day!
K. Hen. What 's he that wishes so?
My cousin Westmoreland? No, my fair
    cousin.
If we are mark'd to die, we are enow
To do our country loss; and if to live,
The fewer men, the greater share of
    honour.
God's will! I pray thee, wish not one
    man more.
By Jove, I am not covetous for gold,
Nor care I who doth feed upon my cost;
It yearns me not if men my garments
    wear;
Such outward things dwell not in my de-
    sires;
But if it be a sin to covet honour,
I am the most offending soul alive.
No, faith, my coz, wish not a man from
    England.
God's peace! I would not lose so great
    an honour
As one man more, methinks, would share
    from me
For the best hope I have. O, do not wish
    one more!
Rather proclaim it, Westmoreland,
    through my host,
That he which hath no stomach to this
    fight,
Let him depart. His passport shall be
    made,

And crowns for convoy put into his purse.
We would not die in that man's company
That fears his fellowship to die with us.
This day is call'd the feast of Crispian.
He that outlives this day, and comes safe
    home,
Will stand a tip-toe when this day is
    named,
And rouse him at the name of Crispian.
He that shall live this day, and see old
    age,
Will yearly on the vigil feast his neigh-
    bours,
And say, "To-morrow is Saint Crispian."
Then will he strip his sleeve and show his
    scars,
And say, "These wounds I had on Cris-
    pin's day."
Old men forget; yet all shall be forgot,
But he 'll remember with advantages
What feats he did that day. Then shall
    our names,
Familiar in his mouth as household
    words,
Harry the King, Bedford, and Exeter,
Warwick and Talbot, Salisbury and
    Gloucester,
Be in their flowing cups freshly remem-
    b'red.
This story shall the good man teach his
    son;
And Crispin Crispian shall ne'er go by,
From this day to the ending of the world,
But we in it shall be remembered,
We few, we happy few, we band of
    brothers.
For he to-day that sheds his blood with
    me
Shall be my brother; be he ne'er so vile,
This day shall gentle his condition;
And gentlemen in England now a-bed
Shall think themselves accurs'd they were
    not here,
And hold their manhoods cheap whiles
    any speaks
That fought with us upon Saint Cris-
    pin's day.

Re-enter SALISBURY.

Sal. My sovereign lord, bestow your-
    self with speed.
The French are bravely in their battles
    set,
And will with all expedience charge on us.
    K. Hen. All things are ready, if our
    minds be so.
West. Perish the man whose mind is
    backward now!
K. Hen. Thou dost not wish more
    help from England, coz?
West. God's will! my liege, would you
    and I alone,
Without more help, could fight this royal
    battle!
    K. Hen. Why, now thou hast un-
    wish'd five thousand men,
Which likes me better than to wish us
    one.
You know your places. God be with you
    all!

Julius Cæsar

Act IV.

Scene I. *A house in Rome.*

Antony, Octavius, *and* Lepidus
[seated at a table].

Ant. These many, then, shall die;
    their names are prick'd.
Oct. Your brother too must die; con-
    sent you, Lepidus?
Lep. I do consent,—
Oct.   Prick him down, Antony.
Lep. Upon condition Publius shall not
    live,
Who is your sister's son, Mark Antony.
    Ant. He shall not live; look, with a
    spot I damn him.
But, Lepidus, go you to Cæsar's house;
Fetch the will hither, and we shall deter-
    mine
How to cut off some charge in legacies.
Lep. What, shall I find you here?
Oct. Or here, or at the Capitol.
             [Exit Lepidus.
Ant. This is a slight unmeritable man,

Meet to be sent on errands; is it fit,
The threefold world divided, he should
    stand
One of the three to share it?
    Oct.   So you thought him;
And took his voice who should be prick'd
    to die,
In our black sentence and proscription.
    Ant. Octavius, I have seen more days
    than you;
And though we lay these honours on this
    man
To ease ourselves of divers slanderous
    loads,
He shall but bear them as the ass bears
    gold,
To groan and sweat under the business,
Either led or driven, as we point the
    way;
And having brought our treasure where
    we will,
Then take we down his load, and turn
    him off,
Like to the empty ass, to shake his ears
And graze in commons.
    Oct.   You may do your will;
But he's a tried and valiant soldier.
    Ant. So is my horse, Octavius; and
    for that
I do appoint him store of provender.
It is a creature that I teach to fight,
To wind, to stop, to run directly on,
His corporal motion govern'd by my
    spirit.
And, in some taste, is Lepidus but so;
He must be taught and train'd and bid
    go forth;
A barren-spirited fellow; one that feeds
On abjects, orts, and imitations,
Which, out of use and stal'd by other
    men,
Begin his fashion. Do not talk of him
But as a property. And now, Octavius,
Listen great things. Brutus and Cassius
Are levying powers; we must straight
    make head;
Therefore let our alliance be combin'd,
Our best friends made, our means
    stretch'd;

And let us presently go sit in council
How covert matters may be best dis-
    clos'd
And open perils surest answered.
    Oct. Let us do so; for we are at the
    stake,
And bay'd about with many enemies;
And some that smile have in their hearts,
    I fear,
Millions of mischiefs.   *[Exeunt.*

Scene II. *Camp near Sardis. Before
        Brutus's tent.*

Drum. Enter Brutus, Lucilius,
[Lucius,] *and the army.* Titinius
and Pindarus *meet them.*
    Bru. Stand, ho!
    Lucil. Give the word, ho! and stand.
    Bru. What now, Lucilius! is Cassius
    near?
    Lucil. He is at hand; and Pindarus is
    come
To do you salutation from his master.
    Bru. He greets me well. Your mas-
    ter, Pindarus,
In his own change, or by ill officers,
Hath given me some worthy cause to
    wish
Things done undone; but, if he be at
    hand,
I shall be satisfied.
    Pin.   I do not doubt
But that my noble master will appear
Such as he is, full of regard and honour.
    Bru. He is not doubted. A word,
    Lucilius:
How he receiv'd you let me be resolv'd.
    Lucil. With courtesy and with respect
    enough;
But not with such familiar instances,
Nor with such free and friendly confer-
    ence,
As he hath us'd of old.
    Bru.   Thou hast describ'd
A hot friend cooling. Ever note, Lucilius,
When love begins to sicken and decay,
It useth an enforced ceremony.

There are no tricks in plain and simple
    faith;
But hollow men, like horses hot at
    hand,
Make gallant show and promise of their
    mettle;   *[Low march within.*
But when they should endure the bloody
    spur
They fall their crests, and, like deceitful
    jades,
Sink in the trial. Comes his army on?
    Lucil. They mean this night in Sardis
      to be quarter'd.
The greater part, the horse in general,
Are come with Cassius.

    Enter CASSIUS *and his Powers.*

    Bru.   Hark! he is arriv'd.
March gently on to meet him.
    Cas. Stand, ho!
    Bru. Stand, ho! Speak the word
      along.
    [1. Sol.] Stand!
    [2. Sol.] Stand!
    [3. Sol.] Stand!
    Cas. Most noble brother, you have
      done me wrong.
    Bru. Judge me, you gods! wrong I
      mine enemies?
And, if not so, how should I wrong a
    brother?
    Cas. Brutus, this sober form of yours
      hides wrongs;
And when you do them—
    Bru.   Cassius, be content;
Speak your griefs softly; I do know you
    well.
Before the eyes of both our armies here,
Which should perceive nothing but love
    from us,
Let us not wrangle. Bid them move
    away;
Then in my tent, Cassius, enlarge your
    griefs,
And I will give you audience.
    Cas.   Pindarus,
Bid our commanders lead their charges
    off
A little from this ground.

    Bru. [Lucius], do you the like; and
    let no man
Come to our tent till we have done our
    conference.
[Lucilius] and Titinius, guard our door.
    [Exeunt.

    SCENE III. *Brutus's tent.*

    [Enter] BRUTUS *and* CASSIUS.

    Cas. That you have wrong'd me doth
      appear in this:
You have condemn'd and noted Lucius
    Pella
For taking bribes here of the Sardians;
Wherein my letters, praying on his side,
Because I knew the man was slighted
    off,—
    Bru. You wrong'd yourself to write
      in such a case.
    Cas. In such a time as this it is not
      meet
That every nice offence should bear his
    comment.
    Bru. Let me tell you, Cassius, you
      yourself
Are much condemn'd to have an itching
    palm,
To sell and mart your offices for gold
To undeservers.
    Cas.   I an itching palm!
You know that you are Brutus that
    speaks this,
Or, by the gods, this speech were else
    your last.
    Bru. The name of Cassius honours
      this corruption,
And chastisement doth therefore hide his
    head.
    Cas. Chastisement!
    Bru. Remember March, the ides of
      March remember:
Did not great Julius bleed for justice'
    sake?
What villain touch'd his body, that did
    stab
And not for justice? What, shall one
    of us,

That struck the foremost man of all this world
But for supporting robbers, shall we now
Contaminate our fingers with base bribes,
And sell the mighty space of our large honours
For so much trash as may be grasped thus?
I had rather be a dog, and bay the moon,
Than such a Roman.

Cas. Brutus, bait not me;
I 'll not endure it. You forget yourself
To hedge me in. I am a soldier, I,
Older in practice, abler than yourself
To make conditions.

Bru. Go to; you are not, Cassius.

Cas. I am.

Bru. I say you are not.

Cas. Urge me no more, I shall forget myself;
Have mind upon your health, tempt me no farther.

Bru. Away, slight man!

Cas. Is 't possible?

Bru. Hear me, for I will speak.
Must I give way and room to your rash choler?
Shall I be frighted when a madman stares?

Cas. O ye gods, ye gods! must I endure all this?

Bru. All this! ay, more. Fret till your proud heart break;
Go show your slaves how choleric you are,
And make your bondmen tremble. Must I budge?
Must I observe you? Must I stand and crouch
Under your testy humour? By the gods,
You shall digest the venom of your spleen,
Though it do split you; for, from this day forth,
I 'll use you for my mirth, yea, for my laughter,
When you are waspish.

Cas. Is it come to this?

Bru. You say you are a better soldier:
Let it appear so; make your vaunting true,
And it shall please me well. For mine own part,
I shall be glad to learn of noble men.

Cas. You wrong me every way; you wrong me, Brutus;
I said an elder soldier, not a better.
Did I say "better"?

Bru. If you did, I care not.

Cas. When Cæsar liv'd, he durst not thus have mov'd me.

Bru. Peace, peace! you durst not so have tempted him.

Cas. I durst not!

Bru. No.

Cas. What, durst not tempt him!

Bru. For your life you durst not.

Cas. Do not presume too much upon my love;
I may do that I shall be sorry for.

Bru. You have done that you should be sorry for.
There is no terror, Cassius, in your threats,
For I am arm'd so strong in honesty
That they pass by me as the idle wind,
Which I respect not. I did send to you
For certain sums of gold, which you deni'd me;
For I can raise no money by vile means.—
By heaven, I had rather coin my heart,
And drop my blood for drachmas, than to wring
From the hard hands of peasants their vile trash
By any indirection.—I did send
To you for gold to pay my legions,
Which you deni'd me. Was that done like Cassius?
Should I have answer'd Caius Cassius so?
When Marcus Brutus grows so covetous
To lock such rascal counters from his friends,

Be ready, gods, with all your thunder-
    bolts;
Dash him to pieces!
   Cas.   I deni'd you not.
   Bru. You did.
   Cas. I did not. He was but a fool
    that brought
My answer back. Brutus hath riv'd my
    heart.
A friend should bear his friend's infirmi-
    ties,
But Brutus makes mine greater than
    they are.
   Bru. I do not, till you practise them
    on me.
   Cas. You love me not.
   Bru.   I do not like your faults.
   Cas. A friendly eye could never see
    such faults.
   Bru. A flatterer's would not, though
    they do appear
As huge as high Olympus.
   Cas. Come, Antony, and young Oc-
    tavius, come,
Revenge yourselves alone on Cassius,
For Cassius is aweary of the world;
Hated by one he loves; brav'd by his
    brother;
Check'd like a bondman; all his faults
    observ'd,
Set in a note-book, learn'd and conn'd by
    rote
To cast into my teeth. O, I could weep
My spirit from mine eyes! There is my
    dagger,
And here my naked breast; within, a
    heart
Dearer than Plutus' mine, richer than
    gold.
If that thou be'st a Roman, take it
    forth;
I, that deni'd thee gold, will give my
    heart.
Strike, as thou didst at Cæsar; for, I
    know,
When thou didst hate him worst, thou
    lov'dst him better
Than ever thou lov'dst Cassius.
   Bru.   Sheathe your dagger.

Be angry when you will, it shall have
    scope.
Do what you will, dishonour shall be
    humour.
O Cassius, you are yoked with a lamb
That carries anger as the flint bears fire;
Who, much enforced, shows a hasty
    spark,
And straight is cold again.
   Cas.   Hath Cassius liv'd
To be but mirth and laughter to his
    Brutus,
When grief and blood ill-temper'd vexeth
    him?
   Bru. When I spoke that, I was ill-
    temper'd too.
   Cas. Do you confess so much? Give
    me your hand.
   Bru. And my heart too.
   Cas.   O Brutus!
   Bru.   What 's the matter?
   Cas. Have not you love enough to
    bear with me,
When that rash humour which my
    mother gave me
Makes me forgetful?
   Bru. Yes, Cassius; and, for hence-
    forth,
When you are over earnest with your
    Brutus,
He 'll think your mother chides, and
    leave you so.
   Poet. [*Within.*] Let me go in to see
    the generals;
There is some grudge between 'em, 't is
    not meet
They be alone.
   Lucil. [*Within.*] You shall not come
    to them.
   Poet. [*Within.*] Nothing but death
    shall stay me.

Enter POET [*followed by* LUCILIUS,
TITINIUS, *and* LUCIUS].

   Cas. How now! what 's the matter?
   Poet. For shame, you generals! what
    do you mean?
Love, and be friends, as two such men
    should be;

For I have seen more years, I 'm sure,
than ye.

Cas. Ha, ha! how vilely doth this
cynic rhyme!

Bru. Get you hence, sirrah; saucy
fellow, hence!

Cas. Bear with him, Brutus; 't is his
fashion.

Bru. I 'll know his humour, when he
knows his time.

What should the wars do with these jig-
ging fools?

Companion, hence!

Cas. Away, away, be gone!
[*Exit Poet.*

Bru. Lucilius and Titinius, bid the
commanders

Prepare to lodge their companies to-
night.

Cas. And come yourselves, and bring
Messala with you

Immediately to us.
[*Exeunt Lucilius and Titinius.*]

Bru. Lucius, a bowl of wine!
[*Exit Lucius.*]

Cas. I did not think you could have
been so angry.

Bru. O Cassius, I am sick of many
griefs.

Cas. Of your philosophy you make no
use

If you give place to accidental evils.

Bru. No man bears sorrow better.
Portia is dead.

Cas. Ha! Portia!

Bru. She is dead.

Cas. How scap'd I killing when I
cross'd you so?

O insupportable and touching loss!

Upon what sickness?

Bru. Impatient of my absence,

And grief that young Octavius with
Mark Antony

Have made themselves so strong,—for
with her death

That tidings came,—with this she fell
distract,

And, her attendants absent, swallow'd
fire.

Cas. And died so?

Bru. Even so.

Cas. O ye immortal gods!

Re-enter Boy [Lucius], *with wine and
tapers.*

Bru. Speak no more of her. Give me
a bowl of wine.

In this I bury all unkindness, Cassius.
[*Drinks.*]

Cas. My heart is thirsty for that
noble pledge.

Fill Lucius, till the wine o'erswell the
cup;

I cannot drink too much of Brutus' love.
[*Drinks.*]

Re-enter TITINIUS, *with* MESSALA.

Bru. Come in, Titinius!
[*Exit Lucius.*]
Welcome, good Messala.

Now sit we close about this taper here,

And call in question our necessities.

Cas. Portia, art thou gone?

Bru. No more, I pray you.

Messala, I have here received letters

That young Octavius and Mark Antony

Come down upon us with a mighty
power,

Bending their expedition toward Philippi.

Mes. Myself have letters of the self-
same tenour.

Bru. With what addition?

Mes. That by proscription and bills
of outlawry,

Octavius, Antony, and Lepidus

Have put to death an hundred senators.

Bru. Therein our letters do not well
agree;

Mine speak of seventy senators that died

By their proscriptions, Cicero being one.

Cas. Cicero one!

Mes. Cicero is dead,

And by that order of proscription.

Had you your letters from your wife, my
lord?

Bru. No, Messala.

Mes. Nor nothing in your letters writ
of her?

Bru. Nothing, Messala.

Mes.   That, methinks, is strange.

Bru. Why ask you? Hear you aught of her in yours?

Mes. No, my lord.

Bru. Now, as you are a Roman, tell me true.

Mes. Then like a Roman bear the truth I tell:

For certain she is dead, and by strange manner.

Bru. Why, farewell, Portia. We must die, Messala.

With meditating that she must die once,

I have the patience to endure it now.

Mes. Even so great men great losses should endure.

Cas. I have as much of this in art as you,

But yet my nature could not bear it so.

Bru. Well, to our work alive. What do you think

Of marching to Philippi presently?

Cas. I do not think it good.

Bru.   Your reason?

Cas.   This it is:

'T is better that the enemy seek us.

So shall he waste his means, weary his soldiers,

Doing himself offence; whilst we, lying still,

Are full of rest, defence, and nimbleness.

Bru. Good reasons must, of force, give place to better.

The people 'twixt Philippi and this ground

Do stand but in a forc'd affection,

For they have grudg'd us contribution.

The enemy, marching along by them,

By them shall make a fuller number up,

Come on refresh'd, new-added, and encourag'd;

From which advantage shall we cut him off

If at Philippi we do face him there,

These people at our back.

Cas.   Hear me, good brother.

Bru. Under your pardon. You must note beside,

That we have tried the utmost of our friends;

Our legions are brim-full, our cause is ripe.

The enemy increaseth every day;

We, at the height, are ready to decline.

There is a tide in the affairs of men,

Which, taken at the flood, leads on to fortune;

Omitted, all the voyage of their life

Is bound in shallows and in miseries.

On such a full sea are we now afloat;

And we must take the current when it serves,

Or lose our ventures.

Cas.   Then, with your will, go on.

We 'll along ourselves, and meet them at Philippi.

Bru. The deep of night is crept upon our talk,

And nature must obey necessity;

Which we will niggard with a little rest.

There is no more to say?

Cas.   No more. Good-night.

Early to-morrow will we rise, and hence.

Bru. Lucius! *(Re-enter Lucius.)*

My gown.   *[Exit Lucius.]*

      Farewell, good Messala!

Good-night, Titinius. Noble, noble Cassius,

Good-night, and good repose.

Cas.   O my dear brother!

This was an ill beginning of the night.

Never come such division 'tween our souls!

Let it not, Brutus.

Re-enter Lucius, *with the gown.*

Bru.   Everything is well.

Cas. Good-night, my lord.

Bru.   Good-night, good brother.

Tit. Mes. Good-night, Lord Brutus.

Bru.   Farewell, every one.

      [Exeunt all but Brutus and Lucius].

Give me the gown. Where is thy instrument?

Luc. Here in the tent.

Bru. What, thou speak'st drowsily?

Poor knave, I blame thee not; thou art
 o'er-watch'd.
Call Claudius and some other of my
 men;
I 'll have them sleep on cushions in my
 tent.
 Luc. Varro and Claudius!

 Enter VARRO *and* CLAUDIUS.

Var. Calls my lord?
 Bru. I pray you, sirs, lie in my tent
 and sleep;
It may be I shall raise you by and by
On business to my brother Cassius.
 Var. So please you, we will stand and
 watch your pleasure.
 Bru. I will not have it so: lie down,
 good sirs;
It may be I shall otherwise bethink me.
   [*Varro and Claudius lie down.*]
Look, Lucius, here 's the book I sought
 for so;
I put it in the pocket of my gown.
 Luc. I was sure your lordship did not
 give it me.
 Bru. Bear with me, good boy, I am
 much forgetful.
Canst thou hold up thy heavy eyes a
 while,
And touch thy instrument a strain or
 two?
 Luc. Ay, my lord, an 't please you.
 Bru.   It does, my boy.
I trouble thee too much, but thou art
 willing.
 Luc. It is my duty, sir.
 Bru. I should not urge thy duty past
 thy might;
I know young bloods look for a time of
 rest.
 Luc. I have slept, my lord, already.
 Bru. It was well done; and thou shalt
 sleep again;
I will not hold thee long. If I do live,
I will be good to thee.
     [*Music, and a song.*
This is a sleepy tune. O murderous
 slumber,
Lay'st thou thy leaden mace upon my boy,

That plays thee music? Gentle knave,
 good-night;
I will not do thee so much wrong to wake
 thee.
If thou dost nod, thou break'st thy instrument.
I 'll take it from thee; and, good boy,
 good-night.
Let me see, let me see; is not the leaf
 turn'd down
Where I left reading? Here it is, I
 think.

 Enter the GHOST *of* CÆSAR.

How ill this taper burns! Ha! who
 comes here?
I think it is the weakness of mine eyes
That shapes this monstrous apparition.
It comes upon me. Art thou anything?
Art thou some god, some angel, or some
 devil,
That mak'st my blood cold and my hair
 to stare?
Speak to me what thou art.
 Ghost. Thy evil spirit, Brutus.
 Bru.   Why com'st thou?
 Ghost. To tell thee thou shalt see me
 at Philippi.
 Bru. Well; then I shall see thee
 again?
 Ghost. Ay, at Philippi.
 Bru. Why, I will see thee at Philippi,
 then.
       [*Exit Ghost.*]
Now I have taken heart thou vanishest.
Ill spirit, I would hold more talk with
 thee.
Boy, Lucius! Varro! Claudius! Sirs,
 awake!
Claudius!
 Luc. The strings, my lord, are false.
 Bru. He thinks he still is at his instru-
 ment.
Lucius, awake!
 Luc. My lord?
 Bru. Didst thou dream, Lucius, that
 thou so criedst out?
 Luc. My lord, I do not know that I
 did cry.

Bru. Yes, that thou didst. Didst thou see anything?

Luc. Nothing, my lord.

Bru. Sleep again, Lucius. Sirrah Claudius!

Fellow thou, awake!

Var. My lord?

Clau. My lord?

Bru. Why did you so cry out, sirs, in your sleep?

Var. Clau. Did we, my lord?

Bru. Ay. Saw you anything?

Var. No, my lord, I saw nothing.

Clau. Nor I, my lord.

Bru. Go and commend me to my brother Cassius;

Bid him set on his powers betimes before,

And we will follow.

Var. Clau. It shall be done, my lord.

[*Exeunt.*

Macbeth

Act III, Scene IV

Hall in the palace.

A banquet prepar'd. Enter MACBETH, LADY MACBETH, ROSS, LENNOX, Lords, *and* Attendants.

Macb. You know your own degrees; sit down. At first

And last, the hearty welcome.

Lords. Thanks to your Majesty.

Macb. Ourself will mingle with society

And play the humble host.

Our hostess keeps her state, but in best time

We will require her welcome.

Lady M. Pronounce it for me, sir, to all our friends,

For my heart speaks they are welcome.

FIRST MURDERER [*appears at the door*].

Macb. See, they encounter thee with their hearts' thanks.

Both sides are even; here I 'll sit i' the midst.

Be large in mirth; anon we'll drink a measure

The table round. [*Approaching the door.*]—There 's blood upon thy face.

Mur. 'T is Banquo's then.

Macb. 'T is better thee without than he within.

Is he dispatch'd?

Mur. My lord, his throat is cut; that I did for him.

Macb. Thou art the best o' the cut-throats; yet he 's good

That did the like for Fleance. If thou didst it,

Thou art the nonpareil.

Mur. Most royal sir,

Fleance is scap'd.

Macb. Then comes my fit again. I had else been perfect,

Whole as the marble, founded as the rock,

As broad and general as the casing air;

But now I am cabin'd, cribb'd, confin'd, bound in

To saucy doubts and fears. But Banquo 's safe?

Mur. Ay, my good lord; safe in a ditch he bides,

With twenty trenched gashes on his head,

The least a death to nature.

Macb. Thanks, for that;

There the grown serpent lies. The worm that 's fled

Hath nature that in time will venom breed,

No teeth for the present. Get thee gone; to-morrow

We 'll hear ourselves again.

[*Exit Murderer.*

Lady M. My royal lord,

You do not give the cheer. The feast is sold

That is not often vouch'd, while 't is a-making,

'T is given with welcome. To feed were best at home;

From thence, the sauce to meat is ceremony;
Meeting were bare without it.

Enter the Ghost *of Banquo, and sits in Macbeth's place.*

Macb.   Sweet remembrancer!
Now, good digestion wait on appetite,
And health on both!
  Len.   May 't please your Highness sit.
  Macb. Here had we now our country's honour roof'd,
Were the grac'd person of our Banquo present,
Who may I rather challenge for unkindness
Than pity for mischance.
  Ross.   His absence, sir,
Lays blame upon his promise. Please 't your Highness
To grace us with your royal company?
  Macb. The table 's full.
  Len.   Here is a place reserv'd, sir.
  Macb. Where?
  Len. Here, my good lord. What is 't that moves your Highness?
  Macb. Which of you have done this?
  Lords.   What, my good lord?
  Macb. Thou canst not say I did it; never shake
Thy gory locks at me.
  Ross. Gentlemen, rise: his Highness is not well.
  Lady M. Sit, worthy friends; my lord is often thus,
And hath been from his youth. Pray you, keep seat;
The fit is momentary; upon a thought
He will again be well. If much you note him,
You shall offend him and extend his passion.
Feed, and regard him not. [*Aside to Macbeth.*] Are you a man?
  Macb. Ay, and a bold one, that dare look on that
Which might appall the devil.
  Lady M. [*Aside to Macbeth.*] O proper stuff!

This is the very painting of your fear;
This is the air-drawn dagger which, you said,
Led you to Duncan. O, these flaws and starts,
Impostors to true fear, would well become
A woman's story at a winter's fire,
Authoriz'd by her grandam. Shame itself!
Why do you make such faces? When all 's done,
You look but on a stool.
  Macb. Prithee, see there! behold! look! lo! how say you?
Why, what care I? If thou canst nod, speak too.
If charnel-houses and our graves must send
Those that we bury back, our monuments
Shall be the maws of kites.
                    [*Ghost vanishes.*]
  Lady M. [*Aside to Macbeth.*] What, quite unmann'd in folly?
  Macb. If I stand here, I saw him.
  Lady M. [*Aside to Macbeth.*] Fie, for shame!
  Macb. Blood hath been shed ere now, i' the olden time,
Ere humane statute purg'd the gentle weal;
Ay, and since too, murders have been perform'd
Too terrible for the ear. The time has been,
That, when the brains were out, the man would die,
And there an end; but now they rise again,
With twenty mortal murders on their crowns,
And push us from our stools. This is more strange
Than such a murder is.
  Lady M.   My worthy lord,
Your noble friends do lack you.
  Macb.   I do forget.

CROMWELL'S FIRST INTERVIEW WITH MILTON

From a painting by David Neal

Do not muse at me, my most worthy friends;

I have a strange infirmity, which is nothing

To those that know me. Come, love and health to all;

Then I 'll sit down. Give me some wine; fill full.

Re-enter Ghost.

I drink to the general joy o' the whole table,

And to our dear friend Banquo, whom we miss;

Would he were here! to all and him we thirst,

And all to all.

    Lords. Our duties, and the pledge.

    Macb. Avaunt! and quit my sight! let the earth hide thee!

Thy bones are marrowless, thy blood is cold;

Thou hast no speculation in those eyes

Which thou dost glare with!

    Lady M. Think of this, good peers,

But as a thing of custom; 't is no other,

Only it spoils the pleasure of the time.

    Macb. What man dare, I dare.

Approach thou like the rugged Russian bear,

The arm'd rhinoceros, or the Hyrcan tiger;

Take any shape but that, and my firm nerves

Shall never tremble. Or be alive again,

And dare me to the desert with thy sword;

If trembling I inhabit then, protest me

The baby of a girl. Hence, horrible shadow!

Unreal mockery, hence!

        [*Ghost vanishes.*]

        Why, so; being gone,

I am a man again. Pray you, sit still.

    Lady M. You have displac'd the mirth, broke the good meeting,

With most admir'd disorder.

    Macb. Can such things be,

And overcome us like a summer's cloud,

Without our special wonder? You make me strange

Even to the disposition that I owe,

When now I think you can behold such sights,

And keep the natural ruby of your cheeks,

When mine is blanch'd with fear.

    Ross. What sights, my lord?

    Lady M. I pray you, speak not; he grows worse and worse;

Question enrages him. At once, good-night.

Stand not upon the order of your going,

But go at once.

    Len. Good-night; and better health

Attend his Majesty!

    Lady M. A kind good-night to all!

        [*Exeunt Lords.*

    Macb. It will have blood, they say; blood will have blood.

Stones have been known to move and trees to speak;

Augures and understood relations have

By maggot-pies and choughs and rooks brought forth

The secret'st man of blood. What is the night?

    Lady M. Almost at odds with morning, which is which.

    Macb. How say'st thou, that Macduff denies his person

At our great bidding?

    Lady M. Did you send to him, sir?

    Macb. I hear it by the way; but I will send.

There 's not a one of them but in his house

I keep a servant fee'd. I will to-morrow,

And betimes I will, to the weird sisters.

More shall they speak; for now I am bent to know,

By the worst means, the worst. For mine own good

All causes shall give way. I am in blood

Stepp'd in so far that, should I wade no more,

Returning were as tedious as go o'er.

Strange things I have in head, that will to hand,

Which must be acted ere they may be
    scann'd.

Lady M. You lack the season of all
    natures, sleep.

Macb. Come, we 'll to sleep. My
    strange and self-abuse
Is the initiate fear that wants hard use;
We are yet but young in deed. [*Exeunt.*

Act V, Scene I.

Dunsinane. Ante-room in the castle.

Enter a Doctor *of* Physic *and a* Waiting
Gentlewoman.

Doct. I have two nights watch'd with
you, but can perceive no truth in your
report. When was it she last walk'd?

Gent. Since his Majesty went into the
field, I have seen her rise from her bed,
throw her nightgown upon her, unlock
her closet, take forth paper, fold it, write
upon 't, read it, afterwards seal it, and
again return to bed; yet all this while in
a most fast sleep.

Doct. A great perturbation in nature,
to receive at once the benefit of sleep,
and do the effects of watching! In this
slumb'ry agitation, besides her walking
and other actual performances, what, at
any time, have you heard her say?

Gent. That, sir, which I will not report after her.

Doct. You may to me; and 't is most
meet you should.

Gent. Neither to you nor any one;
having no witness to confirm my speech.

Enter Lady Macbeth, *with a taper.*

Lo you, here she comes! This is her
very guise; and, upon my life, fast asleep.
Observe her; stand close.

Doct. How came she by that light?

Gent. Why, it stood by her. She has
light by her continually; 't is her command.

Doct. You see, her eyes are open.

Gent. Ay, but their sense are shut.

Doct. What is it she does now? Look,
how she rubs her hands.

Gent. It is an accustom'd action with
her, to seem thus washing her hands. I
have known her continue in this a quarter of an hour.

Lady M. Yet here 's a spot.

Doct. Hark! she speaks. I will set
down what comes from her, to satisfy
my remembrance the more strongly.

Lady M. Out, damned spot! out, I
say!—One: two: why, then 't is time to
do 't.—Hell is murky!—Fie, my lord,
fie! a soldier, and afeard? What need
we fear who knows it, when none can
call our power to account?—Yet who
would have thought the old man to have
had so much blood in him?

Doct. Do you mark that?

Lady M. The thane of Fife had a
wife; where is she now?—What, will
these hands ne'er be clean?—No more o'
that, my lord, no more o' that; you mar
all with this starting.

Doct. Go to, go to; you have known
what you should not.

Gent. She has spoke what she should
not, I am sure of that; Heaven knows
what she has known.

Lady M. Here 's the smell of the
blood still; all the perfumes of Arabia
will not sweeten this little hand. Oh,
oh, oh!

Doct. What a sigh is there! The
heart is sorely charg'd.

Gent. I would not have such a heart
in my bosom for the dignity of the whole
body.

Doct. Well, well, well,—

Gent. Pray God it be, sir.

Doct. This disease is beyond my practice; yet I have known those which have
walk'd in their sleep who have died holily
in their beds.

Lady M. Wash your hands, put on
your nightgown; look not so pale.—I tell
you yet again, Banquo 's buried; he cannot come out on 's grave.

Doct. Even so?

Lady M. To bed, to bed! there 's knocking at the gate. Come, come, come, come, give me your hand. What 's done cannot be undone.—To bed, to bed, to bed!   [*Exit.*

Doct. Will she go now to bed?

Gent. Directly.

Doct. Foul whisp'rings are abroad; unnatural deeds

Do breed unnatural troubles; infected minds

To their deaf pillows will discharge their secrets.

More needs she the divine than the physician.

God, God, forgive us all! Look after her;

Remove from her the means of all annoyance,

And still keep eyes upon her. So, good-night!

My mind she has mated, and amaz'd my sight.

I think, but dare not speak.

Gent.   Good-night, good doctor.
                                [*Exeunt.*

SIR HENRY WOTTON
[1568-1639]

The Character of a Happy Life

How happy is he born and taught
  That serveth not another's will;
Whose armour is his honest thought,
  And simple truth his utmost skill;

Whose passions not his masters are;
  Whose soul is still prepared for death,
Untied unto the world by care
  Of public fame or private breath;

Who envies none that chance doth raise,
  Nor vice; who never understood
How deepest wounds are given by praise,
  Nor rules of state, but rules of good;

Who hath his life from rumours freed;
  Whose conscience is his strong retreat;

Whose state can neither flatterers feed,
  Nor ruin make oppressors great;

Who God doth late and early pray
  More of his grace than gifts to lend;
And entertains the harmless day
  With a religious book or friend—

This man is freed from servile bands
  Of hope to rise or fear to fall:
Lord of himself, though not of lands,
  And, having nothing, yet hath all.

On his Mistress the Queen of Bohemia

You meaner beauties of the night,
  That poorly satisfy our eyes
More by your number than your light,
  You common people of the skies;
  What are you when the moon shall rise?

You curious chanters of the wood,
  That warble forth Dame Nature's lays,
Thinking your passions understood
  By your weak accents; what's your praise
  When Philomel her voice shall raise?

You violets that first appear,
  By your pure purple mantles known
Like the proud virgins of the year,
  As if the spring were all your own;
  What are you when the rose is blown?

So, when my mistress shall be seen
  In form and beauty of her mind,
By virtue first, then choice, a Queen,
  Tell me, if she were not design'd
  Th' eclipse and glory of her kind.

GEORGE WITHER
[1588-1667]

A Christmas Carol

So now is come our joyfulst feast:
  Let every man be jolly,

Each room with ivy leaves is drest
  And every post with holly.
Though some churls at our mirth repine,
Round your foreheads garlands twine,
Drown sorrow in a cup of wine,
  And let us all be merry.

          *   *   *   *   *

Now every lad is wondrous trim,
  And no man minds his labour;
Our lasses have provided them
  A bag-pipe and a tabor.
Young men and maids and girls and boys
Give life to one another's joys,
And you anon shall by their noise
  Perceive that they are merry.

Rank misers now do sparing shun,
  Their hall of music soundeth;
And dogs thence with whole shoulders
    run,
  So all things here aboundeth.
The country folk themselves advance,
For Crowdy-mutton's come out of
    France,
And Jack shall pipe, and Jill shall dance,
  And all the town be merry.

Ned Swash hath fetched his bands from
    pawn,
  And all his best apparel;
Brisk Nell hath bought a ruff of lawn
  With droppings of the barrel.
And those that hardly all the year
Had bread to eat or rags to wear,
Will have both clothes and dainty fare
  And all the day be merry.

          *   *   *   *   *

The wenches with their wassail-bowls
  About the street are singing,
The boys are come to catch the owls,
  The wild-mare in is bringing.
Our kitchen-boy hath broke his box,
And to the dealing of the ox
Our honest neighbours come by flocks,
  And here they will be merry.

          *   *   *   *   *

Then wherefore in these merry days
  Should we I pray be duller?

No, let us sing our roundelays
  To make our mirth the fuller;
And whilest thus inspired we sing
Let all the streets with echoes ring:
Woods, and hills, and every-thing
  Bear witness we are merry.

When we are upon the Seas

On those great waters now I am,
  Of which I have been told,
That whosoever thither came
  Should wonders there behold.
In this unsteady place of fear,
  Be present, Lord, with me;
For in these depths of water here
  I depths of danger see.

A stirring courser now I sit,
  A headstrong steed I ride,
That champs and foams upon the bit
  Which curbs his lofty pride.
The softest whistling of the winds
  Doth make him gallop fast;
And as their breath increased he finds
  The more he maketh haste.

Take Thou, oh Lord! the reins in hand,
  Assume our Master's room;
Vouchsafe Thou at our helm to stand,
  And pilot to become.
Trim Thou the sails, and let good speed
  Accompany our haste;
Sound Thou the channels at our need,
  And anchor for us cast.

A fit and favourable wind
  To further us provide;
And let it wait on us behind,
  Or lackey by our side.
From sudden gusts, from storms, from
    sands,
  And from the raging wave;
From shallows, rocks, and pirates' hands,
  Men, goods, and vessel save.

Preserve us from the wants, the fear,
  And sickness of the seas;
But chiefly from our sins, which are
  A danger worse than these.

Lord! let us also safe arrive
  Where we desire to be;
And for Thy mercies let us give
  Due thanks and praise to Thee.

The Prayer of Old Age

As this my carnal robe grows old,
Soil'd, rent, and worn by length of years,
Let me on that by faith lay hold
Which man in life immortal wears:
  So sanctify my days behind,
  So let my manners be refined,
That when my soul and flesh must part,
There lurk no terrors in my heart.

So shall my rest be safe and sweet
When I am lodgèd in my grave;
And when my soul and body meet,
A joyful meeting they shall have;
  Their essence then shall be divine,
  This muddy flesh shall starlike shine,
And God shall that fresh youth restore
Which will abide for evermore.

ROBERT HERRICK (1591-1674)

Corinna's Going a-Maying

Get up, get up for shame! The bloom-
  ing morn
  Upon her wings presents the god un-
    shorn.
See how Aurora throws her fair
Fresh-quilted colours through the air:
Get up, sweet slug-a-bed, and see
The dew bespangling herb and tree!
Each flower has wept and bow'd toward
  the east
Above an hour since, yet you not drest;
  Nay! not so much as out of bed?
  When all the birds have matins said
  And sung their thankful hymns, 'tis sin,
  Nay, profanation, to keep in,
Whereas a thousand virgins on this day
Spring sooner than the lark, to fetch in
  May.

Rise and put on your foliage, and be seen
To come forth, like the spring-time, fresh
  and green,
  And sweet as Flora. Take no care
  For jewels for your gown or hair:
  Fear not; the leaves will strew
  Gems in abundance upon you:
Besides, the childhood of the day has
  kept,
Against you come, some orient pearls
  unwept.
  Come, and receive them while the light
  Hangs on the dew-locks of the night:
  And Titan on the eastern hill
  Retires himself, or else stands still
Till you come forth! Wash, dress, be
  brief in praying:
Few beads are best when once we go
  a-Maying.

Come, my Corinna, come; and coming,
  mark
How each field turns a street, each street
  a park,
  Made green and trimm'd with trees!
    see how
  Devotion gives each house a bough
  Or branch! each porch, each door, ere
    this,
  An ark, a tabernacle is,
Made up of white-thorn neatly inter-
  wove,
As if here were those cooler shades of
  love.
  Can such delights be in the street
  And open fields, and we not see 't?
  Come, we'll abroad: and let 's obey
  The proclamation made for May,
And sin no more, as we have done, by
  staying;
But, my Corinna, come, let 's go
  a-Maying.

There's not a budding boy or girl this
  day
But is got up and gone to bring in May.
  A deal of youth ere this is come
  Back, and with white-thorn laden
    home.

Some have despatch'd their cakes and
    cream,
Before that we have left to dream:
And some have wept and woo'd, and
    plighted troth,
And chose their priest, ere we can cast off
    sloth:
Many a green-gown has been given,
Many a kiss, both odd and even:
Many a glance, too, has been sent
From out the eye, love's firmament:
Many a jest told of the keys betraying
This night, and locks pick'd: yet we're
    not a-Maying!

Come, let us go, while we are in our
    prime,
And take the harmless folly of the time!
    We shall grow old apace, and die
    Before we know our liberty.
    Our life is short, and our days run
    As fast away as does the sun.
And, as a vapour or a drop of rain,
Once lost, can ne'er be found again,
    So when or you or I are made
    A fable, song, or fleeting shade,
    All love, all liking, all delight
    Lies drown'd with us in endless night.
Then, while time serves, and we are but
    decaying,
Come, my Corinna, come, let's go
    a-Maying.

The Night Piece

HER eyes the glow-worm lend thee,
The shooting stars attend thee;
    And the elves also,
    Whose little eyes glow
Like the sparks of fire, befriend thee.

No Will-o'-the-wisp mislight thee,
Nor snake or slow-worm bite thee;
    But on, on thy way
    Not making a stay,
Since ghost there's none to affright thee.

Let not the dark thee cumber:
What though the moon does slumber?

The stars of the night
Will lend thee their light
Like tapers clear without number.

Then, Julia, let me woo thee,
Thus, thus to come unto me;
    And when I shall meet
    Thy silv'ry feet,
My soul I'll pour into thee.

To Daffodils

FAIR daffodils, we weep to see
    You haste away so soon;
As yet the early-rising sun
    Has not attain'd his noon.
        Stay, stay
    Until the hasting day
        Has run
    But to the evensong;
And, having pray'd together, we
    Will go with you along.

We have short time to stay, as you,
    We have as short a spring;
As quick a growth to meet decay,
    As you, or anything.
        We die
    As your hours do, and dry
        Away
    Like to the summer's rain;
Or as the pearls of morning's dew,
    Ne'er to be found again.

Upon Julia's Clothes

WHENAS in silks my Julia goes,
Then, then, methinks, how sweetly flows
The liquefaction of her clothes!

Next, when I cast mine eyes and see
That brave vibration each way free,
—O how that glittering taketh me!

To the Virgins, to make much of Time

GATHER ye rosebuds while ye may,
    Old Time is still a-flying:

And this same flower that smiles to-day
　　To-morrow will be dying.

The glorious lamp of heaven, the sun,
　　The higher he 's a-getting,
The sooner will his race be run,
　　And nearer he 's to setting.

That age is best which is the first,
　　When youth and blood are warmer;
But being spent, the worse, and worst
　　Times still succeed the former.

Then be not coy, but use your time,
　　And while ye may, go marry:
For having lost but once your prime,
　　You may for ever tarry.

THOMAS CAREW (1595?-1639?)

Epitaph on the Lady Mary Villiers

THE Lady Mary Villiers lies
Under this stone; with weeping eyes
The parents that first gave her birth,
And their sad friends, laid her in earth.
If any of them, Reader, were
Known unto thee, shed a tear;
Or if thyself possess a gem
As dear to thee, as this to them,
Though a stranger to this place,
Bewail in theirs thine own hard case:

For thou perhaps at thy return
May'st find thy Darling in an urn.

JAMES SHIRLEY (1596-1666)

A Dirge

THE glories of our blood and state
　　Are shadows, not substantial things;
There is no armour against Fate;
　　Death lays his icy hand on kings:
　　　　Sceptre and Crown
　　　　Must tumble down,
And in the dust be equal made
With the poor crookèd scythe and spade.
Some men with swords may reap the field,
　　And plant fresh laurels where they kill:
But their strong nerves at last must yield;
　　They tame but one another still:
　　　　Early or late
　　　　They stoop to fate,
And must give up their murmuring breath
When they, pale captives, creep to death.

The garlands wither on your brow;
　　Then boast no more your mighty deeds!
Upon Death's purple altar now
　　See where the victor-victim bleeds.
　　　　Your heads must come
　　　　To the cold tomb:
Only the actions of the just
Smell sweet and blossom in their dust.

SIR THOMAS BROWNE (1605-1682)

From RELIGIO MEDICI

Faith in Mysteries

As for those wingy Mysteries in Divinity, and airy subtleties in Religion, which have unhing'd the brains of better heads, they never stretched the *Pia Mater* of mine. Methinks there be not impossibilities enough in Religion for an active faith; the deepest Mysteries ours contains have not only been illustrated, but maintained, by Syllogism and the rule of Reason. I love to lose my self in a mystery, to pursue my Reason to an *O altitudo!* 'Tis my solitary recreation to pose my apprehension with those involved Ænigmas and riddles of the Trinity, with Incarnation, and Resurrection.   I can answer all the Objections of Satan and my rebellious reason with that odd resolution I learned of Tertullian, *Certum est, quia impossibile est.*   I desire to exercise my faith in the difficultest point; for to credit ordinary and visible objects is not faith, but perswasion.   Some believe the better for seeing CHRIST's Sepulchre; and, when they have seen the Red Sea, doubt not of the Miracle.   Now, contrarily, I bless my self and am thankful that I lived not in the days of Miracles, that I never saw CHRIST nor His Disciples.   I would not have been one of those Israelites that pass'd the Red Sea, nor one of CHRIST's patients on whom He wrought His wonders; then had my faith been thrust upon me, nor should I enjoy that greater blessing pronounced to all that believe and saw not.   'Tis an easie and necessary belief, to credit what our eye and sense hath examined.   I believe He was dead, and buried, and rose again; and desire to see Him in His glory, rather than to contemplate Him in His Cenotaphe or Sepulchre.   Nor is this much to believe; as we have reason, we owe this faith unto History: *they* only had the advantage of a bold and noble Faith, who lived before His coming, who upon obscure prophesies and mystical Types could raise a belief, and expect apparent impossibilities.

The Soul Illimitable

Now for my life, it is a miracle of thirty years, which to relate, were not a History, but a piece of Poetry, and would sound to common ears like a Fable.   For the World, I count it not an Inn, but an Hospital; and a place not to live, but to dye in.   The world that I regard is my self; it is the Microcosm of my own frame that I cast mine eye on; for the other, I use it but like my Globe, and turn it round sometimes for my recreation.   Men that look upon my outside, perusing only my condition and Fortunes, do err in my Altitude; for I am above Atlas his shoulders. The earth is a point not only in respect of the Heavens above us, but of that heavenly and celestial part within us; that mass of Flesh that circumscribes me, limits not my mind: that surface that tells the Heavens it hath an end, cannot persuade me I have any: I take my circle to be above three hundred and sixty; though the number of the Ark do measure my body, it comprehendeth not my mind: whilst I study to find how I am a Microcosm, or little World, I find my self something more than the great.   There is surely a piece of Divinity in us, something that was before the Elements, and owes no homage unto the Sun.   Nature tells me

I am the Image of GOD, as well as Scripture: he that understands not thus much, hath not his introduction or first lesson, and is yet to begin the Alphabet of man. Let me not injure the felicity of others, if I say I am as happy as any: *Ruat cœlum, fiat voluntas Tua,* salveth all; so that whatsoever happens, it is but what our daily prayers desire. In brief, I am content; and what should Providence add more? Surely this is it we call Happiness, and this do I enjoy; with this I am happy in a dream, and as content to enjoy a happiness in a fancy, as others in a more apparent truth and realty. There is surely a neerer apprehension of any thing that delights us in our dreams, than in our waked senses: without this I were unhappy; for my awaked judgment discontents me, ever whispering unto me, that I am from my friend; but my friendly dreams in the night requite me, and make me think I am within his arms. I thank GOD for my happy dreams, as I do for my good rest; for there is a satisfaction in them unto reasonable desires, and such as can be content with a fit of happiness: and surely it is not a melancholy conceit to think we are all asleep in this World, and that the conceits of this life are as meer dreams to those of the next; as the Phantasms of the night, to the conceits of the day. There is an equal delusion in both, and the one doth but seem to be the embleme or picture of the other: we are somewhat more than our selves in our sleeps, and the slumber of the body seems to be but the waking of the soul. It is the ligation of sense, but the liberty of reason; and our waking conceptions do not match the Fancies of our sleeps. At my Nativity my Ascendant was the watery sign of Scorpius; I was born in the Planetary hour of Saturn, and I think I have a piece of that Leaden Planet in me. I am no way facetious, nor disposed for the mirth and galliardize of company; yet in one dream I can compose a whole Comedy, behold the action, apprehend the jests, and laugh my self awake at the conceits thereof. Were my memory as faithful as my reason is then fruitful, I would never study but in my dreams; and this time also would I chuse for my devotions: but our grosser memories have then so little hold of our abstracted understandings, that they forget the story, and can only relate to our awaked souls, a confused and broken tale of that that hath passed. Aristotle, who had written a singular Tract *Of Sleep,* hath not, methinks, throughly defined it; nor yet Galen, though he seem to have corrected it; for those Noctambuloes and night-walkers, though in their sleep, do yet injoy the action of their senses. We must therefore say that there is something in us that is not in the jurisdiction of Morpheus; and that those abstracted and ecstatick souls do walk about in their own corps, as spirits with the bodies they assume, wherein they seem to hear, see, and feel, though

indeed the Organs are destitute of sense, and their natures of those
faculties that should inform them.   Thus it is observed, that men sometimes, upon the hour of their departure, do speak and reason above
themselves; for then the soul, beginning to be freed from the ligaments
of the body, begins to reason like her self, and to discourse in a strain
above mortality.

From HYDRIOTAPHIA; OR URNE BURIALL

The Vanity of Ambition

Now since these dead bones have already out-lasted the living ones of
Methuselah, and in a yard under ground, and thin walls of clay, out-worn
all the strong and specious buildings above it; and quietly rested under
the drums and tramplings of three conquests; what Prince can promise
such diuturnity unto his Reliques, or might not gladly say,

Sic ego componi versus in ossa velim.

Time which antiquates Antiquities, and hath an art to make dust of all
things, hath yet spared these *minor* Monuments.

In vain we hope to be known by open and visible conservatories, when
to be unknown was the means of their continuation and obscurity their
protection: If they dyed by violent hands, and were thrust into their
Urnes, these bones become considerable, and some old Philosophers
would honour them, whose souls they conceived most pure, which were
thus snatched from their bodies; and to retain a stranger propension unto
them: whereas they weariedly left a languishing corps, and with faint
desires of reunion.   If they fell by long and aged decay, yet wrapt up
in the bundle of time, they fall into indistinction, and make but one blot
with Infants.   If we begin to die when we live, and long life be but a
prolongation of death; our life is a sad composition; We live with death,
and die not in a moment.   How many pulses made up the life of
Methuselah, were work for *Archimedes:* Common Counters summe up
the life of *Moses* his man.   Our dayes become considerable like petty
sums by minute accumulations; where numerous fractions make up but
small round numbers; and our dayes of a span long make not one little
finger.

If the nearnesse of our last necessity, brought a nearer conformity
into it, there were a happinesse in hoary hairs, and no calamity in half
senses.   But the long habit of living indisposeth us for dying; when
Avarice makes us the sport of death; When even *David* grew politickly

cruell; and *Solomon* could hardly be said to be the wisest of men. But many are too early old, and before the date of age. Adversity stretcheth our dayes, misery makes *Alcmenas* nights, and time hath no wings unto it. But the most tedious being is that which can unwish itself, content to be nothing, or never to have been, which was beyond the *male*content of *Job,* who cursed not the day of his life, but his Nativity: Content to have so farre been, as to have a Title to future being; Although he had lived here but in an hidden state of life, and as it were an abortion.

What Song the *Syrens* sang, or what name *Achilles* assumed when he hid himself among women, though puzling Questions, are not beyond all conjecture. What time the persons of these Ossuaries entred the famous Nations of the dead, and slept with Princes and Counsellours, might admit a wide solution. But who were the proprietaries of these bones, or what bodies these ashes made up, were a question above Anti- quarism. Not to be resolved by man, nor easily perhaps by spirits, except we consult the Provinciall Guardians, or tutellary Observators. Had they made as good provision for their names, as they have done for their Reliques, they had not so grosly erred in the art of perpetuation. But to subsist in bones, and be but Pyramidally extant, is a fallacy in duration. Vain ashes, which in the oblivion of names, persons, times, and sexes, have found unto themselves, a fruitless continuation, and only arise unto late posterity, as Emblemes of mortall vanities; Antidotes against pride, vain-glory, and madding vices. Pagan vain-glories which thought the world might last for ever, had encouragement for ambition, and, finding no *Atropos* unto the immortality of their Names, were never dampt with the necessity of oblivion. Even old ambitions had the ad- vantage of ours, in the attempts of their vain-glories, who acting early, and before the probable Meridian of time, have by this time found great accomplishment of their designes, whereby the ancient *Heroes* have already out-lasted their Monuments, and Mechanicall preservations. But in this latter Scene of time, we cannot expect such mummies unto our memories, when ambition may fear the Prophecy of *Elias,* and *Charles* the fifth can never hope to live within two *Methuselas* of *Hector.*

And therefore restlesse inquietude for the diuturnity of our memories unto present considerations, seems a vanity almost out of date, and superannuated peece of folly. We cannot hope to live so long in our names, as some have done in their persons, one face of *Janus* holds no proportion unto the other. 'Tis too late to be ambitious. The great mutations of the world are acted, or time may be too short for our de- signes. To extend our memories by Monuments, whose death we daily pray for, and whose duration we cannot hope, without injiury to our expectations, in the advent of the last day, were a contradiction to our beliefs. We whose generations are ordained in this setting part of time, are providentially taken off from such imaginations; And being necessitated to eye the remaining particle of futurity, are naturally constituted unto thoughts of the next word, and cannot excusably decline the consideration of that duration, which maketh Pyramids pillars of snow, and all that's past a moment.

From THE GARDEN OF CYRUS

Sleep

BUT the quincunx of heaven runs low, and 'tis time to close the five ports of knowledge. We are unwilling to spin out our awaking thoughts into the phantasms of sleep, which often continueth precogitations; making cables of cobwebs, and wildernesses of handsome groves. Beside Hippocrates hath spoke so little, and the oneirocritical masters have left such frigid interpretations from plants, that there is little encouragement to dream of Paradise itself. Nor will the sweetest delight of gardens afford much comfort in sleep; wherein the dulness of that sense shakes hands with delectable odours; and though in the bed of Cleopatra, can hardly with any delight raise up the ghost of a rose.

Night, which Pagan theology could make the daughter of Chaos, affords no advantage to the description of order; although no lower than that mass can we derive its genealogy. All things began in order, so shall they end, and so shall they begin again; according to the ordainer of order and mystical mathematicks of the city of heaven.

Though Somnus in Homer be sent to rouse up Agamemnon, I find no such effects in these drowsy approaches of sleep. To keep our eyes open longer, were but to act our Antipodes. The huntsmen are up in America, and they are already past their first sleep in Persia. But who can be drowsy at that hour which freed us from everlasting sleep? or have slumbering thoughts at that time, when sleep itself must end, and, as some conjecture, all shall awake again?

EDMUND WALLER (1606-1687)

Go, lovely Rose

Go, lovely Rose!
Tell her that wastes her time and me,
That now she knows,
When I resemble her to thee
How sweet and fair she seems to be.

Tell her that's young,
And shuns to have her graces spied,
That had'st thou sprung
In deserts where no men abide,
Thou must have uncommended died.

Small is the worth
Of beauty from the light retired;
Bid her come forth!
Suffer herself to be desired,
And not blush so to be admired.

Then die: that she
The common fate of all things rare
May read in thee;
How small a part of time they share,
They are so wondrous sweet and fair.

On a Girdle

THAT which her slender waist con-
fined,
Shall now my joyful temples bind;
No monarch but would give his crown
His arms might do what this has done.

It was my Heaven's extremest sphere,
The pale which held that lovely deer;
My joy, my grief, my hope, my love,
Did all within this circle move.

A narrow compass! and yet there
Dwelt all that's good, and all that's
fair;
Give me but what this ribband bound,
Take all the rest the sun goes round.

JOHN MILTON (1608-1674)

On the Morning of Christ's Nativity

IT was the Winter wilde,
While the Heav'n-born-childe,
All meanly wrapt in the rude manger
lies;
Nature in aw to him
Had dofft her gawdy trim,
With her great Master so to sym-
pathize:
It was no season then for her
To wanton with the Sun her lusty
Paramour.

Only with speeches fair
She woo's the gentle Air
To hide her guilty front with innocent
Snow,
And on her naked shame,
Pollute with sinfull blame,
The Saintly Vail of Maiden white to
throw,
Confounded, that her Makers eyes
Should look so neer upon her foul de-
formities.

But he her fears to cease,
Sent down the meek-eyd Peace,
She crown'd with Olive green, came
softly sliding
Down through the turning sphear
His ready Harbinger,
With Turtle wing the amorous clouds
dividing,
And waving wide her mirtle wand,
She strikes a universall Peace through
Sea and Land.

No War, or Battails sound
Was heard the World around,
The idle spear and shield were high up
hung;
The hookèd Chariot stood
Unstain'd with hostile blood,
The Trumpet spake not to the armèd
throng,

And Kings sate still with awfull eye,
As if they surely knew their sovran Lord
    was by.

But peacefull was the night
Wherein the Prince of light
    His raign of peace upon the earth
    began:
The Windes with wonder whist,
Smoothly the waters kist,
    Whispering new joyes to the milde
    Ocean,
Who now hath quite forgot to rave,
While Birds of Calm sit brooding on the
    charmèd wave.

The Stars with deep amaze
Stand fixt in stedfast gaze,
    Bending one way their pretious in-
    fluence,
And will not take their flight,
For all the morning light,
    Or Lucifer that often warn'd them
    thence;
But in their glimmering Orbs did glow,
Untill their Lord himself bespake, and
    bid them go.

And though the shady gloom
Had given day her room,
    The Sun himself with-held his wonted
    speed,
And hid his head for shame,
As his inferiour flame,
    The new enlightn'd world no more
    should need;
He saw a greater Sun appear
Then his bright Throne, or burning
    Axletree could bear.

The Shepherds on the Lawn,
Or ere the point of dawn,
    Sate simply chatting in a rustick row;
Full little thought they than,
That the mighty Pan
    Was kindly come to live with them
    below;
Perhaps their loves, or els their sheep,
Was all that did their silly thoughts so
    busie keep.

When such musick sweet
Their hearts and ears did greet,
    As never was by mortall finger
    strook,
Divinely-warbled voice
Answering the stringèd noise,
    As all their souls in blisfull rapture
    took
The Air such pleasure loth to lose,
With thousand echo's still prolongs each
    heav'nly close.

Nature that heard such sound
Beneath the hollow round
    Of Cynthia's seat, the Airy region
    thrilling,
Now was almost won
To think her part was don,
    And that her raign had here its last
    fulfilling;
She knew such harmony alone
Could hold all Heav'n and Earth in
    happier union.

At last surrounds their sight
A Globe of circular light,
    That with long beams the shame-fac't
    night array'd,
The helmèd Cherubim,
And sworded Seraphim,
    Are seen in glittering ranks with wings
    displaid,
Harping in loud and solemn quire,
With unexpressive notes to Heav'ns new-
    born Heir.

Such musick (as 'tis said)
Before was never made,
    But when of old the sons of morning
    sung,
While the Creator Great
His constellations set,
    And the well-ballanc't world on hinges
    hung,
And cast the dark foundations deep,
And bid the weltring waves their oozy
    channel keep.

Ring out ye Crystall sphears,
Once bless our human ears,
  (If ye have power to touch our senses
    so)
And let your silver chime
Move in melodious time;
  And let the Base of Heav'ns deep
    Organ blow
And with your ninefold harmony
Make up full consort to th'Angelike
    symphony.

For if such holy Song
Enwrap our fancy long,
  Time will run back, and fetch the age
    of gold,
And speckl'd vanity
Will sicken soon and die,
  And leprous sin will melt from earthly
    mould,
And Hell it self will pass away,
And leave her dolorous mansions to the
    peering day.

Yea Truth, and Justice then
Will down return to men,
  Th'enameld Arras of the Rain-bow
    wearing,
And Mercy set between,
Thron'd in Celestiall sheen,
  With radiant feet the tissued clouds
    down stearing,
And Heav'n as at som festivall,
Will open wide the Gates of her high
    Palace Hall.

But wisest Fate sayes no,
This must not yet be so,
  The Babe lies yet in smiling Infancy,
That on the bitter cross
Must redeem our loss;
  So both himself and us to glorifie:
Yet first to those ychain'd in sleep,
The wakefull trump of doom must thun-
    der through the deep,

With such a horrid clang
As on mount Sinai rang
  While the red fire, and smouldring
    clouds out brake:

The agèd Earth agast
With terrour of that blast,
  Shall from the surface to the center
    shake;
When at the worlds last session,
The dreadfull Judge in middle Air shall
    spread his throne.

And then at last our bliss
Full and perfect is,
  But now begins; for from this happy
    day
Th'old Dragon under ground
In straiter limits bound,
  Not half so far casts his usurpèd sway,
And wrath to see his Kingdom fail,
Swindges the scaly Horrour of his
    foulded tail.

The Oracles are dumm,
No voice or hideous humm
  Runs through the archèd roof in words
    deceiving.
Apollo from his shrine
Can no more divine,
  With hollow shreik the steep of Del-
    phos leaving.
No nightly trance, or breathèd spell,
Inspire's the pale-ey'd Priest from the
    prophetic cell.

The lonely mountains o're,
And the resounding shore,
  A voice of weeping heard, and loud
    lament;
From haunted spring, and dale
Edg'd with poplar pale,
  The parting Genius is with sighing
    sent,
With flowre-inwov'n tresses torn
The Nimphs in twilight shade of tangled
    thickets mourn.

In consecrated Earth,
And on the holy Hearth,
  The Lars, and Lemures moan with
    midnight plaint,
In Urns, and Altars round,
A drear, and dying sound

Affrights the Flamins at their service
　　quaint;
And the chill Marble seems to sweat,
While each peculiar power forgoes his
　　wonted seat.

Peor, and Baalim,
Forsake their Temples dim,
　　With that twise-batter'd god of Pales-
　　tine,
And moonèd Ashtaroth,
Heav'ns Queen and Mother both,
　　Now sits not girt with Tapers holy
　　shine,
The Libyc Hammon shrinks his horn,
In vain the Tyrian Maids their wounded
　　Thamuz mourn.

And sullen Moloch fled,
Hath left in shadows dred,
　　His burning Idol all of blackest hue,
In vain with Cymbals ring,
They call the grisly king,
　　In dismall dance about the furnace
　　blue;
The brutish gods of Nile as fast,
Isis and Orus, and the Dog Anubis hast.

Nor is Osiris seen
In Memphian Grove, or Green,
　　Trampling the unshowr'd Grasse with
　　lowings loud:
Nor can he be at rest
Within his sacred chest,
　　Naught but profoundest Hell can be
　　his shroud,
In vain with Timbrel'd Anthems dark
The sable-stolèd Sorcerers bear his wor-
　　shipt Ark.

He feels from Juda's Land
The dredded Infants hand,
　　The rayes of Bethlehem blind his dusky
　　eyn;
Nor all the gods beside,
Longer dare abide,
　　Not Typhon huge ending in snaky
　　twine:

Our Babe to shew his Godhead true,
Can in his swadling bands controul the
　　damnèd crew.

So when the Sun in bed,
Curtain'd with cloudy red,
　　Pillows his chin upon an Orient wave,
The flocking shadows pale,
Troop to th'infernall jail,
　　Each fetter'd Ghost slips to his severall
　　grave,
And the yellow-skirted Fayes,
Fly after the Night-steeds, leaving their
　　Moon-lov'd maze.

But see the Virgin blest,
Hath laid her Babe to rest.
　　Time is our tedious Song should here
　　have ending,
Heav'ns youngest teemèd Star,
Hath fixt her polisht Car,
　　Her sleeping Lord with Handmaid
　　Lamp attending:
And all about the Courtly Stable,
Bright-harnest Angels sit in order serv-
　　iceable.

L'Allegro

HENCE, loathèd Melancholy,
　　Of Cerberus and blackest Midnight
　　born,
In Stygian cave forlorn
　　'Mongst horrid shapes, and shrieks,
　　and sights unholy!
Find out some uncouth cell
　　Where brooding Darkness spreads his
　　jealous wings
And the night-raven sings;
　　There under ebon shades, and low-
　　browed rocks
As ragged as thy locks,
　　In dark Cimmerian desert ever dwell.

But come, thou Goddess fair and free,
In heaven ycleped Euphrosyne,
And by men, heart-easing Mirth,
Whom lovely Venus at a birth
With two sister Graces more

To ivy-crownèd Bacchus bore;
Or whether (as some sager sing)
The frolic wind that breathes the spring,
Zephyr, with Aurora playing,
As he met her once a-Maying,
There on beds of violets blue
And fresh-blown roses washt in dew
Filled her with thee, a daughter fair,
So buxom, blithe, and debonair.
   Haste thee, Nymph, and bring with
     thee
Jest, and youthful jollity,
Quips, and cranks, and wanton wiles,
Nods, and becks, and wreathèd smiles
Such as hang on Hebe's cheek,
And love to live in dimple sleek;
Sport that wrinkled Care derides,
And Laughter holding both his sides.
Come, and trip it as ye go
On the light fantastic toe;
And in thy right hand lead with thee
The mountain Nymph, sweet Liberty;
And if I give thee honour due
Mirth, admit me of thy crew,
To live with her, and live with thee
In unreprovèd pleasures free;
To hear the lark begin his flight
And singing startle the dull night
From his watch-tower in the skies,
Till the dappled Dawn doth rise;
Then to come, in spite of sorrow,
And at my window bid good-morrow
Through the sweetbriar, or the vine,
Or the twisted eglantine:
While the cock with lively din
Scatters the rear of Darkness thin,
And to the stack, or the barn-door,
Stoutly struts his dames before:
Oft list'ning how the hounds and horn
Cheerly rouse the slumbring Morn,
From the side of some hoar hill,
Through the high wood echoing shrill:
Sometime walking, not unseen,
By hedge-row elms, on hillocks green,
Right against the eastern gate
Where the great Sun begins his state
Robed in flames and amber light,
The clouds in thousand liveries dight;
While the ploughman, near at hand,

Whistles o'er the furrowed land,
And the milkmaid singeth blithe,
And the mower whets his scythe,
And every shepherd tells his tale
Under the hawthorn in the dale.
   Straight mine eye hath caught new
     pleasures
Whilst the lantskip round it measures:
Russet lawns, and fallows gray,
Where the nibbling flocks do stray;
Mountains, on whose barren breast
The labouring clouds do often rest;
Meadows trim with daisies pied,
Shallow brooks, and rivers wide;
Towers and battlements it sees
Bosomed high in tufted trees,
Where perhaps some Beauty lies,
The Cynosure of neighbouring eyes.
Hard by, a cottage chimney smokes
From betwixt two aged oaks,
Where Corydon and Thyrsis met
Are at their savoury dinner set
Of herbs and other country messes,
Which the neat-handed Phillis dresses;
And then in haste her bower she leaves
With Thestylis to bind the sheaves;
Or, if the earlier season lead,
To the tanned haycock in the mead.
   Sometimes with secure delight
The upland hamlets will invite,
When the merry bells ring round,
And the jocund rebecks sound
To many a youth and many a maid,
Dancing in the chequered shade;
And young and old come forth to play
On a sun-shine holyday,
Till the live-long day-light fail:
Then to the spicy nut-brown ale,
With stories told of many a feat,
How fairy Mab the junkets eat:—
She was pincht and pulled, she said;
And he, by Friar's lantern led,
Tells how the drudging goblin sweat
To earn his cream-bowl duly set,
When in one night, ere glimpse of morn,
His shadowy flail hath threshed the corn
That ten day-labourers could not end;
Then lies him down, the lubbar fend,
And stretcht out all the chimney's length,

Basks at the fire his hairy strength,
And crop-full out of doors he flings,
Ere the first cock his matin rings.

Thus done the tales, to bed they creep,
By whispering winds soon lulled asleep.

Towered cities please us then,
And the busy hum of men,
Where throngs of knights and barons
   bold,
In weeds of peace, high triumphs hold,
With store of ladies, whose bright eyes
Rain influence, and judge the prize
Of wit or arms, while both contend
To win her grace, whom all commend.
There let Hymen oft appear
In saffron robe, with taper clear,
And pomp, and feast, and revelry,
With mask and antique pageantry;
Such sights as youthful poets dream
On summer eves by haunted stream.
Then to the well-trod stage anon,
If Jonson's learnèd sock be on,
Or sweetest Shakspere, Fancy's child,
Warble his native wood-notes wild.

And ever against eating cares,
Lap me in soft Lydian airs,
Married to immortal verse,
Such as the meeting soul may pierce,
In notes with many a winding bout
Of linkèd sweetness long drawn out,
With wanton heed and giddy cunning,
The melting voice through mazes run-
   ning,
Untwisting all the chains that tie
The hidden soul of harmony;
That Orpheus' self may heave his head
From golden slumber on a bed
Of heapt Elysian flowers, and hear
Such strains as would have won the ear
Of Pluto to have quite set free
His half-regained Eurydice.

These delights if thou canst give,
Mirth, with thee I mean to live.

Il Penseroso

HENCE, vain deluding Joys,
   The brood of Folly without father
   bred!

How little you bestead,
   Or fill the fixèd mind with all your
   toys!
Dwell in some idle brain,
   And fancies fond with gaudy shapes
   possess,
As thick and numberless
   As the gay motes that people the sun-
   beams,
Or likest hovering dreams,
   The fickle pensioners of Morpheus'
   train.

But hail, thou Goddess sage and holy!
Hail, divinest Melancholy!
Whose saintly visage is too bright
To hit the sense of human sight,
And therefore to our weaker view
O'erlaid with black, staid Wisdom's hue;
Black, but such as in esteem
Prince Memnon's sister might beseem,
Or that starred Ethiop Queen that
   strove
To set her beauty's praise above
The Sea-Nymphs, and their powers of-
   fended.
Yet thou art higher far descended:
Thee bright-haired Vesta, long of yore
To solitary Saturn bore;
His daughter she; in Saturn's reign
Such mixture was not held a stain.
Oft in glimmering bowers and glades
He met her, and in secret shades
Of woody Ida's inmost grove,
While yet there was no fear of Jove.

Come, pensive Nun, devout and pure,
Sober, steadfast, and demure,
All in a robe of darkest grain,
Flowing with majestic train,
And sable stole of cypress lawn
Over thy decent shoulders drawn.
Come; but keep thy wonted state,
With even step, and musing gait,
And looks commercing with the skies,
Thy rapt soul sitting in thine eyes:
There, held in holy passion still,
Forget thyself to marble, till
With a sad leaden downward cast
Thou fix them on the earth as fast.

And join with thee calm Peace, and
    Quiet,
Spare Fast, that oft with gods doth diet,
And hears the Muses in a ring
Aye round about Jove's altar sing;
And add to these retired Leisure,
That in trim gardens takes his pleasure;
But, first and chiefest, with thee bring
Him that yon soars on golden wing,
Guiding the fiery-wheelèd throne,
The Cherub Contemplation;
And the mute Silence hist along,
'Less Philomel will deign a song,
In her sweetest saddest plight,
Smoothing the rugged brow of Night,
While Cynthia checks her dragon yoke
Gently o'er th' accustomed oak.
—Sweet bird, that shunn'st the noise of
    folly,
Most musical, most melancholy!
Thee, Chauntress, oft the woods among
I woo, to hear thy even-song;
And, missing thee, I walk unseen
On the dry smooth-shaven green,
To behold the wandering Moon,
Riding near her highest noon,
Like one that had been led astray
Through the heaven's wide pathless way,
And oft, as if her head she bowed,
Stooping through a fleecy cloud.

  Oft, on a plat of rising ground,
I hear the far-off curfew sound
Over some wide-watered shore,
Swinging slow with sullen roar;
Or, if the air will not permit,
Some still removèd place will fit,
Where glowing embers through the room
Teach light to counterfeit a gloom,
Far from all resort of mirth,
Save the cricket on the hearth,
Or the Bellman's drowsy charm
To bless the doors from nightly harm.

  Or let my lamp, at midnight hour,
Be seen in some high lonely tower,
Where I may oft out-watch the Bear,
With thrice-great Hermes, or unsphere
The spirit of Plato, to unfold
What worlds or what vast regions hold
Th' immortal mind that hath forsook

Her mansion in this fleshly nook;
And of those Dæmons that are found
In fire, air, flood, or under ground,
Whose power hath a true consent
With planet or with element.
Sometime let gorgeous Tragedy
In sceptred pall come sweeping by,
Presenting Thebes, or Pelops' line,
Or the tale of Troy divine,
Or what (though rare) of later age
Ennobled hath the buskined stage.

  But, O sad Virgin! that thy power
Might raise Musæus from his bower;
Or bid the soul of Orpheus sing
Such notes as, warbled to the string,
Drew iron tears down Pluto's cheek,
And made hell grant what Love did
    seek;
Or call up him that left half-told
The story of Cambuscan bold,
Of Camball, and of Algarsife,
And who had Canace to wife
That owned the virtuous ring and glass,
And of the wondrous horse of brass
On which the Tartar King did ride;
And if aught else great Bards beside
In sage and solemn tunes have sung
Of turneys, and of trophies hung,
Of forests, and enchantments drear,
Where more is meant than meets the ear.

  Thus, Night oft see me in thy pale
    career,
Till civil-suited Morn appear,
Not tricked and frounced, as she was
    wont
With the Attic Boy to hunt,
But kerchieft in a comely cloud,
While rocking winds are piping loud,
Or ushered with a shower still,
When the gust hath blown his fill,
Ending on the rustling leaves,
With minute drops from off the eaves.
And, when the sun begins to fling
His flaring beams, me, Goddess, bring
To archèd walks of twilight groves,
And shadows brown, that Sylvan loves,
Or pine, or monumental oak,
Where the rude axe with heavèd stroke
Was never heard the Nymphs to daunt,

Or fright them from their hallowed
　　haunt.
There, in close covert, by some brook,
Where no profaner eye may look,
Hide me from Day's garish eye,
While the bee with honeyed thigh,
That at her flowery work doth sing,
And the waters murmuring,
With such consort as they keep,
Entice the dewy-feathered Sleep.
And let some strange mysterious dream,
Wave at his wings in airy stream,
Of lively portraiture displayed,
Softly on my eyelids laid.
And as I wake, sweet music breathe
Above, about, or underneath,
Sent by some Spirit to mortals good,
Or th' unseen Genius of the wood.
　　But let my due feet never fail
To walk the studious cloister's pale,
And love the high-embowèd roof,
With antic pillars massy proof,
And storied windows richly dight,
Casting a dim religious light.
There let the pealing organ blow,
To the full-voiced Quire below,
In service high and anthems clear,
As may with sweetness, through mine ear,
Dissolve me into ecstasies,
And bring all Heaven before mine eyes.
　　And may at last my weary age
Find out the peaceful hermitage,
The hairy gown and mossy cell,
Where I may sit and rightly spell,
Of every star that Heaven doth shew,
And every herb that sips the dew;
Till old experience do attain
To something like prophetic strain.
　　These pleasures, Melancholy, give,
And I with thee will choose to live.

Lycidas

YET once more, O ye Laurels, and once
　　more
Ye Myrtles brown, with ivy never sere,
I come to pluck your berries harsh and
　　crude,

And with forced fingers rude
Shatter your leaves before the mellowing
　　year.
Bitter constraint and sad occasion dear
Compels me to disturb your season due;
For Lycidas is dead, dead ere his prime,
Young Lycidas, and hath not left his
　　peer.
Who would not sing for Lycidas? he
　　knew
Himself to sing, and build the lofty
　　rhyme.
He must not float upon his watery bier
Unwept, and welter to the parching wind,
Without the meed of some melodious
　　tear.
　　Begin then, Sisters of the sacred well
That from beneath the seat of Jove doth
　　spring;
Begin, and somewhat loudly sweep the
　　string.
Hence with denial vain and coy excuse:
So may some gentle Muse
With lucky words favour *my* destined
　　urn,
And as he passes, turn
And bid fair peace be to my sable shroud!
For we were nursed upon the self-same
　　hill,
Fed the same flock, by fountain, shade,
　　and rill:
　　Together both, ere the high lawns ap-
　　peared
Under the opening eyelids of the Morn,
We drove a-field, and both together
　　heard
What time the grey-fly winds her sultry
　　horn,
Battening our flocks with the fresh dews
　　of night,
Oft till the star that rose at evening
　　bright
Toward heaven's descent had sloped his
　　westering wheel.
Meanwhile the rural ditties were not
　　mute;
Tempered to the oaten flute
Rough Satyrs danced, and Fauns with
　　cloven heel

From the glad sound would not be absent
    long;
And old Damœtas loved to hear our
    song.
  But, oh! the heavy change, now thou
    art gone,
Now thou art gone and never must re-
    turn!
Thee, Shepherd, thee the woods and
    desert caves
With wild thyme and the gadding vine
    o'er-grown,
And all their echoes, mourn.
The willows, and the hazel copses green,
Shall now no more be seen
Fanning their joyous leaves to thy soft
    lays.
As killing as the canker to the rose,
Or taint-worm to the weanling herds
    that graze,
Or frost to flowers that their gay ward-
    robe wear
When first the white-thorn blows;
Such, Lycidas, thy loss to shepherd's ear.
  Where were ye, Nymphs, when the re-
    morseless deep
Closed o'er the head of your loved
    Lycidas?
For neither were ye playing on the
    steep
Where your old bards, the famous
    Druids, lie,
Nor on the shaggy top of Mona high,
Nor yet where Deva spreads her wizard
    stream.
Ay me! I fondly dream
"Had ye been there" . . . For what
    could that have done?
What could the Muse herself that Or-
    pheus bore,
The Muse herself, for her enchanting
    son,
Whom universal nature did lament,
When, by the rout that made the hideous
    roar,
His gory visage down the stream was
    sent,
Down the swift Hebrus to the Lesbian
    shore?

  Alas! what boots it with uncessant
    care
To tend the homely, slighted, Shepherd's
    trade
And strictly meditate the thankless
    Muse?
Were it not better done, as others use,
To sport with Amaryllis in the shade,
Or with the tangles of Neæra's hair?
Fame is the spur that the clear spirit doth
    raise
(That last infirmity of noble mind)
To scorn delights, and live labourious
    days;
But the fair guerdon when we hope to
    find,
And think to burst out into sudden blaze,
Comes the blind Fury with the abhorrèd
    shears
And slits the thin-spun life. "But not
    the praise,"
Phœbus replied, and touched my trem-
    bling ears:
"Fame is no plant that grows on mortal
    soil,
Nor in the glistering foil
Set off to the world, nor in broad rumour
    lies,
But lives and spreads aloft by those pure
    eyes
And perfect witness of all-judging Jove;
As he pronounces lastly on each deed,
Of so much fame in heaven expect thy
    meed."
  O fountain Arethuse, and thou hon-
    oured flood,
Smooth-sliding Mincius, crowned with
    vocal reeds,
That strain I heard was of a higher
    mood.
But now my oat proceeds,
And listens to the Herald of the Sea
That came in Neptune's plea.
He asked the waves, and asked the felon
    winds,
What hard mishap hath doomed this
    gentle swain?
And questioned every gust of rugged
    wings

That blows from off each beaked prom-
ontory.
They knew not of his story;
And sage Hippotades their answer brings,
That not a blast was from his dungeon
strayed:
The air was calm, and on the level brine
Sleek Panope with all her sisters played.
It was that fatal and perfidious bark,
Built in th' eclipse, and rigged with curses
dark,
That sunk so low that sacred head of
thine.

  Next Camus, reverend Sire, went foot-
ing slow,
His mantle hairy, and his bonnet sedge,
Inwrought with figures dim, and on the
edge
Like to that sanguine flower inscribed
with woe.
"Ah! who hath reft," quoth he, "my
dearest pledge!"
Last came, and last did go,
The Pilot of the Galilean lake;
Two massy keys he bore of metals twain
(The golden opes, the iron shuts amain)
He shook his mitred locks, and stern
bespake:—
"How well could I have spared for thee,
young swain,
Enow of such, as for their bellies' sake
Creep, and intrude, and climb into the
fold!
Of other care they little reck'ning make
Than how to scramble at the shearers'
feast,
And shove away the worthy bidden guest.
Blind mouths! that scarce themselves
know how to hold
A sheep-hook, or have learnèd aught else
the least
That to the faithful herdsman's art be-
longs!
What recks it them? What need they?
They are sped;
And, when they list, their lean and flashy
songs
Grate on their scrannel pipes of wretched
straw;

The hungry sheep look up, and are not
fed,
But swoln with wind and the rank mist
they draw
Rot inwardly, and foul contagion spread;
Besides what the grim wolf with privy
paw
Daily devours apace, and nothing said.
—But that two-handed engine at the door
Stands ready to smite once, and smite no
more."
  Return, Alpheus; the dread voice is
past
That shrunk thy streams; return, Sicilian
Muse,
And call the vales, and bid them hither
cast
Their bells and flowerets of a thousand
hues.
Ye valleys low, where the mild whispers
use
Of shades, and wanton winds, and gush-
ing brooks,
On whose fresh lap the swart star
sparely looks,
Throw hither all your quaint enamelled
eyes,
That on the green turf suck the honeyed
showers,
And purple all the ground with vernal
flowers.
Bring the rathe primrose that forsaken
dies,
The tufted crow-toe, and pale jessamine,
The white pink, and the pansy freaked
with jet,
The glowing violet,
The musk-rose, and the well-attired
woodbine,
With cowslips wan that hang the pensive
head,
And every flower that sad embroidery
wears.
Bid amaranthus all his beauty shed,
And daffodillies fill their cups with
tears,
To strew the laureat hearse where Lycid
lies.
For so, to interpose a little ease,

Let our frail thoughts dally with false
  surmise.
Ay me! whilst thee the shores and sound-
  ing seas
Wash far away, where'er thy bones are
  hurled;
Whether beyond the stormy Hebrides,
Where thou perhaps under the whelm-
  ing tide
Visit'st the bottom of the monstrous
  world;
Or whether thou, to our moist vows
  denied,
Sleep'st by the fable of Bellerus old,
Where the great Vision of the guarded
  mount
Looks toward Namancos and Bayona's
  hold.
Look homeward, Angel, now, and melt
  with ruth:
And, O ye dolphins, waft the hapless
  youth!
  Weep no more, woeful shepherds, weep
    no more,
For Lycidas, your sorrow, is not dead,
Sunk though he be beneath the watery
  floor.
So sinks the day-star in the ocean-bed,
And yet anon repairs his drooping head
And tricks his beams, and with new-
  spangled ore
Flames in the forehead of the morning
  sky:
So Lycidas sunk low, but mounted
  high
Through the dear might of Him that
  walked the waves;
Where, other groves and other streams
  along,
With nectar pure his oozy locks he laves,
And hears the unexpressive nuptial song,
In the blest kingdoms meek of joy and
  love.
There entertain him all the Saints above
In solemn troops, and sweet societies,
That sing, and singing in their glory
  move,
And wipe the tears for ever from his
  eyes.

Now, Lycidas, the shepherds weep no
  more;
Henceforth thou art the Genius of the
  shore
In thy large recompense, and shalt be
  good
To all that wander in that perilous flood.
  Thus sang the uncouth swain to the
    oaks and rills,
While the still morn went out with san-
  dals grey:
He touched the tender stops of various
  quills,
With eager thought warbling his Doric
  lay:
And now the sun had stretched out all
  the hills,
And now was dropt into the western bay.
At last he rose, and twitched his mantle
  blue:
To-morrow to fresh woods, and pastures
  new.

When the Assault was Intended to the City

CAPTAIN or Colonel, or Knight in Arms,
Whose chance on these defenceless doors
  may seize,
If deed of honour did thee ever please,
Guard them, and him within protect
  from harms.
He can requite thee; for he knows the
  charms
That call fame on such gentle acts as
  these,
And he can spread thy name o'er lands
  and seas,
Whatever clime the sun's bright circle
  warms.
Lift not thy spear against the Muses'
  bower:
The great Emathian conqueror bid spare
The house of Pindarus, when temple and
  tower
Went to the ground; and the repeated air
Of sad Electra's poet had the power
To save the Athenian walls from ruin
  bare.

On the Late Massacre in Piedmont

AVENGE, O Lord! Thy slaughtered
    Saints, whose bones
Lie scattered on the Alpine mountains
    cold;
Even them who kept Thy truth so pure
    of old
When all our fathers worshiped stocks
    and stones,
Forget not: in Thy book record their
    groans
Who were Thy sheep, and in their an-
    cient fold
Slain by the bloody Piemontese, that
    rolled
Mother with infant down the rocks.
    Their moans
The vales redoubled to the hills, and they
To Heaven. Their martyred blood and
    ashes sow
O'er all the Italian fields, where still
    doth sway
The triple Tyrant: that from these may
    grow
A hundred-fold, who, having learnt Thy
    way,
Early may fly the Babylonian woe.

On his Blindness

WHEN I consider how my light is spent,
Ere half my days in this dark world and
    wide,
And that one Talent which is death to
    hide
Lodged with me useless, though my soul
    more bent
To serve therewith my Maker, and
    present
My true account, lest He returning chide,
"Doth God exact day-labour, light de-
    nied?"
I fondly ask. But patience, to prevent
That murmur, soon replies: "God doth
    not need
Either man's work, or His own gifts. Who best

Bear His mild yoke, they serve Him
    best. His state
Is kingly: thousands at His bidding speed
And post o'er land and ocean without
    rest.
They also serve who only stand and
    wait."

To Mr. Lawrence

LAWRENCE of virtuous Father virtuous
    Son,
Now that the Fields are dank, and ways
    are mire,
Where shall we sometimes meet, and by
    the fire
Help waste a sullen day; what may be
    won
From the hard Season gaining: time will
    run
On smoother, till Favonius re-inspire
The frozen earth; and clothe in fresh
    attire
The Lily and Rose, that neither sow'd
    nor spun.
What neat repast shall feast us, light
    and choice,
Of Attic taste with Wine, whence we
    may rise
To hear the Lute well toucht, or art-
    full voice
Warble immortal Notes and Tuscan
    Air?
He who of those delights can judge, and
    spare
To interpose them oft, is not unwise.

To Cyriack Skinner

CYRIACK, whose grandsire on the royal
    bench
Of British Themis, with no mean ap-
    plause,
Pronounced, and in his volumes taught,
    our laws,
Which others at their bar so often
    wrench,
To-day deep thoughts resolve with me to
    drench

In mirth that after no repenting draws;
Let Euclid rest, and Archimedes pause,
And what the Swede intend, and what
the French.
To measure life learn thou betimes, and
know
Toward solid good what leads the near-
est way;
For other things mild Heaven a time
ordains,
And disapproves that care, though wise
in show,
That with superfluous burden loads the
day,
And, when God sends a cheerful hour,
refrains.

To the Same

Cyriack, this three years' day these eyes,
though clear,
To outward view, of blemish or of spot,
Bereft of light, their seeing have forgot;
Nor to their idle orbs doth sight appear
Of sun, or moon, or star, throughout the
year,
Or man, or woman. Yet I argue not
Against Heaven's hand or will, nor bate
a jot
Of heart or hope, but still bear up and
steer
Right onward. What supports me, dost
thou ask?
The conscience, friend, to have lost them
overplied

In Liberty's defence, my noble task,
Of which all Europe rings from side to
side.
This thought might lead me through the
world's vain mask
Content, though blind, had I no better
guide.

On his Deceased Wife

Methought I saw my late espousèd
Saint
Brought to me like Alcestis from the
grave,
Whom Jove's great Son to her glad Hus-
band gave,
Rescued from death by force though
pale and faint.
Mine, as whom washt from spot of
child-bed taint,
Purification in the old Law did save,
And such as yet once more I trust to
have
Full sight of her in Heaven without re-
straint,
Came vested all in white, pure as her
mind:
Her face was veiled, yet to my fancied
sight,
Love, sweetness, goodness, in her person
shined
So clear, as in no face with more delight.
But oh, as to embrace me she inclined
I waked, she fled, and day brought back
my night.

EDWARD, EARL OF CLARENDON (1609–1674)

From The History of the Rebellion and Civil Wars in England

The Character of Lord Falkland

But I must here take leave a little longer to discontinue this narration; and if the celebrating the memory of eminent and extraordinary
persons, and transmitting their great virtues, for the imitation of posterity, be one of the principal ends and duties of history, it will not be
thought impertinent, in this place, to remember a loss which no time will

suffer to be forgotten, and no success or good fortune could repair. In this unhappy battle was slain the Lord Viscount Falkland; a person of such prodigious parts of learning and knowledge, of that inimitable sweetness and delight in conversation, of so flowing and obliging a humanity and goodness to mankind, and of that primitive simplicity and integrity of life, that if there were no other brand upon this odious and accursed civil war, than that single loss, it must be most infamous and execrable to all posterity.

Turpe mori, post te, solo non posse dolore.

Before this parliament, his condition of life was so happy that it was hardly capable of improvement. Before he came to twenty years of age, he was master of a noble fortune, which descended to him by the gift of a grandfather, without passing through his father or mother, who were then both alive and not well enough contented to find themselves passed by in the descent. His education for some years had been in Ireland, where his father was lord deputy; so that, when he returned into England, to the possession of his fortune, he was unentangled with any acquaintance or friends, which usually grow up by the custom of conversation; and therefore was to make a pure election of his company; which he chose by other rules than were prescribed to the young nobility of that time. And it cannot be denied, though he admitted some few to his friendship for the agreeableness of their natures, and their undoubted affection to him, that his familiarity and friendship, for the most part, was with men of the most eminent and sublime parts, and of untouched reputation in point of integrity; and such men had a title to his bosom.

He was a great cherisher of wit and fancy and good parts in any man; and if he found them clouded with poverty or want, a most liberal and bountiful patron towards them, even above his fortune; of which, in those administrations, he was such a dispenser as if he had been trusted with it to such uses, and if there had been the least of vice in his expense he might have been thought too prodigal. He was constant and pertinacious in whatsoever he resolved to do, and not to be wearied by any pains that were necessary to that end. And therefore having once resolved not to see London, which he loved above all places, till he had perfectly learned the Greek tongue, he went to his own house in the country, and pursued it with that indefatigable industry, that it will not be believed in how short a time he was master of it, and accurately read all the Greek historians.

In this time, his house being within ten miles of Oxford, he contracted familiarity and friendship with the most polite and accurate men of that university; who found such an immenseness of wit, and such a solidity of judgment in him, so infinite a fancy, bound in by a most logical ratiocination, such a vast knowledge, that he was not ignorant in any thing, yet such an excessive humility, as if he had known nothing, that they frequently resorted, and dwelt with him, as in a college situated in a purer air; so that his house was a university bound in a less volume; whither they came not so much for repose as study, and to examine and refine those grosser propositions which laziness and consent made current in vulgar conversation.

Many attempts were made upon him by the instigation of his mother (who was a lady of another persuasion in religion, and of a most masculine understanding, allayed with the passion and infirmities of her own sex) to pervert him in his piety to the church of England, and to reconcile him to that of Rome; which they prosecuted with the more confidence, because he declined no opportunity or occasion of conference with those of that religion, whether priests or laics; having diligently studied the controversies and exactly read all or the choicest of the Greek and Latin fathers, and having a memory so stupendous, that he remembered on all occasions whatsoever he read. And he was so great an enemy to that passion and uncharitableness which he saw produced by difference of opinion in matters of religion, that in all those disputations with priests and others of the Roman church, he affected to manifest all possible civility to their persons, and estimation of their parts; which made them retain still some hope of his reduction; even when they had given over offering farther reasons to him to that purpose. But this charity towards them was much lessened, and any correspondence with them quite declined, when, by sinister arts, they had corrupted his two younger brothers, being both children, and stolen them from his house, and transported them beyond seas, and perverted his sisters: upon which occasion he writ two large discourses against the principal positions of that religion, with that sharpness of style, and full weight of reason, that the church is deprived of great jewels in the concealment of them, and that they are not published to the world.

He was superior to all those passions and affections which attend vulgar minds, and was guilty of no other ambition than of knowledge, and to be reputed a lover of all good men; and that made him too much a contemner of those arts which must be indulged to in the transaction of human affairs. In the last short parliament he was a burgess in the house of commons; and from the debates, which were then managed with all imaginable gravity and sobriety, he contracted such a reverence to parliaments, that he thought it really impossible that they could ever produce mischief or inconvenience to the kingdom, or that the kingdom could be tolerably happy in the intermission of them. And from the unhappy and unseasonable dissolution of that convention, he harboured, it may be, some jealousy and prejudice of the court, towards which he was not before immoderately inclined; his father having wasted a full fortune there, in those offices and employments by which other men use to obtain a greater. He was chosen again this parliament to serve in the same place, and, in the beginning of it, declared himself very sharply and severely against those exorbitancies which had been most grievous to the state; for he was so rigid an observer of established laws and rules, that he could not endure the least breach or deviation from them; and thought no mischief so intolerable as the presumption of ministers of state to break positive rules for reason[s] of state; or judges to transgress known laws, upon the title of conveniency or necessity; which made him so severe against the earl of Strafford and the lord Finch, contrary to his natural gentleness and temper: insomuch as they who did not know his composition to be as free from revenge as it was from pride, thought that the sharpness to the former might proceed from the memory of some unkindnesses, not without a mixture of injustice, from him towards his father. But without doubt he was free from those temptations, and was only misled by the authority of those who he believed understood the laws perfectly; of which himself was utterly ignorant; and if the assumption, which was scarce controverted, had been true, that an endeavour to overthrow the fundamental laws of the kingdom had been treason, a strict understanding might make reasonable conclusions to satisfy his own judgment, from the exorbitant parts of their several charges.

The great opinion he had of the uprightness and integrity of those persons who appeared most active, especially of Mr. Hambden, kept him longer from suspecting any design against the peace of the kingdom; and though he differed commonly from them in conclusions, he believed long their purposes were honest. When he grew better informed what was law, and discerned [in them] a desire to control that law by a vote of one or both houses, no man more opposed those attempts, and gave the adverse party more trouble by reason and argumentation; insomuch as he was, by degrees, looked upon as an advocate for the court, to which he contributed so little, that he declined those addresses, and even those invitations which he was obliged almost by civility to entertain. And he was so jealous of the least imagination that he should incline to preferment, that he affected even a morosity to the court and to the courtiers; and left nothing undone which might prevent and divert the king's or queen's favour towards him, but the deserving it. For when the king sent for him once or twice to speak with him, and to give him thanks for his excellent comportment in those councils, which his majesty graciously termed doing him service, his answers were more negligent and less satisfactory than might be expected; as if he cared only that his actions should be just, not that they should be acceptable, and that his majesty should think that they proceeded only from the impulsion of conscience, without any sympathy in his affections; which from a stoical and sullen nature might not have been misinterpreted; yet, from a person of so perfect a habit of generous and obsequious compliance with all good men, might very well have been interpreted by the king as more than an ordinary averseness to his service: so that he took more pains, and more forced his nature to actions unagreeable and unpleasant to it, that he might not be thought to incline to the court, than any man hath done to procure an office there. And if any thing but not doing his duty could have kept him from receiving a testimony of the king's grace and trust at that time, he had not been called to his council; not that he was in truth averse to the court or from receiving public employment; for he had a great devotion to the king's person, and had before used some small endeavour to be recommended to him for a foreign negociation, and had once a desire to be sent ambassador into France; but he abhorred an imagination or doubt should sink into the thoughts of any man, that, in the discharge of his trust and duty in parliament, he had any bias to the court, or that the king himself should apprehend that he looked for a reward for being honest.

For this reason, when he heard it first whispered that the king had a purpose to make him a counsellor, for which in the beginning there was no other ground but because he was known sufficient, (*haud semper errat fama, aliquando et eligit,*) he resolved to decline it; and at last suffered himself only to be overruled by the advice and persuasions of his friends to submit to it. Afterwards, when he found that the king intended to make him his secretary of state, he was positive to refuse it; declaring to his friends that he was most unfit for it, and that he must either do that which would be great disquiet to his own nature, or leave that undone which was most necessary to be done by one that was honoured with that place; for that the most just and honest men did every day that which he could not give himself leave to do. And indeed he was so exact and strict an observer of justice and truth, *ad amussim,* that he believed those necessary condescensions and applications to the weakness of other men, and those arts and insinuations which are necessary for discoveries and prevention of ill, would be in him a declension from the rule which he acknowledged fit, and absolutely necessary to be practised in those employments; and was, [in truth,] so precise in the practick principles he prescribed to himself, (to all others he was as indulgent,) as if he had lived *in republica Platonis, non in fæce Romuli.*

Two reasons prevailed with him to receive the seals, and but for those he had resolutely avoided them. The first, the consideration that it [his refusal] might bring some blemish upon the king's affairs, and that men would have believed that he had refused so great an honour and trust because he must have been with it obliged to do somewhat else not justifiable. And this he made matter of conscience, since he knew the king made choice of him before other men especially because he thought him more honest than other men. The other was, lest he might be thought to avoid it out of fear to do an ungracious thing to the house of commons, who were sorely troubled at the displacing sir Harry Vane, whom they looked upon as removed for having done them those offices they stood in need of; and the disdain of so popular an incumbrance wrought upon him next to the other. For as he had a full appetite of fame by just and generous actions, so he had an equal contempt of it by any servile expedients: and he so much the more consented to and approved the justice upon sir Harry Vane, in his own private judgment, by how much he surpassed most men in the religious observation of a trust, the violation whereof he would not admit of any excuse for.

For these reasons, he submitted to the king's command, and became his secretary, with as humble and devout an acknowledgment of the greatness of the obligation as could be expressed, and as true a sense of it in his heart. Yet two things he could never bring himself to whilst he continued in that office, that was to his death; for which he was contented to be reproached, as for omissions in a most necessary part of his place. The one, employing of spies, or giving any countenance or entertainment to them. I do not mean such emissaries as with danger would venture to view the enemy's camp, and bring intelligence of their number or quartering, or such generals as such an observation can comprehend; but those who, by communication of guilt, or dissimulation of manners, wound themselves into such trusts and secrets as enabled them to make discoveries for the benefit of the state. The other, the liberty of opening letters upon a suspicion that they might contain matter of dangerous consequence. For the first, he would say, such instruments must be void of all ingenuity and common honesty, before they could be of use; and afterwards they could never be fit to be credited: and that no single preservation could be worth so general a wound and corruption of human society, as the cherishing such persons would carry with it. The last, he thought such a violation of the law of nature, that no qualification by office could justify a single person in the trespass; and though he was convinced, by the necessity and iniquity of the time, that those advantages of information were not to be declined, and were necessarily to be practised, he found means to shift it from himself; when he confessed he needed excuse and pardon for the omission: so unwilling he was to resign any thing in his nature to an obligation in his office.

In all other particulars he filled his place plentifully, being sufficiently versed in languages to understand any that [are] used in business, and to make himself again understood. To speak of his integrity, and his high disdain of any bait that might seem to look towards corruption, *in tanto viro, injuria virtutum fuerit.* Some sharp expressions he used against the archbishop of Canterbury; and his concurring in the first bill to take away the votes of bishops in the house of peers, gave occasion to some to believe, and opportunity to others to conclude and publish, that he was no friend to the church, and the established government of it; and troubled his very friends much, who were more confident of the contrary than prepared to answer the allegations.

The truth is, he had unhappily contracted some prejudice to the archbishop; and having only known him enough to observe his passion, when, it may be, multiplicity of business or other indisposition had possessed him, did wish him less entangled and engaged in the business of the court or state: though, I speak it knowingly, he had a singular estimation and reverence of his great learning and confessed integrity; and really thought his letting himself to those expressions, which implied a disesteem of him, or at least an acknowledgment of his infirmities, would enable him to shelter him from part of the storm he saw raised for his destruction; which he abominated with his soul.

The giving his consent to the first bill for the displacing the bishops did proceed from two grounds: the first, his not understanding the original of their right and suffrage there: the other, an opinion, that the combination against the whole government of the church by bishops, was so violent and furious, that a less composition than the dispensing with their intermeddling in secular affairs would not preserve the order. And he was presuaded to this by the profession of many persons of honour, who declared, they did desire the one, and would then not press the other; which, in that particular, misled many men. But when his observation and experience made him discern more of their intentions than he before suspected, with great frankness he opposed the second bill that was preferred for that purpose; and had, without scruple, the order itself in perfect reference; and thought too great encouragement could not possibly be given to learning, nor too great rewards to learned men; and was never in the least degree swayed or moved by the objections which were made against that government, (holding them most ridiculous,) or affected to the other, which those men fancied to themselves.

He had a courage of the most clear and keen temper, and so far from fear, that he was not without appetite of danger; and therefore, upon any occasion of action, he always engaged his person in those troops which he thought, by the forwardness of the commanders, to be most like to be farthest engaged; and in all such encounters he had about him a strange cheerfulness and companiableness, without at all affecting the execution that was then principally to be attended, in which he took no delight, but took pains to prevent it, where it was not, by resistance, necessary: insomuch that at Edgehill, when the enemy was routed, he was like to have incurred great peril, by interposing to save those who had thrown away their arms, and against whom, it may be, others were more fierce for their having thrown them away: insomuch as a man might think, he came into the field only out of curiosity to see the face of danger, and charity to prevent the shedding of blood. Yet in his natural inclination he acknowledged he was addicted to the profession of a soldier; and shortly after he came to his fortune, and before he came to age, he went into the Low Countries with a resolution of procuring command, and to give himself up to it, from which he was converted by the complete inactivity of that summer: and so he returned into England, and shortly after entered upon that vehement course of study we mentioned before, till the first alarum from the north; and then again he made ready for the field, and though he received some repulse in the command of a troop of horse, of which he had a promise, he went a volunteer with the earl of Essex.

From the entrance into this unnatural war, his natural cheerfulness and vivacity grew clouded, and a kind of sadness and dejection of spirit stole upon him, which he had never been used to; yet being one of those who believed that one battle would end all differences, and that there would be so great a victory on one side, that the other would be compelled to submit to any conditions from the victor, (which supposition and conclusion generally sunk into the minds of most men, [and] prevented the looking after many advantages which might then have been laid hold of,) he resisted those indispositions, *et in luctu, bellum inter remedia erat*. But after the king's return from Brentford, and the furious resolution of the two houses not to admit any treaty for peace, those indispositions, which had before touched him, grew into a perfect habit of uncheerfulness; and he, who had been so exactly unreserved and affable to all men, that his face and countenance was always present and vacant to his company, and held any cloudiness and less pleasantness of the visage a kind of rudeness or incivility, became, on a sudden, less communicable; and thence, very sad, pale, and exceedingly affected with the spleen. In his clothes and habit, which he had intended before always with more neatness and industry and expense than is usual to so great a mind, he was not now only incurious, but too negligent; and in his reception of suitors, and the necessary or casual addresses to his place, so quick and sharp and severe, that there wanted not some men (who were strangers to his nature and disposition) who believed him proud and imperious, from which no mortal man was ever more free.

The truth is, that as he was of a most incomparable gentleness, application, and even a demissness and submission to good and worthy and entire men, so he was naturally (which could not but be more evident in his place, which objected him to another conversation and intermixture than his own election had done) *adversus malos injucundus;* and was so ill a dissembler of his dislike and disinclination to ill men, that it was not possible for such not to discern it. There was once in the house of commons such a declared acceptation of the good service an eminent member had done to them, and, as they said, to the whole kingdom, that it was moved, he being present, that the speaker might, in the name of the whole house, give him thanks; and then, that every member might, as a testimony of his particular acknowledgment, stir or move his hat towards him; the which (though not ordered) when very many did, the lord Falkland, (who believed the service itself not to be of that moment, and that an honourable and generous person could not have stooped to it for any recompense,) instead of moving his hat, stretched both his arms out, and clasped his hands together upon the crown of his hat, and held it close down to his head; that all men might see how odious that flattery was to him, and the very approbation of the person, though at that time most popular.

When there was any overture or hope of peace, he would be more erect and vigorous, and exceedingly solicitous to press any thing which he thought might promote it; and sitting amongst his friends, often, after a deep silence and frequent sighs, would, with a shrill and sad accent, ingeminate the word *Peace, Peace;* and would passionately profess, that the very agony of the war, and the view of the calamities and desolation of the kingdom did and must endure, took his sleep from him, and would shortly break his heart. This made some think, or pretend to think, that he was so much enamoured on peace, that he would have been glad the king should have bought it at any price; which was a most unreasonable calumny. As if a man, that was himself the most punctual and precise in every circumstance that might reflect upon conscience or honour, could have wished the king to have committed a trespass against either. And yet this senseless scandal made some impression upon him, or at least he used it for an excuse of the daringness of his spirit; for at the leaguer before Gloucester, when his friends passionately reprehended him for exposing his person unnecessarily to danger, (as he delighted to visit the trenches and nearest approaches, and to discover what the enemy did,) as being so much beside the duty of his place, that it might be understood against it, he would say merrily, that his office could not take away the privileges of his age; and that a secretary in war might be present at the greatest secret of danger; but withal alleged seriously, that it concerned him to be more active in enterprises of hazard than other men, that all might see that his impatiency for peace proceeded not from pusillanimity, or fear to adventure his own person.

In the morning before the battle, as always upon action, he was very cheerful, and put himself into the first rank of the lord Byron's regiment, who was then advancing upon the enemy, who had lined the hedges on both sides with musketeers; from whence he was shot with a musket in the lower part of the belly, and in the instant falling from his horse, his body was not found till the next morning; till when, there was some hope he might have been a prisoner; though his nearest friends, who knew his temper, received small comfort from that imagination. Thus fell that incomparable young man, in the four and thirtieth year of his age, having so much despatched the business of life, that the oldest rarely attain to that immense knowledge, and the youngest enter not into the world with more innocence: and whosoever leads such a life needs not care upon how short warning it be taken from him.

From The Life of Edward, Earl of Clarendon

The Stuart Family

The truth is, it was the unhappy fate and constitution of that family, that they trusted naturally the judgments of those who were as much inferior to them in understanding as they were in quality, before their own, which was very good; and suffered even their natures, which disposed them to virtue and justice, to be prevailed upon and altered and corrupted by those who knew how to make use of some one infirmity that they discovered in them; and by complying with that, and cherishing and serving it, they by degrees wrought upon the mass, and sacrificed all the other good inclinations to that single vice. They were too much inclined to like men at first sight, and did not love the conversation of men of many more years than themselves, and thought age not only troublesome but impertinent. They did not love to deny, and less to strangers than to their friends; not out of bounty or generosity, which was a flower that did never grow naturally in the heart of either of the families, that of Stuart or the other of Bourbon, but out of an unskilfulness and defect in the countenance; and when they prevailed with themselves to make some pause rather than to deny, importunity removed all resolution, which they knew neither how to shut out nor to defend themselves against, even when it was evident enough that they had much rather not consent; which often made that which would have looked like bounty lose all its grace and lustre.

The Character of Charles I

To speak first of his private qualifications as a man, before the mention of his princely and royal virtues; he was, if ever any, the most worthy of the title of an honest man; so great a lover of justice, that no temptation could dispose him to a wrongful action, except it were so disguised to him that he believed it to be just. He had a tenderness and compassion of nature, which restrained him from ever doing a hard-hearted thing; and therefore he was so apt to grant pardon to malefactors, that his judges represented to him the damage and insecurity to the public that flowed from such his indulgence. And then he restrained himself from pardoning either murders or highway robberies, and quickly discerned the fruits of his severity by a wonderful reformation of those enormities. He was very punctual and regular in his devotions; so that he was never known to enter upon his recreations or sports, though never so early in the morning, before he had been at public prayers; so that on hunting days his chaplains were bound to a very early attendance. And he was likewise very strict in observing the hours of his private cabinet devotions; and was so severe an exactor of gravity and reverence in all mention of religion, that he could never endure any light or profane word, with what sharpness of wit soever it was covered: and though he was well pleased and delighted with reading verses made upon any occasion, no man durst bring before him any thing that was profane or unclean. That kind of wit had never any countenance then. He was so great an example of conjugal affection, that they who did not imitate him in that particular did not brag of their liberty: and he did not only permit, but direct his bishops to prosecute those scandalous vices, in the ecclesiastical courts, against persons of eminence and near relation to his service.

His kingly virtues had some mixture and allay, that hindered them from shining in full lustre, and from producing those fruits they should have been attended with. He was not in his nature bountiful, though he gave very much: which appeared more after the duke of Buckingham's death, after which those showers fell very rarely; and he paused too long in giving, which made those to whom he gave less sensible of the benefit. He kept state to the full, which made his court very orderly; no man presuming to be seen in a place where he had no pretence to be. He saw and observed men long, before he received any about his person, and did not love strangers, nor very confident men. He was a patient hearer of causes; which he frequently accustomed himself to at the council board; and judged very well, and was dexterous in the mediating part: so that he often put an end to causes by persuasion, which the stubbornness of men's humours made dilatory in courts of justice.

He was very fearless in his person, but not enterprising; and had an excellent understanding, but was not confident enough of it; which made him oftentimes change his own opinion for a worse, and follow the advice of a man that did not judge so well as himself. And this made him more irresolute than the conjuncture of his affairs would admit: if he had been of a rougher and more imperious nature, he would have found more respect and duty. And his not applying some severe cures to approaching evils proceeded from the lenity of his nature and the tenderness of his conscience, which, in all cases of blood, made him choose the softer way, and not hearken to severe counsels, how reasonably soever urged. This only restrained him from pursuing his advantage in the first Scottish expedition, when, humanly speaking, he might have reduced that nation to the most slavish obedience that could have been wished. But no man can say he had then many who advised him to it, but the contrary, by a wonderful indisposition all his council had to fighting, or any other fatigue. He was always an immoderate lover of the Scottish nation, having not only been born there, but educated by that people, and besieged by them always, having few English about him till he was king; and the major number of his servants being still of [that nation,] who he thought could never fail him. And then, no man had such an ascendant over him, by the lowest and humblest insinuations, as duke Hamilton had.

As he excelled in all other virtues, so in temperance he was so strict, that he abhorred all debauchery to that degree, that, at a great festival solemnity, where he once was, when very many of the nobility of the

English and Scots were entertained, [being] told by one who withdrew from thence, what vast draughts of wine they drank, and that there was one earl who had drank most of the rest down, and was not himself moved or altered, the king said that he deserved to be hanged; and that earl coming shortly [after] into the room where his majesty was, in some gayety, to shew how unhurt he was from that battle, the king sent one to bid him withdraw from his majesty's presence; nor did he in some days after appear before the king.

There were so many miraculous circumstances contributed to his ruin, that men might well think that heaven and earth conspired it, and that the stars designed it. Though he was, from the first declension of his power, so much betrayed by his own servants, that there were very few who remained faithful to him, yet that treachery proceeded not from any treasonable purpose to do him any harm, but from particular and personal animosities against other men. And, afterwards, the terror all men were under of the parliament, and the guilt they were conscious of themselves, made them watch all opportunities to make themselves gracious to those who could do them good; and so they became spies upon their master, and from one piece of knavery were hardened and confirmed to undertake another; till at last they had no hope of preservation but by the destruction of their master. And after all this, when a man might reasonably believe that less than a universal defection of three nations could not have reduced a great king to so ugly a fate, it is most certain, that in that very hour, when he was thus wickedly murdered in the sight of the sun, he had as great a share in the hearts and affections of his subjects in general, was as much beloved, esteemed, and longed for by the people in general of the three nations, as any of his predecessors had ever been. To conclude, he was the worthiest gentleman, the best master, the best friend, the best husband, the best father, and the best Christian, that the age in which he lived had produced. And if he were not the best king, if he [were] without some parts and qualities which have made some kings great and happy, no other prince was ever unhappy who was possessed of half his virtues and endowments, and so much without any kind of vice.

The Character of Cromwell

He was one of those men, *quos vituperare ne inimici quidem possunt, nisi ut simul laudent;* [whom his very enemies could not condemn without commending him at the same time:] for he could never have done half that mischief without great parts of courage and industry and judgment. And he must have had a wonderful understanding in the natures and humours of men, and as great a dexterity in the applying them, who from a private and obscure birth, (though of a good family,) without interest of estate, alliance or friendship, could raise himself to such a height, and compound and knead such opposite and contradictory tempers, humours, and interests into a consistence that contributed to his designs and to their own destruction; whilst himself grew insensibly powerful enough to cut off those by whom he had climbed, in the instant that they projected to demolish their own building. What Velleius Paterculus said of Cinna may very justly be said of him, *ausum eum, quæ nemo auderet bonus; perfecisse, quæ a nullo, nisi fortissimo, perfici possent:* [he attempted those things which no good man durst have ventured on; and achieved those in which none but a valiant and great man could have succeeded.] Without doubt, no man with more wickedness ever attempted any thing, or brought to pass what he desired more wickedly, more in the face and contempt of religion and moral honesty; yet wickedness as great as his could never have accomplished those trophies, without the assistance of a great spirit, an admirable circumspection and sagacity, and a most magnanimous resolution.

When he appeared first in the parliament, he seemed to have a person in no degree gracious, no ornament of discourse, none of those talents which use to reconcile the affections of the standers by: yet as he grew into place and authority, his parts seemed to be renewed, as if he had concealed faculties, till he had occasion to use them; and when he was to act the part of a great man, he did it without any indecency through the want of custom.

After he was confirmed and invested protector by *The humble petition and advice,* he consulted with very few upon any action of importance, nor communicated any enterprise he resolved upon with more than those who were to have principal parts in the execution of it; nor to them sooner than was absolutely necessary. What he once resolved, in which he was not rash, he would not be dissuaded from, nor endure any contradiction of his power and authority, but extorted obedience from them who were not willing to yield it.

When he had laid some very extraordinary tax upon the city, one Cony, an eminent fanatic, and one who had heretofore served him very notably, positively refused to pay his part, and loudly dissuaded others from submitting to it, as an imposition notoriously against the law and the propriety of the subject, which all honest men were bound to defend. Cromwell sent for him, and cajoled him with the memory of the old kindness and friendship that had been between them, and that of all men he did not expect this opposition from him, in a matter that was so necessary for the good of the commonwealth. But it was always his fortune to meet with the most rude and obstinate behaviour from those who had formerly been absolutely governed by him, and they commonly put him in mind of some expressions and sayings of his own in cases of the like nature; so this man remembered him how great an enemy he had expressed himself to such grievances, and declared that all who submitted to them, and paid illegal taxes, were more to blame, and greater enemies to their country, than they who imposed them, and that the tyranny of princes could never be grievous but by the tameness and stupidity of the people. When Cromwell saw that he could not convert him, he told him that he had a will as stubborn as his, and he would try, which of them two should be master. And thereupon, with some terms of reproach and contempt, he committed the man to prison; whose courage was nothing abated by it; but as soon as the term came, he brought his habeas corpus in the king's bench, which they then called the upper bench. Maynard, who was of council with the prisoner, demanded his liberty with great confidence, both upon the illegality of the commitment, and the illegality of the imposition, as being laid without any lawful authority. The judges could not maintain or defend either, but enough declared what their sentence would be; and therefore the protector's attorney required a farther day to answer what had been urged. Before that day, Maynard was committed to the Tower, for presuming to question or make doubt of his authority; and the judges were sent for, and severely reprehended for suffering that license; and when they with all humility mentioned the law and magna charta, Cromwell told them, their magna charta should not control his actions, which he knew were for the safety of the commonwealth. He asked them who made them judges; [whether] they had any authority to sit there but what he gave them; and that if his authority were at an end, they knew well enough what would become of themselves; and therefore advised them to be more tender of that which could only preserve them; and so dismissed them with caution, that they should not suffer the lawyers to prate what it would not become them to hear.

Thus he subdued a spirit that had been often troublesome to the most sovereign power, and made Westminster-hall as obedient and subservient to his commands as any of the rest of his quarters. In all other matters, which did not concern the life of his jurisdiction, he seemed to have great reverence for the law, and rarely interposed between party and party. And as he proceeded with this kind of indignation and haughtiness with those who were refractory, and dared to contend with his greatness, so towards those who complied with his good pleasure, and courted his protection, he used a wonderful civility, generosity, and bounty.

To reduce three nations, which perfectly hated him, to an entire obedience to all his dictates; to awe and govern those nations by an army that was indevoted to him, and wished his ruin, was an instance of a very prodigious address. But his greatness at home was but a shadow of the glory he had abroad. It was hard to discover which feared him most, France, Spain, or the Low Countries, where his friendship was current at the value he put upon it. And as they did all sacrifice their honour and their interest to his pleasure, so there is nothing he could have demanded, that either of them would have denied him. To manifest which, there need only two instances. The first is, when those of the valley of Lucerne had unwarily rebelled against the duke of Savoy, which gave occasion to the pope and the neighbour princes of Italy to call and solicit for their extirpation, which their prince positively resolved upon, Cromwell sent his agent to the duke of Savoy, a prince with whom he had no correspondence or commerce, and so engaged the cardinal, and even terrified the pope himself, without so much as doing any grace to the English [Roman] catholics, (nothing being more usual than his saying that his ships in the Mediterranean should visit Civita Vecchia, and that the sound of his cannon should be heard in Rome,) that the duke of Savoy thought it necessary to restore all that he had taken from them, and did renew all those privileges they had formerly enjoyed, and newly forfeited.

The other instance of his authority was yet greater, and more incredible. In the city of Nismes, which is one of the fairest in the province of Languedoc, and where those of the religion do most abound, there was a great faction at that season when the consuls (who are the chief magistrates) were to be chosen. Those of the [reformed] religion had the confidence to set up one of themselves for that magistracy; which they of the Roman religion resolved to oppose with all their power. The dissension between them made so much noise, that the intendant of the province, who is the supreme minister in all civil affairs throughout the whole province, went thither to prevent any disorder that might happen. When the day of the election came, those of the religion possessed themselves with many armed men of the town-house, where the election was to be made. The magistrates sent to know what their meaning was; to which they answered, they were there to give their voices for the choice of the new consuls, and to be sure that the election should be fairly made. The bishop of the city, the intendant of the province, with all the officers of the church, and the present magistrates of the town, went together in their robes to be present at the election, without any suspicion that there would be any force used. When they came near the gate of the town-house, which was shut, and they supposed would be opened when they came, they within poured out a volley of musket-shot upon them, by which the dean of the church, and two or three of the magistrates of the town were killed upon the place, and very many others wounded; whereof some died shortly after. In this confusion, the magistrates put themselves into as good a posture to defend themselves as they could, without any purpose of offending the other, till they should be better provided; in order to which they sent an express to the court with a plain relation of the whole matter of fact, and that there appeared to be no manner of combination with those of the religion in other places of the province; but that it was an insolence in those of the place, upon their presumption of their great numbers, which were little inferior to those of the catholics. The court was glad of the occasion, and resolved that this provocation, in which other places were not involved, and which nobody could excuse, should warrant all kind of severity in that city, even to the pulling down their temples, and expelling many of them for ever out of the city; which, with the execution and forfeiture of many of the principal persons, would be a general mortification to all of the religion in France; with whom they were heartily offended; and a part of the army was forthwith ordered to march towards Nismes, to see this executed with the utmost rigour.

Those of the religion in the town were quickly sensible into what condition they had brought themselves; and sent with all possible submission to the magistrates to excuse themselves, and to impute what had been done to the rashness of particular men, who had no order for what they did. The magistrates answered, that they were glad they were sensible of their miscarriage; but they could say nothing upon the subject till the king's pleasure should be known; to whom they had sent a full relation of all that had passed. The other very well knew what the king's pleasure would be, and forthwith sent an express, one Moulins a Scotchman, who had lived many years in that place and in Montpelier, to Cromwell, to desire his protection and interposition. The express made so much haste, and found so good a reception the first hour he came, that Cromwell, after he had received the whole account, bade him refresh himself after so long a journey, and he would take such care of his business, that by the time he came to Paris he should find it despatched; and that night, sent away another messenger to his ambassador Lockhart; who, by the time Moulins came thither, had so far prevailed with the cardinal, that orders were sent to stop the troops, which were upon their march towards Nismes; and within a few days after, Moulins returned with a full pardon and amnesty from the king, under the great seal of France, so fully confirmed with all circumstances, that there was never farther mention made of it, but all things passed as if there had never been any such thing. So that nobody can wonder that his memory remains still in those parts and with those people in great veneration.

He would never suffer himself to be denied any thing he ever asked of the cardinal, alleging that the people would not be otherwise satisfied; which he [the cardinal] bore very heavily, and complained of to those with whom he would be free. One day he visited madam Turenne, and when he took his leave of her, she, according to her custom, besought him to continue gracious to the churches. Whereupon the cardinal told her that he knew not how to behave himself; if he advised the king to punish and suppress their insolence, Cromwell threatened [him] to join with the Spaniard; and if he shewed any favour to them, at Rome they accounted him an heretic.

He was not a man of blood, and totally declined Machiavel's method, which prescribes, upon any alteration of a government, as a thing absolutely necessary, to cut off all the heads of those, and extirpate their families, who are friends to the old [one]. And it was confidently reported, that in the council of officers it was more than once proposed that there might be a general massacre of all the royal party, as the only expedient to secure the government; but Cromwell would never consent to it; it may be, out of too much contempt of his enemies. In a word, as he had all the wickednesses against which damnation is denounced, and for which hell-fire is prepared, so he had some virtues which have caused the memory of some men in all ages to be celebrated; and he will be looked upon by posterity as a brave bad man.

SIR JOHN SUCKLING (1609-1642)

A Ballad upon a Wedding

I TELL thee, Dick, where I have been,
Where I the rarest things have seen;
  O, things without compare!
Such sights again cannot be found
In any place on English ground,
  Be it at wake or fair.

At Charing-Cross, hard by the way,
Where we (thou know'st) do sell our hay,
  There is a house with stairs;

And there did I see coming down
Such folk as are not in our town,
  Forty at least, in pairs.

Amongst the rest, one pest'lent fine
(His beard no bigger though than thine)
  Walked on before the rest:
Our landlord looks like nothing to him:
The King (God bless him) 'twould undo him,
  Should he go still so drest.

At Course-a-Park, without all doubt,
He should have first been taken out
  By all the maids i' th' town:

Though lusty Roger there had been,
Or little George upon the Green,
  Or Vincent of the Crown.

But wot you what? the youth was going
To make an end of all his wooing;
  The parson for him stay'd:
Yet by his leave (for all his haste)
He did not so much wish all past
  (Perchance), as did the maid.

The maid (and thereby hangs a tale),
For such a maid no Whitsun-ale
  Could ever yet produce:
No grape, that's kindly ripe, could be
So round, so plump, so soft as she,
  Nor half so full of juice.

Her finger was so small, the ring,
Would not stay on, which they did bring,
  It was too wide a peck:
And to say truth (for out it must)
It looked like the great collar (just)
  About our young colt's neck.

Her feet beneath her petticoat,
Like little mice, stole in and out,
  As if they fear'd the light:
But O she dances such a way!
No sun upon an Easter-day
  Is half so fine a sight.

Her cheeks so rare a white was on,
No daisy makes comparison,
  (Who sees them is undone),
For streaks of red were mingled there,
Such as are on a Catherine pear
  The side that's next the sun.

Her lips were red, and one was thin,
Compar'd to that was next her chin
  (Some bee had stung it newly);
But, Dick, her eyes so guard her face;
I durst no more upon them gaze
  Than on the sun in July.

Her mouth so small, when she does
    speak,
Thou'dst swear her teeth her words did
    break,
  That they might passage get;

But she so handled still the matter,
They came as good as ours, or better,
  And are not spent a whit.

Just in the nick the cook knocked thrice,
And all the waiters in a trice
  His summons did obey;
Each serving-man, with dish in hand,
Marched boldly up, like our trained band,
  Presented, and away.

When all the meat was on the table,
What man of knife or teeth was able
  To stay to be intreated?
And this the very reason was,
Before the parson could say grace,
  The company was seated.

The business of the kitchen's great,
For it is fit that men should eat;
  Nor was it there denied:
Passion o' me, how I run on!
There's that that would be thought upon
  (I trow) besides the bride.

Now hats fly off, and youths carouse;
Healths first go round, and then the
    house,
  The bride's came thick and thick:
And when 'twas nam'd another's health,
Perhaps he made it hers by stealth;
  And who could help it, Dick?

On the sudden up they rise and dance;
Then sit again and sigh, and glance:
  Then dance again and kiss:
Thus several ways the time did pass,
Whilst ev'ry woman wished her place,
  And every man wished his.

RICHARD LOVELACE [1618-1658]

To Althea from Prison

WHEN love with unconfinèd wings
  Hovers within my gates,
And my divine Althea brings
  To whisper at the grates;
When I lie tangled in her hair,
  And fetter'd to her eye,

The birds that wanton in the air
　　Know no such liberty.

When flowing cups run swiftly round
　　With no allaying Thames,
Our careless heads with roses crown'd,
　　Our hearts with loyal flames;
When thirsty grief in wine we steep,
　　When healths and draughts go free—
Fishes that tipple in the deep
　　Know no such liberty.

When, like committed linnets, I
　　With shriller throat shall sing
The sweetness, mercy, majesty,
　　And glories of my King;
When I shall voice aloud, how good
　　He is, how great should be,
Enlargèd winds that curl the flood
　　Know no such liberty.

Stone walls do not a prison make,
　　Nor iron bars a cage;
Minds innocent and quiet take
　　That for an hermitage;
If I have freedom in my love—
　　And in my soul am free,
Angels alone, that soar above,
　　Enjoy such liberty.

To Lucasta, on Going beyond Seas

If to be absent were to be
　　Away from thee;
Or that when I am gone
　　You or I were alone;
Then, my Lucasta, might I crave
Pity from blustering wind, or swallowing
　　wave.

But I'll not sigh one blast or gale
　　To swell my sail,
Or pay a tear to 'suage
　　The foaming blue-god's rage;
For whether he will let me pass
Or no, I'm still as happy as I was.

Though seas and land betwixt us both,
　　Our faith and troth,

Like separated souls,
　　All time and space controls:
Above the highest sphere we meet
Unseen, unknown, and greet as Angels
　　greet.

So then we do anticipate
　　Our after-fate,
And are alive i' the skies,
　　If thus our lips and eyes
Can speak like spirits unconfined
In Heaven, their earthy bodies left be-
　　hind.

To Lucasta, on Going to the Wars

Tell me not, Sweet, I am unkind,
　　That from the nunnery
Of thy chaste breast and quiet mind
　　To war and arms I fly.

True, a new mistress now I chase,
　　The first foe in the field;
And with a stronger faith embrace
　　A sword, a horse, a shield.

Yet this inconstancy is such
　　As you too shall adore—
I could not love thee, Dear, so much,
　　Loved I not honour more.

ANDREW MARVELL [1621-1678]

Song of the Emigrants in Bermuda

Where the remote Bermudas ride
In th' ocean's bosom unespy'd,
From a small boat that row'd along
The list'ning winds received this song.
　　"What should we do but sing His
　　praise
That led us through the wat'ry maze
Unto an isle so long unknown,
And yet far kinder than our own?
Where He the huge sea-monsters wracks,
That lift the deep upon their backs;
He lands us on a grassy stage,
Safe from the storms, and prelate's rage:

He gave us this eternal Spring
Which here enamels everything,
And sends the fowls to us in care
On daily visits through the air.
He hangs in shades the orange bright
Like golden lamps in a green night,
And does in the pomegranates close
Jewels more rich than Ormus shows:
He makes the figs our mouths to meet
And throws the melons at our feet;
But apples, plants of such a price,
No tree could ever bear them twice.
With cedars chosen by His hand
From Lebanon He stores the land;
And makes the hollow seas that roar
Proclaim the ambergris on shore.
He cast (of which we rather boast)
The Gospel's pearl upon our coast;
And in these rocks for us did frame
A temple where to sound His name.
Oh! let our voice His praise exalt
Till it arrive at Heaven's vault,
Which thence (perhaps) rebounding may
Echo beyond the Mexique bay!"
—Thus sung they in the English boat
A holy and a cheerful note:
And all the way, to guide their chime,
With falling oars they kept the time.

Thoughts in a Garden

How vainly men themselves amaze
To win the palm, the oak, or bays,
And their uncessant labours see
Crown'd from some single herb or tree,
Whose short and narrow-vergèd shade
Does prudently their toils upbraid;
While all the flowers and trees do close
To weave the garlands of repose.

Fair Quiet, have I found thee here,
And Innocence thy sister dear!
Mistaken long, I sought you then
In busy companies of men:
Your sacred plants, if here below,
Only among the plants will grow:
Society is all but rude
To this delicious solitude.

No white nor red was ever seen
So am'rous as this lovely green.
Fond lovers, cruel as their flame,
Cut in these trees their mistress' name;
Little, alas, they know or heed
How far these beauties hers exceed!
Fair trees! wheres'e'er your barks I
        wound,
No name shall but your own be found.

When we have run our passions' heat
Love hither makes his best retreat:
The gods, who mortal beauty chase,
Still in a tree did end their race;
Apollo hunted Daphne so
Only that she might laurel grow;
And Pan did after Syrinx speed
Not as a nymph, but for a reed.

What wondrous life is this I lead!
Ripe apples drop about my head;
The luscious clusters of the vine
Upon my mouth do crush their wine;
The nectarine and curious peach
Into my hands themselves do reach;
Stumbling on melons, as I pass,
Ensnared with flowers, I fall on grass.

Meanwhile the mind, from pleasure less,
Withdraws into its happiness;
The mind, that ocean where each kind
Does straight its own resemblance find;
Yet it creates, transcending these,
Far other worlds, and other seas;
Annihilating all that's made
To a green thought in a green shade.

Here at the fountain's sliding foot
Or at some fruit-tree's mossy root,
Casting the body's vest aside
My soul into the boughs does glide;
There, like a bird, it sits and sings,
Then whets and claps its silver wings,
And, till prepared for longer flight,
Waves in its plumes the various light.

Such was that happy Garden-state
While man there walk'd without a mate:
After a place so pure and sweet,
What other help could yet be meet!

But 'twas beyond a mortal's share
To wander solitary there:
Two paradises 'twere in one
To live in Paradise alone.

How well the skilful gardner drew
Of flowers and herbs this dial new!

Where, from above, the milder sun
Does through a fragrant zodiac run:
And, as it works, th' industrious bee
Computes its time as well as we.
How could such sweet and wholesome
    hours
Be reckon'd, but with herbs and flowers!

JOHN BUNYAN (1628-1688)

From THE PILGRIM'S PROGRESS

Christian's Victory over Apollyon

The Pilgrim's Progress is the account of a dream, representing in allegorical narrative the life of a Christian, from his conversion to his death. In *Revelation*, IX, 11, Apollyon is mentioned as "the angel of the bottomless pit, whose name in the Hebrew tongue is Abaddon, but in the Greek hath his name Apollyon." The struggle of Christian with Apollyon, therefore, represents his struggle with the Evil One.

BUT now in this Valley of Humiliation poor Christian was hard put to it, for he had gone but a little way before he espied a foul fiend coming over the field to meet him; his name is Apollyon. Then did Christian begin to be afraid, and to cast in his mind whether to go back, or to stand his ground. But he considered again, that he had no armor for his back, and therefore thought that to turn the back to him, might give him greater advantage with ease to pierce him with his darts; therefore he resolved to venture, and stand his ground. For, thought he, had I no more in mine eye than the saving of my life, 'twould be the best way to stand.

So he went on, and Apollyon met him. Now the monster was hideous to behold: he was clothed with scales like a fish (and they are his pride); he had wings like a dragon, feet like a bear, and out of his belly came fire and smoke; and his mouth was as the mouth of a lion. When he was come up to Christian, he beheld him with a disdainful countenance, and thus began to question with him.

APOL. Whence come you? and whither are you bound?

CHR. I am come from the City of Destruction, which is the place of all evil, and am going to the City of Zion.

APOL. By this I perceive thou art one of my subjects, for all that country is mine; and I am the prince and god of it. How is it then that thou hast run away from thy king? Were it not that I hope thou mayest do me more service, I would strike thee now at one blow to the ground.

CHR. I was born indeed in your dominions, but your service was hard, and your wages such as a man could not live on, "for the wages of sin is death"; therefore when I was come to years, I did as other considerate persons do, look out, if perhaps I might mend myself.

APOL. There is no prince that will thus lightly lose his subjects, neither will I as yet lose thee: but since thou complainest of thy service and wages, be content to go back; what our country will afford, I do here promise to give thee.

CHR. But I have let myself to another, even to the King of princes, and how can I with fairness go back with thee?

APOL. Thou hast done in this, according to the proverb, changed a bad for a worse; but it is ordinary for those who have professed themselves his servants, after a while to give him the slip, and return again to me. Do thou so too, and all shall be well.

CHR. I have given him my faith, and sworn my allegiance to him; how then can I go back from this, and not be hanged as a traitor?

APOL. Thou didst the same to me, and yet I am willing to pass by all, if now thou wilt yet turn again and go back.

CHR. What I promised thee was in my nonage; and besides, I count that the Prince under whose banner now I stand, is able to absolve me; yea and to pardon also what I did as to my compliance with thee: and besides (O thou destroying Apollyon), to speak truth, I like his service, his wages, his servants, his government, his company, and country better than thine; and therefore leave off to persuade me further, I am his servant, and I will follow him.

APOL. Consider again when thou art in cold blood, what thou art like to meet with in the way that thou goest. Thou knowest that for the most part, his servants come to an ill end, because they are transgressors against me and my ways. How many of them have been put to shameful deaths! and besides, thou countest his service better than mine, whereas he never came yet from the place where he is, to deliver any that served him out of our hands; but as for me, how many times, as all the world very well knows, have I delivered, either by power or fraud, those that have faithfully served me, from him and his, though taken by them, and so I will deliver thee.

CHR. His forbearing at present to deliver them is on purpose to try their love, whether they will cleave to him to the end: and as for the ill end thou sayest they come to, that is most glorious in their account: For for present deliverance, they do not much expect it; for they stay for their glory, and then they shall have it, when their Prince comes in his, and the glory of the angels.

APOL. Thou hast already been unfaithful in thy service to him, and how dost thou think to receive wages of him?

CHR. Wherein, O Apollyon, have I been unfaithful to him?

APOL. Thou didst faint at first setting out, when thou wast almost choked in the Gulf of Despond; thou didst attempt wrong ways to be rid of thy burden, whereas thou shouldest have stayed till thy Prince had taken it off; thou didst sinfully sleep and lose thy choice thing; thou wast also almost persuaded to go back at the sight of the lions; and when thou talkest of thy journey, and of what thou hast heard and seen, thou art inwardly desirous of vainglory in all that thou sayest or doest.

CHR. All this is true, and much more, which thou hast left out; but the Prince whom I serve and honor is merciful, and ready to forgive; but besides, these infirmities possessed me in thy country, for there I sucked them in, and I have groaned under them, been sorry for them, and have obtained pardon of my Prince.

APOL. Then Apollyon broke out into a grievous rage, saying, I am an enemy to this Prince; I hate his person, his laws, and people; I am come out on purpose to withstand thee.

CHR. Apollyon, beware what you do, for I am in the King's highway, the way of holiness, therefore take heed to yourself.

APOL. Then Apollyon straddled quite over the whole breadth of the way, and said, I am void of fear in this matter, prepare thyself to die; for I swear by my infernal den thou shalt go no further; here will I spill thy soul.

And with that he threw a flaming dart at his breast, but Christian had a shield in his hand, with which he caught it, and so prevented the danger of that.

Then did Christian draw, for he saw 'twas time to bestir him; and Apollyon as fast made at him, throwing darts as thick as hail; by the which, notwithstanding all that Christian could do to avoid it, Apollyon wounded him in his head, his hand, and foot. This made Christian give a little back; Apollyon, therefore, followed his work amain, and Christian again took courage, and resisted as manfully as he could. This sore combat lasted for above half a day, even till Christian was almost quite spent. For you must know that Christian, by reason of his wounds, must needs grow weaker and weaker.

Then Apollyon, espying his opportunity, began to gather up close to Christian, and wrestling with him, gave him a dreadful fall; and with that Christian's sword flew out of his hand. Then said Apollyon, I am sure of thee now! and with that, he had almost pressed him to death, so that Christian began to despair of life. But as God would have it, while Apollyon was fetching of his last blow, thereby to make a full end of this good man, Christian nimbly reached out his hand for his sword, and caught it, saying, "Rejoice not against me, O mine enemy! when I fall, I shall arise"; and with that gave him a deadly thrust, which made him give back, as one that had received his mortal wound. Christian perceiving that, made at him again, saying, "Nay, in all these things we are more than conquerors." And with that Apollyon spread forth his dragon's wings, and sped him away, that Christian saw him no more.

JOHN DRYDEN (1631-1700)

From ANNUS MIRABILIS

The Fire of London

SUCH was the rise of this prodigious fire,
  Which, in mean buildings first ob-
    scurely bred,
From thence did soon to open streets
    aspire,
  And straight to palaces and temples
    spread.

The diligence of trades, and noiseful gain,
  And luxury, more late, asleep were
    laid;
All was the Night's, and in her silent
    reign
  No sound the rest of Nature did in-
    vade.

In this deep quiet, from what source un-
    known,
  Those seeds of fire their fatal birth
    disclose;
And first few scattering sparks about
    were blown,
  Big with the flames that to our ruin
    rose.

Then in some close-pent room it crept
    along,
  And, smouldering as it went, in silence
    fed;
Till the infant monster, with devouring
    strong,
  Walked boldly upright with exalted
    head.

Now, like some rich or mighty murderer,
  Too great for prison which he breaks
    with gold,
Who fresher for new mischiefs does ap-
    pear,
  And dares the world to tax him with
    the old,

So scapes the insulting fire his narrow
    jail,
  And makes small outlets into open
    air;
There the fierce winds his tender force
    assail,
  And beat him downward to his first
    repair.

The winds, like crafty courtesans, with-
    held
  His flames from burning but to blow
    them more:
And, every fresh attempt, he is repelled
  With faint denials, weaker than before.

And now, no longer letted of his prey,
  He leaps up at it with enraged desire,
O'erlooks the neighbours with a wide
    survey,
  And nods at every house his threaten-
    ing fire.

The ghosts of traitors from the Bridge
    descend,
  With bold fanatic spectres to rejoice;
About the fire into a dance they bend,
  And sing their sabbath notes with
    feeble voice.

Our guardian angel saw them where they
 sate,
 Above the palace of our slumbering
  King;
He sighed, abandoning his charge to
 Fate,
 And drooping oft looked back upon the
  wing.

At length the crackling noise and dreadful blaze
 Called up some waking lover to the
  sight;
And long it was ere he the rest could
 raise,
 Whose heavy eyelids yet were full of
  night.

The next to danger, hot pursued by fate,
 Half-clothed, half-naked, hastily re-
  tire;
And frighted mothers strike their breasts
 too late
 For helpless infants left amidst the fire.

Their cries soon waken all the dwellers
 near;
 Now murmuring noises rise in every
  street;
The more remote run stumbling with
 their fear,
 And in the dark men justle as they
  meet.

So weary bees in little cells repose;
 But if night-robbers lift the well-
  stored hive,
An humming through their waxen city
 grows,
 And out upon each other's wings they
  drive.

Now streets grow thronged and busy as
 by day;
 Some run for buckets to the hallowed
  quire;
Some cut the pipes, and some the engines
 play,
 And some more bold mount ladders to
  the fire.

In vain; for from the east a Belgian
 wind
 His hostile breath through the dry
  rafters sent;
The flames impelled soon left their foes
 behind,
 And forward with a wanton fury went.

A key of fire ran all along the shore,
 And lightened all the river with a
  blaze;
The wakened tides began again to roar,
 And wondering fish in shining waters
  gaze.

Old Father Thames raised up his reverend head,
 But feared the fate of Simois would
  return;
Deep in his ooze he sought his sedgy bed,
 And shrank his waters back into his
  urn.

The fire meantime walks in a broader
 gross;
 To either hand his wings he opens
  wide;
He wades the streets, and straight he
 reaches 'cross
 And plays his longing flames on the
  other side.

At first they warm, then scorch, and then
 they take;
 Now with long necks from side to side
  they feed;
At length, grown strong, their mother-
 fire forsake,
 And a new colony of flames succeed.

To every nobler portion of the town
 The curling billows roll their restless
  tide;
In parties now they straggle up and
 down,
 As armies unopposed for prey divide.

One mighty squadron, with a sidewind
 sped,
 Through narrow lanes his cumbered
  fire does haste,

By powerful charms of gold and silver
led
The Lombard bankers and the Change
to waste.

Another backward to the Tower would
go,
And slowly eats his way against the
wind;
But the main body of the marching foe
Against the imperial palace is designed.

Now day appears; and with the day the
King,
Whose early care had robbed him of
his rest;
Far off the cracks of falling houses ring,
And shrieks of subjects pierce his ten-
der breast.

Near as he draws, thick harbingers of
smoke
With gloomy pillars cover all the
place;
Whose little intervals of night are broke
By sparks that drive against his sacred
face.

More than his guards his sorrows made
him known,
And pious tears which down his cheeks
did shower;
The wretched in his grief forgot their
own;
So much the pity of a king has power.

He wept the flames of what he loved so
well,
And what so well had merited his love;
For never prince in grace did more excel,
Or royal city more in duty strove.

From ABSALOM AND ACHITOPHEL,

Part I

Achitophel

Absalom and Achitophel (later known
as Part I) appeared anonymously on November 17, 1681. At the moment, Charles
II was exerting every effort to secure the
Catholic succession in England. The opposition, led by the Earl of Shaftesbury,
was equally intent upon securing the passage of the Exclusion Bill, which would
have prevented Charles's brother from
succeeding to the throne, and cleared the
way for the eventual accession of the
King's natural son, the Duke of Monmouth.

In the poem, Monmouth figures as Absalom, Shaftesbury as Achitophel, Charles
as David, Cromwell as Saul, the Roman
Catholics as Jebusites, the Dissenters as
Levites. "The Plot" mentioned in the following selection is the so-called Popish
Plot, of which Titus Oates (Corah in the
poem) had accused the Catholics, in 1678.
Shaftesbury had made great capital among
the populace of the charge that the Catholics had plotted to kill King Charles and
put at once on the throne his brother
James, who was to bring about a return
of England to the faith. The poem relates
that Shaftesbury persuaded Monmouth to
rebellion; that the King, after taking counsel, determined to draw the sword of "justice" against his foes; and that, with the
consent of the Almighty, he succeeded.
The strongest satiric elements appear in
the descriptions of the leaders of the rebellion: Shaftesbury as Achitophel, and
George Villiers, the second Duke of Buckingham, as Zimri. He had ridiculed Dryden as Bayes, in *The Rehearsal.*

OF these the false Achitophel was first,
A name to all succeeding ages curst:
For close designs and crooked counsels
fit,
Sagacious, bold, and turbulent of wit,
Restless, unfixed in principles and place,
In power unpleased, impatient of dis-
grace;
A fiery soul which, working out its way,
Fretted the pigmy body to decay
And o'er-informed the tenement of clay.
A daring pilot in extremity,
Pleased with the danger, when the waves
went high,
He sought the storms; but, for a calm
unfit,
Would steer too nigh the sands to boast
his wit.
Great wits are sure to madness near
allied,
And thin partitions do their bounds
divide;

Else, why should he, with wealth and honour blest,
Refuse his age the needful hours of rest?
Punish a body which he could not please,
Bankrupt of life, yet prodigal of ease?
And all to leave what with his toil he won
To that unfeathered two-legged thing, a son,
Got, while his soul did huddled notions try,
And born a shapeless lump, like anarchy.
In friendship false, implacable in hate,
Resolved to ruin or to rule the state;
To compass this the triple bond he broke,
The pillars of the public safety shook,
And fitted Israel for a foreign yoke;
Then, seized with fear, yet still affecting fame,
Usurped a patriot's all-atoning name.
So easy still it proves in factious times
With public zeal to cancel private crimes.
How safe is treason and how sacred ill,
Where none can sin against the people's will,
Where crowds can wink and no offence be known,
Since in another's guilt they find their own!
Yet fame deserved no enemy can grudge;
The statesman we abhor, but praise the judge.
In Israel's courts ne'er sat an Abbethdin
With more discerning eyes or hands more clean,
Unbribed, unsought, the wretched to redress,
Swift of despatch and easy of access.
Oh! had he been content to serve the crown
With virtues only proper to the gown,
Or had the rankness of the soil been freed
From cockle that oppressed the noble seed,
David for him his tuneful harp had strung
And Heaven had wanted one immortal song.

But wild ambition loves to slide, not stand,
And Fortune's ice prefers to Virtue's land.
Achitophel, grown weary to possess
A lawful fame and lazy happiness,
Disdained the golden fruit to gather free,
And lent the crowd his arm to shake the tree.
Now, manifest of crimes contrived long since,
He stood at bold defiance with his Prince,
Held up the buckler of the people's cause
Against the crown, and skulked behind the laws.
The wished occasion of the Plot he takes;
Some circumstances finds, but more he makes;
By buzzing emissaries fills the ears
Of listening crowds with jealousies and fears
Of arbitrary counsels brought to light,
And proves the King himself a Jebusite.
Weak arguments! which yet he knew full well
Were strong with people easy to rebel.
For, governed by the moon, the giddy Jews
Tread the same track when she the prime renews.
And once in twenty years their scribes record,
By natural instinct they change their lord.

From ABSALOM AND ACHITOPHEL,

Part II

The Malcontents. Zimri

See the note prefixed to "Achitophel," above. In this passage, the Levites are the Presbyterian leaders, and the Solymaean rout are the rabble of London dissenters.

To FURTHER this, Achitophel unites
The malcontents of all the Israelites,
Whose differing parties he could wisely join

For several ends to serve the same design;
The best, (and of the princes some were such,)
Who thought the power of monarchy too much;
Mistaken men and patriots in their hearts,
Not wicked, but seduced by impious arts;
By these the springs of property were bent
And wound so high they cracked the government.
The next for interest sought to embroil the state
To sell their duty at a dearer rate,
And make their Jewish markets of the throne,
Pretending public good to serve their own.
Others thought kings an useless heavy load,
Who cost too much and did too little good.
These were for laying honest David by
On principles of pure good husbandry.
With them joined all the haranguers of the throng
That thought to get preferment by the tongue.
Who follow next a double danger bring,
Not only hating David, but the King;
The Solymaean rout, well versed of old
In godly faction and in treason bold,
Cowering and quaking at a conqueror's sword,
But lofty to a lawful prince restored,
Saw with disdain an Ethnic plot begun
And scorned by Jebusites to be outdone.
Hot Levites headed these; who, pulled before
From the ark which in the Judges' days they bore,
Resumed their cant, and with a zealous cry
Pursued their old beloved theocracy,
Where Sanhedrin and priest enslaved the nation,
And justified their spoils by inspiration;

For who so fit for reign as Aaron's race,
If once dominion they could found in grace?
These led the pack; though not of surest scent,
Yet deepest mouthed against the government.
A numerous host of dreaming saints succeed
Of the true old enthusiastic breed:
'Gainst form and order they their power employ,
Nothing to build and all things to destroy.
But far more numerous was the herd of such
Who think too little and who talk too much.
These out of mere instinct, they knew not why,
Adored their fathers' God and property,
And by the same blind benefit of Fate
The Devil and the Jebusite did hate:
Born to be saved even in their own despite,
Because they could not help believing right.
Such were the tools; but a whole Hydra more
Remains of sprouting heads too long to score.
Some of their chiefs were princes of the land;
In the first rank of these did Zimri stand,
A man so various that he seemed to be
Not one, but all mankind's epitome:
Stiff in opinions, always in the wrong,
Was everything by starts and nothing long;
But in the course of one revolving moon
Was chymist, fiddler, statesman, and buffoon;
Then all for women, painting, rhyming, drinking,
Besides ten thousand freaks that died in thinking.
Blest madman, who could every hour employ

With something new to wish or to en-
joy!
Railing and praising were his usual
themes,
And both, to show his judgment, in ex-
tremes:
So over violent or over civil
That every man with him was God or
Devil.
In squandering wealth was his peculiar
art;
Nothing went unrewarded but desert.
Beggared by fools whom still he found
too late,
He had his jest, and they had his estate.
He laughed himself from Court; then
sought relief
By forming parties, but could ne'er be
chief:
For spite of him, the weight of business
fell
On Absalom and wise Achitophel;
Thus wicked but in will, of means bereft,
He left not faction, but of that was left.

A Song for St. Cecilia's Day

FROM harmony, from heavenly harmony
   This universal frame began:
  When Nature underneath a heap
   Of jarring atoms lay
  And could not heave her head,
The tuneful voice was heard from high,
   "Arise, ye more than dead!"
Then cold, and hot, and moist, and dry,
In order to their stations leap,
  And Music's power obey.
From harmony, from heavenly harmony
   This universal frame began:
   From harmony to harmony
Thro' all the compass of the notes it ran,
The diapason closing full in Man.

What passion cannot Music raise and
   quell!
  When Jubal struck the chorded shell
  His listening brethren stood around,
  And, wondering, on their faces fell

To worship that celestial sound.
Less than a god they thought there could
  not dwell
  Within the hollow of that shell
  That spoke so sweetly and so well.
What passion cannot Music raise and
  quell!

  The trumpet's loud clangor
   Excites us to arms,
  With shrill notes of anger
   And mortal alarms.
The double double double beat
  Of the thundering drum
  Cries: "Hark! the foes come;
Charge, charge, 'tis too late to retreat!"

The soft complaining flute
  In dying notes discovers
  The woes of hopeless lovers,
Whose dirge is whisper'd by the warbling
  lute.

  Sharp violins proclaim
Their jealous pangs and desperation,
Fury, frantic indignation,
Depth of pains, and height of passion
  For the fair disdainful dame.

But oh! what art can teach,
What human voice can reach
  The sacred organ's praise?
Notes inspiring holy love,
Notes that wing their heavenly ways
  To mend the choirs above.

Orpheus could lead the savage race,
And trees unrooted left their place
  Sequacious of the lyre:
But bright Cecilia raised the wonder
  higher:
When to her Organ vocal breath was
  given
An Angel heard, and straight appear'd—
  Mistaking earth for heaven.

GRAND CHORUS

As from the power of sacred lays
  The spheres began to move,

And sung the great Creator's praise
  To all the blest above;
So when the last and dreadful hour
This crumbling pageant shall devour,
The trumpet shall be heard on high,
The dead shall live, the living die,
And Music shall untune the sky.

Alexander's Feast; or, The Power of Music

I

'TWAS at the royal feast for Persia won
  By Philip's warlike son:
  Aloft in awful state
  The godlike hero sate
  On his imperial throne;
His valiant peers were placed around;
Their brows with roses and with myrtles
  bound:
(So should desert in arms be crown'd.)
The lovely Thais, by his side,
Sate like a blooming Eastern bride,
In flower of youth and beauty's pride.
    Happy, happy, happy pair!
      None but the brave,
      None but the brave,
      None but the brave deserves the
        fair.

CHORUS

  Happy, happy, happy pair!
    None but the brave,
    None but the brave,
    None but the brave deserves the
      fair.

II

  Timotheus, placed on high
    Amid the tuneful choir,
  With flying fingers touch'd the lyre:
    The trembling notes ascend the sky,
    And heavenly joys inspire.
  The song began from Jove,
  Who left his blissful seats above,
  (Such is the power of mighty love)

A dragon's fiery form belied the god:
Sublime on radiant spires he rode,
  When he to fair Olympia press'd;
  And while he sought her snowy
    breast:
Then, round her slender waist he
  curl'd,
And stamp'd an image of himself, a sov-
    ereign of the world.
The listening crowd admire the lofty
    sound,
"A present deity," they shout around;
"A present deity," the vaulted roofs
    rebound:
    With ravished ears
    The monarch hears,
    Assumes the god,
    Affects to nod,
    And seems to shake the spheres.

CHORUS: With ravished ears, etc.

III

The praise of Bacchus then the sweet
    musician sung,
  Of Bacchus, ever fair and ever young.
  The jolly god in triumph comes;
  Sound the trumpets, beat the drums;
    Flush'd with a purple grace
    He shows his honest face:
Now give the hautboys breath; he comes,
    he comes.
  Bacchus, ever fair and young,
    Drinking joys did first ordain;
  Bacchus' blessings are a treasure,
  Drinking is the soldier's pleasure;
    Rich the treasure,
    Sweet the pleasure,
    Sweet is pleasure after pain.

CHORUS: Bacchus' blessings are a treasure, etc.

IV

Sooth'd with the sound, the king grew
    vain;
    Fought all his battles o'er again;
And thrice he routed all his foes, and
    thrice he slew the slain.

The master saw the madness rise,
His glowing cheeks, his ardent eyes;
And while he heaven and earth defied,
Changed his hand, and check'd his
    pride.
  He chose a mournful Muse,
    Soft pity to infuse;
He sung Darius great and good,
  By too severe a fate,
Fallen, fallen, fallen, fallen,
  . Fallen from his high estate,
And weltering in his blood;
Deserted at his utmost need
By those his former bounty fed; -
On the bare earth exposed he lies,
With not a friend to close his eyes.

With downcast looks the joyless victor
    sate,
  Revolving in his alter'd soul
    The various turns of chance be-
      low:
  And, now and then, a sigh he stole,
    And tears began to flow.

CHORUS: Revolving in his alter'd soul,
etc.

V

The mighty master smiled to see
That love was in the next degree;
'Twas but a kindred sound to move,
For pity melts the mind to love.
  Softly sweet, in Lydian measures,
  Soon he soothed his soul to pleasures.
"War," he sung, "is toil and trouble;
Honour but an empty bubble;
  Never ending, still beginning,
Fighting still, and still destroying:
  If the world be worth thy winning,
Think, O think it worth enjoying:
  Lovely Thais sits beside thee,
  Take the good the gods provide
    thee."

The many rend the skies with loud ap-
    plause:
So Love was crown'd, but Music won
    the cause.

The prince, unable to conceal his
    pain,
  Gazed on the fair
  Who caused his care,
And sigh'd and look'd, sigh'd and
    look'd,
Sigh'd and look'd, and sigh'd again;
At length, with love and wine at once
    oppress'd,
The vanquish'd victor sunk upon her
    breast.

CHORUS: The prince, unable to conceal
his pain, etc.

VI

Now strike the golden lyre again;
A louder yet, and yet a louder strain.
Break his bands of sleep asunder,
And rouse him, like a rattling peal of
    thunder.
  Hark, hark, the horrid sound
    Has raised up his head;
    As awaked from the dead,
  And, amazed, he stares around.
"Revenge, revenge!" Timotheus cries;
  "See the Furies arise;
    See the snakes that they rear,
    How they hiss in their hair,
And the sparkles that flash from their
    eyes!
  Behold a ghastly band,
  Each a torch in his hand!
Those are Grecian ghosts, that in battle
    were slain,
    And unburied remain
    Inglorious on the plain:
    Give the vengeance due
    To the valiant crew.
Behold how they toss their torches on
    high,
    How they point to the Persian
    abodes,
And glittering temples of their hostile
    gods."
The princes applaud with a furious joy;
And the king seized a flambeau with zeal
    to destroy;

Thais led the way,
To light him to his prey,
And, like another Helen, fired another
Troy.

CHORUS: And the king seized a flambeau
with zeal to destroy, etc.

And added length to solemn sounds,
With nature's mother wit, and arts un-
known before.
Let old Timotheus yield the prize,
Or both divide the crown:
He raised a mortal to the skies;
She drew an angel down.

VII

Thus, long ago,
Ere heaving bellows learned to blow,
While organs yet were mute,
Timotheus, to his breathing flute
And sounding lyre,
Could swell the soul to rage, or kindle
soft desire.
At last divine Cecilia came,
Inventress of the vocal frame;
The sweet enthusiast, from her sacred
store,
Enlarged the former narrow bounds,

GRAND CHORUS

At last divine Cecilia came,
Inventress of the vocal frame;
The sweet enthusiast, from her sacred
store,
Enlarged the former narrow bounds,
And added length to solemn sounds,
With nature's mother wit, and arts un-
known before.
Let old Timotheus yield the prize,
Or both divide the crown:
He raised a mortal to the skies;
She drew an angel down.

DANIEL DEFOE (1659?-1731)

From ROBINSON CRUSOE, Part II

Friday and the Bear

BUT never was a fight managed so hardily, and in such a surprising manner, as that which followed between Friday and the bear, which gave us all, though at first we were surprised and afraid for him, the greatest diversion imaginable. As the bear is a heavy, clumsy creature, and does not gallop as the wolf does, who is swift and light, so he has two particular qualities, which generally are the rule of his actions: first, as to men, who are not his proper prey; I say, not his proper prey, because, though I cannot say what excessive hunger might do, which was now their case, the ground being all covered with snow; but as to men, he does not usually attempt them, unless they first attack him. On the contrary, if you meet him in the woods, if you don't meddle with him, he won't meddle with you; but then you must take care to be very civil to him, and give him the road, for he is a very nice gentleman. He won't go a step out of his way for a prince; nay, if you are really afraid, your best way is to look another way, and keep going on, for sometimes if you stop;

and stand still, and look steadily at him, he takes it for an affront; but if you throw or toss anything at him, and it hits him, though it were but a bit of a stick as big as your finger, he takes it for an affront, and sets all his other business aside to pursue his revenge; for he will have satisfaction in point of honour. That is his first quality; the next is, that if he be once affronted, he will never leave you, night or day, till he has his revenge, but follows, at a good round rate, till he overtakes you.

My man Friday had delivered our guide, and when we came up to him he was helping him off from his horse; for the man was both hurt and frighted, and indeed the last more than the first; when, on the sudden, we spied the bear come out of the wood, and a vast monstrous one it was, the biggest by far that ever I saw. We were all a little surprised when we saw him; but when Friday saw him, it was easy to see joy and courage in the fellow's countenance. "O! O! O!" says Friday, three times pointing to him. "O master! you give me te leave; me shakee te hand with him; me make you good laugh."

I was surprised to see the fellow so pleased. "You fool you," says I, "he will eat you up." "Eatee me up! eatee me up!" says Friday, twice over again; "me eatee him up; me make you good laugh; you all stay here, me show you good laugh." So down he sits, and gets his boots off in a moment, and put on a pair of pumps, as we call the flat shoes they wear, and which he had in his pocket, gives my other servant his horse, and with his gun away he flew, swift like the wind.

The bear was walking softly on, and offered to meddle with nobody till Friday, coming pretty near, calls to him, as if the bear could understand him, "Hark ye, hark ye," says Friday, "me speakee wit you." We followed at a distance; for now being come down on the Gascoign side of the mountains, we were entered a vast great forest, where the country was plain and pretty open, though many trees in it scattered here and there.

Friday, who had, as we say, the heels of the bear, came up with him quickly, and takes up a great stone and throws at him, and hit him just on the head, but did him no more harm than if he had thrown it against a wall. But it answered Friday's end, for the rogue was so void of fear, that he did it purely to make the bear follow him, and show us some laugh, as he called it.

As soon as the bear felt the stone, and saw him, he turns about, and comes after him, taking devilish long strides, and shuffling along at a strange rate, so as would have put a horse to a middling gallop. Away runs Friday, and takes his course as if he run towards us for help; so we all resolved to fire at once upon the bear, and deliver my man; though

I was angry at him heartily for bringing the bear back upon us, when he was going about his own business another way; and especially I was angry, that he had turned the bear upon us, and then run away; and I called out, "You dog," said I, "is this your making us laugh? Come away, and take your horse, that we may shoot the creature." He hears me, and cries out, "No shoot, no shoot; stand still, you get much laugh." And as the nimble creature run two feet for the beast's one, he turned on a sudden, on one side of us, and seeing a great oak tree fit for his purpose, he beckoned to us to follow; and doubling his pace, he gets nimbly up the tree, laying his gun down upon the ground, at about five or six yards from the bottom of the tree.

The bear soon came to the tree, and we followed at a distance. The first thing he did, he stopped at the gun, smelt to it, but let it lie, and up he scrambles into the tree, climbing like a cat, though so monstrously heavy. I was amazed at the folly, as I though it, of my man, and could not for my life see anything to laugh at yet, till seeing the bear get up the tree, we all rode nearer to him.

When we came to the tree, there was Friday got out to the small end of a large limb of the tree, and the bear got about half way to him. As soon as the bear got out to that part where the limb of the tree was weaker, "Ha!" says he to us, "now you see me teachee the bear dance." So he falls a-jumping and shaking the bough, at which the bear began to totter, but stood still, and began to look behind him, to see how he should get back. Then, indeed, we did laugh heartily. But Friday had not done with him by a great deal. When he sees him stand still, he calls out to him again, as if he had supposed the bear could speak English, "What, you no come farther? pray you come farther;" so he left jumping and shaking the tree; and the bear, just as if he had understood what he said, did come a little farther; then he fell a-jumping again, and the bear stopped again.

We thought now was a good time to knock him on the head, and I called to Friday to stand still, and we would shoot the bear; but he cried out earnestly, "O pray! O pray no shoot, me shoot by and then;" he would have said by-and-by. However, to shorten the story, Friday danced so much, and the bear stood so ticklish, that we had laughing enough indeed, but still could not imagine what the fellow would do: for first we thought he depended upon shaking the bear off; and we found the bear was too cunning for that too; for he would not go out far enough to be thrown down, but clings fast with his great broad claws and feet, so that we could not imagine what would be the end of it, and where the jest would be at last.

But Friday put us out of doubt quickly; for seeing the bear cling fast to the bough, and that he would not be persuaded to come any farther, " Well, well," says Friday, " you no come farther, me go, me go; you no come to me, me go come to you;" and upon this he goes out to the smallest end of the bough, where it would bend with his weight, and gently lets himself down by it, sliding down the bough till he came near enough to jump down on his feet and away he ran to his gun, takes it up, and stands still.

" Well," said I to him, " Friday, what will you do now? Why don't you shoot him? " " No shoot," says Friday, " no yet; me shoot now, me no kill; me stay, give you one more laugh." And indeed, so he did, as you will see presently; for when the bear sees his enemy gone, he comes back from the bough where he stood, but did it mighty leisurely, looking behind him every step, and coming backward till he got into the body of the tree; then with the same hinder end foremost he comes down the tree, grasping it with his claws, and moving one foot at a time, very leisurely. At this juncture, and just before he could set his hind feet upon the ground, Friday stepped up close to him, clapped the muzzle of his piece into his ear, and shot him dead as a stone.

Then the rogue turned about to see if we did not laugh; and when he saw we were pleased by our looks, he falls a-laughing himself very loud. " So we kill bear in my country," says Friday. " So you kill them? " says I; " why, you have no guns." " No," says he, " no gun, but shoot great much long arrow."

From A JOURNAL OF THE PLAGUE YEAR

The Story of the Piper

The full title of the work from which the following selection is taken, is "A Journal of the Plague Year: being observations or memorials of the most remarkable occurrences, as well public as private, which happened in London during the last visitation in 1665. Written by a Citizen who continued all the while in London. Never made public before." The book appeared in 1722, when the English public were alarmed at the outbreak of the plague in Marseilles in 1720-21. The *Journal* is, ostensibly, the work of a saddler, who lived, with a house-keeper, maid-servant, and two apprentices, "without Aldgate, about midway between Aldgate Church and Whitechapel Bars, on the left hand, or north side, of the street." Defoe himself was but six years of age at the time of the great plague; when he produced the *Journal*, however, he had accumulated much information from the reminiscences of survivors and from authoritative books written at the time. Its realism, at any rate, is unsurpassed.

IT was under this John Hayward's care, and within his bounds, that the story of the piper, with which people have made themselves so merry, happened, and he assured me that it was true. It is said that it was a blind piper; but, as John told me, the fellow was not blind, but an ignorant, weak, poor man, and usually walked his rounds about ten o'clock at night and went piping along from door to door, and the people usually took him in at public-houses where they knew him, and would give him drink and victuals, and sometimes farthings; and he in return would pipe and sing and talk simply, which diverted the people; and thus he lived. It was but a very bad time for this diversion while things were as I have told, yet the poor fellow went about as usual, but was almost starved; and when anybody asked how he did he would answer, the dead cart had not taken him yet, but that they had promised to call for him next week.

It happened one night that this poor fellow, whether somebody had given him too much drink or no—John Hayward said he had not drink in his house, but that they had given him a little more victuals than ordinary at a public-house in Coleman Street—and the poor fellow, having not usually had a bellyful for perhaps not a good while, was laid all along upon the top of a bulk or stall, and fast asleep, at a door in the street near London Wall, towards Cripplegate, and that upon the same bulk or stall the people of some house, in the alley of which the house was a corner, hearing a bell, which they always rang before the cart came, had laid a body really dead of the plague just by him, thinking, too, that this poor fellow had been a dead body, as the other was, and laid there by some of the neighbours.

Accordingly, when John Hayward with his bell and the cart came along, finding two dead bodies lie upon the stall, they took them up with the instrument they used and threw them into the cart, and all this while the piper slept soundly.

From hence they passed along and took in other dead bodies, till, as honest John Hayward told me, they almost buried him alive in the cart; yet all this while he slept soundly. At length the cart came to the place where the bodies were to be thrown into the ground, which, as I do remember, was at Mount Mill; and as the cart usually stopped some time before they were ready to shoot out the melancholy load they had in it, as soon as the cart stopped the fellow awaked and struggled a little to get his head out from among the dead bodies, when, raising himself up in the cart, he called out, "Hey! where am I?" This frighted the fellow that attended about the work; but after some pause John Hayward, recovering himself, said, "Lord, bless us! There's somebody in the cart not quite dead!" So another called to him and said, "Who are you?" The fellow answered, "I am the poor piper. Where am I?" "Where are you?" says Hayward. "Why, you are in the dead-cart, and we are going to bury you." "But I an't dead though, am I?" says the piper, which made them laugh a little, though, as John said, they were heartily frighted at first; so they helped the poor fellow down, and he went about his business.

I know the story goes he set up his pipes in the cart and frighted the bearers and others so that they ran away; but John Hayward did not tell the story so, nor say anything of his piping at all; but that he was a poor piper, and that he was carried away as above I am fully satisfied of the truth of.

JONATHAN SWIFT (1667-1745)

From THE BATTLE OF THE BOOKS

The Spider and the Bee

The Battle of the Books appeared in 1704. It was suggested by a controversy that had originated in France, and had been carried on in England, about the relative merits of the Ancients and the Moderns. In Homeric style, it narrates "the terrible fight that happened on Friday last, between the ancient and modern books, in the king's library." The argument between the spider and the bee in St. James's library comes just before the actual commencement of hostilities. The spider, with his skill in fortification and mathematics, represents the excellences and other qualities of modern learning; the bee, with his wings and his voice, stands for the ancient. "Sweetness and light," the final words of the fable, provided the title of Matthew Arnold's famous essay on the Hebraic and Hellenistic elements of our spiritual inheritance.

THINGS were at this crisis, when a material accident fell out. For, upon the highest corner of a large window, there dwelt a certain spider, swollen up to the first magnitude by the destruction of infinite numbers of flies, whose spoils lay scattered before the gates of his palace, like human bones before the cave of some giant. The avenues to his castle were guarded with turnpikes and palisadoes, all after the modern way of fortification. After you had passed several courts, you came to the centre, wherein you might behold the constable himself in his own lodgings, which had windows fronting to each avenue, and ports to sally out, upon all occasions of prey or defence. In this mansion he had for some time dwelt in peace and plenty, without danger to his person by swallows from above, or to his palace, by brooms from below; when it was the pleasure of fortune to conduct thither a wandering bee, to whose curiosity a broken pane in the glass had discovered itself, and in he went; where, expatiating a while, he at last happened to alight upon one of the outward walls of the spider's citadel; which, yielding to the unequal weight, sunk down to the very foundation. Thrice he endeavoured to force his passage, and thrice the centre shook. The spider within, feeling the terrible convulsion, supposed at first that nature was approaching to her final dissolution; or else, that Beelzebub, with all his legions, was come to revenge the death of many thousands of his subjects, whom his enemy had slain and devoured. However, he at length valiantly resolved to issue forth, and meet his fate. Meanwhile the bee had acquitted himself of his toils, and, posted securely at some distance, was employed in cleansing his wings, and disengaging them from the ragged remnants of the cobweb. By this time the spider was adventured out, when, beholding the chasms, the ruins, and dilapidations of his fortress, he was very near at his wit's end; he stormed and swore like a madman, and swelled till he was ready to burst. At length, casting his eye upon the bee, and wisely gathering causes from events, (for they knew each other by sight) : "A plague split you," said he, "for a giddy son of a . . . Is it you, with a vengeance, that have made this litter here? Could not you look before you, and be d—d? Do you think I have nothing else to do (in the devil's name) but to mend and repair after you . . .?"—"Good words, friend," said the bee, (having now pruned himself, and being disposed to droll,) "I'll give you my hand and word to come near your kennel no more; I was never in such a confounded pickle since I was born."—"Sirrah," replied the spider, "if it were not for breaking an old custom in our family, never to stir abroad against an enemy, I should come and teach you better manners."—"I pray have patience," said the bee, "or you'll spend your substance, and, for aught I see, you may stand in need of it all, toward the repair of your house."—"Rogue, rogue," replied the spider, "yet, methinks you should have more respect to a person, whom all the world allows to be so much your betters."—"By my troth," said the bee, "the comparison will amount to a very good jest, and you will do me a favour to let me know the reasons that all the world is pleased to use in so hopeful a dispute." At this the spider, having swelled himself into the size and posture of a disputant, began his argument in the true spirit of controversy, with resolution to be heartily scurrilous and angry, to urge on his own reasons, without the least regard to the answers or objections of his opposite, and fully predetermined in his mind against all conviction.

"Not to disparage myself," said he, "by the comparison with such a rascal, what art thou but a vagabond without house or home, without stock or inheritance? Born to no possession of your own, but a pair of wings and a drone-pipe. Your livelihood is a universal plunder upon nature; a freebooter over fields and gardens; and, for the sake of stealing, will rob a nettle as easily as a violet. Whereas I am a domestic animal, furnished with a native stock within myself. This large castle (to shew my improvements in the mathematics) is all built with my own hands, and the materials extracted altogether out of my own person."

"I am glad," answered the bee, "to hear you grant at least that I am come honestly by my wings and my voice; for then, it seems, I am obliged to Heaven alone for my flights and my music; and Providence would never have bestowed on me two such gifts, without designing them for the noblest ends. I visit indeed all the flowers and blossoms of the field and garden; but whatever I collect thence, enriches myself, without the least injury to their beauty, their smell, or their taste. Now, for you and your skill in architecture, and other mathematics, I have little to say: In that building of yours there might, for aught I know, have been labour and method enough; but, by woful experience for us both, it is plain, the materials are naught, and I hope you will henceforth take warning, and consider duration and matter, as well as method and art. You boast, indeed, of being obliged to no other creature, but of drawing and spinning out all from yourself; that is to say, if we may judge of the liquor in the vessel by what issues out, you possess a good plentiful store of dirt and poison in your breast; and, though I would by no means lessen or disparage your genuine stock of either, yet, I doubt you are somewhat obliged, for an increase of both, to a little foreign assistance. Your inherent portion of dirt does not fail of acquisitions, by sweepings exhaled from below; and one insect furnishes you with a share of poison to destroy another. So that, in short, the question comes all to this— Whether is the nobler being of the two, that which, by a lazy contemplation of four inches round, by an overweening pride, feeding and engendering on itself, turns all into excrement and venom, producing nothing at all, but flybane and a cobweb; or that which, by a universal range, with long search, much study, true judgment, and distinction of things, brings home honey and wax."

This dispute was managed with such eagerness, clamour, and warmth, that the two parties of books, in arms below, stood silent a while, waiting in suspense what would be the issue, which was not long undetermined: For the bee, grown impatient at so much loss of time, fled straight away to a bed of roses, without looking for a reply, and left the spider, like an orator, collected in himself, and just prepared to burst out.

It happened upon this emergency, that Æsop broke silence first. He had been of late most barbarously treated by a strange effect of the regent's humanity, who had tore off his title-page, sorely defaced one

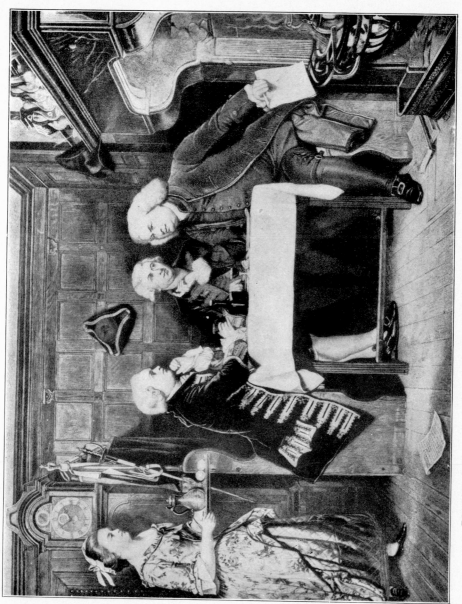

DR. JOHNSON, GOLDSMITH AND BOSWELL AT THE MITRE TAVERN, FLEET STREET

From an engraving by R. B. Parks after the picture by Eyre Crowe, A. R. A.

half of his leaves, and chained him fast among a shelf of Moderns. Where, soon discovering how high the quarrel was likely to proceed, he tried all his arts, and turned himself to a thousand forms. At length, in the borrowed shape of an ass, the regent mistook him for a Modern; by which means he had time and opportunity to escape to the Ancients, just when the spider and the bee were entering into their contest, to which he gave his attention with a world of pleasure; and when it was ended, swore in the loudest key, that in all his life he had never known two cases so parallel and adapt to each other, as that in the window, and this upon the shelves. "The disputants," said he, "have admirably managed the dispute between them, have taken in the full strength of all that is to be said on both sides, and exhausted the substance of every argument *pro* and *con*. It is but to adjust the reasonings of both to the present quarrel, then to compare and apply the labours and fruits of each, as the bee has learnedly deduced them, and we shall find the conclusion fall plain and close upon the Moderns and us. For, pray, gentlemen, was ever anything so modern as the spider in his air, his turns, and his paradoxes? He argues in the behalf of you his brethren and himself, with many boastings of his native stock and great genius; that he spins and spits wholly from himself, and scorns to own any obligation or assistance from without. Then he displays to you his great skill in architecture, and improvement in the mathematics. To all this the bee, as an advocate, retained by us the Ancients, thinks fit to answer—that, if one may judge of the great genius or inventions of the Moderns by what they have produced, you will hardly have countenance to bear you out, in boasting of either. Erect your schemes with as much method and skill as you please; yet if the materials be nothing but dirt, spun out of your own entrails (the guts of modern brains) the edifice will conclude at last in a cobweb, the duration of which, like that of other spiders' webs, may be imputed to their being forgotten, or neglected, or hid in a corner. For anything else of genuine that the Moderns may pretend to, I cannot recollect; unless it be a large vein of wrangling and satire, much of a nature and substance with the spider's poison; which, however they pretend to spit wholly out of themselves, is improved by the same arts, by feeding upon the insects and vermin of the age. As for us the Ancients, we are content, with the bee, to pretend to nothing of our own, beyond our wings and our voice, that is to say, our flights and our language. For the rest, whatever we have got, has been by infinite labour and search, and ranging through every corner of nature; the difference is, that, instead of dirt and poison, we have rather chosen to fill our hives with honey and wax, thus furnishing mankind with the two noblest of things, which are sweetness and light."

When I Come to be Old

NOT to marry a young Woman,

Not to keep young Company unless they really desire it.

Not to be peevish or morose, or suspicious.

Not to scorn present Ways, or Wits, or Fashions, or Men, or War, &c.

Not to be fond of Children, *or let them come near me hardly.*

Not to tell the same story over and over to the same People.

Not to be covetous.

Not to neglect decency, or cleanliness, for fear of falling into Nastiness.

Not to be over severe with young People, but give Allowances for their youthful follies and weaknesses.

Not to be influenced by, or give ear to knavish tattling servants, or others.

Not to be too free of advise, nor trouble any but those that desire it.

To desire some good Friends to inform me which of these Resolutions I break, or neglect, and wherein; and reform accordingly.

Not to talk much, nor of myself.

Not to boast of my former beauty, or strength, or favor with Ladies, &c.

Not to hearken to Flatteries, nor conceive I can be beloved by a young woman, et eos qui hereditatem captant, odisse ac vitare.

Not to be positive or opiniative.

Not to set up for observing all these Rules; for fear I should observe none.

From THE JOURNAL TO STELLA

The Killing of Duke Hamilton

London, *Nov.* 15, 1712.

BEFORE this comes to your hands you will have heard of the most terrible accident that hath almost ever happened. This morning at eight my man brought me word that Duke Hamilton had fought with Lord Mohun, and killed him, and was brought home wounded. I immediately sent him to the Duke's house, in St. James's Square; but the porter could hardly answer for tears, and a great rabble was about the house. In short, they fought at seven this morning. The dog Mohun was killed on the spot; and, while the Duke was over him, Mohun shortened his sword, stabbed him in at the shoulder to the heart. The Duke was helped toward the cakehouse by the ring in Hyde Park (where they fought), and died on the grass, before he could reach the house; and was brought home in his coach by eight, while the poor Duchess was asleep. Macartney and one Hamilton were the seconds, who fought likewise, and are both fled. I am told that a footman of Lord Mohun's stabbed Duke Hamilton, and some say Macartney did so too. Mohun gave the affront, and yet sent the challenge. I am infinitely concerned for the poor Duke, who was a frank, honest, good-natured man. I loved him very well, and I think he loved me better. He had the greatest mind in the world to have me go with him to France, but durst not tell it me; and those he did tell said

I could not be spared, which was true. They have removed the poor Duchess to a lodging in the neighbourhood, where I have been with her two hours, and am just come away. I never saw so melancholy a scene; for indeed all reasons for real grief belong to her; nor is it possible for anybody to be a greater loser in all regards. She has moved my very soul. The lodging was inconvenient, and they would have removed her to another; but I would not suffer it, because it had no room backward, and she must have been tortured with the noise of the Grub Street screamers mentioning her husband's murder in her ears.

From GULLIVER'S TRAVELS

Gulliver and the Lilliputians

WHAT became of my companions in the boat, as well as of those who escaped on the rock, or were left in the vessel, I cannot tell; but conclude they were all lost. For my own part, I swam as fortune directed me, and was pushed forward by wind and tide. I often let my legs drop, and could feel no bottom; but when I was almost gone, and able to struggle no longer, I found myself within my depth; and by this time the storm was much abated. The declivity was so small, that I walked near a mile before I got to the shore, which I conjectured was about eight o'clock in the evening. I then advanced forward near half a mile, but could not discover any sign of houses or inhabitants; at least I was in so weak a condition, that I did not observe them. I was extremely tired, and with that, and the heat of the weather, and about half a pint of brandy that I drank as I left the ship, I found myself much inclined to sleep. I lay down on the grass which was very short and soft, where I slept sounder than ever I remember to have done in my life, and, as I reckoned, about nine hours; for when I awaked, it was just day-light. I attempted to rise, but was not able to stir: for as I happened to lie on my back, I found my arms and legs were strongly fastened on each side to the ground; and my hair, which was long and thick, tied down in the same manner. I likewise felt several slender ligatures across my body, from my arm-pits to my thighs. I could only look upwards, the sun began to grow hot, and the light offended my eyes. I heard a confused noise about me, but in the posture I lay, could see nothing except the sky. In a little time I felt something alive moving on my left leg, which advanced gently forward over my breast, came almost up to my chin; when bending my eyes downwards as much as I could, I perceived it to be a human creature not six inches high, with a bow and arrow in his hands, and a quiver at his back.

In the mean time, I felt at least forty more of the same kind (as I conjectured) following the first. I was in the utmost astonishment, and roared so loud, that they all ran back in fright; and some of them, as I was afterwards told, were hurt with the falls they got by leaping from my sides upon the ground. However, they soon returned, and one of them, who ventured so far as to get a full sight of my face, lifting up his hands and eyes by way of admiration, cried out in a shrill, but distinct voice, *Hekinah degul:* the others repeated the same words several times, but then I knew not what they meant. I lay all this while, as the reader may believe, in great uneasiness: at length, struggling to get loose, I had the fortune to break the strings, and wrench out the pegs that fastened my left arm to the ground; for, by lifting it up to my face, I discovered the methods they had to bind me, and at the same time with a violent pull, which gave me excessive pain, I a little loosened the strings that tied down my hair on the left side, so that I was just able to turn my head about two inches. But the creatures ran off a second time, before I could seize them; whereupon there was a great shout in a very shrill accent, and after it ceased, I heard one of them cry aloud *Tolgo phonac;* when in an instant I felt above an hundred arrows discharged on my left hand, which pricked me like so many needles; and besides, they shot another flight into the air, as we do bombs in Europe, whereof many, I suppose, fell on my body, (though I felt them not) and some on my face, which I immediately covered with my left hand. When this shower of arrows was over, I fell agroaning with grief and pain, and then striving again to get loose, they discharged another volley larger than the first, and some of them attempted with spears to stick me in the sides; but, by good luck, I had on a buff jerkin, which they could not pierce. I thought it the most prudent method to lie still, and my design was to continue so till night, when, my left hand being already loose, I could easily free myself: and as for the inhabitants, I had reason to believe I might be a match for the greatest armies they could bring against me, if they were all of the same size with him that I saw. But fortune disposed otherwise of me. When the people observed I was quiet, they discharged no more arrows; but by the noise I heard, I knew their numbers increased; and about four yards from me, over against my right ear, I heard a knocking for above an hour, like that of people at work; when turning my head that way, as well as the pegs and strings would permit me, I saw a stage erected, about a foot and a half from the ground, capable of holding four of the inhabitants, with two or three ladders to mount it: from whence one of them, who seemed to be a person of quality, made me a long speech, whereof I understood not one syllable. But I should have mentioned, that before the principal person began his oration, he cried out three times, *Langro dehul san:* (these words and the former were afterwards repeated and explained to me). Whereupon immediately about fifty of the inhabitants came and cut the strings that fastened the left side of my head, which gave me the liberty of turning it to the right, and of observing the person and gesture of him that was to speak. He appeared to be of a middle age, and taller than any of the other three who attended him, whereof one was a page that held up his train, and seemed to be somewhat longer than my middle finger; the other two stood one on each side to support him. He acted every part of an orator, and I could observe many periods of threatenings, and others of promises, pity and kindness. I answered in a few words, but in the most submissive manner, lifting up my left hand, and both my eyes to the sun, as calling him for a witness; and being almost famished with hunger, having not eaten a morsel for some hours before I left the ship, I found the demands of nature so strong upon me, that I could not forbear showing my impatience (perhaps against the strict rules of decency) by putting my finger frequently on my mouth, to signify that I wanted food. The *Hurgo* (for so they call a great lord, as I afterwards learnt) understood me very well. He descended from the stage, and commanded that several ladders should be applied to my sides, on which above an hundred of the inhabitants mounted and walked towards my mouth, laden with baskets full of meat, which had been provided and sent thither by the King's orders, upon the first intelligence he received of me. I observed there was the flesh of several animals, but could not distinguish them by the taste. There were shoulders, legs, and loins, shaped like those of mutton, and very well dressed, but smaller than the wings of a lark. I eat them by two or three at a mouthful, and took three loaves at a time, about the bigness of musket bullets. They supplied me as fast as they could, showing a thousand marks of wonder and astonishment at my bulk and appetite. I then made another sign that I wanted a drink. They found by my eating, that a small quantity would not suffice me; and being a most ingenious people, they slung up with great dexterity one of their largest hogsheads, then rolled it towards my hand, and beat out the top; I drank it off at a draught, which I might well do, for it did not hold half a pint, and tasted like a small wine of Burgundy, but much more delicious. They brought me a second hogshead, which I drank in the same manner, and made signs for more, but they had none to give me. When I had performed these wonders, they shouted for joy, and danced upon my breast, repeating several times as they did at first, *Hekinah degul.* They made me a sign that I should throw down the two hogsheads, but first warning the people below to stand out of the way, crying aloud, *Borach mivola*, and when they saw the vessels in the air, there was an universal shout of *Hekinah degul.* I confess I was often tempted, while they were passing backwards and forwards on my body, to seize forty or fifty of the first that came in my reach, and dash them against the ground. But the remembrance of what I had felt, which probably might not be the worst they could do, and the promise of honour I made them, for so I interpreted my submissive behavior, soon drove out these imaginations. Besides, I now considered myself as bound by the laws of hospitality to a people who had treated me with so much expense and magnificence. However, in my thoughts, I could not sufficiently wonder at the intrepidity of these diminutive mortals, who durst venture to mount and walk upon my body, while one of my hands was at liberty, without trembling at the very sight of so prodigious a creature as I must appear to them. After some time, when they observed that I made no more demands for meat, there appeared before me a person of high rank from his Imperial Majesty. His Excellency, having mounted on the small of my right leg, advanced forwards up to my face, with about a dozen of his retinue. And producing his credentials under the Signet Royal, which he applied close to my eyes, spoke about ten minutes, without any signs of anger, but with a kind of determinate resolution; often pointing forwards, which, as I afterwards found, was towards the capital city, about half a mile distant, whither it was agreed by his Majesty in council that I must be conveyed. I answered in few words, but to no purpose, and made a sign with my hand that was loose, putting it to the other (but over his Excellency's head for fear of hurting him or his train) and then to my own head and body, to signify that I desired my liberty. It appeared that he understood me well enough, for he shook his head by way of disapprobation, and held his hand in a posture to show that I must be carried as a prisoner. However, he made other signs to let me understand that I should have meat and drink enough, and very good treatment. Whereupon I once more thought of attempting to break my bonds; but again, when I felt the smart of their arrows, upon my face and hands, which were all in blisters, and many of the darts still sticking in them, and observing likewise that the number of my enemies increased, I gave tokens to let them know that they might do with me what they pleased. Upon this, the *Hurgo* and his train withdrew, with much civility and cheerful countenances. Soon after I heard a general shout, with frequent repetitions of the words, *Peplom selan,* and I felt great numbers of people on my left side relaxing the cords to such a degree, that I was able to turn upon my right, and to ease myself. . . . But before this, they had daubed my face and both hands with a sort of ointment very pleasant to the smell, which in a few minutes removed all the smart of their arrows. These circumstances, added to the refreshment I had received by their victuals and drink, which were very nourishing, disposed me to sleep. I slept about eight hours, as I was afterwards assured; and it was no wonder, for the physicians, by the Emperor's order, had mingled a sleepy potion in the hogshead of wine.

It seems that upon the first moment I was discovered sleeping on the ground after my landing, the Emperor had early notice of it by an express; and determined in council that I should be tied in the manner I have related, (which was done in the night while I slept) that plenty of meat and drink should be sent to me, and a machine prepared to carry me to the capital city.

This resolution perhaps may appear very bold and dangerous, and I am confident would not be imitated by any prince in Europe on the like occasion; however, in my opinion, it was extremely prudent, as well as generous: for supposing these people had endeavoured to kill me with their spears and arrows while I was asleep, I should certainly have awaked with the first sense of smart, which might so far have roused my rage and strength, as to have enabled me to break the strings wherewith I was tied; after which, as they were not able to make resistance, so they could expect no mercy.

These people are most excellent mathematicians, and arrived to a great perfection in mechanics, by the countenance and encouragement of the Emperor, who is a renowned patron of learning. This prince hath several machines fixed on wheels, for the carriage of trees and other great weights. He often builds his largest men of war, whereof some are nine foot long, in the woods where the timber grows, and has them carried on these engines three or four hundred yards to the sea. Five hundred carpenters and engineers were immediately set at work to prepare the greatest engine they had. It was a frame of wood raised three inches from the ground, about seven foot long and four wide, moving upon twenty-two wheels. The shout I heard was upon the arrival of this engine, which it seems set out in four hours after my landing. It was brought parallel to me as I lay. But the principal difficulty was to raise and place me in this vehicle. Eighty poles, each of one foot high, were erected for this purpose, and very strong cords of the bigness of packthread were fastened by hooks to many bandages, which the work-men had girt round my neck, my hands, my body, and my legs. Nine hundred of the strongest men were employed to draw up these cords by many pulleys fastened on the poles, and thus, in less than three hours, I was raised and slung into the engine, and there tied fast. All this I was told, for, while the whole operation was performing, I lay in a profound sleep, by the force of that soporiferous medicine infused into my liquor. Fifteen hundred of the Emperor's largest horses, each about four inches and a half high, were employed to draw me towards the metropolis, which, as I said, was half a mile distant.

About four hours after we began our journey, I awaked by a very ridiculous accident; for the carriage being stopped a while to adjust something that was out of order, two or three of the young natives had the curiosity to see how I looked when I was asleep; they climbed up into the engine, and advancing very softly to my face, one of them, an officer in the guards, put the sharp of his half-spike a good way up into my left nostril, which tickled my nose like a straw, and made me sneeze violently: whereupon they stole off unperceived, and it was three weeks before I knew the cause of my awaking so suddenly. We made a long march the remaining part of that day, and rested at night with five hundred guards on each side of me, half with torches, and half with bows and arrows, ready to shoot me if I should offer to stir. The next morning at sunrise, we continued our march, and arrived within two hundred yards of the city gates about noon. The Emperor, and all his court, came to meet us; but his great officers would by no means suffer his Majesty to endanger his person by mounting on my body.

At the place where the carriage stopped, there stood an ancient temple, esteemed to be the largest in the whole kingdom; which having been polluted some years before by an unnatural murder, was, according to the zeal of those people, looked upon as profane, and therefore had been applied to common uses, and all the ornaments and furniture carried away. In this edifice it was determined I should lodge. The great gate fronting to the north was about four foot high, and almost two foot wide, through which I could easily creep. On each side of the gate was a small window not above six inches from the ground: into that on the left side, the King's smiths conveyed fourscore and eleven chains, like those that hang to a lady's watch in Europe, and almost as large, which were locked to my left leg with six and thirty padlocks. Over-against this temple, on t'other side of the great highway, at twenty foot distance, there was a turret at least five foot high. Here the Emperor ascended, with many principal lords of his court, to have an opportunity of viewing me, as I was told, for I could not see them. It was reckoned that above an hundred thousand inhabitants came out of the town upon the same errand; and, in spite of my guards, I believe there could not be fewer than ten thousand at several times, who mounted my body by the help of ladders. But a proclamation was soon issued to forbid it upon the pain of death. When the workmen found it was impossible for me to break loose, they cut all the strings that bound me; whereupon I rose up, with as melancholy a disposition as ever I had in my life. But the noise and astonishment of the people at seeing me rise and walk, are not to be expressed. The chains that held my left leg were about two yards long, and gave me not only the liberty of walking backwards and forwards in a semi-circle; but, being fixed within four inches of the gate, allowed me to creep in, and lie at my full length in the temple.

The Struldbrugs

ONE day in much good company I was asked by a person of quality, whether I had seen any of their *Struldbrugs,* or *Immortals.* I said I had not, and desired he would explain to me what he meant by such an appellation applied to a mortal creature. He told me, that sometimes, though very rarely, a child happened to be born in a family with a red circular spot in the forehead, directly over the left eyebrow, which was an infallible mark that it should never die. The spot, as he described it, was about the compass of a silver threepence, but in the course of time grew larger, and changed its colour; for at twelve years old it became green, so continued till five and twenty, then turned to a deep blue: at five and forty it grew coal black, and as large as an English shilling, but never admitted any further alteration. He said these births were so rare, that he did not believe there could be above eleven hundred *struldbrugs* of both sexes in the whole kingdom, of which he computed about fifty in the metropolis, and among the rest a young girl born about three years ago. That these productions were not peculiar to any family, but a mere effect of chance; and the children of the *struldbrugs* themselves, were equally mortal with the rest of the people.

After this preface, he gave me a particular account of the *struldbrugs* among them. He said they commonly acted like mortals, till about thirty years old, after which by degrees they grew melancholy and dejected, increasing in both till they came to fourscore. This he learned from their own confession: for otherwise there not being above two or three of that species born in an age, they were too few to form a general observation by. When they came to fourscore years, which is reckoned the extremity of living in this country, they had not only all the follies and infirmities of other old men, but many more which arose from the dreadful prospect of never dying. They were not only opinionative, peevish, covetous, morose, vain, talkative, but uncapable of friendship, and dead to all natural affection, which never descended below their grandchildren. Envy and impotent desires are their prevailing passions. But those objects against which their envy seems principally directed, are the vices of the younger sort, and the deaths of the old. By reflecting on the former, they find themselves cut off from all possibility of pleasure; and whenever they see a funeral, they lament and repine that others have gone to a harbour of rest, to which they themselves never can hope to arrive. They have no remembrance of anything but what they learned and observed in their youth and middle age, and even that is very imperfect. And for the truth or particulars of any fact, it is safer to depend on common traditions than upon their best recollections. The least miserable among them appear to be those who turn to dotage, and entirely lose their memories; these meet with more pity and assistance, because they want many bad qualities which abound in others.

If a *struldbrug* happen to marry one of his own kind, the marriage is dissolved of course by the courtesy of the kingdom, as soon as the younger of the two comes to be fourscore. For the law thinks it a reasonable indulgence, that those who are condemned without any fault of their own to a perpetual continuance in the world, should not have their misery doubled by the load of a wife.

As soon as they have completed the term of eighty years, they are looked on as dead in law; their heirs immediately succeed to their estates, only a small pittance is reserved for their support, and the poor ones are maintained at the public charge. After that period they are held incapable of any employment of trust or profit, they cannot purchase lands or take leases, neither are they allowed to be witnesses in any cause, either civil or criminal, not even for the decision of meers and bounds.

At ninety they lose their teeth and hair, they have at that age no distinction of taste, but eat and drink whatever they can get, without relish or appetite. The diseases they were subject to still continue without increasing or diminishing. In talking they forget the common appellation of things, and the names of persons, even of those who are their nearest friends and relations. For the same reason, they never can amuse themselves with reading, because their memory will not serve to carry them from the beginning of a sentence to the end; and by this defect they are deprived of the only entertainment whereof they might otherwise be capable.

The language of this country being always upon the flux, the *struldbrugs* of one age do not understand those of another, neither are they able after two hundred years to hold any conversation (farther than by a few general words) with their neighbours the mortals; and thus they lie under the disadvantage of living like foreigners in their own country.

This was the account given me of the *struldbrugs,* as near as I can remember. I afterwards saw five or six of different ages, the youngest not above two hundred years old, who were brought to me at several times by some of my friends; but although they were told that I was a great traveller, and had seen all the world, they had not the least curiosity to ask me a question; only desired I would give them *slumskudask,* or a token of remembrance, which is a modest way of begging, to avoid the law that strictly forbids it, because they are provided for by the public, although indeed with a very scanty allowance.

They are despised and hated by all sorts of people; when one of them is born, it is reckoned ominous, and their birth is recorded very particularly: so that you may know their age by consulting the registry, which however hath not been kept above a thousand years past, or at least hath been destroyed by time or public disturbances. But the usual way of computing how old they are, is by asking them what kings or great persons they can remember, and then consulting history, for infallibly the last prince in their mind did not begin his reign after they were fourscore years old.

They were the most mortifying sight I ever beheld, and the women more horrible than the men. Besides the usual deformities in extreme old age, they acquired an additional ghastliness in proportion to their number of years, which is not to be described; and among half a dozen, I soon distinguished which was the eldest, although there was not above a century or two between them.

SIR RICHARD STEELE (1672-1729)

The Tatler, No. 101, June 6, 1710: On Sorrow and Memory

—— Dies, ni fallor, adest, quem semper acerbum,
Semper honoratum, sic dii voluistis habebo.

THERE are those among mankind, who can enjoy no relish of their being, except the world is made acquainted with all that relates to them, and think everything lost that passes unobserved; but others find a solid delight in stealing by the crowd, and modeling their life after such a manner, as is as much above the approbation as the practice of the vulgar. Life being too short to give instances great enough of true friendship or good will, some sages have thought it pious to preserve a certain reverence for the *Manes* of their deceased friends; and have withdrawn

themselves from the rest of the world at certain seasons, to com-
memorate in their own thoughts such of their acquaintance who have
gone before them out of this life. And indeed, when we are advanced
in years, there is not a more pleasing entertainment, than to recollect in
a gloomy moment the many we have parted with, that have been dear
and agreeable to us, and to cast a melancholy thought or two after those,
with whom, perhaps, we have indulged ourselves in whole nights of mirth
and jollity. With such inclinations in my heart I went to my closet yesterday in the evening, and resolved to be sorrowful; upon which occasion
I could not but look with disdain upon myself, that though all the reasons
which I had to lament the loss of many of my friends are now as forcible
as at the moment of their departure, yet did not my heart swell with the
same sorrow which I felt at that time; but I could, without tears, reflect
upon many pleasing adventures I have had with some, who have long been
blended with common earth.

Though it is by the benefit of nature, that length of time thus blots
out the violence of afflictions; yet with tempers too much given to
pleasure, it is almost necessary to revive the old places of grief in our
memory; and ponder step by step on past life, to lead the mind into that
sobriety of thought which poises the heart, and makes it beat with due
time, without being quickened with desire, or retarded with despair,
from its proper and equal motion. When we wind up a clock that is
out of order, to make it go well for the future, we do not immediately
set the hand to the present instant, but we make it strike the round of all
its hours, before it can recover the regularity of its time. Such, thought
I, shall be my method this evening; and since it is that day of the year
which I dedicate to the memory of such in another life as I much delighted in when living, an hour or two shall be sacred to sorrow and their
memory, while I run over all the melancholy circumstances of this kind
which have occurred to me in my whole life. The first sense of sorrow
I ever knew was upon the death of my father at which time I was not
quite five years of age; but was rather amazed at what all the house
meant, than possessed with a real understanding why nobody was willing
to play with me. I remember I went into the room where his body lay,
and my mother sat weeping alone by it. I had my battledore in my hand,
and I fell a-beating the coffin, and calling papa; for, I know not how, I
had some slight idea that he was locked up there. My mother catched
me in her arms, and, transported beyond all patience of the silent grief
she was before in, she almost smothered me in her embraces; and told me,
in a flood of tears, "Papa could not hear me, and would play with me no
more, for they were going to put him under ground, whence he could

never come to us again." She was a very beautiful woman, of a noble spirit, and there was a dignity in her grief amidst all the wildness of her transport, which, methought, struck me with an instinct of sorrow, that, before I was sensible of what it was to grieve, seized my very soul, and has made pity the weakness of my heart ever since. The mind in infancy is, methinks, like the body in embryo, and receives impressions so forcible, that they are as hard to be removed by reason, as any mark, with which a child is born, is to be taken away by any future application. Hence it is, that good-nature in me is no merit; but having been so frequently overwhelmed with her tears before I knew the cause of any affliction, or could draw defenses from my own judgment. I imbibed commiseration, remorse, and an unmanly gentleness of mind, which has since ensnared me into ten thousand calamities; from whence I can reap no advantage, except it be, that, in such a humor as I am now in, I can the better indulge myself in the softnesses of humanity, and enjoy that sweet anxiety which arises from the memory of past afflictions.

We, that are very old, are better able to remember things which befel us in our distant youth, than the passages of later days. For this reason it is, that the companions of my strong and vigorous years present themselves more immediately to me in this office of sorrow. Untimely and unhappy deaths are what we are most apt to lament; so little are we able to make it indifferent when a thing happens, though we know it must happen. Thus we groan under life, and bewail those who are relieved from it. Every object that returns to our imagination raises different passions, according to the circumstances of their departure. Who can have lived in an army, and in a serious hour reflect upon the many gay and agreeable men that might long have flourished in the arts of peace, and not join with the imprecations of the fatherless and widow on the tyrant to whose ambition they fell sacrifices? But gallant men, who are cut off by the sword, move rather our veneration than our pity; and we gather relief enough from their own contempt of death, to make that no evil, which was approached with so much cheerfulness, and attended with so much honor. But when we turn our thoughts from the great parts of life on such occasions, and instead of lamenting those who stood ready to give death to those from whom they had the fortune to receive it; I say, when we let our thoughts wander from such noble objects, and consider the havoc which is made among the tender and the innocent, pity enters with an unmixed softness, and possesses all our souls at once.

Here (were there words to express such sentiments with proper tenderness) I should record the beauty, innocence and untimely death, of the first object my eyes ever beheld with love. The beauteous virgin!

how ignorantly did she charm, how carelessly excel! Oh Death! thou
hast right to the bold, to the ambitious, to the high, and to the haughty;
but why this cruelty to the humble, to the meek, to the undiscerning, to
the thoughtless? Nor age, nor business, nor distress, can erase the dear
image from my imagination. In the same week, I saw her dressed for a
ball, and in a shroud. How ill did the habit of death become the pretty
trifler? I still behold the smiling earth—— A large train of disasters
were coming on to my memory, when my servant knocked at my closet
door, and interrupted me with a letter, attended with a hamper of wine,
of the same sort with that which is to be put to sale, on Thursday next,
at Garraway's coffee-house. Upon the receipt of it, I sent for three of
my friends. We are so intimate, that we can be company in whatever
state of mind we meet, and can entertain each other without expecting
always to rejoice. The wine we found to be generous and warming,
but with such an heat as moved us rather to be cheerful than frolicsome.
It revived the spirits, without firing the blood. We commended it until
two of the clock this morning; and having to-day met a little before
dinner, we found, that though we drank two bottles a man, we had much
more reason to recollect than forget what had passed the night before.

The Spectator, No. 468, Wednesday, August 27, 1712: On the Death of Estcourt

*Erat homo ingeniosus, acutus, acer, et qui plurimum et salis haberet et fellis,
nec candoris minus.*—Plin., Epist.

My paper is in a kind a letter of news, but it regards rather what
passes in the world of conversation than that of business. I am very
sorry that I have at present a circumstance before me which is of very
great importance to all who have a relish for gaiety, wit, mirth, or
humour. I mean the death of Dick Estcourt. I have been obliged
to him for so many hours of jollity, that it is but a small recompense,
though all I can give him, to pass a moment or two in sadness for the
loss of so agreeable a man. Poor Estcourt! the last time I saw him, we
were plotting to show the town his great capacity for acting in its full
light, by introducing him as dictating to a set of young players, in what
manner to speak this sentence, and utter t'other passion—he had so
exquisite a discerning of what was defective in any object before him,
that in an instant he could show you the ridiculous side of what would
pass for beautiful and just, even to men of no ill judgment, before he had
pointed at the failure. He was no less skilful in the knowledge of beauty;

and, I dare say, there is no one who knew him well but can repeat more well-turned compliments, as well as smart repartees, of Mr. Estcourt's than of any other man in England. This was easily to be observed in his inimitable faculty of telling a story, in which he would throw in natural and unexpected incidents, to make his court to one part, and rally the other part of the company. Then he would vary the usage he gave them, according as he saw them bear kind or sharp language. He had the knack to raise up a pensive temper, and mortify an impertinently gay one, with the most agreeable skill imaginable. There are a thousand things which crowd into my memory, which make me too much concerned to tell on about him. Hamlet, holding up the skull which the gravedigger threw to him with an account that it was the head of the king's jester, falls into very pleasing reflections, and cries out to his companion:—

"Alas, poor Yorick!—I knew him, Horatio: a fellow of infinite jest, of most excellent fancy: he hath borne me on his back a thousand times; and now, how abhorred in my imagination it is! my gorge rises at it. Here hung those lips, that I have kissed I know not how oft. Where be your gibes now? your gambols? your songs? your flashes of merriment, that were wont to set the table on a roar? Not one now, to mock your own grinning? quite chap-fallen? Now get you to my lady's chamber, and tell her, let her paint an inch thick, to this favour she must come; make her laugh at that."

It is an insolence natural to the wealthy to affix, as much as in them lies, the character of a man to his circumstances. Thus it is ordinary with them to praise faintly the good qualities of those below them, and say it is very extraordinary in such a man as he is, or the like, when they are forced to acknowledge the value of him whose lowness upbraids their exaltation. It is to this humour only that it is to be ascribed that a quick wit in conversation, a nice judgment upon any emergency that could arise, and a most blameless inoffensive behaviour, could not raise this man above being received only upon the foot of contributing to mirth and diversion. But he was as easy under that condition as a man of so excellent talents was capable; and since they would have it that to divert was his business, he did it with all the seeming alacrity imaginable, though it stung him to the heart that it was his business. Men of sense, who could taste his excellences, were well satisfied to let him lead the way in conversation, and play after his own manner; but fools, who provoked him to mimicry, found he had the indignation to let it be at their expense who called for it, and he would show the form of conceited heavy fellows as jests to the company at their own request, in revenge for interrupting him from being a companion to put on the character of a jester.

What was peculiarly excellent in this memorable companion was, that in the accounts he gave of persons and sentiments, he did not only hit the figure of their faces and manner of their gestures, but he would in his narration fall into their very way of thinking, and this when he recounted passages wherein men of the best wit were concerned, as well as such wherein were represented men of the lowest rank of understanding. It is certainly as great an instance of self-love to a weakness, to be impatient of being mimicked, as any can be imagined. There were none but the vain, the formal, the proud, or those who were incapable of amending their faults, that dreaded him; to others he was in the highest degree pleasing; and I do not know any satisfaction of any indifferent kind I ever tasted so much, as having got over an impatience of seeing myself in the air he could put me when I have displeased him. It is indeed to his exquisite talent this way, more than any philosophy I could read on the subject, that my person is very little of my care; and it is indifferent to me what is said of my shape, my air, my manner, my speech, or my address. It is to poor Estcourt I chiefly owe that I am arrived at the happiness of thinking nothing a diminution to me, but what argues a depravity of my will.

It has as much surprised me as anything in Nature to have it frequently said that he was not a good player: but that must be owing to a partiality for former actors in the parts in which he succeeded them, and judging by comparison of what was liked before, rather than by the nature of the thing. When a man of his wit and smartness could put on an utter absence of common sense in his face, as he did in the character of Bullfinch in the "Northern Lass," and an air of insipid cunning and vivacity in the character of Pounce in the "Tender Husband," it is folly to dispute his capacity and success, as he was an actor.

Poor Estcourt! let the vain and proud be at rest; they will no more disturb their admiration of their dear selves, and thou art no longer to drudge in raising the mirth of stupids, who know nothing of thy merit, for thy maintenance.

It is natural for the generality of mankind to run into reflections upon our mortality when disturbers of the world are laid at rest, but to take no notice when they who can please and divert are pulled from us: but for my part, I cannot but think the loss of such talents as the man of whom I am speaking was master of, a more melancholy instance of mortality than the dissolution of persons of never so high characters in the world, whose pretensions were that they were noisy and mischievous.

But I must grow more succinct, and, as a Spectator, give an account of this extraordinary man who, in his way, never had an equal in any age before him, or in that wherein he lived. I speak of him as a companion, and a man qualified for conversation. His fortune exposed him to an obsequiousness towards the worst sort of company, but his excellent qualities rendered him capable of making the best figure in the most refined. I have been present with him among men of the most delicate taste a whole night, and have known him (for he saw it was desired) keep the discourse to himself the most part of it, and maintain his good humour with a countenance, in a language so delightful, without offence to any person or thing upon earth, still preserving the distance his circumstances obliged him to; I say, I have seen him do all this in such a charming manner that I am sure none of those I hint at will read this without giving him some sorrow for their abundant mirth, and one gush of tears for so many bursts of laughter. I wish it were any honour to the pleasant creature's memory that my eyes are too much suffused to let me go on—— T.

JOSEPH ADDISON (1672-1719)

The Spectator, No. 13, March 15, 1711: Signior Nicolini and his Lions

Dic mihi, si fueras tu leo, qualis eris?—MART.

THERE is nothing that of late years has afforded matter of greater amusement to the town than Signior Nicolini's combat with a lion in the Haymarket, which has been very often exhibited to the general satisfaction of most of the nobility and gentry in the kingdom of Great Britain. Upon the first rumor of this intended combat, it was confidently affirmed, and is still believed by many in both galleries, that there would be a tame lion sent from the Tower every opera night, in order to be killed by Hydaspes; this report, though altogether groundless, so universally prevailed in the upper regions of the playhouse, that some of the most refined politicians in those parts of the audience gave it out in whisper, that the lion was a cousin-german of the tiger who made his appearance in King William's days, and that the stage would be supplied with lions at the public expense, during the whole session. Many likewise were the conjectures of the treatment which this lion was to meet with from the hands of Signior Nicolini; some supposed that he was to subdue him in recitativo, as Orpheus used to serve the wild beasts in his time, and afterwards to knock him on the head; some fancied that the lion would not pretend to lay his paws upon the hero, by reason of the received opinion, that a lion will not hurt a virgin: several, who pretended to have seen the opera in Italy, had informed their friends, that the lion was to act a part in High-Dutch, and roar twice or thrice to a thorough-base, before he fell at the feet of Hydaspes. To clear up a matter that was so variously reported, I have made it my business to examine whether this pretended lion is really the savage he appears to be, or only a counterfeit.

But before I communicate my discoveries, I must acquaint the reader, that upon my walking behind the scenes last winter, as I was thinking on something else, I accidentally justled against a monstrous animal that extremely startled me, and upon my nearer survey of it, appeared to be a lion rampant. The lion, seeing me very much surprised, told me, in a gentle voice, that I might come by him if I pleased: "for," (says he,) "I do not intend to hurt anybody." I thanked him very kindly, and passed by him. And in a little time after saw him leap upon the stage, and act his part with great applause. It has been observed by several, that the lion has changed his manner of acting twice or thrice since his first appearance; which will not seem strange, when I acquaint my reader that the lion has been changed upon the audience three several times. The first lion was a candle-snuffer, who being a fellow of a testy, choleric temper, overdid his part, and would not suffer himself to be killed so easily as he ought to have done; besides, it was observed of him, that he grew more surly every time he came out of the lion, and having dropt some words in ordinary conversation, as if he had not fought his best, and that he suffered himself to be thrown upon his back in the scuffle, and that he would wrestle with Mr. Nicolin for what he pleased, out of his lion's skin, it was thought proper to discard him: and it is verily believed, to this day, that had he been brought upon the stage another time, he could certainly have done mischief. Besides, it was objected against the first lion, that he reared himself so high upon his hinder paws, and walked in so erect a posture, that he looked more like an old man than a lion.

The second lion was a tailor by trade, who belonged to the play-house, and had the character of a mild and peaceable man in his profession. If the former was too furious, this was too sheepish, for his part; insomuch that after a short modest walk upon the stage, he would fall at the first touch of Hydaspes, without grappling with him, and giving him an opporunity of showing his variety of Italian trips: it is said indeed, that he once gave him a rip in his flesh-colour doublet; but this was only to make work for himself, in his private character of a tailor. I must not omit that it was this second lion who treated me with so much humanity behind the scenes.

The acting lion at present is, as I am informed, a country gentleman, who does it for his diversion, but desires his name may be concealed. He says very handsomely in his own excuse, that he does not act for gain, that he indulges an innocent pleasure in it; and that it is better to pass away an evening in this manner, than in gaming and drinking: but at the same time says, with a very agreeable raillery upon himself, that if his name should be known, the ill-natured world might call him "The ass in the lion's skin." This gentleman's temper is made out of such a happy mixture of the mild and the choleric, that he outdoes both his predecessors, and has drawn together greater audiences than have been known in the memory of man.

I must not conclude my narrative, without taking notice of a groundless report that has been raised, to a gentleman's disadvantage of whom I must declare myself an admirer; namely, that Signior Nicolini and the lion have been seen sitting peaceably by one another, and smoking a pipe together, behind the scenes; by which their common enemies would insinuate, that it is but a sham combat which they represent upon the stage: but, upon inquiry I find, that if any such correspondence has passed between them, it was not till the combat was over, when the lion was to be looked upon as dead, according to the received rules of the drama. Besides, this is what is practised every day in Westminster hall, where nothing is more usual than to see a couple of lawyers, who have been tearing each other to pieces in the court, embracing one another as soon as they are out of it.

I would not be thought, in any part of this relation, to reflect upon Signior Nicolini, who in acting this part only complies with the wretched taste of his audience; he knows very well, that the lion has many more admirers than himself; as they say of the famous equestrian statue on the Pont-Neuf at Paris, that more people go to see the horse, than the king who sits upon it. On the contrary, it gives me a just indignation to see a person whose action gives new majesty to kings, resolution to heroes, and softness to lovers, thus sinking from the greatness of his behavior, and degraded into the character of the London Prentice. I have often wished that our tragedians would copy after this great master in action. Could they make the same use of their arms and legs, and inform their faces with as significant looks and passions, how glorious would an English tragedy appear with that action, which is capable of giving a dignity to the forced thoughts, cold conceits, and unnatural expressions of an Italian opera. In the mean time, I have related this combat of the lion, to show what are at present the reigning entertainments of the politer part of Great Britain.

Audiences have often been reproached by writers for the coarseness of their tastes; but our present grievance does not seem to be the want of a good taste, but of common sense.

The Spectator, No. 159, September 1, 1711: The Vision of Mirzah

—Omnem, quæ nunc obducta tuenti
Mortales hebetat visus tibi, et humida circum
Caligat, nubem eripiam—
—VIRG. Æn. ii. 604.

WHEN I was at Grand Cairo, I picked up several Oriental manuscripts, which I have still by me. Among others I met with one entitled The Visions of Mirza, which I have read over with great pleasure. I intend to give it to the public when I have no other entertainment for them; and shall begin with the first vision, which I have translated word for word as follows:—

"On the fifth day of the moon, which according to the custom of my forefathers I always keep holy, after having washed myself, and offered up my morning devotions, I ascended the high hills of Bagdad, in order to pass the rest of the day in meditation and prayer. As I was here airing myself on the tops of the mountains, I fell into a profound contemplation on the vanity of human life; and passing from one thought to another, 'Surely,' said I, 'man is but a shadow, and life a dream.' Whilst I was thus musing, I cast my eyes towards the summit of a rock that was not far from me, where I discovered one in the habit of a shepherd, with a musical instrument in his hand. As I looked upon him he applied it to his lips, and began to play upon it. The sound of it was exceedingly sweet, and wrought into a variety of tunes that were inexpressibly melodious, and altogether different from anything I had ever heard. They put me in mind of those heavenly airs that are played to the departed souls of good men upon their first arrival in Paradise, to wear out the impressions of their last agonies, and qualify them for the pleasures of that happy place. My heart melted away in secret raptures.

"I had been often told that the rock before me was the haunt of a Genius; and that several had been entertained with music who had passed by it, but never heard that the musician had before made himself visible. When he had raised my thoughts by those transporting airs which he played to taste the pleasures of his conversation, as I looked upon him like one astonished, he beckoned to me, and by the waving of his hand directed me to approach the place where he sat. I drew near with that reverence which is due to a superior nature; and as my heart was entirely subdued by the captivating strains I had heard, I fell down at his feet and wept. The Genius smiled upon me with a look of compassion and affability that familiarized him to my imagination, and at once dispelled all the fears and apprehensions with which I approached him. He lifted me from the ground, and taking me by the hand, ' Mirza,' said he, ' I have heard thee in thy soliloquies; follow me.'

" He then led me to the highest pinnacle of the rock, and placing me on the top of it, ' Cast thy eyes eastward,' said he, ' and tell me what thou seest.' ' I see,' said I, ' a huge valley, and a prodigious tide of water rolling through it.' ' The valley that thou seest,' said he, ' is the Vale of Misery, and the tide of water that thou seest is part of the great Tide of Eternity.' ' What is the reason,' said I, ' that the tide I see rises out of a thick mist at one end, and again loses itself in a thick mist at the other? ' 'What thou seest,' said he, ' is that portion of eternity which is called time, measured out by the sun, and reaching from the beginning of the world to its consummation. Examine now,' said he, ' this sea that is bounded with darkness at both ends, and tell me what thou discoverest in it.' 'I see a bridge,' said I, ' standing in the midst of the tide.' ' The bridge thou seest,' said he, ' is Human Life: consider it attentively.' Upon a more leisurely survey of it, I found that it consisted of three score and ten entire arches, with several broken arches, which added to those that were entire, made up the number about a hundred. As I was counting the arches, the Genius told me that this bridge consisted at first of a thousand arches; but that a great flood swept away the rest, and left the bridge in the ruinous condition I now beheld it. ' But tell me farther,' said he, ' what thou discoverest on it.' ' I see multitudes of people passing over it,' said I, ' and a black cloud hanging on each end of it.' As I looked more attentively, I saw several of the passengers dropping through the bridge into the great tide that flowed underneath it; and upon farther examination, perceived there were innumerable trap-doors that lay concealed in the bridge, which the passengers no sooner trod upon, but they fell through them into the tide, and immediately disappeared. These hidden pitfalls were set very thick at the entrance of the bridge, so that throngs of people no sooner broke through the cloud, but many of them fell into them. They grew thinner towards the middle, but multiplied and lay closer together towards the end of the arches that were entire.

" There were indeed some persons, but their number was very small, that continued a kind of hobbling march on the broken arches, but fell through one after another, being quite tired and spent with so long a walk.

"I passed some time in the contemplation of this wonderful structure, and the great variety of objects which it presented. My heart was filled with a deep melancholy to see several dropping unexpectedly in the midst of mirth and jollity, and catching at everything that stood by them to save themselves. Some were looking up towards the heavens in a thoughtful posture, and in the midst of a speculation stumbled and fell out of sight. Multitudes were very busy in the pursuit of bubbles that glittered in their eyes and danced before them; but often when they thought themselves within the reach of them, their footing failed and down they sunk. In this confusion of objects, I observed some with scimitars in their hands, and others with urinals, who ran to and fro upon the bridge, thrusting several persons on trap-doors which did not seem to lie in their way, and which they might have escaped had they not been thus forced upon them.

"The Genius seeing me indulge myself on this melancholy prospect, told me I had dwelt long enough upon it. 'Take thine eyes off the bridge,' said he, 'and tell me if thou yet seest anything thou dost not comprehend.' Upon looking up, 'What mean,' said I, 'those great flights of birds that are perpetually hovering about the bridge, and settling upon it from time to time? I see vultures, harpies, ravens, cormorants, and among many other feathered creatures several little winged boys, that perch in great numbers upon the middle arches.' 'These,' said the Genius, 'are Envy, Avarice, Superstition, Despair, Love, with the like cares and passions that infest human life.'

"I here fetched a deep sigh. 'Alas,' said I, 'Man was made in vain! how is he given away to misery and mortality! tortured in life, and swallowed up in death!' The Genius being moved with compassion towards me, bid me quit so uncomfortable a prospect. 'Look no more,' said he, 'on man in the first stage of his existence, in his setting out for eternity; but cast thine eye on that thick mist into which the tide bears the several generations of mortals that fall into it.' I directed my sight as I was ordered, and (whether or no the good Genius strengthened it with any supernatural force, or dissipated part of the mist that was before too thick for the eye to penetrate) I saw the valley opening at the farther end, and spreading forth into an immense ocean, that had a huge rock of adamant running through the midst of it, and dividing it into two equal parts. The clouds still rested on one half of it, insomuch that I could discover nothing in it; but the other appeared to me a vast ocean planted with innumerable islands, that were covered with fruits and flowers, and interwoven with a thousand little shining seas that ran among them. I could see persons dressed in glorious habits with garlands upon their heads, passing among the trees, lying down by the sides of fountains, or resting on beds of flowers; and could hear a confused harmony of singing birds, falling waters, human voices, and musical instruments. Gladness grew in me upon the discovery of so delightful a scene. I wished for the wings of an eagle, that I might fly away to those happy seats; but the Genius told me there was no passage to them, except through the gates of death that I saw opening every moment upon the bridge. 'The islands,' said he, 'that lie so fresh and green before thee, and with which the whole face of the ocean appears spotted as far as thou canst see, are more in number than the sands on the seashore: there are myriads of islands behind those which thou here discoverest, reaching farther than thine eye, or even thine imagination can extend itself. These are the mansions of good men after death, who, according to the degree and kinds of virtue in which they excelled, are distributed among these several islands, which abound with pleasures of different kinds and degrees, suitable to the relishes and perfections of those who are settled in them: every island is a paradise accommodated to its respective inhabitants. Are not these, O Mirza, habitations worth contending for? Does life appear miserable that gives thee opportunities of earning such a reward? Is death to be feared that will convey thee to so happy an existence? Think not man was made in vain, who has such an eternity reserved for him.' I gazed with inexpressible pleasure on these happy islands. At length, said I, 'Show me now, I beseech thee, the secrets that lie hid under those dark clouds which cover the ocean on the other side of the rock of adamant.' The Genius making me no answer, I turned me about to address myself to him a second time, but I found that he had left me; I then turned again to the vision which I had been so long contemplating; but instead of the rolling tide, the arched bridge, and the happy islands, I saw nothing but the long hollow valley of Bagdad, with oxen, sheep, and camels grazing upon the sides of it."

C.

ALEXANDER POPE (1688-1744)

Ode on Solitude

HAPPY the man, whose wish and care
A few paternal acres bound,
Content to breathe his native air
    In his own ground:

Whose herds with milk, whose fields with
    bread,
Whose flocks supply him with attire;
Whose trees in summer yield him shade,
    In winter fire:

Blest, who can unconcern'dly find
Hours, days, and years slide soft away
In health of body, peace of mind,
    Quiet by day:

Sound sleep by night; study and ease
Together mixt, sweet recreation,
And innocence, which most does please
    With meditation.

Thus let me live, unseen, unknown;
Thus unlamented let me die;
Steal from the world, and not a stone
    Tell where I lie.

From THE RAPE OF THE LOCK

At the suggestion of Mr. John Caryll, a gentleman who was secretary to Queen Mary, wife of James II, Pope wrote the "heroi-comical poem," *The Rape of the Lock,* in order to put an end, by this sparkling satire, to a quarrel that had arisen between two noble families, on the occasion of Lord Petre's having cut off a lock of Miss Arabella Fermor's hair. The machinery of sylphs is based on the Rosicrucian ideas of spirits living in the elements.

FOR lo! the board with cups and spoons
    is crowned,
The berries crackle, and the mill turns
    round;
On shining altars of Japan they raise
The silver lamp; the fiery spirits blaze;
From silver spouts the grateful liquors
    glide,
While China's earth receives the smoking
    tide:

At once they gratify their scent and taste,
And frequent cups prolong the rich repast,
Straight hover round the fair her airy
    band;
Some, as she sipped, the fuming liquor
    fanned,
Some o'er her lap their careful plumes
    displayed,
Trembling, and conscious of the rich
    brocade.
Coffee (which makes the politician wise,
And see through all things with his halfshut eyes)
Sent up in vapours to the baron's brain
New stratagems the radiant lock to gain.
Ah, cease, rash youth! desist ere 'tis too
    late!
Fear the just gods, and think of Scylla's
    fate!
Changed to a bird, and sent to flit in air,
She dearly pays for Nisus' injured hair!
    But when to mischief mortals bend
    their will,
How soon they find fit instruments of ill!
Just then Clarissa drew with tempting
    grace
A two-edged weapon from her shining
    case:
So ladies in romance assist their knight,
Present the spear, and arm him for the
    fight.
He takes the gift with reverence, and extends
The little engine on his fingers' ends;
This just behind Belinda's neck he spread,
As o'er the fragant steam she bends her
    head.
Swift to the lock a thousand sprites repair,
A thousand wings, by turns, blow back
    the hair;
And thrice they twitched the diamond in
    her ear;
Thrice she looked back, and thrice the foe
    drew near.
Just in that instant, anxious Ariel sought
The close recesses of the virgin's thought;
As on the nosegay in her breast reclined,

He watched th' ideas rising in her mind,
Sudden he viewed, in spite of all her art,
An earthly lover lurking at her heart.
Amazed, confused, he found his power
 expired,
Resigned to fate, and with a sigh retired.
 The peer now spreads the glittering
  forfex wide,
T' inclose the lock; now joins it, to di-
 vide.
E'en then, before the fatal engine closed,
A wretched sylph too fondly interposed;
Fate urged the shears, and cut the sylph
 in twain,
(But airy substance soon unites again).

The meeting points the sacred hair dis-
 sever
From the fair head, forever, and forever!
 Then flashed the living lightning from
  her eyes,
And screams of horror rend th' affrighted
 skies.
Not louder shrieks to pitying Heaven are
 cast,
When husbands, or when lap-dogs
 breathe their last;
Or when rich China vessels fallen from
 high,
In glittering dust and painted fragments
 lie!

HENRY FIELDING (1707-1754)

From TOM JONES

Partridge Sees Garrick's "Hamlet"

The party attending Garrick's performance of *Hamlet,* in the following selection, consists of Mrs. Miller, her younger daughter, Tom Jones, and Partridge. Partridge is Mr. Jones's attendant, faithful, observant, and not without shrewdness, but somewhat simple, and innocent of common sense. In his earlier days in the country, he had been a harmless failure as a schoolmaster and a husband; he had been a clerk also, and had had a sexton under him, as he informs us here.

IN the first row then of the first gallery did Mr. Jones, Mrs. Miller, her youngest daughter, and Partridge, take their places. Partridge immediately declared that it was the finest place he had ever been in. When the first music was played, he said, "It was a wonder how so many fiddlers could play at one time, without putting one another out." While the fellow was lighting the upper candles, he cried out to Mrs. Miller, "Look, look, madam, the very picture of the man in the end of the common-prayer book before the gunpowder-treason service." Nor could he help observing, with a sigh, when all the candles were lighted, "That here were candles enough burnt in one night, to keep an honest poor family for a whole twelvemonth."

As soon as the play, which was Hamlet, Prince of Denmark, began, Partridge was all attention, nor did he break silence till the entrance of the ghost; upon which he asked Jones, "What man that was in the strange dress; something," said he, "like what I have seen in a picture? Sure it is not armour, is it?" Jones answered, "That is the ghost."

To which Partridge replied with a smile, "Persuade me to that, sir, if you can. Though I can't say I ever actually saw a ghost in my life, yet I am certain I should know one, if I saw him, better than that comes to. No, no, sir, ghosts don't appear in such dresses as that, neither." In this mistake, which caused much laughter in the neighbourhood of Partridge, he was suffered to continue, till the scene between the ghost and Hamlet, when Partridge gave that credit to Mr. Garrick, which he had denied to Jones, and fell into so violent a trembling, that his knees knocked against each other. Jones asked him what was the matter, and whether he was afraid of the warrior upon the stage? "O la! sir," said he, "I perceive now it is what you told me. I am not afraid of anything; for I know it is but a play. And if it was really a ghost, it could do one no harm at such a distance, and in so much company; and yet if I was frightened, I am not the only person." "Why, who," cries Jones, "dost thou take to be such a coward here besides thyself?" "Na, you may call me coward if you will; but if that little man there upon the stage is not frightened, I never saw any man frightened in my life. Ay, ay: go along with you: Ay, to be sure! Who's fool then? Will you? Lud have mercy upon such fool-hardiness!—Whatever happens, it is good enough for you.——Follow you? I'd follow the devil as soon. Nay, perhaps it is the devil—— for they say he can put on what likeness he pleases.—Oh! here he is again.——No farther! No, you have gone far enough already; farther than I'd have gone for all the king's dominions." Jones offered to speak, but Partridge cried, "Hush, hush! dear sir, don't you hear him?" And during the whole speech of the ghost, he sat with his eyes fixed partly on the ghost and partly on Hamlet, and with his mouth open; the same passions which succeeded each other in Hamlet, succeeding likewise in him.

When the scene was over, Jones said, "Why, Partridge, you exceed my expectations. You enjoy the play more than I conceived possible." "Nay, sir," answered Partridge, "if you are not afraid of the devil, I can't help it; but to be sure, it is natural to be surprised at such things, though I know there is nothing in them: not that it was the ghost that surprised me, neither; for I should have known that to have been only a man in a strange dress; but when I saw the little man so frightened himself, it was that which took hold of me." "And dost thou imagine, then, Partridge," cries Jones, "that he was really frightened?" "Nay, sir," said Partridge, "did not you yourself observe afterwards, when he found it was his own father's spirit, and how he was murdered in the garden, how his fear forsook him by degrees, and he was struck dumb with sorrow, as it were, just as I should have been, had it been my own case?—But hush! O la! what noise is that? There he is again.——Well to be certain, though I know there is nothing at all in it, I am glad I am not down yonder, where those men are." Then turning his eyes again upon Hamlet, "Ay, you may draw your sword; what signifies a sword against the power of the devil?"

During the second act, Partridge made very few remarks. He greatly admired the fineness of the dresses; nor could he help observing upon the king's countenance. "Well," said he, "how people may be deceived by faces! *Nulla fides fronti* is, I find, a true saying. Who would think, by looking in the king's face, that he had ever committed a murder?" He then inquired after the ghost; but Jones, who intended he should be surprised, gave him no other satisfaction, than, "that he might possibly see him again soon, and in a flash of fire."

Partridge sat in a fearful expectation of this; and now, when the ghost made his next appearance, Partridge cried out, "There, sir, now; what say you now? is he frightened now or no? As much frightened as you think me, and, to be sure, nobody can help some fears. I would not be in so bad a condition as what's his name, squire Hamlet, is there, for all the world. Bless me! what's become of the spirit? As I am a living soul, I thought I saw him sink into the earth." "Indeed, you saw right," answered Jones. "Well, well," cries Partridge, "I know it is only a play: and besides, if there was anything in all this, Madam Miller would not laugh so; for as to you, sir, you would not be afraid, I believe, if the devil was here in person.—There, there—Ay, no wonder you are in such a passion, shake the vile wicked wretch to pieces. If she was my own mother, I would serve her so. To be sure, all duty to a mother is forfeited by such wicked doings.——Ay, go about your business, I hate the sight of you."

Our critic was now pretty silent till the play, which Hamlet introduces before the king. This he did not at first understand, till Jones explained it to him; but he no sooner entered into the spirit of it, than he began to bless himself that he had never committed murder. Then turning to Mrs. Miller, he asked her, "If she did not imagine the king looked as if he was touched; though he is," said he, "a good actor, and doth all he can to hide it. Well, I would not have so much to answer for, as that wicked man there hath, to sit upon a much higher chair than he sits upon. No wonder he run away; for your sake I'll never trust an innocent face again."

The grave-digging scene next engaged the attention of Partridge, who expressed much surprise at the number of skulls thrown upon the stage. To which Jones answered, " That it was one of the most famous burial-places about town." " No wonder then," cries Partridge, " that the place is haunted. But I never saw in my life a worse grave-digger. I had a sexton, when I was clerk, that should have dug three graves while he is digging one. The fellow handles a spade as if it was the first time he had ever had one in his hand. Ay, ay, you may sing. You had rather sing than work, I believe."—Upon Hamlet's taking up the skull, he cried out, " Well! it is strange to see how fearless some men are: I never could bring myself to touch anything belonging to a dead man, on any account.—He seemed frightened enough too at the ghost, I thought. *Nemo omnibus horis sapit.*"

Little more worth remembering occurred during the play, at the end of which Jones asked him, " Which of the players he had liked best? " To this he answered, with some appearance of indignation at the question, " The king, without doubt." " Indeed, Mr. Partridge," says Mrs. Miller, " you are not of the same opinion with the town; for they are all agreed, that Hamlet is acted by the best player who ever was on the stage." " He is the best player! " cries Partridge, with a contemptuous sneer, " why, I could act as well as he myself. I am sure, if I had seen a ghost, I should have looked in the very same manner, and done just as he did. And then, to be sure, in that scene, as you called it, between him and his mother, where you told me he acted so fine, why, Lord help me, any man, that is, any good man, that had such a mother, would have done exactly the same. I know you are only joking with me; but indeed, madam, though I was never at a play in London, yet I have seen acting before in the country; and the king for my money; he speaks all his words distinctly, half as loud again as the other.—Anybody may see he is an actor."

Thus ended the adventure at the playhouse; where Partridge had afforded great mirth, not only to Jones and Mrs. Miller, but to all who sat within hearing, who were more attentive to what he said, than to anything that passed on the stage.

He durst not go to bed all that night, for fear of the ghost; and for many nights after sweated two or three hours before he went to sleep, with the same apprehensions, and waked several times in great horrors, crying out, " Lord have mercy upon us! there it is."

SAMUEL JOHNSON (1709-1784)

The Vanity of Human Wishes

LET observation with extensive view,
Survey mankind, from China to Peru;
Remark each anxious toil, each eager
  strife,
And watch the busy scenes of crowded
  life;
Then say how hope and fear, desire and
  hate,
O'erspread with snares the clouded maze
  of fate,
Where wav'ring man, betray'd by
  vent'rous pride,
To tread the dreary paths without a
  guide;
As treach'rous phantoms in the mist de-
  lude,
Shuns fancied ills, or chases airy good.
How rarely reason guides the stubborn
  choice,
Rules the bold hand, or prompts the sup-
  pliant voice;
How nations sink, by darling schemes
  oppress'd,
When vengeance listens to the fool's re-
  quest.
Fate wings with ev'ry wish th' afflictive
  dart,
Each gift of nature, and each grace of
  art;
With fatal heat impetuous courage
  glows,
With fatal sweetness elocution flows;
Impeachment stops the speaker's pow'rful
  breath,
And restless fire precipitates on death.
  But scarce observ'd, the knowing and
  the bold
Fall in the gen'ral massacre of gold;
Wide-wasting pest; that rages unconfin'd,
And crowds with crimes the records of
  mankind;
For gold his sword the hireling ruffian
  draws,
For gold the hireling judge distorts the
  laws;

Wealth heap'd on wealth, nor truth nor
  safety buys,
The dangers gather as the treasures rise.
  Let hist'ry tell where rival kings com-
  mand,
And dubious title shakes the madded
  land,
When statutes glean the refuse of the
  sword,
How much more safe the vassal than the
  lord,
Low skulks the hind beneath the rage of
  pow'r,
And leaves the wealthy traitor in the
  Tow'r,
Untouch'd his cottage, and his slumbers
  sound,
Tho' confiscation's vultures hover round.
  The needy traveller, serene and gay,
Walks the wild heath, and sings his toil
  away.
Does envy seize thee? crush th' upbraid-
  ing joy,
Increase his riches, and his peace destroy;
New fears in dire vicissitude invade,
The rustling brake alarms, and quiv'ring
  shade;
Nor light nor darkness bring his pain
  relief,
One shews the plunder, and one hides the
  thief.
  Yet still one gen'ral cry the skies
  assails,
And gain and grandeur load the tainted
  gales;
Few know the toiling statesman's fear or
  care,
Th' insidious rival and the gaping heir.
  Once more, Democritus, arise on earth,
With cheerful wisdom and instructive
  mirth,
See motley life in modern trappings
  dress'd,
And feed with varied fools th' eternal
  jest:
Thou who couldst laugh where want
  enchain'd caprice,
Toil crush'd conceit, and man was of a
  piece;

Where wealth unlov'd without a mourner
dy'd;
And scarce a sycophant was fed by pride;
Where ne'er was known the form of
mock debate,
Or seen a new-made mayor's unwieldy
state;
Where change of fav'rites made no
change of laws,
And senates heard before they judg'd a
cause;
How wouldst thou shake at Britain's
modish tribe,
Dart the quick taunt, and edge the pierc-
ing gibe?
Attentive truth and nature to decry,
And pierce each scene with philosophic
eye,
To thee were solemn toys or empty show,
The robes of pleasure and the veils of
woe:
All aid the farce, and all thy mirth main-
tain,
Whose joys are causeless, or whose griefs
are vain.
  Such was the scorn that fill'd the sage's
  mind,
Renew'd at ev'ry glance on human kind;
How just that scorn ere yet thy voice
declare,
Search every state, and canvass ev'ry
pray'r.
  Unnumber'd suppliants crowd Prefer-
  ment's gate,
Athirst for wealth, and burning to be
great;
Delusive Fortune hears th' incessant call,
They mount, they shine, evaporate, and
fall.
On ev'ry stage the foes of peace attend,
Hate dogs their flight, and insult mocks
their end.
Love ends with hope, the sinking states-
man's door
Pours in the morning worshipper no
more;
For growing names the weekly scribbler
lies,
To growing wealth the dedicator flies;

From ev'ry room descends the painted
face,
That hung the bright Palladium of the
place,
And smok'd in kitchens, or in auctions
sold,
To better features yields the frame of
gold;
For now no more we trace in ev'ry line
Heroic worth, benevolence divine:
The form distorted justifies the fall,
And detestation rids th' indignant wall.
  But will not Britain hear the last
  appeal,
Sign her foes' doom, or guard her
fav'rites' zeal?
Thro' Freedom's sons no more remon-
strance rings,
Degrading nobles and controlling kings;
Our supple tribes repress their patriot
throats,
And ask no questions but the price of
votes;
With weekly libels and septennial ale,
Their wish is full to riot and to rail.
  In full-blown dignity, see Wolsey
  stand,
Law in his voice, and fortune in his hand:
To him the church, the realm, their
pow'rs consign,
Thro' him the rays of regal bounty shine,
Still to new heights his restless wishes
tow'r.
Claim leads to claim, and pow'r advances
pow'r;
Till conquest unresisted ceas'd to please,
And rights submitted, left him none to
seize.
At length his sovereign frowns—the train
of state
Mark the keen glance, and watch the sign
to hate.
Where'er he turns he meets a stranger's
eye,
His suppliants scorn him, and his fol-
lowers fly;
At once is lost the pride of awful state,
The golden canopy, the glitt'ring plate,
The regal palace, the luxurious board,

The liv'ried army, and the menial lord.
With age, with cares, with maladies
    oppress'd,
He seeks the refuge of monastic rest.
Grief aids disease, remember'd folly
    stings,
And his last sighs reproach the faith of
    kings.
  Speak thou, whose thoughts at humble
    peace repine,
Shall Wolsey's wealth, with Wolsey's
    end, be thine?
Or liv'st thou now, with safer pride
    content,
The wisest justice on the banks of Trent?
For why did Wolsey near the steeps of
    fate,
On weak foundations raise th' enormous
    weight?
Why but to sink beneath misfortune's
    blow,
With louder ruin to the gulphs below?
  What gave great Villiers to th' as-
    sassin's knife,
And fix'd disease on Harley's closing
    life?
What murder'd Wentworth, and what
    exil'd Hyde,
By kings protected, and to kings ally'd?
What but their wish indulg'd in courts to
    shine,
And pow'r too great to keep, or to re-
    sign?
  When first the college rolls receive his
    name,
The young enthusiast quits his ease for
    fame;
Through all his veins the fever of re-
    nown
Spreads from the strong contagion of the
    gown;
O'er Bodley's dome his future labours
    spread,
And Bacon's mansion trembles o'er his
    head.
Are these thy views? proceed, illustrious
    youth,
And virtue guard thee to the throne of
    Truth!

Yet should thy soul indulge the gen'rous
    heat,
Till captive Science yields her last re-
    treat;
Should Reason guide thee with her
    brightest ray,
And pour on misty Doubt resistless day;
Should no false Kindness lure to loose
    delight,
Nor Praise relax, nor Difficulty fright;
Should tempting Novelty thy cell refrain,
And Sloth effuse her opiate fumes in vain;
Should Beauty blunt on fops her fatal
    dart,
Nor claim the triumph of a letter'd heart;
Should no Disease thy torpid veins in-
    vade,
Nor Melancholy's phantoms haunt thy
    shade;
Yet hope not life from grief or danger
    free,
Nor think the doom of man revers'd for
    thee:
Deign on the passing world to turn thine
    eyes,
And pause awhile from letters, to be
    wise;
There mark what ills the scholar's life
    assail,
Toil, envy, want, the patron, and the jail.
See nations slowly wise, and meanly just,
To buried merit raise the tardy bust.
If dreams yet flatter, once again attend,
Hear Lydiat's life, and Galileo's end.
  Nor deem, when Learning her last
    prize bestows,
The glitt'ring eminence exempt from
    woes;
See when the vulgar 'scape, despis'd or
    aw'd,
Rebellion's vengeful talons seize on Laud.
From meaner minds, tho' smaller fines
    content
The plunder'd palace or sequester'd rent;
Mark'd out by dang'rous parts he meets
    the shock,
And fatal learning leads him to the block:
Around his tomb let Art and Genius
    weep,

But hear his death, ye blockheads, hear
  and sleep.
  The festal blazes, the triumphal show,
The ravish'd standard, and the captive
  foe,
The senate's thanks, the gazette's pom-
  pous tale,
With force resistless o'er the brave pre-
  vail.
Such bribes the rapid Greek o'er Asia
  whirl'd,
For such the steady Romans shook the
  world;
For such in distant lands the Britons
  shine,
And stain with blood the Danube or the
  Rhine;
This pow'r has praise, that virtue scarce
  can warm,
Till fame supplies the universal charm.
Yet Reason frowns on War's unequal
  game,
Where wasted nations raise a single
  name,
And mortgag'd states their grandsires'
  wreaths regret,
From age to age in everlasting debt;
Wreaths which at last the dear-bought
  right convey
To rust on medals, or on stones decay.
  On what foundation stands the war-
  rior's pride,
How just his hopes, let Swedish Charles
  decide;
A frame of adamant, a soul of fire,
No dangers fright him, and no labours
  tire;
O'er love, o'er fear, extends his wide
  domain,
Unconquer'd lord of pleasure and of
  pain;
No joys to him pacific sceptres yield,
War sounds the trump, he rushes to the
  field;
Behold surrounding kings their pow'rs
  combine,
And one capitulate, and one resign;
Peace courts his hand, but spreads her
  charms in vain;

"Think nothing gain'd," he cries, "till
  nought remain,
On Moscow's walls till Gothic standards
  fly,
And all be mine beneath the polar sky."
The march begins in military state,
And nations on his eye suspended wait;
Stern Famine guards the solitary coast,
And Winter barricades the realms of
  Frost;
He comes, nor want nor cold his course
  delay;—
Hide, blushing Glory, hide Pultowa's
  day:
The vanquish'd hero leaves his broken
  bands,
And shews his miseries in distant lands;
Condemn'd a needy supplicant to wait,
While ladies interpose, and slaves debate.
But did not Chance at length her error
  mend?
Did no subverted empire mark his end?
Did rival monarchs give the fatal wound?
Or hostile millions press him to the
  ground?
His fall was destin'd to a barren strand,
A petty fortress, and a dubious hand;
He left the name, at which the world
  grew pale,
To point a moral, or adorn a tale.
  All times their scenes of pompous woes
  afford,
From Persia's tyrant, to Bavaria's lord.
In gay hostility, and barb'rous pride,
With half mankind embattled at his side,
Great Xerxes comes to seize the certain
  prey,
And starves exhausted regions in his
  way;
Attendant Flatt'ry counts his myriads
  o'er,
Till counted myriads soothe his pride no
  more;
Fresh praise is try'd till madness fires his
  mind,
The waves he lashes, and enchains the
  wind;
New pow'rs are claim'd, new pow'rs are
  still bestow'd,

Till rude resistance lops the spreading
god;
The daring Greeks deride the martial
show,
And heap their valleys with the gaudy
foe;
Th' insulted sea with humbler thoughts
he gains,
A single skiff to speed his flight remains;
Th' incumber'd oar scarce leaves the
dreaded coast
Through purple billows and a floating
host.
    The bold Bavarian, in a luckless hour,
Tries the dread summits of Cæsarian
pow'r,
With unexpected legions bursts away,
And sees defenceless realms receive his
sway;
Short sway! fair Austria spreads her
mournful charms,
The queen, the beauty, sets the world in
arms;
From hill to hill the beacons' rousing
blaze
Spreads wide the hope of plunder and of
praise;
The fierce Croatian, and the wild
Hussar,
And all the sons of ravage crowd the
war;
The baffled prince in honour's flatt'ring
bloom
Of hasty greatness finds the fatal doom,
His foes derision, and his subjects blame,
And steals to death from anguish and
from shame.
    Enlarge my life with multitude of days,
In health, in sickness, thus the suppliant
prays;
Hides from himself his state, and shuns
to know,
That life protracted, is protracted woe.
Time hovers o'er, impatient to destroy,
And shuts up all the passages of joy:
In vain their gifts the bounteous seasons
pour,
The fruit autumnal, and the vernal
flow'r,

With listless eyes the dotard views the
store,
He views, and wonders that they please
no more:
Now pall the tasteless meats, and joyless
wines,
And Luxury with sighs her slave resigns.
Approach, ye minstrels, try the soothing
strain,
And yield the tuneful lenitives of pain:
No sounds, alas, would touch th' im-
pervious ear
Though dancing mountains witness'd
Orpheus near,
Nor lute nor lyre his feeble pow'r attend,
Nor sweeter musick of a virtuous friend,
But everlasting dictates crowd his tongue,
Perversely grave or positively wrong.
The still returning tale, and ling'ring
jest,
Perplex the fawning niece and pamper'd
guest,
While growing hopes scarce awe the
gath'ring sneer,
And scarce a legacy can bribe to hear;
The watchful guests still hint the last
offence,
The daughter's petulance, the son's ex-
pence,
Improve his heady rage with treach'rous
skill,
And mould his passions till they make his
will.
    Unnumber'd maladies his joints invade,
Lay siege to life, and press the dire
blockade;
But unextinguish'd Av'rice still remains,
And dreaded losses aggravate his pains;
He turns, with anxious heart and crippled
hands,
His bonds of debt, and mortgages of
lands;
Or views his coffers with suspicious eyes,
Unlocks his gold, and counts it till he
dies.
    But grant, the virtues of a temp'rate
prime
Bless with an age exempt from scorn or
crime;

An age that melts in unperceiv'd decay,
And glides in modest innocence away;
Whose peaceful day Benevolence endears,
Whose night congratulating Conscience
  cheers;
The gen'ral fav'rite as the gen'ral friend:
Such age there is, and who could wish its
  end?
    Yet ev'n on this her load Misfortune
  flings,
To press the weary minutes' flagging
  wings:
New sorrow rises as the day returns,
A sister sickens, or a daughter mourns.
Now kindred Merit fills the sable bier,
Now lacerated Friendship claims a tear.
Year chases year, decay pursues decay,
Still drops some joy from with'ring life
  away;
New forms arise, and diff'rent views
  engage,
Superfluous lags the vet'ran on the stage,
Till pitying Nature signs the last release,
And bids afflicted worth retire to peace.
    But few there are whom hours like
  these await,
Who set unclouded in the gulphs of Fate.
From Lydia's monarch should the search
  descend,
By Solon caution'd to regard his end;
In life's last scene what prodigies sur-
  prise,
Fears of the brave, and follies of the
  wise?
From Marlb'rough's eyes the streams of
  dotage flow,
And Swift expires a driv'ler and a show.
    The teeming mother, anxious for her
  race,
Begs for each birth the fortune of a
  face:
Yet Vane could tell what ills from beauty
  spring;
And Sedley curs'd the form that pleas'd a
  king.
Ye nymphs of rosy lips and radiant eyes,
Whom Pleasure keeps too busy to be
  wise,
Whom joys with soft varieties invite,

By day the frolick, and the dance by
  night,
Who frown with vanity, who smile with
  art,
And ask the latest fashion of the heart,
What care, what rules your heedless
  charms shall save,
Each nymph your rival, and each youth
  your slave?
Against your fame with fondness hate
  combines,
The rival batters, and the lover mines.
With distant voice neglected Virtue calls,
Less heard and less, the faint remon-
  strance falls;
Tir'd with contempt, she quits the slipp'ry
  reign,
And Pride and Prudence take her seat in
  vain.
In crowd at once, where none the pass
  defend,
The harmless Freedom, and the private
  Friend.
The guardians yield, by force superior
  ply'd;
To Int'rest, Prudence; and to Flatt'ry,
  Pride.
Now Beauty falls betray'd, despis'd, dis-
  tress'd,
And hissing Infamy proclaims the rest.
    Where then shall Hope and Fear their
  objects find?
Must dull Suspense corrupt the stagnant
  mind?
Must helpless man, in ignorance sedate,
Roll darkling down the torrent of his
  fate?
Must no dislike alarm, no wishes rise
No cries attempt the mercies of the
  skies?
Inquirer, cease, petitions yet remain,
Which heav'n may hear, nor deem re-
  ligion vain.
Still raise for good the supplicating voice,
But leave to heav'n the measure and the
  choice.
Safe in his pow'r, whose eyes discern afar
The secret ambush of a specious pray'r;
Implore his aid, in his decisions rest,

Secure whate'er he gives, he gives the
best.
Yet when the sense of sacred presence
fires,
And strong devotion to the skies aspires,
Pour forth thy fervours for a healthful
mind,
Obedient passions, and a will resign'd;
For love, which scarce collective man can
fill;
For patience, sov'reign o'er transmuted
ill;
For faith, that, panting for a happier seat,
Counts death kind Nature's signal of
retreat:
These goods for man the laws of heav'n
ordain,
These goods he grants, who grants the
pow'r to gain;
With these celestial Wisdom calms the
mind,
And makes the happiness she does not
find.

On the Death of Dr. Robert Levett

Boswell informs us that Dr. Robert
Levett was "an obscure practiser of physick amongst the lower people, his fees
being sometimes very small sums, sometimes whatever provisions his patients
could afford him; but of such extensive
practice in that way, that Mrs. Williams
has told me, his walk was from Houns-
ditch to Marybone." Dr. Levett for many
years had lodging in Dr. Johnson's house,
or his chambers, "and waited on Dr.
Johnson every morning, through the whole
course of his late and tedious breakfast."
"He was of a strange grotesque appearance, stiff and formal in his manner, and
seldom said a word while any company
was present." He died in 1782. Boswell
quotes the following memorandum by
Johnson: "January 20, Sunday. Robert
Levett was buried in the church-yard of
Bridewell, between one and two in the
afternoon. He died on Thursday 17, about
seven in the morning, by an instantaneous
death. He was an old and faithful friend;
I have known him from about 46. *Com-*

mendavi. May God have mercy on him.
May he have mercy on me."

CONDEMN'D to Hope's delusive mine,
　As on we toil from day to day,
By sudden blasts or slow decline
　Our social comforts drop away.

Well tried through many a varying year,
　See Levett to the grave descend,
Officious, innocent, sincere,
　Of every friendless name the friend.

Yet still he fills affection's eye,
　Obscurely wise and coarsely kind;
Nor, letter'd Arrogance, deny
　Thy praise to merit unrefined.

When fainting nature call'd for aid,
　And hov'ring death prepared the blow,
His vig'rous remedy display'd
　The power of art without the show.

In Misery's darkest cavern known,
　His useful care was ever nigh,
Where hopeless Anguish pour'd his groan,
　And lonely Want retired to die.

No summons mock'd by chill delay,
　No petty gain disdain'd by pride;
The modest wants of every day
　The toil of every day supplied.

His virtues walk'd their narrow round,
　Nor made a pause, nor left a void;
And sure th' Eternal Master found
　The single talent well employ'd.

The busy day, the peaceful night,
　Unfelt, uncounted, glided by;
His frame was firm—his powers were
　　bright,
　　Though now his eightieth year was
　　nigh.

Then with no fiery throbbing pain,
　No cold gradations of decay,
Death broke at once the vital chain,
　And freed his soul the nearest way.

Letter to Lord Chesterfield

In 1747, Dr. Johnson's difficult and highly important work, his *Dictionary of the English Language,* was announced to the world by the publication of its *Plan,* addressed to Philip Dormer, Earl of Chesterfield, then one of his Majesty's Principal Secretaries of State. Boswell describes the Earl as "a nobleman who was very ambitious of literary distinction, and who, upon being informed of the design, had expressed himself in terms very favourable to its success." Many years later, Johnson told Boswell, "Sir, the way in which the *Plan* of my *Dictionary* came to be inscribed to Lord Chesterfield was this: I had neglected to write it by the time appointed. Dodsley (one of the booksellers who had contracted with Johnson for the execution of the work) suggested a desire to have it addressed to Lord Chesterfield. I laid hold of this as a pretext for delay, that it might be better done, and let Dodsley have his desire. I said to my friend, Dr. Bathurst, 'Now if any good comes of my addressing to Lord Chesterfield, it will be ascribed to deep policy, when, in fact, it was only a casual excuse for laziness.'"

In 1754, the *Dictionary* was near publication. During the intervening years, Lord Chesterfield had behaved toward Johnson with coldness and neglect. Now, however, in the hope that Johnson would dedicate the work to him, he attempted to conciliate him by writing two papers in *The World,* commending the undertaking. Johnson then sent to Lord Chesterfield the following letter. It became famous through the peculiar circumstance that Lord Chesterfield, affecting unconcern, kept it lying on his table where anybody might see it, and even read it to Dodsley, with the remark that "this man has great powers." Johnson was reluctant to have the letter published. It was not until 1781 that Boswell, at great pains and after long delay on Johnson's part, secured a copy. He published it separately, in 1790, the year before his *Life of Johnson* came out, and six years after Johnson's death.

" To the Right Honourable the Earl of Chesterfield.

" February 7, 1755.

" My Lord, I have been lately informed, by the proprietor of *The World,* that two papers, in which my Dictionary is recommended to the publick, were written by your Lordship. To be so distinguished, is an honour, which, being very little accustomed to favours from the great, I know not well how to receive, or in what terms to acknowledge.

" When, upon some slight encouragement, I first visited your Lordship, I was overpowered, like the rest of mankind, by the enchantment of your address; and could not forbear to wish that I might boast myself *Le vainqueur du vainqueur de la terre;*—that I might obtain that regard for which I saw the world contending; but I found my attendance so little encouraged, that neither pride nor modesty would suffer me to continue it. When I had once addressed your Lordship in publick, I had exhausted all the art of pleasing which a retired and uncourtly scholar can possess. I had done all that I could; and no man is well pleased to have his all neglected, be it ever so little.

" Seven years, my Lord, have now past, since I waited in your outward rooms, or was repulsed from your door; during which time I have been pushing on my work through difficulties, of which it is useless to complain, and have brought it, at last, to the verge of publication, without one act of assistance, one word of encouragement, or one smile of favour. Such treatment I did not expect, for I never had a Patron before.

" The shepherd in Virgil grew at last acquainted with Love, and found him a native of the rocks.

" Is not a Patron, my Lord, one who looks with unconcern on a man struggling for life in the water, and, when he has reached ground, encumbers him with help? The notice which you have been pleased to take of my labours, had it been early, had been kind; but it has been delayed till I am indifferent, and cannot enjoy it; till I am solitary, and cannot impart it; till I am known, and do not want it. I hope it is no very cynical asperity not to confess obligations where no benefit has been received, or to be unwilling that the Publick should consider me as owing that to a Patron, which Providence has enabled me to do for myself.

" Having carried on my work thus far with so little obligation to any favourer of learning, I shall not be disappointed though I should conclude it, if less be possible, with less; for I have been long wakened from that dream of hope, in which I once boasted myself with so much exultation, my Lord, your Lordship's most humble, most obedient servant,

" Sam Johnson."

JAMES BOSWELL (1740-1795)

From The Life of Samuel Johnson, LL.D.

Johnson Dines with Jack Wilkes at Mr. Dilly's

At the close of the following account of the dinner at Mr. Dilly's, Boswell compliments himself on his successful negotiation of the meeting between Dr. Johnson and Mr. Wilkes, "two men, who though so widely different, had so many things in common—classical learning, modern literature, wit, and humour, and ready repartee—that it would have been much to be regretted if they had been for ever at a distance from each other." Johnson, a firm Tory, had written of Wilkes, in 1770, "Lampoon itself would disdain to speak ill of him, of whom no man speaks well." He called him "a retailer of sedition and obscenity"; and, in regard to the question of allowing Wilkes to take his seat in Parliament, after being twice expelled for seditious libel, said, "We are now disputing . . . whether Middlesex shall be represented, or not, by a criminal from a gaol." Wilkes, in his paper, *The North Briton,* had referred to Johnson, with very slight indirectness, as "a slave of state, hired by a stipend to obey his master." This fierce and formidable radical was, from all accounts, a most polished, urbane, charming person.

But I conceived an irresistible wish, if possible, to bring Dr. Johnson and Mr. Wilkes together. How to manage it, was a nice and difficult matter.

My worthy booksellers and friends, Messieurs Dilly in the Poultry, at whose hospitable and well-covered table I have seen a greater number of literary men, than at any other, except that of Sir Joshua Reynolds, had invited me to meet Mr. Wilkes and some more gentlemen on Wednesday, May 15. "Pray (said I,) let us have Dr. Johnson."—"What with Mr. Wilkes? not for the world, (said Mr. Edward Dilly:) Dr. Johnson would never forgive me."—"Come, (said I,) if you'll let me negociate for you, I will be answerable that all shall go well." DILLY. "Nay, if you will take it upon you, I am sure I shall be very happy to see them both here."

Notwithstanding the high veneration which I entertained for Dr. Johnson, I was sensible that he was sometimes a little actuated by the spirit of contradiction, and by means of that I hoped I should gain my point. I was persuaded that if I had come upon him with a direct proposal, "Sir, will you dine in company with Jack Wilkes?" he would have flown into a passion, and would probably have answered, "Dine with Jack Wilkes, Sir! I'd as soon dine with Jack Ketch." I therefore, while we were sitting quietly by ourselves at his house in an evening, took occasion to open my plan thus:—"Mr. Dilly, Sir, sends his respectful compliments to you, and would be happy if you would do him the honour to dine with him on Wednesday next along with me, as I must soon go to Scotland." JOHNSON. "Sir, I am obliged to Mr. Dilly. I will wait upon him—" BOSWELL. "Provided, Sir, I suppose, that the company which he is to have, is agreeable to you." JOHNSON. "What do you mean, Sir? What do you take me for? Do you think I am so ignorant of the world as to imagine that I am to prescribe to a gentleman what company he is to have at his table?" BOSWELL. "I beg your pardon, Sir, for wishing to prevent you from meeting people whom you might not like. Perhaps he may have some of what he calls his patriotick friends with him." JOHNSON. "Well, sir, and what then? What care I for his *patriotick friends?* Poh!" BOSWELL. "I should not be surprized to find Jack Wilkes there." JOHNSON. "And if Jack Wilkes *should* be there, what is that to *me,* Sir? My dear friend, let us have no more of this. I am sorry to be angry with you; but really it is treating me strangely to talk to me as if I could not meet any company whatever, occasionally." BOSWELL. "Pray forgive me, Sir: I meant well. But you shall meet whoever comes, for me." Thus I secured him, and told Dilly that he would find him very well pleased to be one of his guests on the day appointed.

Upon the much-expected Wednesday, I called on him about half an hour before dinner, as I often did when we were to dine out together, to see that he was ready in time, and to accompany him. I found him buffeting his books, as upon a former occasion, covered with dust, and making no preparation for going abroad. "How is this, Sir? (said I.) Don't you recollect that you are to dine at Mr. Dilly's?" JOHNSON. "Sir, I did not think of going to Dilly's: it went out of my head. I have ordered dinner at home with Mrs. Williams." BOSWELL. "But, my dear Sir, you know you were engaged to Mr. Dilly, and I told him so. He will expect you, and will be much disappointed if you don't come." JOHNSON. "You must talk to Mrs. Williams about this."

Here was a sad dilemma. I feared that what I was so confident I had secured would yet be frustrated. He had accustomed himself to shew Mrs. Williams such a degree of humane attention, as frequently imposed some restraint upon him; and I knew that if she should be obstinate, he would not stir. I hastened down stairs to the blind lady's room, and told her I was in great uneasiness, for Dr. Johnson had engaged to me to dine this day at Mr. Dilly's, but that he had told me he had forgotten his engagement, and had ordered dinner at home. "Yes, Sir, (said she, pretty peevishly,) Dr. Johnson is to dine at home."—"Madam, (said I,) his respect for you is such, that I know he will not leave you unless you absolutely desire it. But as you have so much of his company, I hope you will be good enough to forego it for a day; as Mr. Dilly is a very worthy man, has frequently had agreeable parties at his house for Dr. Johnson, and will be vexed if the Doctor neglects him to-day. And then, Madam, be pleased to consider my situation; I carried the message, and I assured Mr. Dilly that Dr. Johnson was to come, and no doubt he has made a dinner, and invited a company, and boasted of the honour he expected to have. I shall be quite disgraced if the Doctor is not there." She gradually softened to my solicitations, which were certainly as earnest as most entreaties to ladies upon any occasion, and was graciously pleased to empower me to tell Dr. Johnson, "That all things considered, she thought he should certainly go." I flew back to him, still in dust, and careless of what should be the event, "indifferent in his choice to go or stay"; but as soon as I had announced to him Mrs. Williams' consent, he roared, "Frank, a clean shirt," and was very soon drest. When I had him fairly seated in a hackney-coach with me, I exulted as much as a fortune-hunter who has got an heiress into a post-chaise with him to set out for Gretna-Green.

When we entered Mr. Dilly's drawing room, he found himself in the midst of a company he did not know. I kept myself snug and silent, watching how he would conduct himself. I observed him whispering to Mr. Dilly, "Who is that gentleman, Sir?"—"Mr. Arthur Lee."—JOHNSON. "Too, too, too," (under his breath,) which was one of his habitual mutterings. Mr. Arthur Lee could not but be very obnoxious to Johnson, for he was not only a *patriot* but an *American*. He was afterwards minister from the United States at the court of Madrid. "And who is the gentleman in lace?"—"Mr. Wilkes, Sir." This information confounded him still more; he had some difficulty to restrain himself, and taking up a book, sat down upon a window-seat and read, or at least kept his eye upon it intently for some time, till he composed himself. His feelings, I dare say, were awkward enough. But he no doubt recollected his having rated me for supposing that he could be at all disconcerted by any company, and he, therefore, resolutely set himself to behave quite as an easy man of the world, who could adapt himself at once to the disposition and manners of those whom he might chance to meet.

The cheering sound of "Dinner is upon the table," dissolved his reverie, and we *all* sat down without any symptom of ill humour. There were present, beside Mr. Wilkes, and Mr. Arthur Lee, who was an old companion of mine when he studied physick at Edinburgh, Mr. (now Sir John) Miller, Dr. Lettsom, and Mr. Slater the druggist. Mr. Wilkes placed himself next to Dr. Johnson, and behaved to him with so much attention and politeness, that he gained upon him insensibly. No man eat more heartily than Johnson, or loved better what was nice and delicate. Mr. Wilkes was very assiduous in helping him to some fine veal. "Pray give me leave, Sir:—It is better here—A little of the brown— Some fat, Sir—A little of the stuffing—Some gravy—Let me have the pleasure of giving you some butter—Allow me to recommend a squeeze of this orange;—or the lemon, perhaps, may have more zest."—"Sir, Sir, I am obliged to you, Sir," cried Johnson, bowing, and turning his head to him with a look for some time of "surly virtue," but, in a short while, of complacency.

Foote being mentioned, Johnson said, "He is not a good mimick." One of the company added, "A merry Andrew, a buffoon." JOHNSON. "But he has wit too, and is not deficient in ideas, or in fertility and variety of imagery and not empty of reading; he has knowledge enough to fill up his part. One species of wit he has in an eminent degree, that of escape. You drive him into a corner with both hands; but he's gone, Sir, when you think you have got him—like an animal that jumps over your head. Then he has a great range for wit; he never lets truth stand between him and a jest, and he is sometimes mighty coarse. Garrick is under many restraints from which Foote is free." WILKES. "Garrick's wit is more like Lord Chesterfield's." JOHNSON. "The first time I was in company with Foote was at Fitzherbert's. Having no good opinion of the fellow, I was resolved not to be pleased; and it is very difficult to please a man against his will. I went on eating my dinner pretty sullenly, affecting not to mind him. But the dog was so very comical, that I was obliged to lay down my knife and fork, throw myself back upon my chair, and fairly laugh it out. No, Sir, he was irresistible. He upon one occasion experienced, in an extraordinary degree, the efficacy of his powers of entertaining. Amongst the many and various modes which he tried of getting money, he became a partner with a small-beer brewer, and he was to have a share of the profits for procuring customers amongst his numerous acquaintance. Fitzherbert was one who took his small-beer; but it was so bad that the servants resolved not to drink it. They were at some loss how to notify their resolution, being afraid of offending their master, who they knew liked Foote much as a companion. At last they fixed upon a little black boy, who was rather a favourite, to be their deputy, and deliver their remonstrance; and having invested him with the whole authority of the kitchen, he was to inform Mr. Fitzherbert, in all their names, upon a certain day, that they would drink Foote's small-beer no longer. On that day Foote happened to dine at Fitzherbert's, and this boy served at table; he was so delighted with Foote's stories, and merriment, and grimace, that when he went down stairs, he told them, 'This is the finest man I have ever seen. I will not deliver your message. I will drink his small-beer.' "

Somebody observed that Garrick could not have done this. WILKES. "Garrick would have made the small-beer still smaller. He is now leaving the stage; but he will play *Scrub* all his life." I knew that Johnson would let nobody attack Garrick but himself, as Garrick once said to me, and I had heard him praise his liberality; so to bring out his commendation of his celebrated pupil, I said, loudly, "I have heard Garrick is liberal." JOHNSON. "Yes, Sir, I know that Garrick has given away more money than any man in England that I am acquainted with, and that not from ostentatious views. Garrick was very poor when he began life; so when he came to have money, he probably was very unskilful in giving away, and saved when he should not. But Garrick began to be liberal as soon as he could; and I am of opinion, the reputation of avarice which he has had, has been very lucky for him, and prevented his having many enemies. You despise a man for avarice, but do not hate him. Garrick might have been much better attacked for living with more splendour than is suitable to a player: if they had had the wit to have assaulted him in that quarter, they might have galled him more. But they have kept clamouring about his avarice, which has rescued him from much obloquy and envy."

Talking of the great difficulty of obtaining authentick information for biography, Johnson told us, "When I was a young fellow I wanted to write the *Life of Dryden,* and in order to get materials, I applied to the only two persons then alive who had seen him; these were old Swinney, and old Cibber. Swinney's information was no more than this, 'That at Will's coffee-house Dryden had a particular chair for himself, which was set by the fire in winter, and was then called his winter-chair; and that it was carried out for him to the balcony in summer, and was then called his summer-chair.' Cibber could tell no more but 'That he remembered him a decent old man, arbiter of critical disputes at Will's.' You are to consider that Cibber was then at a great distance from Dryden, had perhaps one leg only in the room, and durst not draw in the other." BOSWELL. "Yet Cibber was a man of observation?" JOHNSON. "I think not." BOSWELL. "You will allow his *Apology* to be well done." JOHNSON. "Very well done, to be sure, Sir. That book is a striking proof of the justice of Pope's remark:

> "'Each might his several province well command
> Would all but stoop to what they understand.'"

BOSWELL. "And his plays are good." JOHNSON. "Yes; but that was his trade; *l'esprit du corps:* he had been all his life among players and play-writers. I wondered that he had so little to say in conversation, for he had kept the best company, and learnt all that can be got by the ear. He abused Pindar to me, and then shewed me an Ode of his own, with an absurd couplet, making a linnet soar on an eagle's wing. I told him that when the ancients made a simile, they always made it like something real."

Mr. Wilkes remarked, that "among all the bold flights of Shakspeare's imagination, the boldest was making Birnam wood march to Dunsinane; creating a wood where there never was a shrub; a wood in Scotland! ha! ha! ha!" And he also observed, that "the clannish slavery of the Highlands of Scotland was the single exception to Milton's remark of 'The Mountain Nymph, sweet Liberty,' being worshipped in all hilly countries."—"When I was at Inverary (said he,) on a visit to my old friend, Archibald, Duke of Argyle, his dependents congratulated me on being such a favourite of his Grace. I said, 'It is then, gentlemen, truely lucky for me; for if I had displeased the Duke, and he had wished it, there is not a Campbell among you but would have been ready to bring John Wilkes's head to him in a charger. It would have been only

"'Off with his head! So much for Aylesbury.'

I was then member for Aylesbury."

Mr. Arthur Lee mentioned some Scotch who had taken possession of a barren part of America, and wondered why they should choose it. JOHNSON. "Why, Sir, all barrenness is comparative. The *Scotch* would not know it to be barren." BOSWELL. "Come, come, he is flattering the English. You have now been in Scotland, Sir, and say if you did not see meat and drink enough there." JOHNSON. "Why, yes, Sir; meat and drink enough to give the enhabitants sufficient strength to run away from home." All these quick and lively sallies were said sportively, quite in jest, and with a smile, which showed that he meant only wit. Upon this topick he and Mr. Wilkes could perfectly assimilate; here was a bond of union between them, and I was conscious that as both of them had visited Caledonia, both were fully satisfied of the strange narrow ignorance of those who imagine that it is a land of famine. But they amused themselves with persevering in the old jokes. When I claimed a superiority for Scotland over England in one respect, that no man can be arrested there for a debt merely because another swears it against him; but there must first be the judgement of a court of law ascertaining its justice; and that a seizure of the person, before judgement is obtained, can take place only, if his creditor should swear that he is about to fly from the country, or, as it is technically expressed, is *in meditatione fugæ:* WILKES. "That, I should think, may be safely sworn of all the Scotch nation." JOHNSON. (to Mr. Wilkes,) "You must know, Sir, I lately took my friend Boswell and shewed him genuine civilised life in an English provincial town. I turned him loose at Lichfield, my native city, that he might see for once real civility: for you know he lives among savages in Scotland, and among rakes in London." WILKES. "Except when he is with grave, sober, decent people like you and me." JOHNSON. (smiling,) "And we ashamed of him."

LAURENCE STERNE (1713-1768)

From TRISTRAM SHANDY

The Story of Le Fever

Lieutenant Le Fever is a poor officer, dying from want and sickness, one of the many recipients of kindness from good Uncle Toby, the central figure in *Tristram Shandy.*

IT was to my uncle *Toby's* eternal honour,——though I tell it only for the sake of those, who, when coop'd in betwixt a natural and a positive law, know not, for their souls, which way in the world to turn themselves——That notwithstanding my uncle *Toby* was warmly engaged at that time in carrying on the siege of *Dendermond,* parallel with the allies, who pressed theirs on so vigorously, that they scarce allowed him time to get his dinner——that nevertheless he gave up *Dendermond,* though he had already made a lodgment upon the counterscarp;—and bent his whole thoughts towards the private distresses at the inn; and except that he ordered the garden gate to be bolted up, by which he might be said to have turned the siege of *Dendermond* into a blockade,——he left *Dendermond* to itself——to be relieved or not by the *French* king, as the *French* king thought good; and only considered how he himself should relieve the poor lieutenant and his son.

——That kind BEING, who is a friend to the friendless, shall recompence thee for this.

Thou hast left this matter short, said my uncle *Toby* to the corporal, as he was putting him to bed,——and I will tell thee in what, *Trim.*—— In the first place, when thou madest an offer of my services to *Le Fever,* ——as sickness and travelling are both expensive, and thou knowest he was but a poor lieutenant, with a son to subsist as well as himself out of his pay,—that thou didst not make an offer to him of my purse; because, had he stood in need, thou knowest, *Trim,* he had been as welcome to it as myself.——Your honour knows, said the corporal, I had no orders;——True, quoth my uncle *Toby,*——thou didst very right, *Trim,* as a soldier,——but certainly very wrong as a man.

In the second place, for which, indeed, thou hast the same excuse, continued my uncle *Toby,*——when thou offeredst him whatever was in my house,——thou shouldst have offered him my house too:——A sick brother officer should have the best quarters, *Trim,* and if we had him with us,——we could tend and look to him:——Thou art an excellent nurse thyself, *Trim,*——and what with thy care of him, and the old woman's, and his boy's, and mine together, we might recruit him again at once, and set him upon his legs.——

——In a fortnight or three weeks, added my uncle *Toby,* smiling, ——he might march.——He will never march; an' please your honour, in this world, said the corporal:——He will march; said my uncle *Toby,* rising up, from the side of the bed, with one shoe off:——An' please your honour, said the corporal, he will never march but to his grave:—— He shall march, cried my uncle *Toby,* marching the foot which had a shoe on, though without advancing an inch,——he shall march to his regiment.——He cannot stand it, said the corporal;——He shall be supported, said my uncle *Toby;*——He'll drop at last, said the corporal, and what will become of his boy?——He shall not drop, said my uncle *Toby,* firmly.——A-well-o'-day,——do what we can for him, said *Trim,* maintaining his point,——the poor soul will die:——He shall not die, by G——, cried my uncle *Toby.*

——The ACCUSING SPIRIT, which flew up to heaven's chancery with the oath, blush'd as he gave it in;——and the RECORDING ANGEL, as he wrote it down, dropp'd a tear upon the word, and blotted it out for ever.

——My uncle *Toby* went to his bureau,——put his purse into his breeches pocket, and having ordered the corporal to go early in the morning for a physician,——he went to bed, and fell asleep.

The sun looked bright the morning after, to every eye in the village but *Le Fever's* and his afflicted son's; the hand of death press'd heavy upon his eye-lids,——and hardly could the wheel at the cistern turn round its circle,——when my uncle *Toby,* who had rose up an hour before his wonted time, entered the lieutenant's room, and without preface or apology, sat himself down upon the chair by the bed-side, and, independently of all modes and customs, opened the curtain in the manner an old friend and brother officer would have done it, and asked him how he did,——how he had rested in the night,——what was his complaint, ——where was his pain,——and what he could do to help him:——and without giving him time to answer any one of the enquiries, went on, and told him of the little plan which he had been concerting with the corporal the night before for him.——

——You shall go home directly, *Le Fever,* said my uncle *Toby,* to my house,——and we'll send for a doctor to see what's the matter,—— and we'll have an apothecary,——and the corporal shall be your nurse; ——and I'll be your servant, *Le Fever.*

There was a frankness in my uncle *Toby,*——not the *effect* of familiarity,——but the *cause* of it,——which let you at once into his soul, and shewed you the goodness of his nature; to this, there was something in his looks, and voice, and manner, superadded, which eternally beckoned to the unfortunate to come and take shelter under him; so that before my uncle *Toby* had half finished the kind offers he was making to the father, had the son insensibly pressed up close to his knees, and had taken hold of the breast of his coat, and was pulling it towards him.—— The blood and spirits of *Le Fever,* which were waxing cold and slow within him, and were retreating to their last citadel, the heart——rallied back,——the film forsook his eyes for a moment——he looked up wishfully in my uncle *Toby's* face,——then cast a look upon his boy,——and that *ligament,* fine as it was,——was never broken.——

Nature instantly ebb'd again,——the film returned to its place,——the pulse fluttered——stopp'd——went on——throbb'd——stopp'd again ——moved——stopp'd.

Tristram and the Ass

Tristram was setting forth from his inn at Lyons, to visit *"the tomb of the lovers,"* when he was stopped at the gate by the poor ass that figures in the following narration.

——'TWAS by a poor ass, who had just turned in with a couple of large panniers upon his back, to collect eleemosynary turnip-tops and cabbage-leaves; and stood dubious, with his two fore-feet on the inside of the threshold, and with his two hinder feet towards the street, as not knowing very well whether he was to go in or no.

Now, 'tis an animal (be in what hurry I may) I cannot bear to strike ——there is a patient endurance of sufferings, wrote so unaffectedly in his looks and carriage, which pleads so mightily for him, that it always disarms me; and to that degree, that I do not like to speak unkindly to him: on the contrary, meet him where I will——whether in town or country——in cart or under panniers——whether in liberty or bondage——I have ever something civil to say to him on my part; and as one word begets another (if he has as little to do as I)——I generally fall into conversation with him; and surely never is my imagination so busy as in framing his responses from the etchings of his countenance——and where those carry me not deep enough——in flying from my own heart into his, and seeing what is natural for an ass to think——as well as a man, upon the occasion. In truth, it is the only creature of all the classes of beings below me, with whom I can do this: for parrots, jackdaws, &c. ——I never exchange a word with them——nor with the apes, &c., for pretty near the same reason; they act by rote, as the others speak by it, and equally make me silent: nay my dog and my cat, though I value them both——(and for my dog he would speak if he could)——yet somehow or other, they) neither of them possess the talents for conversation——I can make nothing of a discourse with them, beyond the *proposition,* the *reply,* and *rejoinder,* which terminated my father's and my mother's conversations, in his beds of justice——and those utter'd——there's an end of the dialogue——

——But with an ass, I can commune forever.

Come, *Honesty!* said I,——seeing it was impracticable to pass betwixt him and the gate——art thou for coming in, or going out?

The ass twisted his head round to look up the street——

Well——replied I——we'll wait a minute for thy driver:

——He turned his head thoughtful about, and looked wistfully the opposite way——

I understand thee perfectly, answered I——If thou takest a wrong step in this affair, he will cudgel thee to death——Well! a minute is but a minute, and if it saves a fellow-creature a drubbing, it shall not be set down as ill spent.

He was eating the stem of an artichoke as this discourse went on, and in the little peevish contentions of nature betwixt hunger and unsavouriness, had dropt it out of his mouth half a dozen times, and pick'd it up again——God help thee, *Jack!* said I, thou hast a bitter breakfast on't——and many a bitter day's labour,——and many a bitter blow, I fear, for its wages——'tis all——all bitterness to thee, whatever life is to others.——And now thy mouth, if one knew the truth of it, is as bitter, I dare say, as soot——(for he had cast aside the stem) and thou hast not a friend perhaps in all this world, that will give thee a macaroon.

——In saying this, I pull'd out a paper of 'em, which I had just purchased, and gave him one——and at this moment that I am telling it, my heart smites me, that there was more of pleasantry in the conceit, of seeing *how* an ass would eat a macaroon——than of benevolence in giving him one, which presided in the act.

When the ass had eaten his macaroon, I press'd him to come in—— the poor beast was heavy loaded——his legs seem'd to tremble under him——he hung rather backwards, and as I pull'd at his halter, it broke short in my hand——he look'd up pensive in my face——"Don't thrash me with it——but if you will, you may"——If I do, said, I, I'll be d——d.

The word was but one-half of it pronounced, like the abbess of *Andoüillets'*——(so there was no sin in it)——when a person coming in, let fall a thundering bastinado upon the poor devil's crupper, which put an end to the ceremony.

THOMAS GRAY (1716-1771)

The Progress of Poesy

Φωναντα συνετοῖσιν' ἐς
Δὲ τὸ παν ἑρμηνέων χατίζει
PINDAR, *Olymp.* II.

I. 1

Awake, Æolian lyre, awake
And give to rapture all thy trembling
strings.
From Helicon's harmonious springs
A thousand rills their mazy progress
take:
The laughing flowers, that round them
blow,
Drink life and fragrance as they flow.
Now the rich stream of music winds
along
Deep, majestic, smooth, and strong,
Thro' verdant vales, and Ceres' golden
reign:
Now rolling down the steep amain,
Headlong, impetuous, see it pour:
The rocks and nodding groves rebellow
to the roar.

I. 2

Oh! Sovereign of the willing soul,
Parent of sweet and solemn-breathing
airs,
Enchanting shell! the sullen Cares,
And frantic Passions hear thy soft con-
troul.
On Thracia's Hills the Lord of War
Has curb'd the fury of his car,
And drop'd his thirsty lance at thy com-
mand.
Perching on the scept'red hand
Of Jove, thy magic lulls the feather'd
king
With ruffled plumes, and flagging wing:
Quench'd in dark clouds of slumber lie
The terror of his beak, and light'nings of
his eye.

I. 3

Thee the voice, the dance, obey,
Temper'd to thy warbled lay.

O'er Idalia's velvet-green
The rosy-crownèd Loves are seen
On Cytherea's day
With antic sport, and blue-eyed Pleasures,
Frisking light in frolic measures;
Now pursuing, now retreating,
Now in circling troops they meet:
To brisk notes in cadence beating
Glance their many-twinkling feet.
Slow melting strains their Queen's ap-
proach declare:
Where'er she turns the Graces homage
pay.
With arms sublime, that float upon the
air,
In gliding state she wins her easy way:
O'er her warm cheek, and rising bosom,
move
The bloom of young Desire and purple
light of Love.

II. 1

Man's feeble race what ills await,
Labour, and penury, the racks of pain,
Disease, and sorrow's weeping train,
And death, sad refuge from the storms of
fate!
The fond complaint, my song, disprove,
And justify the laws of Jove.
Say, has he given in vain the heavenly
Muse?
Night, and all her sickly dews,
Her spectres wan, and birds of boding
cry,
He gives to range the dreary sky:
Till down the eastern cliffs afar
Hyperion's march they spy, and glittering
shafts of war.

II. 2

In climes beyond the solar road,
Where shaggy forms o'er ice-built moun-
tains roam,
The Muse has broke the twilight-gloom
To cheer the shivering Native's dull
abode.
And oft, beneath the odorous shade
Of Chili's boundless forests laid,
She deigns to hear the savage youth repeat

In loose numbers wildly sweet
Their feather-cinctur'd chiefs, and dusky
    loves.
Her track, where'er the Goddess roves,
Glory pursue, and generous shame,
Th' unconquerable mind, and freedom's
    holy flame.

II. 3

Woods, that wave o'er Delphi's steep,
Isles, that crown th' Ægean deep,
Fields, that cool Ilissus laves,
Or where Mæander's amber waves
In lingering labyrinths creep,
How do your tuneful echoes languish,
Mute, but to the voice of anguish!
Where each old poetic mountain
Inspiration breath'd around;
Ev'ry shade and hallow'd fountain
Murmur'd deep a solemn sound:
Till the sad Nine in Greece's evil hour
Left their Parnassus for the Latian
    plains.
Alike they scorn the pomp of tyrant-
    power,
And coward vice, that revels in her
    chains.
When Latium had her lofty spirit lost,
They sought, oh, Albion! next thy sea-
    encircled coast.

III. 1

Far from the sun and summer-gale,
In thy green lap was Nature's darling
    laid,
What time, where lucid Avon stray'd,
To him the mighty mother did unveil
Her awful face: The dauntless child
Stretch'd forth his little arms, and smil'd
This pencil take (she said) whose colours
    clear
Richly paint the vernal year:
Thine too these golden keys, immortal
    boy!
This can unlock the gates of Joy;
Of horror that, and thrilling fears,
Or ope the sacred source of sympathetic
    tears.

III. 2

Nor second He, that rode sublime
Upon the seraph-wings of extasy,
The secrets of th' abyss to spy.
He pass'd the flaming bounds of place
    and time:
The living throne, the sapphire-blaze,
Where Angels tremble, while they gaze,
He saw; but blasted with excess of light,
Clos'd his eyes in endless night.
Behold where Dryden's less presumptuous
    car,
Wide o'er the fields of glory bear
Two coursers of ethereal race,
With necks in thunder cloth'd, and long-
    resounding pace.

III. 3

Hark, his hands the lyre explore!
Bright-eyed Fancy hovering o'er
Scatters from her pictur'd urn
Thoughts that breathe, and words that
    burn.
But ah! 'tis heard no more——
Oh! Lyre divine, what daring Spirit
Wakes thee now? tho' he inherit
Nor the pride, nor ample pinion,
That the Theban Eagle bear
Sailing with supreme dominion
Thro' the azure deep of air:
Yet oft before his infant eyes would run
Such forms, as glitter in the Muse's ray
With orient hues, unborrow'd of the sun:
Yet shall he mount, and keep his distant
    way
Beyond the limits of a vulgar fate,
Beneath the good how far—but far above
    the great.

Elegy, Written in a Country Churchyard

THE Curfew tolls the knell of parting
    day,
  The lowing herd winds slowly o'er
    the lea,
The plowman homeward plods his weary
    way,

And leaves the world to darkness and
to me.

Now fades the glimmering landscape on
the sight,
And all the air a solemn stillness holds,
Save where the beetle wheels his droning
flight,
And drowsy tinklings lull the distant
folds;

Save that from yonder ivy-mantled tower
The moping owl does to the moon
complain
Of such, as wandering near her secret
bower,
Molest her ancient solitary reign.

Beneath those rugged elms, that yew-
tree's shade,
Where heaves the turf in many a
mouldering heap,
Each in his narrow cell for ever laid,
The rude Forefathers of the hamlet
sleep.

The breezy call of incense-breathing
Morn,
The swallow twittering from the
straw-built shed,
The cock's shrill clarion, or the echoing
horn,
No more shall rouse them from their
lowly bed.

For them no more the blazing hearth
shall burn,
Or busy housewife ply her evening
care:
No children run to lisp their sire's return,
Or climb his knees the envied kiss to
share.

Oft did the harvest to their sickle yield,
Their furrow oft the stubborn glebe
has broke;
How jocund did they drive their team
afield!
How bow'd the woods beneath their
sturdy stroke!

Let not Ambition mock their useful toil,
Their homely joys, and destiny obscure;
Nor Grandeur hear with a disdainful
smile,
The short and simple annals of the
poor.

The boast of heraldry, the pomp of
power,
And all that beauty, all that wealth
e'er gave,
Awaits alike th' inevitable hour.
The paths of glory lead but to the
grave.

Nor you, ye Proud, impute to These the
fault,
If Memory o'er their Tomb no Trophies raise,
Where through the long-drawn aisle and
fretted vault
The pealing anthem swells the note of
praise.

Can storied urn or animated bust
Back to its mansion call the fleeting
breath?
Can Honour's voice provoke the silent
dust,
Or Flattery sooth the dull cold ear of
Death?

Perhaps in this neglected spot is laid
Some heart once pregnant with celestial
fire;
Hands that the rod of empire might
have sway'd,
Or waked to ecstasy the living lyre.

But Knowledge to their eyes her ample
page
Rich with the spoils of time did ne'er
unroll;
Chill Penury repress'd their noble rage,
And froze the genial current of the
soul.

Full many a gem of purest ray serene,
The dark unfathom'd caves of ocean
bear:

Full many a flower is born to blush
   unseen,
    And waste its sweetness on the desert
     air.

Some village Hampden, that with dauntless breast
    The little Tyrant of his fields with-
     stood;
Some mute inglorious Milton here may
   rest,
    Some Cromwell guiltless of his coun-
     try's blood.

Th' applause of listening senates to command,
    The threats of pain and ruin to despise,
To scatter plenty o'er a smiling land,
    And read their history in a nation's
     eyes,

Their lot forbade: nor circumscribed
   alone
    Their growing virtues, but their crimes
     confin'd;
Forbade to wade through slaughter to a
   throne,
    And shut the gates of mercy on man-
     kind,

The struggling pangs of conscious truth
   to hide,
    To quench the blushes of ingenuous
     shame,
Or heap the shrine of Luxury and Pride
    With incense kindled at the Muse's
     flame.

Far from the madding crowd's ignoble
   strife,
    Their sober wishes never learn'd to
     stray;
Along the cool sequester'd vale of life
    They kept the noiseless tenor of their
     way.

Yet even these bones from insult to
   protect,
    Some frail memorial still erected nigh,

With uncouth rhymes and shapeless
   sculpture deck't,
    Implores the passing tribute of a sigh.

Their name, their years, spelt by th' un-
   letter'd Muse,
    The place of fame and elegy supply:
And many a holy text around she strews,
    That teach the rustic moralist to die.

For who to dumb Forgetfulness a prey,
    This pleasing anxious being e'er re-
     sign'd,
Left the warm precincts of the cheerful
   day,
    Nor cast one longing lingering look
     behind?

On some fond breast the parting soul
   relies,
    Some pious drops the closing eye re-
     quires;
Ev'n from the tomb the voice of Nature
   cries,
    Ev'n in our Ashes live their wonted
     Fires.

For thee, who mindful of the unhonour'd
   Dead
    Dost in these lines their artless tale
     relate,
If chance, by lonely Contemplation led,
    Some kindred spirit shall inquire thy
     fate,

Haply some hoary-headed Swain may say,
    "Oft have we seen him at the peep of
     dawn
Brushing with hasty steps the dews away
    To meet the sun upon the upland lawn.

"Hard by yon wood, now smiling as in
   scorn,
    Muttering his wayward fancies he
     would rove;
Now drooping, woeful-wan, like one forlorn,
    Or crazed with care, or cross'd in hope-
     less love.

"One morn I miss'd him on the custom'd hill,
  Along the heath, and near his favourite tree;
Another came; nor yet beside the rill,
  Nor up the lawn, nor at the wood was he;

"The next with dirges due in sad array
  Slow through the church-way path we saw him borne,—
Approach and read (for thou canst read) the lay
  Graved on the stone beneath yon agèd thorn:"

THE EPITAPH

Here rests his head upon the lap of Earth
  A youth, to Fortune and to Fame unknown;
Fair Science frown'd not on his humble birth
  And Melancholy mark'd him for her own.

Large was his bounty, and his soul sincere;
  Heaven did a recompense as largely send:
He gave to Misery (all he had) a tear,
  He gain'd from Heaven ('twas all he wish'd) a friend.

No farther seek his merits to disclose,
  Or draw his frailties from their dread abode
(There they alike in trembling hope repose)
  The bosom of his Father and his God.

OLIVER GOLDSMITH (1728-1774)

The Haunch of Venison

THANKS, my lord, for your venison, for finer or fatter
Ne'er ranged in a forest, or smoked in a platter;
The haunch was a picture for painters to study,
The fat was so white, and the lean was so ruddy;
Though my stomach was sharp, I could scarce help regretting
To spoil such a delicate picture by eating:
I had thoughts, in my chamber, to place it in view,
To be shown to my friends as a piece of virtú:
As in some Irish houses, where things are so so,
One gammon of bacon hangs up for a show;
But, for eating a rasher of what they take pride in,
They'd as soon think of eating the pan it is fried in.
But hold—let me pause—don't I hear you pronounce
This tale of the bacon's a damnable bounce?
Well, suppose it a bounce—sure a poet may try,
By a bounce now and then, to get courage to fly.
  But, my lord, it's no bounce: I protest in my turn,
It's a truth—and your lordship may ask Mr. Byrne.
To go on with my tale—as I gazed on the haunch,
I thought of a friend that was trusty and stanch;
So I cut it, and sent it to Reynolds undress'd,
To paint it, or eat it, just as he liked best:
Of the neck and the breast I had next to dispose;
'Twas a neck and a breast that might rival Monroe's:
But in parting with these I was puzzled again,
With the how, and the who, and the where, and the when.
There's Howard, and Coley, and Hogarth, and Hiff,

I think they love venison—I know they
love beef.
There's my countryman Higgins—Oh!
let him alone,
For making a blunder, or picking a bone.
But hang it—to poets who seldom can
eat,
Your very good mutton's a very good
treat;
Such dainties to them, their health it
might hurt,
It's like sending them ruffles when want-
ing a shirt.
While thus I debated, in reverie centred,
An acquaintance, a friend as he call'd
himself, enter'd:
An underbred, fine spoken fellow was he,
And he smiled as he look'd at the venison
and me.
"What have we got here?—Why, this is
good eating!
Your own, I suppose—or is it in wait-
ing?"
"Why, whose should it be?" cried I with a
flounce;
"I get these things often"—but this was
a bounce:
"Some lords, my acquaintance, that settle
the nation,
Are pleased to be kind—but I hate osten-
tation."
  "If that be the case then," cried he,
very gay,
"I'm glad to have taken this house in my
way.
To-morrow you take a poor dinner with
me;
No words—I insist on't—precisely at
three:
We'll have Johnson, and Burke; all the
wits will be there;
My acquaintance is slight, or I'd ask my
lord Clare.
And, now that I think on't, as I am a
sinner!
We wanted this venison to make out a
dinner.
What say you?—a pasty, it shall, and it
must,

And my wife, little Kitty, is famous for
crust.
Here, porter—this venison with me to
Mile-end;
No stirring, I beg—my dear friend—my
dear friend!"
Thus snatching his hat, he brush'd off
like the wind,
And the porter and eatables follow'd
behind.
  Left alone to reflect, having emptied
my shelf,
And, "nobody with me at sea but my-
self";
Though I could not help thinking my gen-
tleman hasty,
Yet Johnson, and Burke, and a good
venison pasty
Were things that I never disliked in my
life,
Though clogg'd with a coxcomb, and
Kitty his wife.
So next day, in due splendour to make
my approach,
I drove to his door in my own hackney-
coach.
  When come to the place where we
were all to dine,
(A chair-lumber'd closet just twelve feet
by nine),
My friend bade me welcome, but struck
me quite dumb
With tidings that Johnson and Burke
would not come;
"For I knew it," he cried, "both eternally
fail,
The one with his speeches, and t'other
with Thrale;
But no matter, I'll warrant we'll make
up the party
With two full as clever, and ten times as
hearty.
The one is a Scotchman, the other a Jew,
They're both of them merry, and authors
like you;
The one writes the Snarler, the other the
Scourge;
Some think he writes Cinna—he owns to
Panurge."

While thus he described them by trade
and by name,
They enter'd, and dinner was served as
they came.
  At the top a fried liver, and bacon were
seen,
At the bottom was tripe in a swinging
tureen;
At the sides there were spinach and
pudding made hot;
In the middle a place where the pasty—
was not.
Now, my lord, as for tripe, it's my utter
aversion,
And your bacon I hate like a Turk or a
Persian;
So there I sat stuck like a horse in a
pound,
While the bacon and liver went merrily
round:
But what vex'd me most was that d—d
Scottish rogue,
With his long-winded speeches, his smiles,
and his brogue,
And, "madam," quoth he, "may this bit be
my poison,
A prettier dinner I never set eyes on;
Pray, a slice of your liver, though may I
be cursed,
But I've eat of your tripe till I'm ready
to burst."
"The tripe," quoth the Jew, with his
chocolate cheek,
"I could dine on this tripe seven days in
a week:
I like these here dinners so pretty and
small,
But your friend there, the doctor, eats
nothing at all."
"O—ho!" quoth my friend, "he'll come on
in a trice,
He's keeping a corner for something
that's nice;
There's a pasty"—"A pasty!" repeated
the Jew;
"I don't care if I keep a corner for't
too."
"What the de'il, mon, a pasty!" re-echoed
the Scot;

"Though splitting, I'll still keep a corner
for that."—
"We'll all keep a corner," the lady cried
out;
"We'll all keep a corner," was echoed
about.
While thus we resolved, and the pasty
delay'd,
With looks that quite petrified, enter'd
the maid;
A visage so sad, and so pale with affright,
Waked Priam, in drawing his curtains by
night.
But we quickly found out (for who could
mistake her?)
That she came with some terrible news
from the baker:
And so it fell out, for that negligent
sloven
Had shut out the pasty on shutting his
oven.
Sad Philomel thus—but let similes drop—
And now that I think on't the story may
stop.
To be plain, my good lord, it's but labour
misplaced,
To send such good verses to one of your
taste:
You've got an odd something—a kind of
discerning—
A relish—a taste—sicken'd over by learning;
At least it's your temper, as very well
known,
That you think very slightly of all that's
your own:
So, perhaps, in your habits of thinking
amiss,
You may make a mistake, and think
slightly of this.

The Deserted Village

Sweet Auburn! loveliest village of the
plain;
Where health and plenty cheered the
labouring swain,
Where smiling spring its earliest visit
paid,

And parting summer's lingering blooms
delayed:
Dear lovely bowers of innocence and
ease,
Seats of my youth, when every sport
could please,
How often have I loitered o'er thy green,
Where humble happiness endeared each
scene!
How often have I paused on every
charm,
The sheltered cot, the cultivated farm,
The never-failing brook, the busy mill,
The decent church that topt the neigh-
bouring hill,
The hawthorn bush, with seats beneath
the shade
For talking age and whispering lovers
made!
How often have I blest the coming day,
When toil remitting lent its turn to play,
And all the village train, from labour
free,
Led up their sports beneath the spread-
ing tree,
While many a pastime circled in the
shade,
The young contending as the old sur-
veyed;
And many a gambol frolicked o'er the
ground,
And sleights of art and feats of strength
went round.
And still, as each repeated pleasure tired,
Succeeding sports the mirthful band
inspired;
The dancing pair that simply sought re-
nown
By holding out to tire each other down;
The swain mistrustless of his smutted
face,
While secret laughter tittered round the
place;
The bashful virgin's side-long looks of
love,
The matron's glance that would those
looks reprove:
These were thy charms, sweet village!
sports like these,

With sweet succession, taught even toil
to please:
These round thy bowers their cheerful
influence shed:
These were thy charms—but all these
charms are fled.
Sweet smiling village, loveliest of the
lawn,
Thy sports are fled, and all thy charms
withdrawn.
Amidst thy bowers the tyrant's hand is
seen,
And desolation saddens all thy green:
One only master grasps the whole do-
main,
And half a tillage stints thy smiling plain.
No more thy glassy brook reflects the
day,
But, choked with sedges, works its weedy
way;
Along the glades, a solitary guest,
The hollow sounding bittern guards its
nest;
Amidst thy desert walks the lapwing flies,
And tires their echoes with unvaried
cries;
Sunk are thy bowers in shapeless ruin all,
And the long grass o'ertops the mould-
ering wall;
And trembling, shrinking from the
spoiler's hand,
Far, far away thy children leave the
land.
Ill fares the land, to hastening ills a
prey,
Where wealth accumulates, and men
decay:
Princes and lords may flourish, or may
fade;
A breath can make them, as a breath has
made:
But a bold peasantry, their country's
pride,
When once destroyed, can never be sup-
plied.
A time there was, ere England's griefs
began,
When every rood of ground maintained
its man;

For him light labour spread her whole-
  some store,
Just gave what life required, but gave
  no more:
His best companions, innocence and
  health;
And his best riches, ignorance of wealth.
  But times are altered; trade's unfeel-
  ing train
Usurp the land and dispossess the swain;
Along the lawn, where scattered hamlets
  rose,
Unwieldy wealth and cumbrous pomp
  repose,
And every want to opulence allied,
And every pang that folly pays to pride.
These gentle hours that plenty bade to
  bloom,
Those calm desires that asked but little
  room,
Those healthful sports that graced the
  peaceful scene,
Lived in each look, and brightened all
  the green;
These, far departing, seek a kinder shore,
And rural mirth and manners are no
  more.
  Sweet Auburn! parent of the blissful
  hour,
Thy glades forlorn confess the tyrant's
  power,
Here, as I take my solitary rounds
Amidst thy tangling walks and ruined
  grounds,
And, many a year elapsed, return to view
Where once the cottage stood, the haw-
  thorn grew,
Remembrance wakes with all her busy
  train,
Swells at my breast, and turns the past
  to pain.
  In all my wanderings round this world
  of care,
In all my griefs—and God has given my
  share—
I still had hopes, my latest hours to
  crown,
Amidst these humble bowers to lay me
  down;

To husband out life's taper at the close,
And keep the flame from wasting by re-
  pose:
I still had hopes, for pride attends us
  still,
Amidst the swains to show my book-
  learned skill,
Around my fire an evening group to
  draw,
And tell of all I felt, and all I saw;
And, as an hare whom hounds and horns
  pursue
Pants to the place from whence at first
  she flew,
I still had hopes, my long vexations past,
Here to return—and die at home at last.
  O blest retirement, friend to life's de-
  cline,
Retreats from care, that never must be
  mine,
How happy he who crowns in shades like
  these
A youth of labour with an age of ease;
Who quits a world where strong tempta-
  tions try,
And, since 'tis hard to combat, learns to
  fly!
For him no wretches, born to work and
  weep,
Explore the mine, or tempt the dangerous
  deep;
No surly porter stands in guilty state,
To spurn imploring famine from the
  gate;
But on he moves to meet his latter end,
Angels around befriending Virtue's
  friend;
Bends to the grave with unperceived de-
  cay,
While resignation gently slopes the way;
And, all his prospects brightening to the
  last,
His heaven commences ere the world be
  past!
  Sweet was the sound, when oft at eve-
  ning's close
Up yonder hill the village murmur rose.
There, as I passed with careless steps
  and slow,

The mingling notes came softened from
    below;
The swain responsive as the milk-maid
    sung,
The sober herd that lowed to meet their
    young,
The noisy geese that gabbled o'er the
    pool,
The playful children just let loose from
    school,
The watch-dog's voice that bayed the
    whispering wind,
And the loud laugh that spoke the vacant
    mind;—
These all in sweet confusion sought the
    shade,
And filled each pause the nightingale had
    made.
But now the sounds of population fail,
No cheerful murmurs fluctuate in the
    gale,
No busy steps the grass-grown foot-way
    tread,
For all the bloomy flush of life is fled.
All but yon widowed, solitary thing,
That feebly bends beside the plashy
    spring:
She, wretched matron, forced in age, for
    bread,
To strip the brook with mantling cresses
    spread,
To pick her wintry faggot from the
    thorn,
To seek her nightly shed, and weep till
    morn;
She only left of all the harmless train,
The sad historian of the pensive plain.
    Near yonder copse, where once the gar-
       den smiled,
And still where many a garden flower
    grows wild;
There, where a few torn shrubs the place
    disclose,
The village preacher's modest mansion
    rose.
A man he was to all the country dear,
And passing rich with forty pounds a
    year;
Remote from towns he ran his godly race,

Nor e'er had changed, nor wished to
    change his place;
Unpractised he to fawn, or seek for
    power,
By doctrines fashioned to the varying
    hour;
Far other aims his heart had learned to
    prize,
More skilled to raise the wretched than
    to rise.
His house was known to all the vagrant
    train;
He chid their wanderings but relieved
    their pain:
The long-remembered beggar was his
    guest,
Whose beard descending swept his aged
    breast;
The ruined spendthrift, now no longer
    proud,
Claimed kindred there, and had his
    claims allowed;
The broken soldier, kindly bade to stay,
Sat by the fire, and talked the night away,
Wept o'er his wounds, or, tales of sor-
    row done,
Shouldered his crutch and showed how
    fields were won.
Pleased with his guests, the good man
    learned to glow,
And quite forgot their vices in their woe;
Careless their merits or their faults to
    scan,
His pity gave ere charity began.
    Thus to relieve the wretched was his
       pride,
And e'en his failings leaned to Virtue's
    side;
But in his duty prompt at every call,
He watched and wept, he prayed and felt
    for all;
And, as a bird each fond endearment
    tries
To tempt its new-fledged offspring to the
    skies,
He tried each art, reproved each dull
    delay,
Allured to brighter worlds, and led the
    way.

Beside the bed where parting life was
laid,
And sorrow, guilt, and pain by turns dis-
mayed,
The reverend champion stood. At his
control
Despair and anguish fled the struggling
soul;
Comfort came down the trembling
wretch to raise,
And his last faltering accents whispered
praise.
  At church, with meek and unaffected
grace,
His looks adorned the venerable place;
Truth from his lips prevailed with double
sway,
And fools, who came to scoff, remained
to pray.
The service past, around the pious man,
With steady zeal, each honest rustic ran;
Even children followed with endearing
wile,
And plucked his gown to share the good
man's smile.
His ready smile a parent's warmth ex-
prest;
Their welfare pleased him, and their
cares distrest:
To them his heart, his love, his griefs
were given,
But all his serious thoughts had rest in
heaven.
As some tall cliff that lifts its awful
form,
Swells from the vale, and midway leaves
the storm,
Tho' round its breast the rolling clouds
are spread,
Eternal sunshine settles on its head.
  Beside yon straggling fence that skirts
the way,
With blossom'd furze unprofitably gay,
There, in his noisy mansion, skill'd to
rule,
The village master taught his little
school.
A man severe he was, and stern to view;
I knew him well, and every truant knew;

Well had the boding tremblers learned
to trace
The day's disasters in his morning face;
Full well they laughed with counterfeited
glee
At all his jokes, for many a joke had he;
Full well the busy whisper circling round
Conveyed the dismal tidings when he
frowned.
Yet he was kind, or, if severe in aught,
The love he bore to learning was in
fault;
The village all declared how much he
knew:
'Twas certain he could write, and cipher
too;
Lands he could measure, terms and tides
presage,
And even the story ran that he could
gauge;
In arguing, too, the parson owned his
skill,
For, even tho' vanquished, he could argue
still;
While words of learned length and thun-
dering sound
Amazed the gazing rustics ranged
around;
And still they gazed, and still the wonder
grew,
That one small head could carry all he
knew.
  But past is all his fame. The very
spot
Where many a time he triumphed is
forgot.
Near yonder thorn, that lifts its head on
high,
Where once the sign-post caught the
passing eye,
Low lies that house where nut-brown
draughts inspired,
Where graybeard mirth and smiling toil
retired,
Where village statesmen talked with
looks profound,
And news much older than their ale went
round.
Imagination fondly stoops to trace

The parlour splendours of that festive place:
The white-washed wall, the nicely sanded floor,
The varnished clock that clicked behind the door:
The chest contrived a double debt to pay,
A bed by night, a chest of drawers by day;
The pictures placed for ornament and use,
The twelve good rules, the royal game of goose;
The hearth, except when winter chill'd the day,
With aspen boughs and flowers and fennel gay;
While broken tea-cups, wisely kept for show,
Ranged o'er the chimney, glistened in a row.
　Vain transitory splendours! could not all
Reprieve the tottering mansion from its fall?
Obscure it sinks, nor shall it more impart
An hour's importance to the poor man's heart.
Thither no more the peasant shall repair
To sweet oblivion of his daily care;
No more the farmer's news, the barber's tale,
No more the woodman's ballad shall prevail;
No more the smith his dusky brow shall clear,
Relax his ponderous strength, and lean to hear;
The host himself no longer shall be found
Careful to see the mantling bliss go round;
Nor the coy maid, half willing to be prest,
Shall kiss the cup to pass it to the rest.
　Yes! let the rich deride, the proud disdain,
These simple blessings of the lowly train;
To me more dear, congenial to my heart,
One native charm, than all the gloss of art.
Spontaneous joys, where Nature has its play,
The soul adopts, and owns their first born sway;
Lightly they frolic o'er the vacant mind,
Unenvied, unmolested, unconfined.
But the long pomp, the midnight masquerade,
With all the freaks of wanton wealth arrayed—
In these, ere triflers half their wish obtain,
The toiling pleasure sickens into pain;
And, e'en while fashion's brightest arts decoy,
The heart distrusting asks if this be joy.
　Ye friends to truth, ye statesmen who survey
The rich man's joy increase, the poor's decay,
'Tis yours to judge, how wide the limits stand
Between a splendid and an happy land.
Proud swells the tide with loads of freighted ore,
And shouting Folly hails them from her shore;
Hoards e'en beyond the miser's wish abound,
And rich men flock from all the world around.
Yet count our gains! This wealth is but a name
That leaves our useful products still the same.
Not so the loss. The man of wealth and pride
Takes up a space that many poor supplied;
Space for his lake, his park's extended bounds,
Space for his horses, equipage, and hounds:
The robe that wraps his limbs in silken sloth
Has robbed the neighbouring fields of half their growth;

His seat, where solitary sports are seen,
Indignant spurns the cottage from the green:
Around the world each needful product flies,
For all the luxuries the world supplies;
While thus the land adorned for pleasure all
In barren splendour feebly waits the fall.
  As some fair female unadorned and plain,
Secure to please while youth confirms her reign,
Slights every borrowed charm that dress supplies,
Nor shares with art the triumph of her eyes;
But when those charms are past, for charms are frail,
When time advances, and when lovers fail,
She then shines forth, solicitous to bless,
In all the glaring impotence of dress.
Thus fares the land by luxury betrayed:
In nature's simplest charms at first arrayed,
But verging to decline, its splendours rise,
Its vistas strike, its palaces surprise;
While, scourged by famine from the smiling land
The mournful peasant leads his humble band,
And while he sinks, without one arm to save,
The country blooms—a garden and a grave.
  Where then, ah! where, shall poverty reside,
To 'scape the pressure of contiguous pride?
If to some common's fenceless limits strayed,
He drives his flock to pick the scanty blade,
Those fenceless fields the sons of wealth divide,
And even the bare-worn common is denied.

If to the city sped—what waits him there?
To see profusion that he must not share;
To see ten thousand baneful arts combined
To pamper luxury, and thin mankind;
To see those joys the sons of pleasure know
Extorted from his fellow-creature's woe.
Here while the courtier glitters in brocade,
There the pale artist plies the sickly trade;
Here while the proud their long-drawn pomps display,
There the black gibbet glooms beside the way.
The dome where pleasure holds her midnight reign
Here, richly deckt, admits the gorgeous train:
Tumultuous grandeur crowds the blazing square,
The rattling chariots clash, the torches glare.
Sure scenes like these no troubles e'er annoy!
Sure these denote one universal joy!
Are these thy serious thoughts?—Ah, turn thine eyes
Where the poor houseless shivering female lies.
She once, perhaps, in village plenty blest,
Has wept at tales of innocence distrest;
Her modest looks the cottage might adorn,
Sweet as the primrose peeps beneath the thorn:
Now lost to all; her friends, her virtue fled,
Near her betrayer's door she lays her head,
And, pinch'd with cold, and shrinking from the shower,
With heavy heart deplores that luckless hour,
When idly first, ambitious of the town,
She left her wheel and robes of country brown.

Do thine, sweet Auburn,—thine, the
  loveliest train,—
Do thy fair tribes participate her pain?
Even now, perhaps, by cold and hunger
  led,
At proud men's doors they ask a little
  bread!
  Ah, no! To distant climes, a dreary
    scene,
Where half the convex world intrudes
  between,
Through torrid tracts with fainting steps
  they go,
Where wild Altama murmurs to their
  woe.
Far different there from all that charmed
  before
The various terrors of that horrid shore;
Those blazing suns that dart a down-
  ward ray,
And fiercely shed intolerable day;
Those matted woods, where birds forget
  to sing,
But silent bats in drowsy clusters cling;
Those poisonous fields with rank luxuri-
  ance crowned,
Where the dark scorpion gathers death
  around;
Where at each step the stranger fears to
  wake
The rattling terrors of the vengeful
  snake;
Where crouching tigers wait their hap-
  less prey,
And savage men more murderous still
  than they;
While oft in whirls the mad tornado
  flies,
Mingling the ravaged landscape with the
  skies.
Far different these from every former
  scene,
The cooling brook, the grassy vested
  green,
The breezy covert of the warbling grove,
That only sheltered thefts of harmless
  love.
  Good Heaven! what sorrows gloomed
    that parting day,

That called them from their native walks
  away;
When the poor exiles, every pleasure
  past,
Hung round the bowers, and fondly
  looked their last,
And took a long farewell, and wished in
  vain
For seats like these beyond the western
  main,
And shuddering still to face the distant
  deep,
Returned and wept, and still returned to
  weep.
The good old sire the first prepared to go
To new found worlds, and wept for
  others' woe;
But for himself, in conscious virtue brave,
He only wished for worlds beyond the
  grave.
His lovely daughter, lovelier in her tears,
The fond companion of his helpless years,
Silent went next, neglected of her charms,
And left a lover's for a father's arms.
With louder plaints the mother spoke
  her woes,
And blest the cot where every pleasure
  rose,
And kist her thoughtless babes with many
  a tear
And claspt them close, in sorrow doubly
  dear,
Whilst her fond husband strove to lend
  relief
In all the silent manliness of grief.
  O luxury! thou curst by Heaven's
    decree,
How ill exchanged are things like these
  for thee!
How do thy potions, with insidious joy,
Diffuse their pleasure only to destroy!
Kingdoms by thee, to sickly greatness
  grown,
Boast of a florid vigour not their own.
At every draught more large and large
  they grow,
A bloated mass of rank unwieldy woe;
Till sapped their strength, and every part
  unsound,

Down, down, they sink, and spread a ruin
round.
Even now the devastation is begun,
And half the business of destruction
done;
Even now, methinks, as pondering here
I stand,
I see the rural virtues leave the land.
Down where yon anchoring vessel
spreads the sail,
That idly waiting flaps with every gale,
Downward they move, a melancholy
band,
Pass from the shore, and darken all the
strand.
Contented Toil, and hospitable Care,
And kind connubial tenderness, are there;
And piety with wishes placed above,
And steady loyalty, and faithful love.
And thou, sweet Poetry, thou loveliest
maid,
Still first to fly where sensual joys in-
vade;
Unfit in these degenerate times of shame
To catch the heart, or strike for honest
fame;
Dear charming nymph, neglected and de-
cried,
My shame in crowds, my solitary pride;
Thou source of all my bliss, and all my
woe,
That found'st me poor at first, and
keep'st me so;
Thou guide by which the nobler arts
excel,
Thou nurse of every virtue, fare thee
well!
Farewell, and oh! where'er thy voice be
tried,
On Torno's cliffs, or Pambamarca's side,
Whether where equinoctial fervours
glow,
Or winter wraps the polar world in
snow,
Still let thy voice, prevailing over time,
Redress the rigours of the inclement
clime;
Aid slighted truth with thy persuasive
strain;

Teach erring man to spurn the rage of
gain;
Teach him, that states of native strength
possest,
Tho' very poor, may still be very blest;
That trade's proud empire hastes to swift
decay,
As ocean sweeps the laboured mole away;
While self-dependent power can time
defy,
As rocks resist the billows and the sky.

Retaliation

Garrick wrote the following account of
the origin of this poem. "At a meeting
of a company of gentlemen who were well
known to each other, and diverting themselves among other things with the peculiar oddities of Dr. Goldsmith, who never
would allow a superior in any art, from
writing poetry down to dancing a horn-
pipe, the Doctor with great eagerness in-
sisted upon trying his epigrammatic powers
with Mr. Garrick, and each of them was
to write the other's epitaph. Mr. Garrick
immediately said that his epitaph was finished, and spoke the following distich ex-
tempore:

Here lies Nolly Goldsmith, for shortness
call'd Noll,
Who wrote like an angel, but talk'd like
poor Poll!

Goldsmith, upon the company's laughing
very heartily, grew very thoughtful and
either would not or could not write anything at that time: however, he set to
work, and some weeks after produced the
. . . poem called 'Retaliation,' which has
been much admired and gone through several editions. The public in general have
been mistaken in imagining that this poem
was written in anger by the Doctor; it
was just the contrary; the whole on all
sides was done with the greatest good
humour" . . .

Other accounts have it that several
members of the company, dining at the
St. James's coffee-house, wrote epitaphs on
Goldsmith, ridiculing his Irish accent, his
person, and his unreadiness in speech.
Garrick's was spoken at once; the others
were read to Goldsmith when he next
appeared at the St. James's coffee-house.
The complete poem was not produced
at once—certainly not "at the next meeting." It was unfinished when Goldsmith
died.

The persons mentioned as of the company
were all good friends of the Doctor's.

"Our Burke" was Edmund Burke; "Garrick," David Garrick; "Reynolds," Sir Joshua Reynolds; and "Tommy Townshend," Mr. T. Townshend, member for Whitchurch. In the course of the poem, Goldsmith refers to the Rev. Dr. Dodd, hanged for forgery; Dr. Kenrick, who read lectures at the Devil Tavern, under the title of "The School of Shakespeare"; James Macpherson, who had lately published a translation of Homer; Hugh Kelly, a popular dramatist; and W. Woodfall, printer of the *Morning Chronicle.*

OF old, when Scarron his companions invited,
Each guest brought his dish, and the feast was united.
If our landlord supplies us with beef and with fish,
Let each guest bring himself, and he brings the best dish:
Our Dean shall be venison, just fresh from the plains,
Our Burke shall be tongue, with the garnish of brains,
Our Will shall be wild fowl, of excellent flavour,
And Dick with his pepper, shall heighten the savour:
Our Cumberland's sweetbread its place shall obtain,
And Douglas is pudding substantial and plain:
Our Garrick's a salad; for in him we see
Oil, vinegar, sugar, and saltness agree:
To make out the dinner full certain I am,
That Ridge is anchovy, and Reynolds is lamb;
That Hickey's a capon, and by the same rule,
Magnanimous Goldsmith a gooseberry fool.
At a dinner so various, at such a repast,
Who'd not be a glutton, and stick to the last?
Here, waiter, more wine, let me sit while I'm able,
Till all my companions sink under the table;
Then, with chaos and blunders encircling my head,
Let me ponder, and tell what I think of the dead.

Here lies the good Dean, reunited to earth,
Who mix'd reason with pleasure, and wisdom with mirth:
If he had any faults, he has left us in doubt,
At least, in six weeks I could not find them out;
Yet some have declared, and it can't be denied them,
That sly-boots was cursedly cunning to hide them.

Here lies our good Edmund, whose genius was such,
We scarcely can praise it, or blame it too much;
Who, born for the universe, narrow'd his mind,
And to party gave up what was meant for mankind:
Tho' fraught with all learning, yet straining his throat
To persuade Tommy Townshend to lend him a vote;
Who, too deep for his hearers, still went on refining,
And thought of convincing, while they thought of dining;
Though equal to all things, for all things unfit;
Too nice for a statesman, too proud for a wit;
For a patriot too cool; for a drudge disobedient;
And too fond of the *right* to pursue the *expedient.*
In short, 'twas his fate, unemploy'd, or in place, sir,
To eat mutton cold, and cut blocks with a razor.

Here lies honest William, whose heart was a mint,
While the owner ne'er knew half the good that was in't;
The pupil of impulse, it forced him along,

His conduct still right, with his argument
wrong;
Still aiming at honour, yet fearing to
roam,
The coachman was tipsy, the chariot
drove home;
Would you ask for his merits? alas! he
had none;
What was good was spontaneous, his
faults were his own.

Here lies honest Richard whose fate I
must sigh at;
Alas! that such frolic should now be so
quiet!
What spirits were his! what wit and
what whim!
Now breaking a jest, and now breaking
a limb!
Now wrangling and grumbling to keep up
the ball!
Now teasing and vexing, yet laughing at
all!
In short, so provoking a devil was
Dick,
That we wish'd him full ten times a day
at Old Nick;
But, missing his mirth and agreeable
vein,
As often we wish'd to have Dick back
again.

Here Cumberland lies, having acted his
parts,
The Terence of England, the mender of
hearts;
A flattering painter, who made it his care
To draw men as they ought to be, not as
they are.
His gallants are all faultless, his women
divine,
And comedy wonders at being so fine:
Like a tragedy queen he has dizen'd her
out,
Or rather like tragedy giving a rout.
His fools have their follies so lost in a
crowd
Of virtues and feelings that folly grows
proud;
And coxcombs, alike in their failings
alone,

Adopting his portraits, are pleased with
their own.
Say, where has our poet this malady
caught?
Or wherefore his characters thus without
fault?
Say, was it that vainly directing his view
To find out men's virtues, and finding
them few,
Quite sick of pursuing each troublesome
elf,
He grew lazy at last, and drew from
himself.

Here Douglas retires from his toils to
relax,
The scourge of impostors, the terror of
quacks:
Come, all ye quack bards, and ye quack-
ing divines,
Come, and dance on the spot where your
tyrant reclines:
When satire and censure encircled his
throne,
I fear'd for your safety, I fear'd for my
own;
But now he is gone, and we want a de-
tector,
Our Dodds shall be pious, our Kenricks
shall lecture;
Macpherson write bombast, and call it a
style;
Our Townshend make speeches, and I
shall compile;
New Lauders and Bowers the Tweed
shall cross over,
No countryman living their tricks to discover;
Detection her taper shall quench to a
spark,
And Scotchman meet Scotchman, and
cheat in the dark.

Here lies David Garrick, describe him
who can,
An abridgment of all that was pleasant
in man:
As an actor, confess'd without rival to
shine;
As a wit, if not first, in the very first
line:

Yet, with talents like these, and an excellent heart,
This man had his failings—a dupe to his
art.
Like an ill judging beauty, his colours
he spread,
And be-plaster'd with rouge his own natural red.
On the stage he was natural, simple,
affecting;
'Twas only that when he was off he was
acting.
With no reason on earth to go out of
his way,
He turn'd and he varied full ten times a
day:
Though secure of our hearts, yet con-
foundedly sick
If they were not his own by finessing and
trick:
He cast off his friends, as a huntsman his
pack,
For he knew when he pleased he could
whistle them back.
Of praise a mere glutton, he swallow'd
what came,
And the puff of a dunce he mistook it for
fame;
Till his relish grown callous, almost to
disease,
Who pepper'd the highest was surest to
please.
But let us be candid, and speak out our
mind,
If dunces applauded, he paid them in
kind.
Ye Kenricks, ye Kellys, and Woodfalls
so grave,
What a commerce was yours while you
got and you gave!
How did Grub-street re-echo the shouts
that you raised,
While he was be-Roscius'd, and you were
be-praised!
But peace to his spirit, wherever it flies,
To act as an angel and mix with the
skies:
Those poets, who owe their best fame to
his skill,

Shall still be his flatterers, go where he
will;
Old Shakespeare receive him with praise
and with love,
And Beaumonts and Bens be his Kellys
above.
  Here Hickey reclines, a most blunt
pleasant creature,
And slander itself must allow him good
nature;
He cherish'd his friend, and he relish'd
a bumper;
Yet one fault he had, and that was a
thumper.
Perhaps you may ask if the man was a
miser?
I answer, no, no, for he always was
wiser:
Too courteous perhaps, or obligingly
flat?
His very worst foe can't accuse him of
that:
Perhaps he confided in men as they
go,
And so was too foolishly honest? Ah
no!
Then what was his failing? come, tell it,
and burn ye,—
He was, could he help it? a special
attorney.
  Here Reynolds is laid, and, to tell you
my mind,
He has not left a wiser or better behind:
His pencil was striking, resistless, and
grand;
His manners were gentle, complying, and
bland;
Still born to improve us in every part,
His pencil our faces, his manners our
heart:
To coxcombs averse, yet most civilly
steering,
When they judged without skill he was
still hard of hearing;
When they talk'd of their Raphaels,
Correggios, and stuff,
He shifted his trumpet, and only took
snuff.
By flattery unspoiled. . . .

WILLIAM COWPER (1731-1800)

The Diverting History of John Gilpin

Showing how he went farther than he
intended, and came safe home again.

JOHN GILPIN was a citizen
　　Of credit and renown,
A train-band captain eke was he
　　Of famous London town.

John Gilpin's spouse said to her dear—
　　Though wedded we have been
These twice ten tedious years, yet we
　　No holiday have seen.

To-morrow is our wedding-day,
　　And we will then repair
Unto the Bell at Edmonton
　　All in a chaise and pair.

My sister, and my sister's child,
　　Myself, and children three,
Will fill the chaise; so you must ride
　　On horseback after we.

He soon replied—I do admire
　　Of womankind but one,
And you are she, my dearest dear,
　　Therefore it shall be done.

I am a linen-draper bold,
　　As all the world doth know,
And my good friend the calender
　　Will lend his horse to go.

Quoth Mrs. Gilpin—That's well said;
　　And, for that wine is dear,
We will be furnish'd with our own,
　　Which is both bright and clear.

John Gilpin kiss'd his loving wife;
　　O'erjoy'd was he to find
That, though on pleasure she was bent,
　　She had a frugal mind.

The morning came, the chaise was
　　brought,
　　But yet was not allow'd

To drive up to the door, lest all
　　Should say that she was proud.

So three doors off the chaise was stay'd,
　　Where they did all get in;
Six precious souls, and all agog
　　To dash through thick and thin!

Smack went the whip, round went the
　　wheels,
　　Were never folk so glad,
The stones did rattle underneath,
　　As if Cheapside were mad.

John Gilpin at his horse's side
　　Seiz'd fast the flowing mane,
And up he got, in haste to ride,
　　But soon came down again;

For saddle-tree scarce reach'd had he,
　　His journey to begin,
When, turning round his head, he saw
　　Three customers come in.

So down he came; for loss of time,
　　Although it griev'd him sore,
Yet loss of pence, full well he knew,
　　Would trouble him much more.

'Twas long before the customers
　　Were suited to their mind,
When Betty screaming came down
　　stairs—
　　"The wine is left behind!"

Good lack! quoth he—yet bring it me,
　　My leathern belt likewise,
In which I bear my trusty sword
　　When I do exercise.

Now mistress Gilpin (careful soul!)
　　Had two stone bottles found,
To hold the liquor that she lov'd,
　　And keep it safe and sound.

Each bottle had a curling ear,
　　Through which the belt he drew,
And hung a bottle on each side,
　　To make his balance true.

Then, over all, that he might be
  Equipp'd from top to toe,
His long red cloak, well brush'd and
    neat,
  He manfully did throw.

Now see him mounted once again
  Upon his nimble steed,
Full slowly pacing o'er the stones,
  With caution and good heed!

But, finding soon a smoother road
  Beneath his well-shod feet,
The snorting beast began to trot,
  Which gall'd him in his seat.

So, Fair and softly, John he cried,
  But John he cried in vain;
That trot became a gallop soon,
  In spite of curb and rein.

So stooping down, as needs he must
  Who cannot sit upright,
He grasp'd the mane with both his
    hands,
  And eke with all his might.

His horse, who never in that sort
  Had handled been before,
What thing upon his back had got
  Did wonder more and more.

Away went Gilpin, neck or nought;
  Away went hat and wig!—
He little dreamt, when he set out,
  Of running such a rig!

The wind did blow, the cloak did fly,
  Like streamer long and gay,
Till, loop and button failing both,
  At last it flew away.

Then might all people well discern
  The bottles he had slung;
A bottle swinging at each side,
  As hath been said or sung.

The dogs did bark, the children scream'd,
  Up flew the windows all;
And ev'ry soul cried out—Well done!
  As loud as he could bawl.

Away went Gilpin—who but he?
  His fame soon spread around—
He carries weight! he rides a race!
  'Tis for a thousand pound!

And still, as fast as he drew near,
  'Twas wonderful to view
How in a trice the turnpike-men
  Their gates wide open threw.

And now, as he went bowing down
  His reeking head full low,
The bottles twain behind his back
  Were shatter'd at a blow.

Down ran the wine into the road,
  Most piteous to be seen,
Which made his horse's flanks to smoke
  As they had basted been.

But still he seem'd to carry weight,
  With leathern girdle brac'd;
For all might see the bottle-necks
  Still dangling at his waist.

Thus all through merry Islington
  These gambols he did play,
And till he came unto the Wash
  Of Edmonton so gay.

And there he threw the wash about
  On both sides of the way,
Just like unto a trundling mop,
  Or a wild goose at play.

At Edmonton his loving wife
  From the balcony spied
Her tender husband, wond'ring much
  To see how he did ride.

Stop, stop, John Gilpin!—Here's the
    house—
  They all at once did cry;
The dinner waits, and we are tir'd:
  Said Gilpin—So am I!

But yet his horse was not a whit
  Inclin'd to tarry there;
For why?—his owner had a house
  Full ten miles off, at Ware.

So like an arrow swift he flew,
  Shot by an archer strong;
So did he fly—which brings me to
  The middle of my song.

Away went Gilpin, out of breath,
  And sore against his will,
Till at his friend the calender's
  His horse at last stood still.

The calender, amaz'd to see
  His neighbour in such trim,
Laid down his pipe, flew to the gate,
  And thus accosted him:—

What news? what news? your tidings
    tell;
  Tell me you must and shall—
Say why bare-headed you are come,
  Or why you come at all?

Now Gilpin had a pleasant wit,
  And lov'd a timely joke;
And thus unto the calender
  In merry guise he spoke:—

I came because your horse would come;
  And, if I well forebode,
My hat and wig will soon be here—
  They are upon the road.

The calender, right glad to find
  His friend in merry pin,
Return'd him not a single word,
  But to the house went in;

Whence straight he came with hat and
    wig;
  A wig that flow'd behind,
A hat not much the worse for wear,
  Each comely in its kind.

He held them up, and, in his turn,
  Thus show'd his ready wit—
My head is twice as big as yours,
  They therefore needs must fit.

But let me scrape the dirt away
  That hangs upon your face;
And stop and eat, for well you may
  Be in a hungry case.

Said John—It is my wedding-day,
  And all the world would stare,
If wife should dine at Edmonton
  And I should dine at Ware!

So, turning to his horse, he said—
  I am in haste to dine;
'Twas for your pleasure you came here,
  You shall go back for mine.

Ah, luckless speech, and bootless boast!
  For which he paid full dear;
For, while he spake, a braying ass
  Did sing most loud and clear;

Whereat his horse did snort, as he
  Had heard a lion roar,
And gallop'd off with all his might,
  As he had done before.

Away went Gilpin, and away
  Went Gilpin's hat and wig!
He lost them sooner than at first—
  For why?—they were too big!

Now, mistress Gilpin, when she saw
  Her husband posting down
Into the country far away,
  She pull'd out half a crown;

And thus unto the youth she said
  That drove them to the Bell—
This shall be yours when you bring back
  My husband safe and well.

The youth did ride, and soon did meet
  John coming back amain;
Whom in a trice he tried to stop,
  By catching at his rein;

But, not performing what he meant,
  And gladly would have done,
The frighted steed he frighted more,
  And made him faster run.

Away went Gilpin, and away
  Went post-boy at his heels!—
The post-boy's horse right glad to miss
  The lumb'ring of the wheels.

Six gentlemen upon the road,
  Thus seeing Gilpin fly,
With post-boy scamp'ring in the rear,
  They rais'd the hue and cry:

Stop thief! stop thief!—a highwayman!
  Not one of them was mute;
And all and each that pass'd that way
  Did join in the pursuit.

And now the turnpike gates again
  Flew open in short space;
The toll-men thinking, as before,
  That Gilpin rode a race.

And so he did—and won it too!—
  For he got first to town;
Nor stopp'd till where he had got up
  He did again get down.

Now let us sing—Long live the king,
  And Gilpin long live he;
And, when he next doth ride abroad,
  May I be there to see!

On the Loss of the Royal George

This poem commemorates the going down of the *Royal George*, in August, 1782, with Rear-Admiral Kempenfelt and all on board. The ship was refitting at Portsmouth, preparatory to proceeding with the fleet under Lord Howe to the relief of Gibraltar. She was careened, to permit the repairing of a leak below waterline. A large piece of her bottom fell out, and she went down at once, with the loss of at least eight hundred persons, for, besides the officers and men, there were many tradesmen and women and children aboard.

Toll for the Brave!
The brave that are no more!
All sunk beneath the wave
Fast by their native shore!

Eight hundred of the brave
Whose courage well was tried,
Had made the vessel heel
And laid her on her side.

A land-breeze shook the shrouds
And she was overset;
Down went the Royal George,
With all her crew complete.

Toll for the brave!
Brave Kempenfelt is gone;
His last sea-fight is fought,
His work of glory done.

It was not in the battle;
No tempest gave the shock;
She sprang no fatal leak,
She ran upon no rock.

His sword was in its sheath,
His fingers held the pen,
When Kempenfelt went down
With twice four hundred men.

—Weigh the vessel up
Once dreaded by our foes!
And mingle with our cup
The tears that England owes.

Her timbers yet are sound,
And she may float again
Full charged with England's thunder,
And plough the distant main:

But Kempenfelt is gone,
His victories are o'er;
And he and his eight hundred
Shall plough the wave no more.

The Poplar Field

The poplars are fell'd, farewell to the
    shade
And the whispering sound of the cool
    colonnade,
The winds play no longer, and sing in
    the leaves,
Nor Ouse on his bosom their image re-
    ceives.

Twelve years have elaps'd since I first
    took a view
Of my favourite field and the bank where
    they grew,

And now in the grass behold they are laid,
And the tree is my seat that once lent me a shade.

The blackbird has fled to another retreat
Where the hazels afford him a screen from the heat,
And the scene where his melody charm'd me before,
Resounds with his sweet-flowing ditty no more.

My fugitive years are all hasting away,
And I must ere long lie as lowly as they,
With a turf on my breast, and a stone at my head,
Ere another such grove shall arise in its stead.

'Tis a sight to engage me, if any thing can,
To muse on the perishing pleasures of man;
Though his life be a dream, his enjoyments, I see,
Have a being less durable even than he.

RICHARD BRINSLEY SHERIDAN (1751-1816)

The Critic; or, A Tragedy Rehearsed

A Dramatic Piece in Three Acts

To Mrs. Greville

Madam,—In requesting your permission to address the following pages to you, which, as they aim themselves to be critical, require every protection and allowance that approving taste or friendly prejudice can give them, I yet ventured to mention no other motive than the gratification of private friendship and esteem. Had I suggested a hope that your implied approbation would give a sanction to their defects, your particular reserve, and dislike to the reputation of critical taste, as well as of poetical talent, would have made you refuse the protection of your name to such a purpose. However, I am not so ungrateful as now to attempt to combat this disposition in you. I shall not here presume to argue that the present state of poetry claims and expects every assistance that taste and example can afford it; nor endeavour to prove that a fastidious concealment of the most elegant productions of judgment and fancy is an ill return for the possession of those endowments. Continue to deceive yourself in the idea that you are known only to be eminently admired and regarded for the valuable qualities that attach private friendships, and the graceful talents that adorn conversation. Enough of what you have written has stolen into full public notice to answer my purpose; and you will, perhaps, be the only person, conversant in elegant literature, who shall read this address and not perceive that by publishing your particular approbation of the following drama, I have a more interested object than to boast the true respect and regard with which I have the honour to be, Madam, your very sincere and obedient humble servant,

R. B. SHERIDAN.

DRAMATIS PERSONÆ

SIR FRETFUL PLAGIARY	INTERPRETER
PUFF	UNDER PROMPTER
DANGLE	MR. HOPKINS
SNEER	MRS. DANGLE
SIGNOR PASTICCIO RITORNELLO	SIGNORE PASTICCIO RITORNELLO

Scenemen, Musicians, *and* Servants.

CHARACTERS OF THE TRAGEDY

LORD BURLEIGH	SON
GOVERNOR OF TILBURY FORT	CONSTABLE
EARL OF LEICESTER	THAMES
SIR WALTER RALEIGH	TILBURINA
SIR CHRISTOPHER HATTON	CONFIDANT
MASTER OF THE HORSE	JUSTICE'S LADY
DON FEROLO WHISKERANDOS	FIRST NIECE
BEEFEATER	SECOND NIECE
JUSTICE	

Knights, Guards, Constables, Sentinels, Servants, Chorus, Rivers, Attendants, &c., &c.

SCENE—LONDON: *in* DANGLE'S *House during the First Act, and throughout the rest of the Play in* DRURY LANE THEATRE.

PROLOGUE

BY THE HONOURABLE RICHARD FITZPATRICK

THE sister Muses, whom these realms obey,
Who o'er the drama hold divided sway,
Sometimes by evil counsellors, 'tis said,
Like earth-born potentates have been misled.
In those gay days of wickedness and wit,
When Villiers criticised what Dryden writ,
The tragic queen, to please a tasteless crowd,
Had learn'd to bellow, rant, and roar so loud,
That frighten'd Nature, her best friend before,
The blustering beldam's company foreswore;
Her comic sister, who had wit 'tis true,
With all her merits, had her failings too:
And would sometimes in mirthful moments use
A style too flippant for a well-bred muse;
Then female modesty abash'd began

To seek the friendly refuge of the fan,
Awhile behind that slight intrenchment stood,
Till driven from thence, she left the stage for good.
In our more pious, and far chaster times,
These sure no longer are the Muse's crimes!
But some complain that, former faults to shun,
The reformation to extremes has run.
The frantic hero's wild delirium past,
Now insipidity succeeds bombast:
So slow Melpomene's cold numbers creep,
Here dulness seems her drowsy court to keep,
And we are scarce awake, whilst you are fast asleep.
Thalia, once so ill-behaved and rude,
Reform'd, is now become an arrant prude;
Retailing nightly to the yawning pit
The purest morals, undefiled by wit!
Our author offers, in these motley scenes,
A slight remonstrance to the drama's queens:
Nor let the goddesses be over nice;
Free-spoken subjects give the best advice.
Although not quite a novice in his trade,
His cause to-night requires no common aid.
To this, a friendly, just, and powerful court,
I come ambassador to beg support.
Can he undaunted brave the critic's rage?
In civil broils with brother bards engage?
Hold forth their errors to the public eye,
Nay more, e'en newspapers themselves defy?
Say, must his single arm encounter all?
By number vanquish'd, e'en the brave may fall;
And though no leader should success distrust,
Whose troops are willing, and whose cause is just;
To bid such hosts of angry foes defiance,
His chief dependence must be, your alliance.

ACT I

SCENE I.—*A Room in* DANGLE'S *House*

MR. *and* MRS. DANGLE *discovered at breakfast, and reading newspapers*

Dang. [*Reading.*] *Brutus to Lord North.—Letter the second on the State of the Army*—Psha! *To the first L dash D of the A dash Y.— Genuine extract of a Letter from St. Kitt's.—Coxheath Intelligence.— It is now confidently asserted that Sir Charles Hardy*—Psha! nothing but about the fleet and the nation!—and I hate all politics but theatrical politics.—Where's the Morning Chronicle?

Mrs. Dang. Yes, that's your Gazette.

Dang. So, here we have it.—[*Reads.*] *Theatrical intelligence extraordinary.—We hear there is a new tragedy in rehearsal at Drury Lane Theatre, called the Spanish Armada, said to be written by Mr. Puff, a gentleman well known in the theatrical world. If we may allow ourselves to give credit to the report of the performers, who, truth to say, are in general but indifferent judges, this piece abounds with the most striking and received beauties of modern composition.*—So! I am very glad my friend Puff's tragedy is in such forwardness.—Mrs. Dangle, my dear, you will be very glad to hear that Puff's tragedy——

Mrs. Dang. Lord, Mr. Dangle, why will you plague me about such nonsense?—Now the plays are begun I shall have no peace.—Isn't it sufficient to make yourself ridiculous by your passion for the theatre, without continually teasing me to join you? Why can't you ride your hobby-horse without desiring to place me on a pillion behind you, Mr. Dangle?

Dang. Nay, my dear, I was only going to read——

Mrs. Dang. No, no; you will never read anything that's worth listening to. You hate to hear about your country; there are letters every day with Roman signatures, demonstrating the certainty of an invasion, and proving that the nation is utterly undone. But you never will read anything to entertain one.

Dang. What has a woman to do with politics, Mrs. Dangle?

Mrs. Dang. And what have you to do with the theatre, Mr. Dangle? Why should you affect the character of a critic? I have no patience with you!—haven't you made yourself the jest of all your acquaintance by your interference in matters where you have no business? Are you not called a theatrical Quidnunc, and a mock Mæcenas to second-hand authors?

Dang. True; my power with the managers is pretty notorious. But is it no credit to have applications from all quarters for my interest—from lords to recommend fiddlers, from ladies to get boxes, from authors to get answers, and from actors to get engagements?

Mrs. Dang. Yes, truly; you have contrived to get a share in all the plague and trouble of theatrical property, without the profit, or even the credit of the abuse that attends it.

Dang. I am sure, Mrs. Dangle, you are no loser by it, however; you have all the advantages of it. Mightn't you, last winter, have had the reading of the new pantomime a fortnight previous to its performance? And doesn't Mr. Fosbrook let you take places for a play before it is advertised, and set you down for a box for every new piece through the season? And didn't my friend, Mr. Smatter, dedicate his last farce to you at my particular request, Mrs. Dangle?

Mrs. Dang. Yes; but wasn't the farce damned, Mr. Dangle? And to be sure it is extremely pleasant to have one's house made the motley rendezvous of all the lackeys of literature; the very high 'Change of trading authors and jobbing critics!—Yes, my drawing-room is an absolute register-office for candidate actors, and poets without character.— Then to be continually alarmed with misses and ma'ams piping hysteric changes on Juliets and Dorindas, Pollys and Ophelias; and the very furniture trembling at the probationary starts and unprovoked rants of would-be Richards and Hamlets!—And what is worse than all, now that the manager has monopolized the Opera House, haven't we the signors and signoras calling here, sliding their smooth semibreves, and gargling glib divisions in their outlandish throats—with foreign emissaries and French spies, for aught I know, disguised like fiddlers and figure dancers?

Dang. Mercy! Mrs. Dangle!

Mrs. Dang. And to employ yourself so idly at such an alarming crisis as this too—when, if you had the least spirit, you would have been at the head of one of the Westminster associations—or trailing a volunteer pike in the Artillery Ground! But you—o' my conscience, I believe, if the French were landed to-morrow, your first inquiry would be, whether they had brought a theatrical troop with them.

Dang. Mrs. Dangle, it does not signify—I say the stage is *the mirror of Nature,* and the actors are *the Abstract and brief Chronicles of the Time:* and pray what can a man of sense study better?—Besides, you will not easily persuade me that there is no credit or importance in being at the head of a band of critics, who take upon them to decide for the whole town, whose opinion and patronage all writers solicit, and whose recommendation no manager dares refuse.

Mrs. Dang. Ridiculous!—Both managers and authors of the least merit laugh at your pretensions.—The public is their critic—without whose fair approbation they know no play can rest on the stage, and with whose applause they welcome such attacks as yours, and laugh at the malice of them, where they can't at the wit.

Dang. Very well, madam—very well!

Enter SERVANT

Ser. Mr. Sneer, sir, to wait on you.

Dang. Oh, show Mr. Sneer up.—[*Exit* SERVANT.]—Plague on't, now we must appear loving and affectionate, or Sneer will hitch us into a story.

Mrs. Dang. With all my heart; you can't be more ridiculous than you are.

Dang. You are enough to provoke—

Enter SNEER

Ha! my dear Sneer, I am vastly glad to see you.—My dear, here's Mr. Sneer.

Mrs. Dang. Good-morning to you, sir.

Dang. Mrs. Dangle and I have been diverting ourselves with the papers. Pray, Sneer, won't you go to Drury Lane Theatre the first night of Puff's tragedy?

Sneer. Yes; but I suppose one shan't be able to get in, for on the first night of a new piece they always fill the house with orders to support it. But here, Dangle, I have brought you two pieces, one of which you must exert yourself to make the managers accept, I can tell you that; for 'tis written by a person of consequence.

Dang. So! now my plagues are beginning.

Sneer. Ay, I am glad of it, for now you'll be happy. Why, my dear Dangle, it is a pleasure to see how you enjoy your volunteer fatigue, and your solicited solicitations.

Dang. It's a great trouble—yet, egad, it's pleasant too.—Why, sometimes of a morning I have a dozen people call on me at breakfast-time, whose faces I never saw before, nor ever desire to see again.

Sneer. That must be very pleasant indeed!

Dang. And not a week but I receive fifty letters, and not a line in them about any business of my own.

Sneer. An amusing correspondence!

Dang. [*Reading.*] *Bursts into tears and exit.*—What, is this a tragedy?

Sneer. No, that's a genteel comedy, not a translation—only taken from the French: it is written in a style which they have lately tried to run down; the true sentimental, and nothing ridiculous in it from the beginning to the end.

Mrs. Dang. Well, if they had kept to that, I should not have been such an enemy to the stage; there was some edification to be got from those pieces, Mr. Sneer!

Sneer. I am quite of your opinion, Mrs. Dangle: the theatre, in proper hands, might certainly be made the school of morality; but now, I am sorry to say it, people seem to go there principally for their entertainment!

Mrs. Dang. It would have been more to the credit of the managers to have kept it in the other line.

Sneer. Undoubtedly, madam; and hereafter perhaps to have had it recorded, that in the midst of a luxurious and dissipated age, they preserved two houses in the capital, where the conversation was always moral at least, if not entertaining!

Dang. Now, egad, I think the worst alteration is in the nicety of the audience!—No *double-entendre,* no smart innuendo admitted; even Vanbrugh and Congreve obliged to undergo a bungling reformation!

Sneer. Yes, and our prudery in this respect is just on a par with the artificial bashfulness of a courtesan, who increases the blush upon her cheek in an exact proportion to the diminution of her modesty.

Dang. Sneer can't even give the public a good word! But what have we here?—This seems a very odd——

Sneer. Oh, that's a comedy on a very new plan; replete with wit and mirth, yet of a most serious moral! You see it is called *The Reformed House-breaker;* where, by the mere force of humour, housebreaking is put in so ridiculous a light, that if the piece has its proper run, I have no doubt but that bolts and bars will be entirely useless by the end of the season.

Dang. Egad, this is new indeed!

Sneer. Yes; it is written by a particular friend of mine, who has discovered that the follies and foibles of society are subjects unworthy the notice of the comic muse, who should be taught to stoop only to the greater vices and blacker crimes of humanity—gibbeting capital offences in five acts, and pillorying petty larcenies in two.—In short, his idea is to dramatize the penal laws, and make the stage a court of ease to the Old Bailey.

DANG. It is truly moral.

Re-enter SERVANT

Ser. Sir Fretful Plagiary, sir.

Dang. Beg him to walk up.—[*Exit* SERVANT.] Now, Mrs. Dangle, Sir Fretful Plagiary is an author to your own taste.

Mrs. Dang. I confess he is a favourite of mine, because everybody else abuses him.

Sneer. Very much to the credit of your charity, madam, if not of your judgment.

Dang. But, egad, he allows no merit to any author but himself, that's the truth on't—though he's my friend.

Sneer. Never.—He is as envious as an old maid verging on the desperation of six and thirty; and then the insidious humility with which he seduces you to give a free opinion on any of his works, can be exceeded only by the petulant arrogance with which he is sure to reject your observations.

Dang. Very true, egad—though he's my friend.

Sneer. Then his affected contempt of all newspaper strictures; though, at the same time, he is the sorest man alive, and shrinks like scorched parchment from the fiery ordeal of true criticism: yet he is so covetous of popularity, that he had rather be abused than not mentioned at all.

Dang. There's no denying it—though he is my friend.

Sneer. You have read the tragedy he has just finished, haven't you?

Dang. Oh, yes; he sent it to me yesterday.

Sneer. Well, and you think it execrable, don't you?

Dang. Why, between ourselves, egad, I must own—though he is my friend—that it is one of the most——He's here—[*Aside.*]—finished and most admirable perform——

Sir Fret. [*Without.*] Mr. Sneer with him did you say?

Enter SIR FRETFUL PLAGIARY

Dang. Ah, my dear friend!—Egad, we were just speaking of your tragedy.—Admirable, Sir Fretful, admirable!

Sneer. You never did anything beyond it, Sir Fretful—never in your life.

Sir Fret. You make me extremely happy; for without a compliment, my dear Sneer, there isn't a man in the world whose judgment I value as I do yours and Mr. Dangle's.

Mrs. Dang. They are only laughing at you, Sir Fretful; for it was but just now that——

Dang. Mrs. Dangle!—Ah, Sir Fretful, you know Mrs. Dangle.— My friend Sneer was rallying just now:—he knows how she admires you, and——

Sir. Fret. O Lord, I am sure Mr. Sneer has more taste and sincerity than to——[*Aside.*] A damned double-faced fellow!

Dang. Yes, yes—Sneer will jest—but a better humoured——

Sir Fret. Oh, I know——

Dang. He has a ready turn for ridicule—his wit costs him nothing.

Sir Fret. No, egad—or I should wonder how he came by it.

[*Aside.*

Mrs. Dang. Because his jest is always at the expense of his friend.

[*Aside.*

Dang. But, Sir Fretful, have you sent your play to the managers yet?—or can I be of any service to you?

Sir Fret. No, no, I thank you: I believe the piece had sufficient recommendation with it.—I thank you though.—I sent it to the manager of Covent Garden Theatre this morning.

Sneer. I should have thought now, that it might have been cast (as the actors call it) better at Drury Lane.

Sir Fret. O Lud! no—never send a play there while I live—hark'ee!

[*Whispers* SNEER.

Sneer. Writes himself!—I know he does.

Sir Fret. I say nothing—I take away from no man's merit—am hurt at no man's good fortune—I say nothing.—But this I will say—through all my knowledge of life, I have observed—that there is not a passion so strongly rooted in the human heart as envy.

Sneer. I believe you have reason for what you say, indeed.

Sir Fret. Besides—I can tell you it is not always so safe to leave a play in the hands of those who write themselves.

Sneer. What, they may steal from them, hey, my dear Plagiary?

Sir Fret. Steal!—to be sure they may; and, egad, serve your best thoughts as gypsies do stolen children, disfigure them to make 'em pass for their own.

Sneer. But your present work is a sacrifice to Melpomene, and he, you know, never——

Sir Fret. That's no security: a dexterous plagiarist may do anything. Why, sir, for aught I know, he might take out some of the best things in my tragedy, and put them into his own comedy.

Sneer. That might be done, I dare be sworn.

Sir Fret. And then, if such a person gives you the least hint or assistance, he is devilish apt to take the merit of the whole——

Dang. If it succeeds.

Sir Fret. Ay, but with regard to this piece, I think I can hit that gentleman, for I can safely swear he never read it.

Sneer. I'll tell you how you may hurt him more.

Sir Fret. How?

Sneer. Swear he wrote it.

Sir Fret. Plague on't now, Sneer, I shall take it ill!—I believe you want to take away my character as an author.

Sneer. Then I am sure you ought to be very much obliged to me.

Sir Fret. Hey!—sir!——

Dang. Oh, you know, he never means what he says.

Sir Fret. Sincerely then—do you like the piece?

Sneer. Wonderfully!

Sir Fret. But come, now, there must be something that you think might be mended, hey——Mr. Dangle, has nothing struck you?

Dang. Why, faith, it is but an ungracious thing for the most part, to——

Sir Fret. With most authors it is just so, indeed; they are in general strangely tenacious! But, for my part, I am never so well pleased as when a judicious critic points out any defect to me; for what is the purpose of showing a work to a friend, if you don't mean to profit by his opinion?

Sneer. Very true.—Why, then, though I seriously admire the piece upon the whole, yet there is one small objection; which, if you'll give me leave, I'll mention.

Sir Fret. Sir, you can't oblige me more.

Sneer. I think it wants incident.

Sir Fret. Good God! you surprise me!—wants incident!

Sneer. Yes; I own I think the incidents are too few.

Sir Fret. Good God! Believe me, Mr. Sneer, there is no person for whose judgment I have a more implicit deference. But I protest to you, Mr. Sneer, I am only apprehensive that the incidents are too crowded.— My dear Dangle, how does it strike you?

Dang. Really I can't agree with my friend Sneer. I think the plot quite sufficient; and the four first acts by many degrees the best I ever read or saw in my life. If I might venture to suggest anything, it is that the interest rather falls off in the fifth.

Sir Fret. Rises, I believe you mean, sir.

Dang. No, I don't upon my word.

Sir Fret. Yes, yes, you do, upon my soul!—it certainly don't fall off, I assure you.—No, no; it don't fall off.

Dang. Now, Mrs. Dangle, didn't you say it struck you in the same light?

Mrs. Dang. No, indeed, I did not.—I did not see a fault in any part of the play, from the beginning to the end.

Sir Fret. Upon my soul, the women are the best judges after all!

Mrs. Dang. Or, if I made any objection, I am sure it was to nothing in the piece; but that I was afraid it was on the whole, a little too long.

Sir Fret. Pray, madam, do you speak as to duration of time; or do you mean that the story is tediously spun out?

Mrs. Dang. O Lud! no.—I speak only with reference to the usual length of acting plays.

Sir Fret. Then I am very happy—very happy indeed—because the

play is a short play, a remarkably short play. I should not venture to
differ with a lady on a point of taste; but on these occasions, the watch,
you know, is the critic.

Mrs. Dang. Then, I suppose it must have been Mr. Dangle's drawl-
ing manner of reading it to me.

Sir Fret. Oh, if Mr. Dangle read it, that's quite another affair!—
But I assure you, Mrs. Dangle, the first evening you can spare me three
hours and a half, I'll undertake to read you the whole, from beginning
to end, with the prologue and epilogue, and allow time for the music
between the acts.

Mrs. Dang. I hope to see it on the stage next.

Dang. Well, Sir Fretful, I wish you may be able to get rid as easily
of the newspaper criticisms as you do of ours.

Sir Fret. The newspapers! Sir, they are the most villainous—
licentious—abominable—infernal.—Not that I ever read them—no—I
make it a rule never to look into a newspaper.

Dang. You are quite right; for it certainly must hurt an author of
delicate feelings to see the liberties they take.

Sir Fret. No, quite the contrary! their abuse is, in fact, the best
panegyric—I like it of all things. An author's reputation is only in
danger from their support.

Sneer. Why, that's true—and that attack, now, on you the other
day——

Sir Fret. What? where?

Dang. Ay, you mean in a paper of Thursday: it was completely
ill-natured, to be sure.

Sir Fret. Oh so much the better.—Ha! ha! ha! I wouldn't have
it otherwise.

Dang. Certainly it is only to be laughed at; for——

Sir Fret. You don't happen to recollect what the fellow said, do
you?

Sneer. Pray, Dangle—Sir Fretful seems a little anxious——

Sir Fret. O Lud, no!—anxious!—not I—not the least.—I—but one
may as well hear, you know.

Dang. Sneer, do you recollect?—[*Aside to* Sneer.] Make out
something.

Sneer. [*Aside to* Dangle.] I will.—[*Aloud.*] Yes, yes, I remember
perfectly.

Sir Fret. Well, and pray now—not that it signifies—what might the
gentleman say?

Sneer. Why, he roundly asserts that you have not the slightest invention or original genius whatever; though you are the greatest traducer of all other authors living.

Sir Fret. Ha! ha! ha!—very good!

Sneer. That as to comedy, you have not one idea of your own, he believes, even in your commonplace-book—where stray jokes and pilfered witticisms are kept with as much method as the ledger of the lost and stolen office.

Sir Fret. Ha! ha! ha!—very pleasant!

Sneer. Nay, that you are so unlucky as not to have the skill even to steal with taste:—but that you glean from the refuse of obscure volumes, where more judicious plagiarists have been before you; so that the body of your work is a composition of dregs and sentiments—like a bad tavern's worst wine.

Sir Fret. Ha! ha!

Sneer. In your more serious efforts, he says, your bombast would be less intolerable, if the thoughts were ever suited to the expression; but the homeliness of the sentiment stares through the fantastic encumbrance of its fine language, like a clown in one of the new uniforms!

Sir Fret. Ha! ha!

Sneer. That your occasional tropes and flowers suit the general coarseness of your style, as tambour sprigs would a ground of linsey-woolsey; while your imitations of Shakspeare resemble the mimicry of Falstaff's page, and are about as near the standard as the original.

Sir Fret. Ha!

Sneer. In short, that even the finest passages you steal are of no service to you; for the poverty of your own language prevents their assimilating; so that they lie on the surface like lumps of marl on a barren moor, encumbering what it is not in their power to fertilize!

Sir Fret. [*After great agitation.*] Now, another person would be vexed at this!

Sneer. Oh! but I wouldn't have told you—only to divert you.

Sir Fret. I know it—I am diverted.—Ha! ha! ha!—not the least invention!—Ha! ha! ha!—very good!—very good!

Sneer. Yes—no genius! ha! ha! ha!

Dang. A severe rogue! ha! ha! ha! But you are quite right, Sir Fretful, never to read such nonsense.

Sir Fret. To be sure—for if there is anything to one's praise, it is a foolish vanity to be gratified at it; and, if it is abuse—why one is always sure to hear of it from one damned good-natured friend or other!

Enter SERVANT

Ser. Sir, there is an Italian gentleman, with a French interpreter, and three young ladies, and a dozen musicians, who say they are sent by Lady Rondeau and Mrs. Fugue.

Dang. Gadso! they come by appointment!—Dear Mrs. Dangle, do let them know I'll see them directly.

Mrs. Dang. You know, Mr. Dangle, I shan't understand a word they say.

Dang. But you hear there's an interpreter.

Mrs. Dang. Well, I'll try to endure their complaisance till you come.
                                                                    [*Exit.*

Ser. And Mr. Puff, sir, has sent word that the last rehearsal is to be this morning, and that he'll call on you presently.

Dang. That's true—I shall certainly be at home.—[*Exit* SERVANT.] —Now, Sir Fretful, if you have a mind to have justice done you in the way of answer, egad, Mr. Puff's your man.

Sir Fret. Psha! sir, why should I wish to have it answered, when I tell you I am pleased at it?

Dang. True, I had forgot that. But I hope you are not fretted at what Mr. Sneer——

Sir Fret. Zounds! no, Mr. Dangle; don't I tell you these things never fret me in the least?

Dang. Nay, I only thought——

Sir Fret. And let me tell you, Mr. Dangle, 'tis damned affronting in you to suppose that I am hurt when I tell you I am not.

Sneer. But why so warm, Sir Fretful?

Sir Fret. Gad's life! Mr. Sneer, you are as absurd as Dangle: how often must I repeat it to you, that nothing can vex me but your supposing it possible for me to mind the damned nonsense you have been repeating to me!—and, let me tell you, if you continue to believe this, you must mean to insult me, gentlemen—and, then, your disrespect will affect me no more than the newspaper criticisms—and I shall treat it with exactly the same calm indifference and philosophic contempt—and so your servant.   [*Exit.*

Sneer. Ha! ha! ha! poor Sir Fretful! Now will he go and vent his philosophy in anonymous abuse of all modern critics and authors.— But, Dangle, you must get your friend Puff to take me to the rehearsal of his tragedy.

Dang. I'll answer for't, he'll thank you for desiring it. But come and help me to judge of this musical family: they are recommended by people of consequence, I assure you.

Sneer. I am at your disposal the whole morning!—but I thought you had been a decided critic in music as well as in literature.

Dang. So I am—but I have a bad ear. I'faith, Sneer, though, I am afraid we were a little too severe on Sir Fretful—though he is my friend.

Sneer. Why, 'tis certain, that unnecessarily to mortify the vanity of any writer is a cruelty which mere dulness never can deserve; but where a base and personal malignity usurps the place of literary emulation, the aggressor deserves neither quarter nor pity.

Dang. That's true, egad!—though he's my friend!

SCENE II.—*A drawing-room in* DANGLE'S *House*

MRS. DANGLE, SIGNOR PASTICCIO RITORNELLO, SIGNORE PASTICCIO RITORNELLO, INTERPRETER, *and* MUSICIANS *discovered.*

Interp. Je dis, madame, j'ai l'honneur to introduce et de vous demander votre protection pour le Signor Pasticcio Ritornello et pour sa charmante famille.

Signor Past. Ah! vosignoria, noi vi preghiamo di favoritevi colla vostra protezione.

1 *Signora Past.* Vosignoria fatevi questi grazie.

2 *Signora Past.* Si, signora.

Interp. Madame—me interpret.—C'est à dire—in English—qu'ils vous prient de leur faire l'honneur——

Mrs. Dang. I say again, gentlemen, I don't understand a word you say.

Signor Past. Questo signore spiegheró——

Interp. Oui—me interpret.—Nous avons les lettres de recommendation pour Monsieur Dangle de——

Mrs. Dang. Upon my word, sir, I don't understand you.

Signor Past. La Contessa Rondeau è nostra padrona.

3 *Signora Past.* Si, padre, et Miladi Fugue.

Interp. O!—me interpret.—Madame, ils disent—in English—Qu'ils ont l'honneur d'être protégés de ces dames.—You understand?

Mrs. Dang. No, sir,—no understand!

Enter DANGLE *and* SNEER

Interp. Ah, voici, Monsieur Dangle!

All Italians. Ah! Signor Dangle!

Mrs. Dang. Mr. Dangle, here are two very civil gentlemen trying to make themselves understood, and I don't know which is the interpreter.

Dang. Eh, bien!

[*The* INTERPRETER *and* SIGNOR PASTICCIO
here speak at the same time.]

Interp. Monsieur Dangle, le grand bruit de vos talens pour la critique, et de votre intérêt avec messieurs les directeurs à tous les théâtres——

Signor Past. Vosignoria siete si famoso par la vostra conoscenza, e vostra interessa colla le direttore da——

Dang. Egad, I think the interpreter is the hardest to be understood of the two!

Sneer. Why, I thought, Dangle, you had been an admirable linguist!

Dang. So I am, if they would not talk so damned fast.

Sneer. Well, I'll explain that—the less time we lose in hearing them the better—for that, I suppose, is what they are brought here for.

[*Speaks to* SIGNOR PASTICCIO—*they sing trios,
&c.,* DANGLE *beating out of time.*]

Enter SERVANT *and whispers* DANGLE

Dang. Show him up.—[*Exit* SERVANT.] Bravo! admirable! bravissimo! admirablissimo!—Ah! Sneer! where will you find voices such as these in England?

Sneer. Not easily.

Dang. But Puff is coming.—Signor and little signoras obligatissimo! —Sposa Signora Danglena—Mrs. Dangle, shall I beg you to offer them some refreshments, and take their address in the next room.

[*Exit* MRS. DANGLE *with* SIGNOR PASTICCIO,
SIGNORE PASTICCIO, MUSICIANS, *and*
INTERPRETER, *ceremoniously.*]

Re-enter SERVANT

Ser. Mr. Puff, sir.   [*Exit.*

Enter PUFF

Dang. My dear Puff!

Puff. My dear Dangle, how is it with you?

Dang. Mr. Sneer, give me leave to introduce Mr. Puff to you.

Puff. Mr. Sneer is this?—Sir, he is a gentleman whom I have long panted for the honour of knowing—a gentleman whose critical talents and transcendent judgment——

Sneer. Dear sir——

Dang. Nay, don't be modest, Sneer; my friend Puff only talks to you in the style of his profession.

Sneer. His profession.

Puff. Yes, sir; I make no secret of the trade I follow: among friends and brother authors, Dangle knows I love to be frank on the subject, and to advertise myself *vivâ voce.*—I am, sir, a practitioner in panegyric, or, to speak more plainly, a professor of the art of puffing, at your service—or anybody else's.

Sneer. Sir, you are very obliging!—I believe, Mr. Puff, I have often admired your talents in the daily prints.

Puff. Yes, sir, I flatter myself I do as much business in that way as any six of the fraternity in town.—Devilish hard work all the summer, friend Dangle,—never worked harder! But, hark'ee,—the winter managers were a little sore, I believe.

Dang. No; I believe they took it all in good part.

Puff. Ay! then that must have been affectation in them: for, egad, there were some of the attacks which there was no laughing at!

Sneer. Ay, the humorous ones.—But I should think, Mr. Puff, that authors would in general be able to do this sort of work for themselves.

Puff. Why, yes—but in a clumsy way. Besides, we look on that as an encroachment, and so take the opposite side. I dare say, now, you conceive half the very civil paragraphs and advertisements you see to be written by the parties concerned, or their friends? No such thing: nine out of ten manufactured by me in the way of business.

Sneer. Indeed!

Puff. Even the auctioneers now—the auctioneers, I say—though the rogues have lately got some credit for their language—not an article of the merit theirs: take them out of their pulpits, and they are as dull as catalogues!—No, sir; 'twas I first enriched their style—'twas I first taught them to crowd their advertisements with panegyrical superlatives, each epithet rising above the other, like the bidders in their own auction rooms! From me they learned to inlay their phraseology with variegated chips of exotic metaphor: by me too their inventive faculties were called forth:—yes, sir, by me they were instructed to clothe ideal walls with gratuitous fruits—to insinuate obsequious rivulets into visionary groves —to teach courteous shrubs to nod their approbation of the grateful soil; or on emergencies to raise upstart oaks, where there never had been an acorn; to create a delightful vicinage without the assistance of a neighbour; or fix the temple of Hygeia in the fens of Lincolnshire!

Dang. I am sure you have done them infinite service; for now, when a gentleman is ruined, he parts with his house with some credit.

Sneer. Service! if they had any gratitude, they would erect a statue to him; they would figure him as a presiding Mercury, the god of traffic and fiction, with a hammer in his hand instead of a caduceus.—But pray, Mr. Puff, what first put you on exercising your talents in this way?

Puff. Egad, sir, sheer necessity!—the proper parent of an art so nearly allied to invention. You must know, Mr. Sneer, that from the first time I tried my hand at an advertisement, my success was such, that for some time after I led a most extraordinary life indeed!

Sneer. How, pray?

Puff. Sir, I supported myself two years entirely by my misfortunes.

Sneer. By your misfortunes!

Puff. Yes, sir, assisted by long sickness, and other occasional disorders: and a very comfortable living I had of it.

Sneer. From sickness and misfortunes! You practised as a doctor and an attorney at once?

Puff. No, egad; both maladies and miseries were my own.

Sneer. Hey! what the plague!

Dang. 'Tis true, i'faith.

Puff. Hark'ee!—By advertisements—*To the charitable and humane!* and *To those whom Providence hath blessed with affluence!*

Sneer. Oh, I understand you.

Puff. And, in truth, I deserved what I got! for, I suppose never man went through such a series of calamities in the same space of time. Sir, I was five times made a bankrupt, and reduced from a state of affluence, by a train of unavoidable misfortunes: then, sir, though a very industrious tradesman, I was twice burned out, and lost my little all both times: I lived upon those fires a month. I soon after was confined by a most excruciating disorder, and lost the use of my limbs: that told very well; for I had the case strongly attested, and went about to collect the subscriptions myself.

Dang. Egad, I believe that was when you first called on me.

Puff. In November last?—O no; I was at that time a close prisoner in the Marshalsea, for a debt benevolently contracted to serve a friend. I was afterwards twice tapped for a dropsy, which declined into a very profitable consumption. I was then reduced to—O no—then, I became a widow with six helpless children, after having had eleven husbands pressed, and being left every time eight months gone with child, and without money to get me into an hospital!

Sneer. And you bore all with patience, I make no doubt?

Puff. Why yes; though I made some occasional attempts at *felo de se;* but as I did not find those rash actions answer, I left off killing myself very soon. Well, sir, at last, what with bankruptcies, fires, gout, dropsies, imprisonments and other valuable calamities, having got together a pretty handsome sum, I determined to quit a business which had always gone rather against my conscience, and in a more liberal way still to indulge my talents for fiction and embellishment, through my favourite channels of diurnal communication—and so, sir, you have my history.

Sneer. Most obligingly communicative indeed! and your confession, if published, might certainly serve the cause of true charity, by rescuing the most useful channels of appeal to benevolence from the cant of imposition. But surely, Mr. Puff, there is no great mystery in your present profession?

Puff. Mystery, sir! I will take upon me to say the matter was never scientifically treated nor reduced to rule before.

Sneer. Reduced to rule!

Puff. O Lud, sir, you are very ignorant, I am afraid!—Yes, sir, puffing is of various sorts; the principal are, the puff direct, the puff preliminary, the puff collateral, the puff collusive, and the puff oblique, or puff by implication. These all assume, as circumstances require, the various forms of Letter to the Editor, Occasional Anecdote, Impartial Critique, Observation from Correspondent, or Advertisement from the Party.

Sneer. The puff direct, I can conceive——

Puff. O yes, that's simple enough! For instance,—a new comedy or farce is to be produced at one of the theatres (though by-the-by they don't bring out half what they ought to do)—the author, suppose Mr. Smatter, or Mr. Dapper, or any particular friend of mine—very well; the day before it is to be performed, I write an account of the manner in which it was received; I have the plot from the author, and only add— "characters strongly drawn—highly coloured—hand of a master—fund of genuine humour—mine of invention—neat dialogue—Attic salt." Then for the performance—"Mr. Dodd was astonishingly great in the character of Sir Harry. That universal and judicious actor, Mr. Palmer, perhaps never appeared to more advantage than in the colonel;—but it is not in the power of language to do justice to Mr. King: indeed he more than merited those repeated bursts of applause which he drew from a most brilliant and judicious audience. As to the scenery—the miraculous powers of Mr. De Loutherbourg's pencil are universally acknowledged. In short, we are at a loss which to admire most, the unrivalled genius of the author, the great attention and liberality of the managers, the wonderful abilities of the painter, or the incredible exertions of all the performers."

Sneer. That's pretty well indeed, sir.

Puff. Oh, cool!—quite cool!—to what I sometimes do.

Sneer. And do you think there are any who are influenced by this?

Puff. O Lud, yes, sir! the number of those who undergo the fatigue of judging for themselves is very small indeed.

Sneer. Well, sir, the puff preliminary.

Puff. Oh, that, sir, does well in the form of a caution. In a matter of gallantry now—Sir Flimsy Gossamer wishes to be well with Lady Fanny Fete—he applies to me—I open trenches for him with a paragraph in the Morning Post.—"It is recommended to the beautiful and accomplished Lady F four stars F dash E to be on her guard against that dangerous character, Sir F dash G; who, however pleasing and insinuating his manners may be, is certainly not remarkable for the *constancy of his attachments!*"—in italics. Here, you see, Sir Flimsy Gossamer is introduced to the particular notice of Lady Fanny, who perhaps never thought of him before—she finds herself publicly cautioned to avoid him, which naturally makes her desirous of seeing him; the observation of their acquaintance causes a pretty kind of mutual embarrassment; this produces a sort of sympathy of interest, which if Sir Flimsy is unable to improve effectually, he at least gains the credit of having their names mentioned together, by a particular set, and in a particular way—which nine times out of ten is the full accomplishment of modern gallantry.

Dang. Egad, Sneer, you will be quite an adept in the business.

Puff. Now, Sir, the puff collateral is much used as an appendage to advertisements, and may take the form of anecdote.—"Yesterday, as the celebrated George Bonmot was sauntering down St. James's Street, he met the lively Lady Mary Myrtle coming out of the park:—'Good God, Lady Mary, I'm surprised to meet you in a white jacket,—for I expected never to have seen you, but in a full-trimmed uniform and a light horseman's cap!'—'Heavens, George, where could you have learned that?'—'Why,' replied the wit, 'I just saw a print of you, in a new publication called the Camp Magazine; which, by-the-by, is a devilish clever thing, and is sold at No. 3, on the right hand of the way, two doors from the printing-office, the corner of Ivy Lane, Paternoster Row, price only one shilling.'"

Sneer. Very ingenious indeed!

Puff. But the puff collusive is the newest of any; for it acts in the disguise of determined hostility. It is much used by bold booksellers and enterprising poets.—"An indignant correspondent observes, that the new poem called *Beelzebub's Cotillon, or Proserpine's Fête Champêtre,* is one of the most unjustifiable performances he ever read. The severity with which certain characters are handled is quite shocking: and as there are many descriptions in it too warmly coloured for female delicacy, the shameful avidity with which this piece is bought by all people of fashion is a reproach on the taste of the times, and a disgrace to the delicacy of the age." Here you see the two strongest inducements are held forth; first that nobody ought to read it; and secondly, that everybody buys it: on the strength of which the publisher boldly prints the tenth edition, before he had Sold ten of the first; and then establishes it by threatening himself with the pillory, or absolutely indicting himself for *scan. mag.*

Dang. Ha! ha! ha!—'gad, I know it is so.

Puff. As to the puff oblique, or puff by implication, it is too various and extensive to be illustrated by an instance: it attracts in titles and presumes in patents; it lurks in the limitation of a subscription, and invites in the assurance of crowd and incommodation at public places; it delights to draw forth concealed merit, with a most disinterested assiduity; and sometimes wears a countenance of smiling censure and tender reproach. It has a wonderful memory for parliamentary debates, and will often give the whole speech of a favoured member with the most flattering accuracy. But, above all, it is a great dealer in reports and suppositions. It has the earliest intelligence of intended preferments that will reflect honour on the patrons; and embryo promotions of modest gentlemen, who know nothing of the matter themselves. It can hint a ribbon for implied services in the air of a common report; and with the carelessness of a casual paragraph, suggest officers into commands, to which they have no pretension but their wishes. This, sir, is the last principal class of the art of puffing—an art which I hope you will now agree with me is of the highest dignity, yielding a tablature of benevolence and public spirit; befriending equally trade, gallantry, criticism, and politics: the applause of genius—the register of charity—the triumph of heroism—the self-defence of contractors—the fame of orators—and the gazette of ministers.

Sneer. Sir, I am completely a convert both to the importance and ingenuity of your profession; and now, sir, there is but one thing which can possibly increase my respect for you, and that is, your permitting me to be present this morning at the rehearsal of your new trage——

Puff. Hush, for heaven's sake!—*My* tragedy!—Egad, Dangle, I take this very ill: you know how apprehensive I am of being known to be the author.

Dang. I'faith I would not have told—but it's in the papers, and your name at length in the Morning Chronicle.

Puff. Ah! those damned editors never can keep a secret!—Well, Mr. Sneer, no doubt you will do me great honour—I shall be infinitely happy—highly flattered——

Dang. I believe it must be near the time—shall we go together?

Puff. No; it will not be yet this hour, for they are always late at that theatre: besides, I must meet you there, for I have some little matters here to send to the papers, and a few paragraphs to scribble before I go. —[*Looking at memorandums.*] Here is *A conscientious Baker, on the subject of the Army Bread; and a Detester of visible Brickwork, in favour of the new invented Stucco;* both in the style of Junius, and promised for to-morrow. The Thames navigation too is at a stand. Misomud or Anti-shoal must go to work again directly.—Here too are some political memorandums—I see; ay—*To take Paul Jones and get the Indiamen out of the Shannon—reinforce Byron—compel the Dutch to*—so!—I must do that in the evening papers, or reserve it for the Morning Herald; for I know that I have undertaken to-morrow, besides, to establish the unanimity of the fleet in the Public Advertiser, and to shoot Charles Fox in the Morning Post.—So, egad, I ha'n't a moment to lose.

Dang. Well, we'll meet in the Green Room.

[*Exeunt severally.*

ACT II

SCENE I.—*The Theatre before the Curtain*

Enter DANGLE, PUFF, *and* SNEER

Puff. No, no, sir; what Shakespeare says of actors may be better applied to the purpose of plays; they ought to be *the abstract and brief chronicles of the time.* Therefore when history, and particularly the history of our own country, furnishes anything like a case in point, to the time in which an author writes, if he knows his own interest, he will take advantage of it; so, sir, I call my tragedy *The Spanish Armada;* and have laid the scene before Tilbury Fort.

Sneer. A most happy thought, certainly!

Dang. Egad it was—I told you so. But pray now, I don't understand how you have contrived to introduce any love into it.

Puff. Love! oh, nothing so easy! for it is a received point among poets, that where history gives you a good heroic outline for a play, you may fill up with a little love at your own discretion: in doing which, nine times out of ten, you only make up a deficiency in the private history of the times. Now, I rather think I have done this with some success.

Sneer. No scandal about Queen Elizabeth, I hope?

Puff. O Lud! no, no;—I only suppose the governor of Tilbury Fort's daughter to be in love with the son of the Spanish admiral.

Sneer. Oh, is that all!

Dang. Excellent, i'faith! I see at once. But won't this appear rather improbable?

Puff. To be sure it will—but what the plague! a play is not to show occurrences that happen every day, but things just so strange, that though they never did, they might happen.

Sneer. Certainly nothing is unnatural, that is not physically impossible.

Puff. Very true—and for that matter Don Ferolo Whiskerandos, for that's the lover's name, might have been over here in the train of the Spanish ambassador, or Tilburina, for that is the lady's name, might have been in love with him, from having heard his character, or seen his picture; or from knowing that he was the last man in the world she ought to be in love with—or for any other good female reason.—However, sir, the fact is, that though she is but a knight's daughter, egad! she is in love like any princess!

Dang. Poor young lady! I feel for her already! for I can conceive how great the conflict must be between her passion and her duty; her love for her country, and her love for Don Ferolo Whiskerandos!

Puff. Oh, amazing!—her poor susceptible heart is swayed to and fro by contending passions like——

Enter UNDER PROMPTER

Und. Promp. Sir, the scene is set, and everything is ready to begin, if you please.

Puff. Egad, then we'll lose no time.

Und. Promp. Though, I believe, sir, you will find it very short, for all the performers have profited by the kind permission you granted them.

Puff. Hey! what?

Und. Promp. You know, sir, you gave them leave to cut out or omit whatever they found heavy or unnecessary to the plot, and I must own they have taken very liberal advantage of your indulgence.

Puff. Well, well.—They are in general very good judges, and I know I am luxuriant.—Now, Mr. Hopkins, as soon as you please.

Und. Promp. [*To the* Orchestra.] Gentlemen, will you play a few bars of something, just to——

Puff. Ay, that's right; for as we have the scenes and dresses, egad, we'll go to't, as if it was the first night's performance;—but you need not mind stopping between the acts—[*Exit* UNDER PROMPTER.—Orchestra *play—then the bell rings.*] Soh! stand clear, gentlemen. Now you know there will be a cry of down! down!—Hats off!—Silence!—Then up curtain, and let us see what our painters have done for us.

[*Curtain rises.*

SCENE II.—*Tilbury Fort*

"*Two* SENTINELS *discovered asleep*"

Dang. Tilbury Fort!—very fine indeed!

Puff. Now, what do you think I open with?

Sneer. Faith, I can't guess——

Puff. A clock.—Hark!—[*Clock strikes.*] I open with a clock striking, to beget an awful attention in the audience: it also marks the time, which is four o'clock in the morning, and saves a description of the rising sun, and a great deal about gilding the eastern hemisphere.

Dang. But pray, are the sentinels to be asleep?

Puff. Fast as watchmen.

Sneer. Isn't that odd though at such an alarming crisis?

Puff. To be sure it is,—but smaller things must give way to a striking scene at the opening; that's a rule. And the case is, that two great men are coming to this very spot to begin the piece; now it is not to be supposed they would open their lips, if these fellows were watching them; so, egad, I must either have sent them off their posts, or set them asleep.

Sneer. Oh, that accounts for it. But tell us, who are these coming?

Puff. These are they—Sir Walter Raleigh, and Sir Christopher Hatton. You'll know Sir Christopher by his turning out his toes—famous, you know, for his dancing. I like to preserve all the little traits of character.—Now attend.

"*Enter* SIR WALTER RALEIGH *and* SIR CHRISTOPHER HATTON.
Sir Christ. True, gallant Raleigh!"

Dang. What, they had been talking before?

Puff. O yes; all the way as they came along.—[*To the* actors.] I beg pardon, gentlemen, but these are particular friends of mine, whose remarks may be of great service to us.—[*To* SNEER *and* DANGLE.] Don't mind interrupting them whenever anything strikes you.

"*Sir Christ.*   True, gallant Raleigh!
              But oh, thou champion of thy country's fame,
              There is a question which I yet must ask:
              A question which I never ask'd before—
              What mean these mighty armaments?
              This general muster? and this throng of chiefs?"

Sneer. Pray, Mr. Puff, how came Sir Christopher Hatton never to ask that question before?

Puff. What, before the play began?—how the plague could he?

Dang. That's true, i'faith!

Puff. But you will hear what he thinks of the matter.

> *"Sir Christ.* Alas! my noble friend, when I behold
> Yon tented plains in martial symmetry
> Array'd; when I count o'er yon glittering lines
> Of crested warriors, where the proud steeds' neigh,
> And valour-breathing trumpet's shrill appeal,
> Responsive vibrate on my listening ear;
> When virgin majesty herself I view,
> Like her protecting Pallas, veil'd in steel,
> With graceful confidence exhort to arms!
> When, briefly, all I hear or see bears stamp
> Of martial vigilance and stern defence,
> I cannot but surmise—forgive, my friend,
> If the conjecture's rash—I cannot but
> Surmise the state some danger apprehends!"

Sneer. A very cautious conjecture that.

Puff. Yes, that's his character; not to give an opinion but on secure grounds.—Now then.

> *"Sir Walt.* O most accomplish'd Christopher!"——

Puff. He calls him by his Christian name, to show that they are on the most familiar terms.

> *"Sir Walt.* O most accomplish'd Christopher! I find
> Thy staunch sagacity still tracks the future,
> In the fresh print of the o'ertaken past."

Puff. Figurative!

> *"Sir Walt.* Thy fears are just.
> *Sir Christ.* But where? whence? when? and what
> The danger is,—methinks I fain would learn.
> *Sir Walt.* You know, my friend, scarce two revolving suns,
> And three revolving moons, have closed their course
> Since haughty Philip, in despite of peace,
> With hostile hand hath struck at England's trade.
> *Sir Christ.* I know it well.
> *Sir Walt.* Philip, you know, is proud Iberia's king!
> *Sir Christ.* He is.
> *Sir Walt.* His subjects in base bigotry
> And Catholic oppression held;—while we,
> You know, the Protestant persuasion hold.
> *Sir Christ.* We do.

Sir Walt.   You know, beside, his boasted armament,
        The famed Armada, by the Pope baptized,
        With purpose to invade these realms——

Sir Christ.   **Is sailed,**
        Our last advices so report.

Sir Walt.   While the Iberian admiral's chief hope,
        His darling son——

Sir Christ.   Ferolo Whiskerandos hight—

Sir Walt.   The same—by chance a prisoner hath been ta'en,
        And in this fort of Tilbury——

Sir Christ.   Is now
        Confined—'tis true, and oft from yon tall turret's top
        I've mark'd the youthful Spaniard's haughty mien—
        Unconquer'd, though in chains.

Sir Walt.   You also know"——

Dang. Mr. Puff, as he knows all this, why does Sir Walter go on telling him?

Puff. But the audience are not supposed to know anything of the matter, are they?

Sneer. True; but I think you manage ill: for there certainly appears no reason why Sir Walter should be so communicative.

Puff. 'Fore Gad, now, that is one of the most ungrateful observations I ever heard!—for the less inducement he has to tell all this, the more, I think, you ought to be obliged to him; for I am sure you'd know nothing of the matter without it.

Dang. That's very true, upon my word.

Puff. But you will find he was not going on.

"*Sir Christ.* Enough, enough—'tis plain—and I no more
        Am in amazement lost!"——

Puff. Here, now you see, Sir Christopher did not in fact ask any one question for his own information.

Sneer. No, indeed: his has been a most disinterested curiosity!

Dang. Really, I find that we are very much obliged to them both.

Puff. To be sure you are. Now then for the commander-in-chief, the Earl of Leicester, who, you know, was no favourite but of the queen's. —We left off—*in amazement lost!*

"*Sir Christ.*   Am in amazement lost.
        But, see where noble Leicester comes! supreme
        In honours and command.

Sir Walt.   And yet, methinks,
        At such a time, so perilous, so fear'd,
        That staff might well become an abler grasp.

Sir Christ. And so, by Heaven! think I; but soft, he's here!"

Puff. Ay, they envy him!

Sneer. But who are these with him?

Puff. Oh! very valiant knights: one is the governor of the fort, the other the master of the horse. And now, I think, you shall hear some better language: I was obliged to be plain and intelligible in the first scene, because there was so much matter of fact in it; but now, i'faith, you have trope, figure, and metaphor, as plenty as noun-substantives.

"Enter EARL OF LEICESTER, GOVERNOR, MASTER OF THE HORSE, KNIGHTS, &c.

Leic. How's this, my friends! is't thus your new-fledged zeal,
   And plumed valour moulds in roosted sloth?
   Why dimly glimmers that heroic flame,
   Whose reddening blaze, by patriot spirit fed,
   Should be the beacon of a kindling realm?
   Can the quick current of a patriot heart
   Thus stagnate in a cold and weedy converse,
   Or freeze in tideless inactivity?
   No! rather let the fountain of your valour
   Spring through each stream of enterprise,
   Each petty channel of conducive daring,
   Till the full torrent of your foaming wrath
   O'erwhelm the flats of sunk hostility!"

Puff. There it is—followed up!

"*Sir Walt.* No more!—the freshening breath of thy rebuke
   Hath fill'd the swelling canvas of our souls!
   And thus, though fate should cut the cable of

              [All take hands.

   Our topmost hopes, in friendship's closing line
   We'll grapple with despair, and if we fall,
   We'll fall in glory's wake!
Leic. There spoke old England's genius!
   Then, are we all resolved?
All. We are—all resolved.
Leic. To conquer—or be free?
All. To conquer, or be free.
Leic. All?
All. All."

Dang. Nem. con. egad!

Puff. O yes!—where they do agree on the stage, their unanimity is wonderful!

"*Leic.* Then let's embrace—and now——   *[Kneels."*

Sneer. What the plague, is he going to pray?

Puff. Yes; hush!—in great emergencies, there is nothing like a prayer.

"Leic.   O mighty Mars!"

Dang. But why should he pray to Mars?
Puff. Hush!

"Leic.   If in thy homage bred,
              Each point of discipline I've still observed;
              Nor but by due promotion, and the right
              Of service, to the rank of major-general
              Have risen; assist thy votary now!
Gov.   Yet do not rise—hear me!   [*Kneels.*
Mast.   And me!   [*Kneels.*
Knight.   And me!   [*Kneels.*
Sir Walt.   And me!   [*Kneels.*"
Sir Christ. And me!

Puff. Now pray altogether.

"All.   Behold thy votaries submissive beg,
              That thou wilt deign to grant them all they ask;
              Assist them to accomplish all their ends,
              And sanctify whatever means they use
              To gain them!"

Sneer. A very orthodox quintetto!
Puff. Vastly well, gentlemen!—Is that well managed or not? Have you such a prayer as that on the stage?
Sneer. Not exactly.
Leic. [*To* PUFF.] But, sir, you haven't settled how we are to get off here.
Puff. You could not go off kneeling, could you?
Sir Walt. [*To* PUFF.] O no, sir; impossible!
Puff. It would have a good effect i' faith, if you could exeunt praying!—Yes, and would vary the established mode of springing off with a glance at the pit.
Sneer. Oh, never mind, so as you get them off!—I'll answer for it, the audience won't care how.
Puff. Well, then, repeat the last line standing, and go off the old way.

"All.   And sanctify whatever means we use
              To gain them.   [*Exeunt.*"

Dang. Bravo! a fine exit.
Sneer. Well, really, Mr. Puff——
Puff. Stay a moment!

"The SENTINELS *get up.*

1 *Sent.*   All this shall to Lord Burleigh's ear.

2 *Sent.*   'Tis meet it should.   [*Exeunt."*

Dang. Hey!—why, I thought those fellows had been asleep?

Puff. Only a pretence; there's the art of it: they were spies of Lord Burleigh's.

Sneer. But isn't it odd they never were taken notice of, not even by the commander-in-chief?

Puff. O Lud, sir! if people who want to listen, or overhear, were not always connived at in a tragedy, there would be no carrying on any plot in the world.

Dang. That's certain.

Puff. But take care, my dear Dangle! the morning gun is going to fire.   [*Cannon fires.*

Dang. Well, that will have a fine effect!

Puff. I think so, and helps to realize the scene.—[*Cannon twice.*] What the plague! three morning guns! there never is but one!—Ay, this is always the way at the theatre: give these fellows a good thing, and they never know when to have done with it.—You have no more cannon to fire?

Und. Promp. [*Within.*] No, sir.

Puff. Now, then, for soft music.

Sneer. Pray, what's that for?

Puff. It shows that Tilburina is coming!—nothing introduces you a heroine like soft music. Here she comes.

Dang. And her confidant, I suppose?

Puff. To be sure! Here they are—inconsolable to the minuet in Ariadne!   [*Soft Music.*

"Enter TILBURINA *and* CONFIDANT.

Tilb.   Now has the whispering breath of gentle morn
          Bid Nature's voice and Nature's beauty rise;
          While orient Phœbus, with unborrow'd hues,
          Clothes the waked loveliness which all night slept
          In heavenly drapery! Darkness is fled.
          Now flowers unfold their beauties to the sun,
          And, blushing, kiss the beam he sends to wake them—
          The striped carnation, and the guarded rose,
          The vulgar wallflower, and smart gillyflower,
          The polyanthus mean—the dapper daisy,
          Sweet-William, and sweet marjoram—and all
          The tribe of single and of double pinks!
          Now, too, the feather'd warblers tune their notes
          Around, and charm the listening grove. The lark!

> The linnet! chaffinch! bullfinch! goldfinch! greenfinch!
> But O, to me no joy can they afford!
> Nor rose, nor wallflower, nor smart gillyflower,
> Nor polyanthus mean, nor dapper daisy,
> Nor William sweet, nor marjoram—nor lark,
> Linnet, nor all the finches of the grove!"

Puff. Your white handkerchief, madam!——

Tilb. I thought, sir, I wasn't to use that till *heart-rending woe.*

Puff. O yes, madam, at *the finches of the grove,* if you please.

"Tilb.   Nor lark,
> Linnet, nor all the finches of the grove!   [*Weeps."*

Puff. Vastly well, madam!

Dang. Vastly well, indeed!

"Tilb.   For, O, too sure, heart-rending woe is now
> The lot of wretched Tilburina!"

Dang. Oh!—it's too much.

Sneer. Oh!—it is indeed.

"Con.   Be comforted, sweet lady; for who knows,
> But Heaven has yet some milk-white day in store?
Tilb.   Alas! my gentle Nora,
> Thy tender youth as yet hath never mourn'd
> Love's fatal dart. Else wouldst thou know, that when
> The soul is sunk in comfortless despair,
> It cannot taste of merriment."

Dang. That's certain.

"Con.   But see where your stern father comes:
> It is not meet that he should find you thus."

Puff. Hey, what the plague!—what a cut is here! Why, what is become of the description of her first meeting with Don Whiskerandos—his gallant behaviour in the sea-fight—and the simile of the canarybird?

Tilb. Indeed, sir, you'll find they will not be missed.

Puff. Very well, very well!

Tilb. [*To* CONFIDANT.] The cue, ma'am, if you please.

"Con.   It is not meet that he should find you thus.
Tilb.   Thou counsel'st right; but 'tis no easy task
> For barefaced grief to wear a mask of joy.

Enter GOVERNOR.

Gov.   How's this!—in tears?—O Tilburina, shame!
> Is this a time for maudling tenderness,
> And Cupid's baby woes?—Hast thou not heard

> That haughty Spain's pope-consecrated fleet
> Advances to our shores, while England's fate,
> Like a clipp'd guinea, trembles in the scale?

Tilb. Then is the crisis of my fate at hand!
> I see the fleets approach—I see——"

Puff. Now, pray, gentlemen, mind. This is one of the most useful figures we tragedy writers have, by which a hero or heroine, in consideration of their being often obliged to overlook things that are on the stage, is allowed to hear and see a number of things that are not.

Sneer. Yes; a kind of poetical second-sight!

Puff. Yes.—Now then, madam.

"Tilb.   I see their decks
> Are clear'd!—I see the signal made!
> The line is form'd!—a cable's length asunder!
> I see the frigates station'd in the rear;
> And now, I hear the thunder of the guns!
> I hear the victor's shouts—I also hear
> The vanquish'd groan!—and now 'tis smoke—and now
> I see the loose sails shiver in the wind!
> I see—I see—what soon you'll see——

Gov. Hold, daughter! peace! this love hath turn'd thy brain:
> The Spanish fleet thou canst not see—because
> —It is not yet in sight!"

Dang. Egad, though, the governor seems to make no allowance for this poetical figure you talk of.

Puff. No, a plain matter-of-fact man;—that's his character.

"Tilb. But will you then refuse his offer?
Gov. I must—I will—I can—I ought—I do.
Tilb. Think what a noble price.
Gov. No more—you urge in vain.
Tilb. His liberty is all he asks."

Sneer. All who asks, Mr. Puff? Who is——

Puff. Egad, sir, I can't tell! Here has been such cutting and slashing, I don't know where they have got to myself.

Tilb. Indeed, sir, you will find it will connect very well.

"—And your reward secure."

Puff. Oh, if they hadn't been so devilish free with their cutting here, you would have found that Don Whiskerandos has been tampering for his liberty, and has persuaded Tilburina to make this proposal to her father. And now, pray observe the conciseness with which the argument is conducted. Egad, the *pro* and *con* goes as smart as hits in a fencing match. It is indeed a sort of small-sword-logic, which we have borrowed from the French.

"*Tilb.*   A retreat in Spain!
Gov.   Outlawry here!
Tilb.   Your daughter's prayer!
Gov.   Your father's oath!
Tilb.   My lover!
Gov.   My country!
Tilb.   Tilburina!
Gov.   England!
Tilb.   A title!
Gov.   Honour!
Tilb.   A pension!
Gov.   Conscience!
Tilb.   A thousand pounds!
Gov.   Ha! thou hast touch'd me nearly!"

Puff. There you see—she threw in *Tilburina.* Quick, parry carte with *England!* Ha! thrust in tierce *a title!*—parried by *honour.* Ha! *a pension* over the arm!—put by by *conscience.* Then flankonade with *a thousand pounds*—and a palpable hit, egad!

"*Tilb.*   Canst thou—
           Reject the suppliant, and the daughter too?
Gov.   No more; I would not hear thee plead in vain:
           The father softens—but the governor
           Is fix'd!   [*Exit.*"

Dang. Ay, that antithesis of persons is a most established figure.

"*Tilb.*   'Tis well,—hence then, fond hopes,—fond passion hence;
           Duty, behold I am all over thine——
Whisk.   [*Without.*] Where is my love—my——
Tilb.   Ha!

Enter Don Ferolo Whiskerandos.

Whisk.   My beauteous enemy!——"

Puff. O dear, ma'am, you must start a great deal more than that! Consider, you had just determined in favour of duty—when, in a moment, the sound of his voice revives your passion—overthrows your resolution—destroys your obedience. If you don't express all that in your start, you do nothing at all.

Tilb. Well, we'll try again.

Dang. Speaking from within has always a fine effect.

Sneer. Very.

"*Whisk.*   My conquering Tilburina! How! Is't thus
            We meet? why are thy looks averse? what means
            That falling tear—that frown of boding woe?
            Ha! now indeed I am a prisoner!
            Yes, now I feel the galling weight of these

	Disgraceful chains—which, cruel Tilburina!
	Thy doting captive gloried in before.—
	But thou art false, and Whiskerandos is undone!
Tilb.	O no! how little dost thou know thy Tilburina!
Whisk.	Art thou then true?—Begone cares, doubts, and fears,
	I make you all a present to the winds;
	And if the winds reject you—try the waves."

Puff. The wind, you know, is the established receiver of all stolen sighs, and cast-off griefs and apprehensions.

"*Tilb.*	Yet must we part!—stern duty seals our doom:
	Though here I call yon conscious clouds to witness,
	Could I pursue the bias of my soul,
	All friends, all right of parents, I'd disclaim,
	And thou, my Whiskerandos, shouldst be father
	And mother, brother, cousin, uncle, aunt,
	And friend to me!
Whisk.	Oh, matchless excellence! and must we part?
	Well, if—we must—we must—and in that case
	The less is said the better."

Puff. Heyday! here's a cut!—What, are all the mutual protestations out?

Tilb. Now, pray, sir, don't interrupt us just here: you ruin our feelings.

Puff. Your feelings!—but, zounds, my feelings, ma'am!

Sneer. No, pray don't interrupt them.

"*Whisk.*	One last embrace.
Tilb.	Now,—farewell, for **ever.**
Whisk.	For ever!
Tilb.	Ay, for ever! [*Going.*"

Puff. 'Sdeath and fury!—Gad's life!—sir! madam! if you go out without the parting look, you might as well dance out. Here, here!

Con. But pray, sir, how am I to get off here?

Puff. You! pshaw! what the devil signifies how you get off! edge away at the top, or where you will—[*Pushes the* CONFIDANT *off.*] Now, ma'am, you see——

Tilb. We understand you, sir.

| | "Ay, for ever. |
| *Both.* | Oh!   [*Turning back, and exeunt.—Scene closes.*" |

Dang. Oh, charming!

Puff. Hey!—'tis pretty well, I believe: you see I don't attempt to strike out anything new—but I take it I improve on the established modes.

Sneer. You do, indeed! But pray is not Queen Elizabeth to appear?

Puff. No, not once—but she is to be talked of for ever; so that, egad, you'll think a hundred times that she is on the point of coming in.

Sneer. Hang it, I think it's a pity to keep her in the green-room all the night.

Puff. O no, that always has a fine effect—it keeps up expectation.

Dang. But are we not to have a battle?

Puff. Yes, yes, you will have a battle at last: but, egad, it's not to be by land, but by sea—and that is the only quite new thing in the piece.

Dang. What, Drake at the Armada, hey?

Puff. Yes, i'faith—fire-ships and all; then we shall end with the procession. Hey, that will do, I think?

Sneer. No doubt on't.

Puff. Come, we must not lose time; so now for the under-plot.

Sneer. What the plague, have you another plot?

Puff. O Lord, yes; ever while you live have two plots to your tragedy. The grand point in managing them is only to let your under-plot have as little connection with your main-plot as possible.—I flatter myself nothing can be more distinct than mine; for as in my chief plot the characters are all great people, I have laid my under-plot in low life, and as the former is to end in deep distress, I make the other end as happy as a farce.—Now, Mr. Hopkins, as soon as you please.

Enter UNDER PROMPTER

Under Promp. Sir, the carpenter says it is impossible you can go to the park scene yet.

Puff. The park scene! no! I mean the description scene here, in the wood.

Under Promp. Sir, the performers have cut it out.

Puff. Cut it out!

Under Promp. Yes, sir.

Puff. What! the whole account of Queen Elizabeth?

Under Promp. Yes, sir.

Puff. And the description of her horse and side-saddle?

Under Promp. Yes, sir.

Puff. So, so; this is very fine indeed!—Mr. Hopkins, how the plague could you suffer this?

Mr. Hop. [*Within.*] Sir, indeed the pruning-knife——

Puff. The pruning-knife—zounds!—the axe! Why, here has been such lopping and topping, I shan't have the bare trunk of my play left presently!—Very well, sir—the performers must do as they please; but, upon my soul, I'll print it every word.

Sneer. That I would, indeed.

Puff. Very well, sir; then we must go on.—Zounds! I would not have parted with the description of the horse!—Well, sir, go on.—Sir, it was one of the finest and most laboured things.—Very well, sir; let them go on.—There you had him and his accoutrements, from the bit to the crupper.—Very well, sir; we must go to the park scene.

Under Promp. Sir, there is the point: the carpenters say, that unless there is some business put in here before the drop, they sha'n't have time to clear away the fort, or sink Gravesend and the river.

Puff. So! this is a pretty dilemma, truly!—Gentlemen, you must excuse me—these fellows will never be ready, unless I go and look after them myself.

Sneer. O dear, sir, these little things will happen.

Puff. To cut out this scene!—but I'll print it—egad, I'll print it every word!   [*Exeunt.*

ACT III

SCENE I.—*The Theatre, before the curtain*

Enter PUFF, SNEER, *and* DANGLE

Puff. Well, we are ready; now then for the justices.

[*Curtain rises.*

"JUSTICES, CONSTABLES, &c., *discovered.*"

Sneer. This, I suppose, is a sort of senate scene.

Puff. To be sure; there has not been one yet.

Dang. It is the under-plot, isn't it?

Puff. Yes.—What, gentlemen, do you mean to go at once to the discovery scene?

Just. If you please, sir.

Puff. Oh, very well!—Hark'ee, I don't choose to say anything more; but, i'faith they have mangled my play in a most shocking manner.

Dang. It's a great pity!

Puff. Now, then, Mr. Justice, if you please.

"*Just.*	Are all the volunteers without?
Const.	They are.
	Some ten in fetters, and some twenty drunk.
Just.	Attends the youth, whose most opprobrious fame
	And clear convicted crimes have stamp'd him soldier?
Const.	He waits your pleasure; eager to repay
	The best reprieve that sends him to the fields

	Of glory, there to raise his branded hand In honour's cause.
Just.	'Tis well—'tis justice arms him! Oh! may he now defend his country's laws With half the spirit he has broke them all! If 'tis your worship's pleasure, bid him enter.
Const.	I fly, the herald of your will. *[Exit."*

Puff. Quick, sir.

Sneer. But, Mr. Puff, I think not only the Justice, but the clown seems to talk in as high a style as the first hero among them.

Puff. Heaven forbid they should not in a free country!—Sir, I am not for making slavish distinctions, and giving all the fine language to the upper sort of people.

Dang. That's very noble in you, indeed.

"Enter Justice's Lady.*"*

Puff. Now, pray mark this scene.

"Lady.	Forgive this interruption, good my love; But as I just now pass'd a prisoner youth, Whom rude hands hither lead, strange bodings seized My fluttering heart, and to myself I said, An' if our Tom had lived, he'd surely been This stripling's height!
Just.	Ha! sure some powerful sympathy directs Us both——

Enter Constable *with* Son.

Son.	What is thy name? My name is Tom Jenkins—*alias* have I none— Though orphan'd, and without a friend!
Just.	Thy parents?
Son.	My father dwelt in Rochester—and was, As I have heard—a fishmonger—no more."

Puff. What, sir, do you leave out the account of your birth, parentage, and education?

Son They have settled it so, sir, here,

Puff. Oh! oh!

"Lady.	How loudly nature whispers to my heart Had he no other name?
Son.	I've seen a bill Of his sign'd Tomkins, creditor.
Just.	This does indeed confirm each circumstance The gypsy told!—Prepare!
Son.	I do.

Just. No orphan, nor without a friend art thou—
      I am thy father; here's thy mother; there
      Thy uncle—this thy first cousin, and those
      Are all your near relations!
Lady. O ecstasy of bliss!
Son.   O most unlook'd for happiness!
Just. O wonderful event! [*They faint alternately in each others arms.*"

Puff. There, you see, relationship, like murder, will out.

"*Just.* Now let's revive—else were this joy too much!
      But come—and we'll unfold the rest within;
      And thou, my boy, must needs want rest and food.
      Hence may each orphan hope, as chance directs,
      To find a father—where he least expects!   [*Exeunt.*"

Puff. What do you think of that?

Dang. One of the finest discovery-scenes I ever saw!—Why, this under-plot would have made a tragedy itself.

Sneer. Ay! or a comedy either.

Puff. And keeps quite clear you see of the other.

    "*Enter* SCENEMEN, *taking away the seats.*"

Puff. The scene remains, does it?

Sceneman. Yes, sir.

Puff. You are to leave one chair, you know.—But it is always awkward in a tragedy, to have you fellows coming in in your play-house liveries to remove things.—I wish that could be managed better.—So now for my mysterious yeoman.

     "*Enter* BEEFEATER.

Beef.   Perdition catch my soul, but I do love thee."

Sneer. Haven't I heard that line before?

Puff. No, I fancy not.—Where, pray?

Dang. Yes, I think there is something like it in Othello.

Puff. Gad! now you put me in mind on't, I believe there is—but that's of no consequence; all that can be said is, that two people happened to hit upon the same thought—and Shakspeare made use of it first, that's all.

Sneer. Very true.

Puff. Now, sir, your soliloquy—but speak more to the pit, if you please—the soliloquy always to the pit, that's a rule.

"*Beef.* Though hopeless love finds comfort in despair,
      It never can endure a rival's bliss!
      But soft—I am observed.
                  [*Exit.*"

Dang. That's a very short soliloquy.

Puff. Yes—but it would have been a great deal longer if he had not been observed.

Sneer. A most sentimental Beefeater that, Mr. Puff!

Puff. Hark'ee—I would not have you be too sure that he is a Beefeater.

Sneer. What, a hero in disguise?

Puff. No matter—I only give you a hint. But now for my principal character. Here he comes—Lord Burleigh in person! Pray, gentlemen, step this way—softly—I only hope the Lord High Treasurer is perfect—if he is but perfect!

"*Enter* LORD BURLEIGH, *goes slowly to a chair, and sits.*"

Sneer. Mr. Puff!

Puff. Hush!—Vastly well, sir! vastly well! a most interesting gravity.

Dang. What, isn't he to speak at all?

Puff. Egad, I thought you'd ask me that!—Yes, it is a very likely thing—that a minister in his situation, with the whole affairs of the nation on his head, should have time to talk!—But hush! or you'll put him out.

Sneer. Put him out; how the plague can that be, if he's not going to say anything?

Puff. There's the reason! why, his part is to think; and how the plague do you imagine he can think if you keep talking?

Dang. That's very true, upon my word!

"LORD BURLEIGH *comes forward, shakes his head, and exit.*"

Sneer. He is very perfect indeed! Now, pray what did he mean by that?

Puff. You don't take it?

Sneer. No, I don't, upon my soul.

Puff. Why, by that shake of the head, he gave you to understand that even though they had more justice in their cause, and wisdom in their measures—yet, if there was not a greater spirit shown on the part of the people, the country would at last fall a sacrifice to the hostile ambition of the Spanish monarchy.

Sneer. The devil! did he mean all that by shaking his head?

Puff. Every word of it—if he shook his head as I taught him.

Dang. Ah! there certainly is a vast deal to be done on the stage by dumb show and expressions of face; and a judicious author knows how much he may trust to it.

Sneer. Oh, here are some of our old acquaintance.

"Enter SIR CHRISTOPHER *and* SIR WALTER RALEIGH.

Sir Christ. My niece and your niece too!
By Heaven! there's witchcraft in't.—He could not else
Have gain'd their hearts.—But see where they approach:
Some horrid purpose lowering on their brows!

Sir Walt. Let us withdraw and mark them.   [*They withdraw."*

Sneer. What is all this?

Puff. Ah! here has been more pruning!—but the fact is, these two young ladies are also in love with Don Whiskerandos.—Now, gentlemen, this scene goes entirely for what we call situation and stage effect, by which the greatest applause may be obtained, without the assistance of language, sentiment, or character: pray mark!

"Enter the two NIECES.

1st Niece. Ellena here!
She is his scorn as much as I—that is
Some comfort still!"

Puff. O dear, madam, you are not to say that to her face!—Aside, ma'am, aside.—The whole scene is to be aside.

"1st Niece. She is his scorn as much as I—that is
Some comfort still!   [*Aside.*

2nd Niece. I know he prizes not Pollina's love;
But Tilburina lords it o'er his heart.   [*Aside.*

1st Niece. But see the proud destroyer of my peace.
Revenge is all the good I've left.   [*Aside.*

2nd Niece. He comes, the false disturber of my quiet.
Now vengeance do thy worst.   [*Aside.*

Enter DON FEROLO WHISKERANDOS.

Whisk. O hateful liberty—if thus in vain
I seek my Tilburina!

Both Nieces.   And ever shalt!

SIR CHRISTOPHER HATTON *and* SIR WALTER RALEIGH *come forward.*

Sir Christ. and Sir Walt. Hold! we will avenge you.

Whisk.   Hold *you*—or see your nieces bleed!

[*The two* NIECES *draw their two daggers to strike* WHISKERANDOS: *the two* UNCLES *at the instant, with their two swords drawn, catch their two* NIECES' *arms, and turn the points of their swords to* WHISKERANDOS, *who immediately draws two daggers, and holds them to the two* NIECES' *bosoms."*

Puff. There's situation for you! there's an heroic group!—You see the ladies can't stab Whiskerandos—he durst not strike them, for fear of their uncles—the uncles durst not kill him, because of their nieces.—

I have them all at a dead lock!—for every one of them is afraid to let go first.

Sneer. Why, then they must stand there for ever!

Puff. So they would, if I hadn't a very fine contrivance for't.—Now mind——

"*Enter* BEEFEATER, *with his halbert.*

Beef.　　　　In the queen's name I charge you all to drop
　　　　　　　Your swords and daggers! [*They drop their swords and daggers.*"

Sneer. That is a contrivance indeed!

Puff. Ay—in the queen's name.

"*Sir Christ.* Come, niece!
Sir Walt. Come, niece!　　　　　　　　　[*Exeunt with the two* NIECES.
Whisk. What's he, who bids us thus renounce our guard?
Beef. Thou must do more—renounce thy love!
Whisk. Thou liest—base Beefeater!
Beef. 　　　　　　　　　　　　　　　Ha! hell! the lie!
　　　　　　By Heaven thou'st roused the lion in my heart!
　　　　　　Off, yeoman's habit!—base disguise! off! off!

[*Discovers himself by throwing off his upper dress, and appearing in a very
　　　fine waistcoat.*
　　　　　　Am I a Beefeater now?
　　　　　　Or beams my crest as terrible as when
　　　　　　In Biscay's Bay I took thy captive sloop?*"

Puff. There, egad! he comes out to be the very captain of the privateer who had taken Whiskerandos prisoner—and was himself an old lover of Tilburina's.

Dang. Admirably managed, indeed!

Puff. Now, stand out of their way.

"*Whisk.* I thank thee, Fortune, that hast thus bestowed
　　　　　　A weapon to chastise this insolent. [*Takes up one of the swords.*
Beef. I take thy challenge, Spaniard, and I thank thee,
　　　　　　Fortune, too! 　　　　　　　　[*Takes up the other sword.*"

Dang. That's excellently contrived!—It seems as if the two uncles had left their swords on purpose for them.

Puff. No, egad, they could not help leaving them.

"*Whisk.* 　　Vengeance and Tilburina!
Beef. 　　　　　　　　　　Exactly so——
　　　[*They fight—and after the usual number of wounds given,* WHISKERANDOS
　　　　　falls.
Whisk. O cursed parry!—that last thrust in tierce
　　　　　　Was fatal.—Captain, thou hast fenced well!
　　　　　　And Whiskerandos quits this bustling scene
　　　　　　For all eter——

Beef. ——nity—he would have added, but stern death
Cut short his being, and the noun at once!"

Puff. Oh, my dear sir, you are too slow: now mind me.—Sir, shall I trouble you to die again?

"Whisk. And Whiskerandos quits this bustling scene
For all eter——

Beef. ——nity—he would have added,——"

Puff. No, sir—that's not it—once more, if you please.

Whisk. I wish, sir, you would practise this without me—I can't stay dying here all night.

Puff. Very well; we'll go over it by-and-by.—[*Exit* WHISKER-ANDOS.] I must humour these gentlemen!

"Beef. Farewell, brave Spaniard! and when next——"

Puff. Dear sir, you needn't speak that speech, as the body has walked off.

Beef. That's true, sir—then I'll join the fleet.

Puff. If you please.—[*Exit* BEEFEATER.] Now, who comes on?

"Enter GOVERNOR, *with his hair properly disordered.*

Gov. A hemisphere of evil planets reign!
And every planet sheds contagious frenzy!
My Spanish prisoner is slain! my daughter,
Meeting the dead corse borne along, has gone
Distract! [*A loud flourish of trumpets.*
But hark! I am summoned to the fort:
Perhaps the fleets have met! amazing crisis!
O Tilburina! from thy aged father's beard
Thou'st pluck'd the few brown hairs which time had left! [*Exit."*

Sneer. Poor gentleman!

Puff. Yes—and no one to blame but his daughter!

Dang. And the planets——

Puff. True.—Now enter Tilburina!

Sneer. Egad, the business comes on quick here.

Puff. Yes, sir—now she comes in stark mad in white satin.

Sneer. Why in white satin?

Puff. O Lord, sir—when a heroine goes mad, she always goes into white satin.—Don't she, Dangle?

Dang. Always—it's a rule.

Puff. Yes—here it is—[*Looking at the book.*] "Enter Tilburina stark mad in white satin, and her confidant stark mad in white linen."

"Enter TILBURINA *and* CONFIDANT, *mad, according to custom."*

Sneer. But, what the deuce! is the confidant to be mad too?

Puff. To be sure she is: the confidant is always to do whatever her mistress does; weep when she weeps, smile when she smiles, go mad when she goes mad.—Now, Madam Confidant—but keep your madness in the background, if you please.

"*Tilb.* The wind whistles—the moon rises—see,
They have kill'd my squirrel in his cage:
Is this a grasshopper?—Ha! no; it is my
Whiskerandos—you shall not keep him—
I know you have him in your pocket—
An oyster may be cross'd in love!—who says
A whale's a bird?—Ha! did you call, my love?—
He's here! he's there!—He's everywhere!
Ah me! he's nowhere!   [*Exit.*"

Puff. There, do you ever desire to see anybody madder than that?

Sneer. Never, while I live!

Puff. You observed how she mangled the metre?

Dang. Yes,—egad, it was the first thing made me suspect she was out of her senses!

Sneer. And pray what becomes of her?

Puff. She is gone to throw herself into the sea, to be sure—and that brings us at once to the scene of action, and so to my catastrophe—my sea-fight, I mean.

Sneer. What, you bring that in at last?

Puff. Yes, yes—you know my play is called *The Spanish Armada;* otherwise, egad, I have no occasion for the battle at all.—Now then for my magnificence!—my battle!—my noise!—and my procession!—You are all ready?

Und. Promp. [*Within.*] Yes, sir.

Puff. Is the Thames dressed?

"*Enter* THAMES *with two* ATTENDANTS."

Thames. Here I am, sir.

Puff. Very well, indeed!—See, gentlemen, there's a river for you! —This is blending a little of the masque with my tragedy—a new fancy, you know—and very useful in my case; for as there must be a procession, I suppose Thames, and all his tributary rivers, to compliment Britannia with a fête in honour of the victory.

Sneer. But pray, who are these gentlemen in green with him?

Puff. Those?—those are his banks.

Sneer. His banks?

Puff. Yes, one crowned with alders, and the other with a villa!— you take the allusions?—But hey! what the plague!—you have got both

your banks on one side.—Here, sir, come round.—Ever while you live,
Thames, go between your banks.—[*Bell rings.*] There, so! now for't!
—Stand aside, my dear friends!—Away, Thames!

[*Exit* THAMES *between his banks.*

[*Flourish of drums, trumpets, cannon, &c., &c. Scene changes to the
sea—the fleets engage—the music plays—"Britons strike home."—
Spanish fleet destroyed by fire-ships, &c.—English fleet advances—
music plays, "Rule Britannia."—The procession of all the English
rivers, and their tributaries, with their emblems, &c., begins with
Handel's water music, ends with a chorus to the march in Judas
Maccabæus.—During this scene,* PUFF *directs and applauds everything—then*

Puff. Well, pretty well—but not quite perfect. So, ladies and gentlemen, if you please, we'll rehearse this piece again to-morrow.

[*Curtain drops.*

WILLIAM BLAKE (1757-1827)

Piping Down the Valleys Wild

PIPING down the valleys wild,
　Piping songs of pleasant glee,
On a cloud I saw a child,
　And he laughing said to me:

"Pipe a song about a Lamb!"
　So I piped with merry cheer,
"Piper, pipe that song again;"
　So I piped: he wept to hear.

"Drop thy pipe, thy happy pipe;
　Sing thy songs of happy cheer!"
So I sung the same again,
　While he wept with joy to hear.

"Piper, sit thee down and write
　In a book that all may read."
So he vanish'd from my sight;
　And I pluck'd a hollow reed,

And I made a rural pen,
　And I stain'd the water clear,
And I wrote my happy songs
　Every child may joy to hear.

The Lamb

LITTLE lamb, who made thee?
Dost thou know who made thee,
Gave thee life and bade thee feed
By the stream and o'er the mead;
Gave thee clothing of delight,
Softest clothing, woolly, bright;
Gave thee such a tender voice,
Making all the vales rejoice?
　Little lamb, who made thee?
　Dost thou know who made thee?

Little lamb, I'll tell thee;
Little lamb, I'll tell thee.
He is callèd by thy name,
For He calls himself a Lamb;
He is meek and He is mild,
He became a little child.
I a child and thou a lamb,
We are callèd by His name.
　Little lamb, God bless thee!
　Little lamb, God bless thee!

The Tiger

TIGER! Tiger! burning bright
In the forests of the night,
What immortal hand or eye
Could frame thy fearful symmetry?

In what distant deeps or skies
Burnt the fire of thine eyes?
On what wings dare he aspire?
What the hand dare seize the fire?

And what shoulder, and what art,
Could twist the sinews of thy heart?
And when thy heart began to beat,
What dread hand? and what dread feet?

What the hammer? what the chain?
In what furnace was thy brain?
What the anvil? what dread grasp
Dare its deadly terrors clasp?

When the stars threw down their spears,
And watered heaven with their tears,
Did he smile his work to see?
Did he who made the Lamb make thee?

Tiger! Tiger! burning bright
In the forests of the night,
What immortal hand or eye
Dare frame thy fearful symmetry?

Holy Thursday

'Twas on a Holy Thursday, their inno-
    cent faces clean,
Came children walking two and two, in
    red, and blue, and green;
Gray-headed beadles walked before, with
    wands as white as snow,
Till into the high dome of Paul's they
    like Thames waters flow.

Oh what a multitude they seemed, these
    flowers of London town!
Seated in companies they sit, with radi-
    ance all their own.
The hum of multitudes was there, but
    multitudes of lambs,
Thousands of little boys and girls raising
    their innocent hands.

Now like a mighty wind they raise to
    heaven the voice of song,
Or like harmonious thunderings the seats
    of heaven among:
Beneath them sit the agèd men, wise
    guardians of the poor.
Then cherish pity, lest you drive an angel
    from your door.

ROBERT BURNS (1759-1796)

John Anderson, my Jo

John Anderson my jo, John,
    When we were first acquent,
Your locks were like the raven,
    Your bonie brow was brent;
But now your brow is beld, John,
    Your locks are like the snaw;
But blessings on your frosty pow,
    John Anderson my jo!

John Anderson my jo, John,
    We clamb the hill thegither;
And monie a cantie day, John,
    We've had wi' ane anither:
Now we maun totter down, John,
    But hand in hand we'll go,
And sleep thegither at the foot,
    John Anderson my jo!

A Red, Red Rose

O, my luve is like a red, red rose,
    That's newly sprung in June.
O, my luve is like the melodie
    That's sweetly play'd in tune.

As fair art thou, my bonie lass,
    So deep in luve am I,
And I will luve thee still, my dear,
    Till a' the seas gang dry.

Till a' the seas gang dry, my dear,
    And the rocks melt wi' the sun!
I will luve thee still, my dear,
    While the sands o' life shall run.

And fare thee weel, my only luve,
    And fare thee weel awhile!
And I will come again, my luve,
    Tho' it were ten thousand mile.

SAMUEL ROGERS (1763-1855)

A Wish

Mine be a cot beside the hill;
A bee-hive's hum shall soothe my ear;

A willowy brook that turns a mill,
With many a fall shall linger near.

The swallow, oft, beneath my thatch
Shall twitter from her clay-built nest;
Oft shall the pilgrim lift the latch,
And share my meal, a welcome guest.

Around my ivied porch shall spring
Each fragrant flower that drinks the
    dew;
And Lucy, at her wheel, shall sing
In russet-gown and apron blue.

The village-church among the trees,
Where first our marriage-vows were
    given,
With merry peals shall swell the breeze
And point with taper spire to Heaven.

WILLIAM WORDSWORTH
(1770-1850)

Lines Written in Early Spring

I HEARD a thousand blended notes,
While in a grove I sate reclined,
In that sweet mood when pleasant
    thoughts
Bring sad thoughts to the mind.

To her fair works did Nature link
The human soul that through me ran;
And much it grieved my heart to think
What man has made of man.

Through primrose tufts, in that green
    bower,
The periwinkle trailed its wreaths;
And 'tis my faith that every flower
Enjoys the air it breathes.

The birds around me hopped and played,
Their thoughts I cannot measure:—
But the least motion which they made,
It seemed a thrill of pleasure.

The budding twigs spread out their fan,
To catch the breezy air;
And I must think, do all I can,
That there was pleasure there.

If this belief from heaven be sent,
If such be Nature's holy plan,
Have I not reason to lament
What man has made of man?

Lines composed a few miles above Tintern Abbey, on revisiting the Banks of the Wye during a Tour. July 13, 1789.

FIVE years have past; five summers, with
    the length
Of five long winters! and again I hear
These waters, rolling from their moun-
    tain-springs
With a soft inland murmur.—Once again
Do I behold these steep and lofty cliffs,
That on a wild secluded scene impress
Thoughts of more deep seclusion; and
    connect
The landscape with the quiet of the
    sky.
The day is come when I again repose
Here, under this dark sycamore, and
    view
These plots of cottage-ground, these
    orchard-tufts,
Which at this season, with their unripe
    fruits,
Are clad in one green hue, and lose
    themselves
'Mid groves and copses. Once again I
    see
These hedge-rows, hardly hedge-rows,
    little lines
Of sportive wood run wild: these pas-
    toral farms,
Green to the very door; and wreaths of
    smoke
Sent up, in silence, from among the
    trees!
With some uncertain notice, as might
    seem
Of vagrant dwellers in the houseless
    woods,
Or of some Hermit's cave, where by his
    fire
The Hermit sits alone.

These beauteous forms,
Through a long absence, have not been
    to me
As is a landscape to a blind man's eye:
But oft, in lonely rooms, and 'mid the din
Of towns and cities, I have owed to
    them,
In hours of weariness, sensations sweet,
Felt in the blood, and felt along the
    heart;
And passing even into my purer mind,
With tranquil restoration:—feelings too
Of unremembered pleasure: such, per-
    haps,
As have no slight or trivial influence
On that best portion of a good man's life,
His little, nameless, unremembered, acts
Of kindness and of love. Nor less, I
    trust,
To them I may have owed another gift,
Of aspect more sublime; that blessed
    mood,
In which the burthen of the mystery,
In which the heavy and the weary weight
Of all this unintelligible world,
Is lightened:—that serene and blessed
    mood,
In which the affections gently lead us
    on,—
Until, the breath of this corporeal frame
And even the motion of our human blood
Almost suspended, we are laid asleep
In body, and become a living soul:
While with an eye made quiet by the
    power
Of harmony, and the deep power of joy,
We see into the life of things.

                    If this
Be but a vain belief, yet, oh! how oft—
In darkness and amid the many shapes
Of joyless daylight; when the fretful stir
Unprofitable, and the fever of the world,
Have hung upon the beatings of my
    heart—
How oft, in spirit, have I turned to thee,
O sylvan Wye! thou wanderer thro' the
    woods,
How often has my spirit turned to thee!

And now, with gleams of half-extin-
    guished thought,
With many recognitions dim and faint,
And somewhat of a sad perplexity,
The picture of the mind revives again:
While here I stand, not only with the
    sense
Of present pleasure, but with pleasing
    thoughts
That in this moment there is life and
    food
For future years. And so I dare to hope,
Though changed, no doubt, from what I
    was when first
I came among these hills; when like a roe
I bounded o'er the mountains, by the
    sides
Of the deep rivers, and the lonely
    streams,
Wherever nature led: more like a man
Flying from something that he dreads
    than one
Who sought the thing he loved. For
    nature then
(The coarser pleasures of my boyish
    days,
And their glad animal movements all
    gone by)
To me was all in all.—I cannot paint
What then I was. The sounding cataract
Haunted me like a passion: the tall rock,
The mountain, and the deep and gloomy
    wood,
Their colours and their forms, were then
    to me
An appetite; a feeling and a love,
That had no need of a remoter charm,
By thought supplied, nor any interest
Unborrowed from the eye.—That time
    is past,
And all its aching joys are now no more,
And all its dizzy raptures. Not for this
Faint I, nor mourn nor murmur; other
    gifts
Have followed; for such loss, I would
    believe,
Abundant recompense. For I have
    learned
To look on nature, not as in the hour

Of thoughtless youth; but hearing often-
times
The still, sad music of humanity,
Nor harsh nor grating, though of ample
power
To chasten and subdue. And I have felt
A presence that disturbs me with the joy
Of elevated thoughts; a sense sublime
Of something far more deeply interfused,
Whose dwelling is the light of setting
suns,
And the round ocean and the living air,
And the blue sky, and in the mind of
man:
A motion and a spirit, that impels
All thinking things, all objects of all
thought,
And rolls through all things. Therefore
am I still
A lover of the meadows and the woods,
And mountains; and of all that we behold
From this green earth; of all the mighty
world
Of eye, and ear,—both what they half
create,
And what perceive; well pleased to rec-
ognise
In nature and the language of the sense
The anchor of my purest thoughts, the
nurse,
The guide, the guardian of my heart, and
soul
Of all my moral being.

                Nor perchance,
If I were not thus taught, should I the
more
Suffer my genial spirits to decay:
For thou art with me here upon the
banks
Of this fair river; thou my dearest
Friend,
My dear, dear Friend; and in thy voice
I catch
The language of my former heart, and
read
My former pleasures in the shooting
lights
Of thy wild eyes. Oh! yet a little while

May I behold in thee what I was once,
My dear, dear Sister! and this prayer I
make,
Knowing that Nature never did betray
The heart that loved her; 'tis her
privilege,
Through all the years of this our life, to
lead
From joy to joy: for she can so inform
The mind that is within us, so impress
With quietness and beauty, and so feed
With lofty thoughts, that neither evil
tongues,
Rash judgments, nor the sneers of selfish
men,
Nor greetings where no kindness is, nor
all
The dreary intercourse of daily life,
Shall e'er prevail against us, or disturb
Our cheerful faith, that all which we
behold
Is full of blessings. Therefore let the
moon
Shine on thee in thy solitary walk;
And let the misty mountain-winds be
free
To blow against thee: and, in after years,
When these wild ecstasies shall be
matured
Into a sober pleasure; when thy mind
Shall be a mansion for all lovely forms,
Thy memory be as a dwelling-place
For all sweet sounds and harmonies;
oh! then,
If solitude, or fear, or pain, or grief,
Should be thy portion, with what healing
thoughts
Of tender joy wilt thou remember me,
And these my exhortations! Nor, per-
chance—
If I should be where I no more can hear
Thy voice, nor catch from thy wild eyes
these gleams
Of past existence—wilt thou then forget
That on the banks of this delightful
stream
We stood together; and that I, so long
A worshipper of Nature, hither came
Unwearied in that service: rather say

With warmer love—oh! with far deeper
  zeal
Of holier love. Nor wilt thou then
  forget
That after many wanderings, many years
Of absence, these steep woods and lofty
  cliffs,
And this green pastoral landscape, were
  to me
More dear, both for themselves and for
  thy sake!

Strange fits of passion have I known

STRANGE fits of passion have I known:
  And I will dare to tell,
But in the Lover's ear alone,
  What once to me befell.

When she I loved looked every day
  Fresh as a rose in June,
I to her cottage bent my way,
  Beneath an evening-moon.

Upon the moon I fixed my eye,
  All over the wide lea;
With quickening pace my horse drew nigh
  Those paths so dear to me.

And now we reached the orchard-plot;
  And, as we climbed the hill,
The sinking moon to Lucy's cot
  Came near, and nearer still.

In one of those sweet dreams I slept,
  Kind Nature's gentlest boon!
And all the while my eyes I kept
  On the descending moon.

My horse moved on; hoof after hoof
  He raised, and never stopped:
When down behind the cottage roof,
  At once, the bright moon dropped.

What fond and wayward thoughts will
  slide
  Into a Lover's head!
"O mercy!" to myself I cried,
  "If Lucy should be dead!"

She dwelt among the untrodden ways

SHE dwelt among the untrodden ways
  Beside the springs of Dove,
A Maid whom there were none to praise
  And very few to love:

A violet by a mossy stone
  Half hidden from the eye!
—Fair as a star, when only one
  Is shining in the sky.

She lived unknown, and few could know
  When Lucy ceased to be;
But she is in her grave, and, oh,
  The difference to me!

I travelled among unknown men

I TRAVELLED among unknown men,
  In lands beyond the sea;
Nor, England! did I know till then
  What love I bore to thee.

'Tis past, that melancholy dream!
  Nor will I quit thy shore
A second time; for still I seem
  To love thee more and more.

Among thy mountains did I feel
  The joy of my desire;
And she I cherished turned her wheel
  Beside an English fire.

Thy mornings showed, thy nights con-
  cealed,
  The bowers where Lucy played;
And thine too is the last green field
  That Lucy's eyes surveyed.

Three years she grew in sun and shower

THREE years she grew in sun and
  shower
Then Nature said, "A lovelier flower
On earth was never sown;

This Child I to myself will take;
She shall be mine, and I will make
A Lady of my own.

"Myself will to my darling be
Both law and impulse: and with me
The Girl, in rock and plain,
In earth and heaven, in glade and
    bower,
Shall feel an overseeing power
To kindle or restrain.

"She shall be sportive as the fawn
That wild witl. glee across the lawn
Or up the mountain springs;
And hers shall be the breathing balm,
And hers the silence and the calm
Of mute insensate things.

"The floating clouds their state shall
    lend
To her; for her the willow bend;
Nor shall she fail to see
Even in the motions of the Storm
Grace that shall mould the Maiden's
    form
By silent sympathy.

"The stars of midnight shall be dear
To her; and she shall lean her ear
In many a secret place
Where rivulets dance their wayward
    round,
And beauty born of murmuring sound
Shall pass into her face.

"And vital feelings of delight
Shall rear her form to stately height,
Her virgin bosom swell;
Such thoughts to Lucy I will give
While she and I together live
Here in this happy dell."

Thus Nature spake—The work was
    done—
How soon my Lucy's race was run!
She died, and left to me
This heath, this calm, and quiet scene;
The memory of what has been,
And never more will be.

A slumber did my spirit seal

A SLUMBER did my spirit seal;
    I had no human fears:
She seemed a thing that could not feel
    The touch of earthly years.

No motion has she now, no force;
    She neither hears nor sees;
Rolled round in earth's diurnal course,
    With rocks, and stones, and trees.

London, 1802

MILTON! thou shouldst be living at this
    hour:
England hath need of thee; she is a fen
Of stagnant waters: altar, sword, and
    pen,
Fireside, the heroic wealth of hall and
    bower,
Have forfeited their ancient English
    dower
Of inward happiness. We are selfish
    men;
Oh! raise us up, return to us again;
And give us manners, virtue, freedom,
    power.
Thy soul was like a Star, and dwelt
    apart:
Thou hadst a voice whose sound was like
    the sea:
Pure as the naked heavens, majestic, free,
So didst thou travel on life's common
    way,
In cheerful godliness; and yet thy heart
The lowliest duties on herself did lay.

It is not to be thought of that the flood

IT is not to be thought of that the flood
Of British freedom, which, to the open
    sea
Of the world's praise, from dark an-
    tiquity
Hath flow'd, "with pomp of waters, un-
    withstood,"—

Roused though it be full often to a mood
Which spurns the check of salutary
    bands,—
That this most famous stream in bogs
    and sands
Should perish; and to evil and to good
Be lost for ever. In our halls is hung
Armoury of the invincible Knights of
    old:
We must be free or die, who speak the
    tongue
That Shakespeare spake; the faith and
    morals hold
Which Milton held.—In everything we
    are sprung
Of Earth's first blood, have titles mani-
    fold.

Ode
Intimations of Immortality from Recollections of early Childhood

The Child is father of the Man;
And I could wish my days to be
Bound each to each by natural piety.

I

THERE was a time when meadow, grove,
    and stream,
The earth, and every common sight,
    To me did seem
    Apparelled in celestial light,
The glory and the freshness of a dream.
It is not now as it hath been of yore;—
    Turn wheresoe'er I may,
    By night or day,
The things which I have seen I now can
    see no more.

II

The Rainbow comes and goes,
And lovely is the Rose,
The Moon doth with delight
Look round her when the heavens are
    bare,
Waters on a starry night
Are beautiful and fair;

The sunshine is a glorious birth;
But yet I know, where'er I go,
That there hath past away a glory from
    the earth.

III

Now, while the birds thus sing a joyous
    song,
    And while the young lambs bound
    As to the tabor's sound,
To me alone there came a thought of
    grief:
A timely utterance gave that thought
    relief,
    And I again am strong:
The cataracts blow their trumpets from
    the steep;
No more shall grief of mine the season
    wrong;
I hear the Echoes through the mountains
    throng.
The Winds come to me from the fields
    of sleep,
    And all the earth is gay;
    Land and sea
Give themselves up to jollity,
    And with the heart of May
Doth every Beast keep holiday;—
    Thou Child of Joy,
Shout round me, let me hear thy shouts,
    thou happy Shepherd-boy!

IV

Ye blessed Creatures, I have heard the
    call
Ye to each other make; I see
The heavens laugh with you in your
    jubilee;
    My heart is at your festival,
    My head hath its coronal,
The fulness of your bliss, I feel—I feel
    it all.
    Oh evil day! if I were sullen
    While Earth herself is adorning,
    This sweet May-morning,
    And the Children are culling
    On every side,
In a thousand valleys far and wide,

Fresh flowers; while the sun shines
    warm,
And the Babe leaps up on his Mother's
    arm:—
    I hear, I hear, with joy I hear!
—But there's a Tree, of many, one,
A single Field which I have looked upon,
Both of them speak of something that is
    gone:
        The Pansy at my feet
        Doth the same tale repeat:
Whither is fled the visionary gleam?
Where is it now, the glory and the
    dream?

V

Our birth is but a sleep and a forgetting:
The Soul that rises with us, our life's
    Star,
        Hath had elsewhere its setting,
        And cometh from afar:
        Not in entire forgetfulness,
        And not in utter nakedness,
But trailing clouds of glory do we come
From God, who is our home:
Heaven lies about us in our infancy!
Shades of the prison-house begin to close
        Upon the growing Boy,
But he beholds the light, and whence it
    flows,
        He sees it in his joy;
The Youth, who daily farther from the
    east
        Must travel, still is Nature's Priest,
        And by the vision splendid
        Is on his way attended;
At length the Man perceives it die away,
And fade into the light of common day.

VI

Earth fills her lap with pleasures of her
    own;
Yearnings she hath in her own natural
    kind,
And, even with something of a Mother's
    mind,
        And no unworthy aim,
        The homely Nurse doth all she can

To make her Foster-child, her Inmate
    Man,
    Forget the glories he hath known,
And that imperial palace whence he came.

VII

Behold the Child among his new-born
    blisses,
A six years' Darling of a pigmy size!
See, where 'mid work of his own hand he
    lies,
Fretted by sallies of his mother's kisses,
With light upon him from his father's
    eyes!
See, at his feet, some little plan or chart,
Some fragment from his dream of human
    life,
Shaped by himself with newly-learned
    art;
        A wedding or a festival,
        A mourning or a funeral;
        And this hath now his heart,
        And unto this he frames his song:
        Then will he fit his tongue
To dialogues of business, love, or strife;
        But it will not be long
        Ere this be thrown aside,
        And with new joy and pride
The little Actor cons another part;
Filling from time to time his "humorous
    stage"
With all the Persons, down to palsied
    Age,
That Life brings with her in her equip-
    age;
        As if his whole vocation
        Were endless imitation.

VIII

Thou, whose exterior semblance doth
    belie
        Thy Soul's immensity;
Thou best Philosopher, who yet dost keep
Thy heritage, thou Eye among the blind,
That, deaf and silent, read'st the eternal
    deep,
Haunted for ever by the eternal mind,—
        Mighty Prophet! Seer blest!
        On whom those truths do rest,

Which we are toiling all our lives to find,
In darkness lost, the darkness of the
    grave;
Thou, over whom thy Immortality
Broods like the Day, a Master o'er a
    Slave,
A Presence which is not to be put by;
Thou little Child, yet glorious in the
    might
Of heaven-born freedom on thy being's
    height,
Why with such earnest pains dost thou
    provoke
The years to bring the inevitable yoke,
Thus blindly with thy blessedness at
    strife?
Full soon thy Soul shall have her earthly
    freight,
And custom lie upon thee with a weight,
Heavy as frost, and deep almost as life!

IX

O joy! that in our embers
Is something that doth live,
That nature yet remembers
What was so fugitive!
The thought of our past years in me doth
    breed
Perpetual benediction: not indeed
For that which is most worthy to be
    blest;
Delight and liberty, the simple creed
Of Childhood, whether busy or at rest,
With new-fledged hope still fluttering in
    his breast:—
Not for these I raise
The song of thanks and praise;
But for those obstinate questionings
Of sense and outward things,
Fallings from us, vanishings;
Blank misgivings of a Creature
Moving about in worlds not realised,
High instincts before which our mortal
    Nature
Did tremble like a guilty Thing sur-
    prised:
But for those first affections,
Those shadowy recollections,

Which, be they what they may,
Are yet the fountain-light of all our day,
Are yet a master-light of all our seeing;
Uphold us, cherish, and have power
    to make
Our noisy years seem moments in the
    being
Of the eternal Silence: truths that wake,
To perish never:
Which neither listlessness, nor mad en-
    deavour,
Nor Man nor Boy,
Nor all that is at enmity with joy,
Can utterly abolish or destroy!
Hence in a season of calm weather
Though inland far we be,
Our Souls have sight of that immortal
    sea
Which brought us hither,
Can in a moment travel thither,
And see the Children sport upon the
    shore,
And hear the mighty waters rolling ever-
    more.

X

Then sing, ye Birds, sing, sing a joyous
    song!
And let the young Lambs bound
As to the tabor's sound!
We in thought will join your throng,
Ye that pipe and ye that play,
Ye that through your hearts today
Feel the gladness of the May!
What though the radiance which was
    once so bright
Be now for ever taken from my sight,
Though nothing can bring back the
    hour
Of splendour in the grass, of glory in the
    flower;
We will grieve not, rather find
Strength in what remains behind;
In the primal sympathy
Which having been must ever be;
In the soothing thoughts that spring
Out of human suffering;
In the faith that looks through death,
In years that bring the philosophic mind.

XI

And O, ye Fountains, Meadows, Hills,
  and Groves,
Forbode not any severing of our loves!
Yet in my heart of hearts I feel your
  might;
I only have relinquished one delight
To live beneath your more habitual sway.
I love the Brooks which down their
  channels fret,
Even more than when I tripped lightly as
  they;
The innocent brightness of a new-born
  Day
  Is lovely yet;
The Clouds that gather round the setting
  sun
Do take a sober colouring from an eye
That hath kept watch o'er man's mor-
  tality;
Another race hath been, and other palms
  are won.
Thanks to the human heart by which we
  live,
Thanks to its tenderness, its joys, and
  fears,
To me the meanest flower that blows can
  give
Thoughts that do often lie too deep for
  tears.

To the Cuckoo

O BLITHE New-comer! I have heard
  I hear thee and rejoice.
O Cuckoo! shall I call thee Bird,
  Or but a wandering Voice?

While I am lying on the grass
  Thy twofold shout I hear;
From hill to hill it seems to pass
  At once far off, and near.

Though babbling only to the Vale,
  Of sunshine and of flowers,
Thou bringest unto me a tale
  Of visionary hours.

Thrice welcome, darling of the Spring!
  Even yet thou art to me
No bird, but an invisible thing,
  A voice, a mystery;

The same whom in my schoolboy days
  I listened to; that Cry
Which made me look a thousand ways
  In bush, and tree, and sky.

To seek thee did I often rove
  Through woods and on the green;
And thou wert still a hope, a love;
  Still longed for, never seen.

And I can listen to thee yet;
  Can lie upon the plain
And listen, till I do beget
  That golden time again.

O blessèd Bird! the earth we pace
  Again appears to be
An unsubstantial, faery place;
  That is fit home for thee!

It is a beauteous evening, calm and free

IT is a beauteous evening, calm and free,
The holy time is quiet as a Nun
Breathless with adoration; the broad sun
Is sinking down in its tranquillity;
The gentleness of heaven broods o'er the
  Sea:
Listen! the mighty Being is awake,
And doth with his eternal motion make
A sound like thunder—everlastingly.
Dear Child! dear Girl! that walkest with
  me here,
If thou appear untouched by solemn
  thought,
Thy nature is not therefore less divine:
Thou liest in Abraham's bosom all the
  year,
And worship'st at the Temple's inner
  shrine,
God being with thee when we know it
  not.

Composed upon Westminster Bridge, September 3, 1802

EARTH has not anything to show more
    fair:
Dull would he be of soul who could pass
    by
A sight so touching in its majesty:
This City now doth, like a garment, wear
The beauty of the morning; silent, bare,
Ships, towers, domes, theatres and tem-
    ples lie
Open unto the fields, and to the sky;
All bright and glittering in the smoke-
    less air.
Never did sun more beautifully steep
In his first splendour, valley, rock, or hill;
Ne'er saw I, never felt, a calm so deep!
The river glideth at his own sweet will:
Dear God! the very houses seem asleep;
And all that mighty heart is lying still!

The Solitary Reaper

BEHOLD her, single in the field,
Yon solitary Highland Lass!
Reaping and singing by herself;
Stop here, or gently pass!
Alone she cuts and binds the grain,
And sings a melancholy strain;
O listen! for the Vale profound
Is overflowing with the sound.

No Nightingale did ever chaunt
More welcome notes to weary bands
Of travellers in some shady haunt,
Among Arabian sands:
A voice so thrilling ne'er was heard
In spring-time from the Cuckoo-bird,
Breaking the silence of the seas
Among the farthest Hebrides.

Will no one tell me what she sings!—
Perhaps the plaintive numbers flow
For old, unhappy, far-off things,
And battles long ago:
Or is it some more humble lay,
Familiar matter of to-day?
Some natural sorrow, loss, or pain,
That has been, and may be again?

Whate'er the theme, the Maiden sang
As if her song could have no ending;
I saw her singing at her work,
And o'er the sickle bending;—
I listened, motionless and still;
And, as I mounted up the hill,
The music in my heart I bore,
Long after it was heard no more.

Stepping Westward

"What, you are stepping westward?"—
    "Yea."
—'Twould be a *wildish* destiny,
If we, who thus together roam
In a strange Land, and far from home,
Were in this place the guests of Chance:
Yet who would stop, or fear to advance,
Though home or shelter he had none,
With such a sky to lead him on?

The dewy ground was dark and cold;
Behind, all gloomy to behold;
And stepping westward seemed to be
A kind of *heavenly* destiny:
I liked the greeting; 'twas a sound
Of something without place or bound;
And seemed to give me spiritual right
To travel through that region bright.

The voice was soft, and she who spake
Was walking by her native lake:
The salutation had to me
The very sound of courtesy:
Its power was felt; and while my eye
Was fixed upon the glowing Sky,
The echo of the voice enwrought
A human sweetness with the thought
Of travelling through the world that lay
Before me in my endless way.

I wandered lonely as a cloud

I WANDERED lonely as a cloud
    That floats on high o'er vales and hills,
When all at once I saw a crowd,
    A host, of golden daffodils;
Beside the lake, beneath the trees,
Fluttering and dancing in the breeze.

Continuous as the stars that shine
  And twinkle on the milky way,
They stretched in never-ending line
  Along the margin of a bay:
Ten thousand saw I at a glance,
Tossing their heads in sprightly dance.

The waves beside them danced; but they
  Out-did the sparkling waves in glee:
A poet could not but be gay,
  In such a jocund company:
I gazed—and gazed—but little thought
What wealth the show to me had
    brought:

For oft, when on my couch I lie
  In vacant or in pensive mood,
They flash upon that inward eye
  Which is the bliss of solitude;
And then my heart with pleasure fills,
And dances with the daffodils.

The world is too much with us; late and soon

THE world is too much with us; late and
    soon,
Getting and spending, we lay waste our
    powers:
Little we see in Nature that is ours;
We have given our hearts away, a sordid
    boon!
This Sea that bares her bosom to the
    moon;
The winds that will be howling at all
    hours,
And are up-gathered now like sleeping
    flowers;
For this, for everything, we are out of
    tune;
It moves us not.—Great God! I'd rather
    be
A Pagan suckled in a creed outworn;
So might I, standing on this pleasant lea,
Have glimpses that would make me less
    forlorn;
Have sight of Proteus rising from the
    sea;
Or hear old Triton blow his wreathèd
    horn.

To a Skylark

ETHEREAL minstrel! pilgrim of the sky!
Dost thou despise the earth where cares
    abound?
Or, while the wings aspire, are heart and
    eye
Both with thy nest upon the dewy
    ground?
Thy nest which thou canst drop into at
    will,
Those quivering wings composed, that
    music still!

Leave to the nightingale her shady wood;
A privacy of glorious light is thine;
Whence thou dost pour upon the world a
    flood
Of harmony, with instinct more divine;
Type of the wise who soar, but never
    roam;
True to the kindred points of Heaven
    and Home!

Yarrow Unvisited

FROM Stirling castle we had seen
  The mazy Forth unravelled;
Had trod the banks of Clyde, and Tay,
  And with the Tweed had travelled;
And when we came to Clovenford,
  Then said my *"winsome Marrow,"*
"Whate'er betide, we'll turn aside,
  And see the Braes of Yarrow."

"Let Yarrow folk, *frae* Selkirk town,
  Who have been buying, selling,
Go back to Yarrow, 'tis their own;
  Each maiden to her dwelling!
On Yarrow's banks let herons feed,
  Hares couch, and rabbits burrow!
But we will downward with the Tweed,
  Nor turn aside to Yarrow.

"There's Galla Water, Leader Haughs,
  Both lying right before us;
And Dryborough, where with chiming
    Tweed
  The lintwhites sing in chorus;

There's pleasant Tiviot-dale, a land
  Made blithe with plough and harrow:
Why throw away a needful day
  To go in search of Yarrow?

"What's Yarrow but a river bare,
  That glides the dark hills under?
There are a thousand such elsewhere
  As worthy of your wonder."
—Strange words they seemed of slight
      and scorn;
  My True-love sighed for sorrow;
And looked me in the face, to think
  I thus could speak of Yarrow!

"Oh, green," said I, "are Yarrow's
      holms,
  And sweet is Yarrow flowing!
Fair hangs the apple frae the rock,
  But we will leave it growing.
O'er hilly path, and open Strath,
  We'll wander Scotland thorough;
But, though so near, we will not turn
  Into the dale of Yarrow.

"Let beeves and home-bred kine partake
  The sweets of Burn-mill meadow;
The swan on still St. Mary's Lake
  Float double, swan and shadow!
We will not see them; will not go,
  To-day, nor yet to-morrow;
Enough if in our hearts we know
  There's such a place as Yarrow.

"Be Yarrow stream unseen, unknown!
  It must, or we shall rue it:
We have a vision of our own;
  Ah! why should we undo it?
The treasured dreams of times long past,
  We'll keep them, winsome Marrow!
For when we're there, although 'tis fair,
  'Twill be another Yarrow!

"If Care with freezing years should come,
  And wandering seem but folly,—
Should we be loth to stir from home,
  And yet be melancholy;
Should life be dull, and spirits low,
  'Twill soothe us in our sorrow,
That earth hath something yet to show,
  The bonny holms of Yarrow!"

Yarrow Visited, September, 1814

AND is this Yarrow?—*This* the Stream
Of which my fancy cherished,
So faithfully, a waking dream?
An image that hath perished!
O that some Minstrel's harp were near,
To utter notes of gladness,
And chase this silence from the air,
That fills my heart with sadness!

Yet why?—a silvery current flows
With uncontrolled meanderings;
Nor have these eyes by greener hills
Been soothed, in all my wanderings.
And, through her depths, Saint Mary's
      Lake
Is visibly delighted;
For not a feature of those hills
Is in the mirror slighted.

A blue sky bends o'er Yarrow vale,
Save where that pearly whiteness
Is round the rising sun diffused,
A tender hazy brightness;
Mild dawn of promise! that excludes
All profitless dejection;
Though not unwilling here to admit
A pensive recollection.

Where was it that the famous Flower
Of Yarrow Vale lay bleeding?
His bed perchance was yon smooth
      mound
On which the herd is feeding:
And haply from this crystal pool,
Now peaceful as the morning,
The water-wraith ascended thrice—
And gave his doleful warning.

Delicious is the Lay that sings
The haunts of happy Lovers,
The path that leads them to the grove,
The leafy grove that covers:
And Pity sanctifies the Verse
That paints, by strength of sorrow,
The unconquerable strength of love;
Bear witness, rueful Yarrow!

But thou, that didst appear so fair
To fond imagination,

Dost rival in the light of day
Her delicate creation:
Meek loveliness is round thee spread,
A softness still and holy;
The grace of forest charms decayed,
And pastoral melancholy.

That region left, the vale unfolds
Rich groves of lofty stature,
With Yarrow winding through the pomp
Of cultivated nature;
And, rising from those lofty groves,
Behold a Ruin hoary!
The shattered front of Newark's Towers,
Renowned in Border story.

Fair scenes for childhood's opening bloom,
For sportive youth to stray in;
For manhood to enjoy his strength;
And age to wear away in!
Yon cottage seems a bower of bliss,
A covert for protection
Of tender thoughts, that nestle there—
The brood of chaste affection.

How sweet, on this autumnal day,
The wild-wood fruits to gather,
And on my True-love's forehead plant
A crest of blooming heather!
And what if I enwreathed my own!
'Twere no offence to reason;
The sober Hills thus deck their brows
To meet the wintry season.

I see—but not by sight alone,
Loved Yarrow, have I won thee;
A ray of fancy still survives—
Her sunshine plays upon thee!
Thy ever-youthful waters keep
A course of lively pleasure;
And gladsome notes my lips can breathe
Accordant to the measure.

The vapours linger round the Heights,
They melt, and soon must vanish;
One hour is theirs, nor more is mine—
Sad thought, which I would banish,
But that I know, where'er I go,
Thy genuine image, Yarrow!
Will dwell with me—to heighten joy,
And cheer my mind in sorrow.

Yarrow Revisited

THE gallant Youth, who may have
    gained,
  Or seeks, a "winsome Marrow,"
Was but an Infant in the lap
  When first I looked on Yarrow;
Once more, by Newark's Castle-gate
  Long left without a warder,
I stood, looked, listened, and with Thee
  Great Minstrel of the Border!

Grave thoughts ruled wide on that sweet
    day,
  Their dignity installing
In gentle bosoms, while sere leaves
  Were on the bough, or falling;
But breezes played, and sunshine
    gleamed—
  The forest to embolden;
Reddened the fiery hues, and shot
  Transparence through the golden.

For busy thoughts the Stream flowed on
  In foamy agitation;
And slept in many a crystal pool
  For quiet contemplation:
No public and no private care
  The freeborn mind enthralling,
We made a day of happy hours,
  Our happy days recalling.

Brisk Youth appeared, the Morn of
    Youth,
  With freaks of graceful folly,—
Life's temperate Noon, her sober Eve,
  Her Night not melancholy;
Past, present, future, all appeared
  In harmony united,
Like guests that meet, and some from far,
  By cordial love invited.

And if, as Yarrow, through the woods
  And down the meadow ranging,
Did meet us with unaltered face,
  Though we were changed and chang-
    ing;
If, *then,* some natural shadows spread
  Our inward prospect over,
The soul's deep valley was not slow
  Its brightness to recover.

Eternal blessings on the Muse,
  And her divine employment!
The blameless Muse, who trains her Sons
  For hope and calm enjoyment;
Albeit sickness, lingering yet,
  Has o'er their pillow brooded;
And Care waylays their steps—a Sprite
  Not easily eluded.

For thee, O Scott! compelled to change
  Green Eildon-hill and Cheviot
For warm Vesuvio's vine-clad slopes;
  And leave thy Tweed and Tiviot
For mild Sorrento's breezy waves;
  May classic Fancy, linking
With native Fancy her fresh aid,
  Preserve thy heart from sinking!

Oh! while they minister to thee,
  Each vying with the other,
May Health return to mellow Age,
  With Strength, her venturous brother;
And Tiber, and each brook and rill
  Renowned in song and story,
With unimagined beauty shine,
  Nor lose one ray of glory!

For Thou, upon a hundred streams,
  By tales of love and sorrow,
Of faithful love, undaunted truth,
  Hast shed the power of Yarrow;
And streams unknown, hills yet unseen,
  Wherever they invite Thee,
At parent Nature's grateful call,
  With gladness must requite Thee.

A gracious welcome shall be thine,
  Such looks of love and honour
As thy own Yarrow gave to me
  When first I gazed upon her;
Beheld what I had feared to see,
  Unwilling to surrender
Dreams treasured up from early days,
  The holy and the tender.

And what, for this frail world, were all
  That mortals do or suffer,
Did no responsive harp, no pen
  Memorial tribute offer?
Yea, what were mighty Nature's self?
  Her features, could they win us,

Unhelped by the poetic voice
  That hourly speaks within us?

Nor deem that localised Romance
  Plays false with our affections;
Unsanctifies our tears—made sport
  For fanciful dejections:
Ah, no! the visions of the past
  Sustain the heart in feeling
Life as she is—our changeful Life,
  With friends and kindred dealing.

Bear witness, Ye, whose thoughts that
    day
  In Yarrow's groves were centred;
Who through the silent portal arch
  Of mouldering Newark entered;
And clomb the winding stair that once
  Too timidly was mounted
By the "last Minstrel," (not the last!)
  Ere he his Tale recounted.

Flow on for ever, Yarrow Stream!
  Fulfil thy pensive duty,
Well pleased that future Bards should
    chant
  For simple hearts thy beauty;
To dream-light dear while yet unseen,
  Dear to the common sunshine,
And dearer still, as now I feel,
  To memory's shadowy moonshine!

Thought of a Briton on the Subjugation of Switzerland

Two Voices are there; one is of the sea,
One of the mountains; each a mighty
    Voice;
In both from age to age thou didst rejoice,
They were thy chosen music, Liberty!
There came a Tyrant, and with holy glee
Thou fought'st against him; but hast
    vainly striven:
Thou from thy Alpine holds at length art
    driven,
Where not a torrent murmurs heard by
    thee.

Of one deep bliss thine ear hath been
    bereft:
Then cleave, O cleave to that which still
    is left;
For, high-souled Maid, what sorrow
    would it be
That Mountain floods should thunder as
    before,
And Ocean bellow from his rocky shore,
And neither awful Voice be heard by
    thee!

JAMES KENNETH STEPHEN
(1859-1892)

A Sonnet

This sonnet embodies in a form of verse
with which Wordsworth had most con-
spicuous success, one of the chief points of
criticism applicable to his work. It paro-
dies in construction and in phrasing two
very famous sonnets of Wordsworth's:
"Thoughts of a Briton on the Subjugation
of Switzerland," which begins with the
line "Two voices are there; one is of the
sea"; and another, which opens with the
words "The world is too much with us."
Both of these sonnets appear in this book,
among the selections from Wordsworth.
The reader familiar with the best and the
worst of Wordsworth will recognize in
single phrases in this parody, allusions to
well-known elements and subjects in
Wordsworth's poetry.

Two voices are there: one is of the deep;
It learns the storm cloud's thunderous
    melody,
Now roars, now murmurs with the
    changing sea,
Now birdlike pipes, now closes soft in
    sleep;
And one is of an old half-witted sheep
Which bleats articulate monotony,
And indicates that two and one are three,
That grass is green, lakes damp, and
    mountains steep:
And, Wordsworth, both are thine: at cer-
    tain times,
Forth from the heart of thy melodious
    rhymes

The form and pressure of high thoughts
    will burst;
At other times—good Lord! I'd rather
    be
Quite unacquainted with the A, B, C,
Than write such hopeless rubbish as thy
    worst.

JAMES HOGG (1770-1835)

The Skylark

BIRD of the wilderness,
    Blithesome and cumberless,
Sweet be thy matin o'er moorland and
    lea!
    Emblem of happiness,
    Blest is thy dwelling-place—
O to abide in the desert with thee!

    Wild is thy lay and loud,
    Far in the downy cloud,
Love gives it energy, love gave it birth,
    Where, on thy dewy wing,
    Where art thou journeying?
Thy lay is in heaven, thy love is on earth.

    O'er fell and fountain sheen,
    O'er moor and mountain green,
O'er the red streamer that heralds the
    day,
    Over the cloudlet dim,
    Over the rainbow's rim,
Musical cherub, soar, singing, away!

    Then, when the gloaming comes,
    Low in the heather blooms
Sweet will thy welcome and bed of love
    be!
    Emblem of happiness,
    Blest is thy dwelling-place—
O to abide in the desert with thee!

A Boy's Song

Where the pools are bright and deep,
Where the grey trout lies asleep,
Up the river and over the lea,
That's the way for Billy and me.

Where the blackbird sings the latest,
Where the hawthorn blooms the sweetest,
Where the nestlings chirp and flee,
That's the way for Billy and me.

Where the mowers mow the cleanest,
Where the hay lies thick and greenest,
There to track the homeward bee,
That's the way for Billy and me.

Where the hazel bank is steepest,
Where the shadow falls the deepest,
Where the clustering nuts fall free,
That's the way for Billy and me.

Why the boys should drive away
Little sweet maidens from the play,
Or love to banter and fight so well,
That's the thing I never could tell.

But this I know, I love to play
Through the meadow, among the hay;
Up the water and over the lea,
That's the way for Billy and me.

Kilmeny

Bonnie Kilmeny gaed up the glen;
But it wasna to meet Duneira's men,
Nor the rosy monk of the isle to see,
For Kilmeny was pure as pure could be.
It was only to hear the yorlin sing,
And pu' the cress-flower round the
    spring;
The scarlet hypp and the hindberrye,
And the nut that hung frae the hazel
    tree;
For Kilmeny was pure as pure could be.
But lang may her minny look o'er the
    wa',
And lang may she seek i' the green-wood
    shaw;
Lang the laird o' Duneira blame,
And lang, lang greet or Kilmeny come
    hame!

When many a day had come and fled,
When grief grew calm, and hope was
    dead,
When mess for Kilmeny's soul had been
    sung,

When the bedesman had pray'd and the
    dead bell rung,
Late, late in gloamin' when all was still,
When the fringe was red on the westlin
    hill,
The wood was sere, the moon i' the wane,
The reek o' the cot hung over the plain,
Like a little wee cloud in the world its
    lane;
When the ingle low'd wi' an eiry leme,
Late, late in the gloamin' Kilmeny came
    hame!

"Kilmeny, Kilmeny, where have you been?
Lang hae we sought baith holt and den;
By linn, by ford, and green-wood tree,
Yet you are halesome and fair to see.
Where gat you that joup o' the lily
    scheen?
That bonnie snood of the birk sae green?
And these roses, the fairest that ever
    were seen?
Kilmeny, Kilmeny, where have you
    been?"

Kilmeny look'd up with a lovely grace,
But nae smile was seen on Kilmeny's
    face;
As still was her look, and as still was
    her e'e,
As the stillness that lay on the emerant
    lea,
Or the mist that sleeps on a waveless sea.
For Kilmeny had been, she knew not
    where,
And Kilmeny had seen what she could
    not declare;
Kilmeny had been where the cock never
    crew,
Where the rain never fell, and the wind
    never blew.
But it seem'd as the harp of the sky had
    rung,
And the airs of heaven play'd round her
    tongue,
When she spake of the lovely forms she
    had seen,
And a land where sin had never been;
A land of love and a land of light,

Withouten sun, or moon, or night;
Where the river swa'd a living stream,
And the light a pure celestial beam;
The land of vision, it would seem,
A still, an everlasting dream.

In yon green-wood there is a waik,
And in that waik there is a wene,
   And in that wene there is a maike,
That neither has flesh, blood, nor bane;
And down in yon green-wood he walks
   his lane.

In that green wene Kilmeny lay,
Her bosom happ'd wi' flowerets gay;
But the air was soft and the silence deep,
And bonnie Kilmeny fell sound asleep.
She kenn'd nae mair, nor open'd her e'e,
Till waked by the hymns of a far coun-
   trye.

She 'waken'd on a couch of the silk sae
   slim,
All striped wi' the bars of the rainbow's
   rim;
And lovely beings round were rife,
Who erst had travell'd mortal life;
And aye they smiled and 'gan to speer,
"What spirit has brought this mortal
   here?"—

"Lang have I journey'd, the world wide,"
A meek and reverend fere replied;
"Baith night and day I have watch'd the
   fair,
Eident a thousand years and mair.
Yes, I have watch'd o'er ilk degree,
Wherever blooms femenitye;
But sinless virgin, free of stain
In mind and body, fand I nane.
Never, since the banquet of time,
Found I a virgin in her prime,
Till late this bonnie maiden I saw
As spotless as the morning snaw:
Full twenty years she has lived as free
As the spirits that sojourn in this coun-
   trye:
I have brought her away frae the snares
   of men,
That sin or death she never may ken."—

They clasp'd her waist and her hands sae
   fair,
They kiss'd her cheek and they kemed her
   hair,
And round came many a blooming fere,
Saying, "Bonnie Kilmeny, ye're welcome
   here!
Women are freed of the littand scorn:
O blest be the day Kilmeny was born!
Now shall the land of the spirits see,
Now shall it ken what a woman may be!
Many a lang year, in sorrow and pain,
Many a lang year through the world
   we've gane,
Commission'd to watch fair womankind,
For it's they who nurice the immortal
   mind.
We have watch'd their steps as the dawn-
   ing shone,
And deep in the green-wood walks alone;
By lily bower and silken bed,
The viewless tears have o'er them shed;
Have soothed their ardent minds to sleep,
Or left the couch of love to weep.
We have seen! we have seen! but the
   time must come,
And the angels will weep at the day of
   doom!

"O would the fairest of mortal kind
Aye keep the holy truths in mind,
That kindred spirits their motions see,
Who watch their ways with anxious e'e,
And grieve for the guilt of humanitye!
O, sweet to Heaven the maiden's prayer,
And the sigh that heaves a bosom sae
   fair!
And dear to Heaven the words of truth,
And the praise of virtue frae beauty's
   mouth!
And dear to the viewless forms of air,
The minds that kyth as the body fair!

"O bonnie Kilmeny! free frae stain,
If ever you seek the world again,
That world of sin, of sorrow and fear,
O tell of the joys that are waiting here;
And tell of the signs you shall shortly
   see;

Of the times that are now, and the times
that shall be"—
They lifted Kilmeny, they led her away,
And she walk'd in the light of a sunless
day;
The sky was a dome of crystal bright,
The fountain of vision, and fountain of
light:
The emerald fields were of dazzling glow,
And the flowers of everlasting blow.
Then deep in the stream her body they
laid,
That her youth and beauty never might
fade;
And they smiled on heaven, when they
saw her lie
In the stream of life that wander'd bye.
And she heard a song, she head it sung,
She kenn'd not where; but sae sweetly
it rung,
It fell on the ear like a dream of the
morn:
"O, blest be the day Kilmeny was born!
Now shall the land of the spirits see,
Now shall it ken what a woman may be!
The sun that shines on the world sae
bright,
A borrow'd gleid frae the fountain of
light;
And the moon that sleeks the sky sae dun,
Like a gouden bow, or a beamless sun,
Shall wear away, and be seen nae mair,
And the angels shall miss them travelling
the air.
But lang, lang after baith night and day,
When the sun and the world have elyed
away;
When the sinner has gane to his waesome
doom,
Kilmeny shall smile in eternal bloom!"—

They bore her away, she wist not how,
For she felt not arm nor rest below;
But so swift they wain'd her through the
light,
'Twas like the motion of sound or sight;
They seem'd to split the gales of air,
And yet nor gale nor breeze was there.
Unnumber'd groves below them grew,

They came, they pass'd, and backward
flew,
Like floods of blossoms gliding on,
In moment seen, in moment gone.
O, never vales to mortal view
Appear'd like those o'er which they flew!
That land to human spirits given,
The lowermost vales of the storied
heaven;
From thence they can view the world
below,
And heaven's blue gates with sapphires
glow,
More glory yet unmeet to know.

They bore her far to a mountain green,
To see what mortal never had seen;
And they seated her high on a purple
sward,
And bade her heed what she saw and
heard,
And note the changes the spirits wrought,
For now she lived in the land of thought.
She look'd, and she saw nor sun nor skies,
But a crystal dome of a thousand dyes:
She look'd, and she saw nae land aright,
But an endless whirl of glory and light:
And radiant beings went and came,
Far swifter than wind, or the linkèd
flame.
She hid her e'en frae the dazzling view;
She look'd again, and the scene was new.

She saw a sun on a summer sky,
And clouds of amber sailing bye;
A lovely land beneath her lay,
And that land had glens and mountains
gray;
And that land had valleys and hoary
piles,
And marlèd seas, and a thousand isles.
Its fields were speckled, its forests green,
And its lakes were all of the dazzling
sheen,
Like magic mirrors, where slumbering lay
The sun and the sky and the cloudlet
gray;
Which heaved and trembled, and gently
swung,

On every shore they seem'd to be hung;
For there they were seen on their down-
 ward plain
A thousand times and a thousand again;
In winding lake and placid firth,
Little peaceful heavens in the bosom of
 earth.
Kilmeny sigh'd and seem'd to grieve,
For she found her heart to that land did
 cleave;
She saw the corn wave on the vale,
She saw the deer run down the dale;
She saw the plaid and the broad clay-
 more,
And the brows that the badge of freedom
 bore;
And she thought she had seen the land
 before.

She saw a lady sit on a throne,
The fairest that ever the sun shone on!
A lion lick'd her hand of milk,
And she held him in a leish of silk;
And a leifu' maiden stood at her knee,
With a silver wand and melting e'e;
Her sovereign shield till love stole in,
And poison'd all the fount within.

Then a gruff untoward bedesman came,
And hundit the lion on his dame;
And the guardian maid wi' the dauntless
 e'e,
She dropp'd a tear, and left her knee;
And she saw till the queen frae the lion
 fled,
Till the bonniest flower of the world lay
 dead;
A coffin was set on a distant plain,
And she saw the red blood fall like rain;
Then bonnie Kilmeny's heart grew sair,
And she turn'd away, and could look nae
 mair.

Then the gruff grim carle girn'd amain,
And they trampled him down, but he rose
 again;
And he baited the lion to deeds of weir,
Till he lapp'd the blood to the kingdom
 dear;
And weening his head was danger-preef,

When crown'd with the rose and clover
 leaf,
He gowl'd at the carle, and chased him
 away
To feed wi' the deer on the mountain
 gray.
He gowl'd at the carle, and geck'd at
 Heaven,
But his mark was set, and his arles given.
Kilmeny a while her e'en withdrew;
She look'd again, and the scene was new.

She saw before her fair, unfurl'd
One half of all the glowing world,
Where oceans roll'd, and rivers ran,
To bound the aims of sinful man.
She saw a people, fierce and fell,
Burst frae their bounds like fiends of
 hell;
Their lilies grew, and the eagle flew;
And she herkèd on her ravening crew,
Till the cities and towers were wrapp'd
 in a blaze,
And the thunder it roar'd o'er the lands
 and the seas.
The widows they wail'd, and the red
 blood ran,
And she threaten'd an end to the race of
 man;
She never lened, nor stood in awe,
Till caught by the lion's deadly paw.
O, then the eagle swink'd for life,
And brainyell'd up a mortal strife;
But flew she north, or flew she south,
She met wi' the gowl o' the lion's mouth.

With a mooted wing and waefu' maen,
The eagle sought her eiry again;
But lang may she cower in her bloody
 nest,
And lang, lang sleek her wounded breast,
Before she sey another flight,
To play wi' the norland lion's might.

But to sing the sights Kilmeny saw,
So far surpassing nature's law,
The singer's voice wad sink away,
And the string of his harp wad cease to
 play.

But she saw till the sorrows of man were
bye,
And all was love and harmony;
Till the stars of heaven fell calmly away,
Like flakes of snaw on a winter day.

Then Kilmeny begg'd again to see
The friends she had left in her own
countrye;
To tell of the place where she had been,
And the glories that lay in the land un-
seen;
To warn the living maidens fair,
The loved of Heaven, the spirits' care,
That all whose minds unmeled remain
Shall bloom in beauty when time is gane.

With distant music, soft and deep,
They lull'd Kilmeny sound asleep;
And when she awaken'd, she lay her lane,
All happ'd with flowers, in the green-
wood wene.
When seven lang years had come and
fled,
When grief was calm, and hope was
dead;
When scarce was remember'd Kilmeny's
name,
Late, late in a gloamin' Kilmeny came
hame!
And O, her beauty was fair to see,
But still and steadfast was her e'e!
Such beauty bard may never declare,
For there was no pride nor passion there;
And the soft desire of maiden's e'en
In that mild face could never be seen.
Her seymar was the lily flower,
And her cheek the moss-rose in the
shower;
And her voice like the distant melodye,
That floats along the twilight sea.
But she loved to raike the lanely glen,
And keepèd afar frae the haunts of men;
Her holy hymns unheard to sing,
To suck the flowers, and drink the spring.
But wherever her peaceful form appear'd,
The wild beasts of the hill were cheer'd;
The wolf play'd blythly round the field,
The lordly byson low'd and kneel'd;

The dun deer woo'd with manner bland,
And cower'd aneath her lily hand.
And when at even the woodlands rung,
When hymns of other worlds she sung
In ecstasy of sweet devotion,
O, then the glen was all in motion!
The wild beasts of the forest came,
Broke from their bughts and faulds the
tame,
And goved around, charm'd and amazed;
Even the dull cattle croon'd and gazed,
And murmur'd and look'd with anxious
pain
For something the mystery to explain.
The buzzard came with the throstle-
cock;
The corby left her houf in the rock;
The blackbird alang wi' the eagle flew;
The hind came tripping o'er the dew;
The wolf and the kid their raike began,
And the tod, and the lamb, and the
leveret ran;
The hawk and the hern attour them
hung,
And the merle and the mavis forhooy'd
their young;
And all in a peaceful ring were hurl'd;
It was like an eve in a sinless world!

When a month and a day had come and
gane,
Kilmeny sought the green-wood wene;
There laid her down on the leaves sae
green,
And Kilmeny on earth was never mair
seen.
But O, the words that fell from her
mouth
Were words of wonder, and words of
truth!
But all the land were in fear and dread,
For they kendna whether she was living
or dead.
It wasna her hame, and she couldna
remain;
She left this world of sorrow and pain,
And return'd to the land of thought
again.